A Theory of Economic Growth

This book provides an in-depth treatment of the overlapping generations model in economics incorporating production. In chapter 1, the
authors investigate competitive equilibria and corresponding dynamics:
existence and uniqueness of equilibrium, global dynamics of capital (including poverty traps), and various extensions of the model. Chapter 2
analyzes the optimality of allocations in this framework, using both the
value function and marginal approaches. Optimality with unbounded
growth is also analyzed. Policy issues, including the Second Welfare
Theorem, pensions, government spending, and optimal taxation, are
discussed in chapter 3. The notion of public debt is introduced in chapter 4, and the sustainability of policies with budget deficits/surpluses is
examined. The last chapter presents extensions of the model including
altruism, education/human capital, and habit formation. Methodolog-
ical emphasis is put on using general preferences and technologies, on
the global study of dynamic aspects of the model, and on furnishing adequate tools to analyze policies involving inter-generational transfers.

David de la Croix is Professor of Economics at the Université
catholique de Louvain and Research Associate of the National Fund
for Scientific Research in Belgium. He has served as a visiting professor at the University of California, Los Angeles. Professor de la Croix's
research interests in macro-economics include demographics, overlapping generations and human capital, and growth and cycles. He has
published articles in leading refereed journals such as the *Journal of
Economic Theory*, *European Economic Review*, *Journal of Economic
Dynamics and Control*, *Journal of Applied Economics*, *Review of Economic Dynamics*, and *Journal of Population Economics*.

Philippe Michel is Professor of Economics at GREQAM, Université de
la Méditerranée (Aix-Marseille II) and a senior member of Institut Uni-
versitaire de France. He taught previously at the Université de Paris I.
The author or coauthor of six books, most recently *Monnaie, Dette,
et Capital* (1999), Professor Michel's research articles have appeared in
prominent journals such as *Econometrica*, *Review of Economic Studies*,
Journal of Economic Theory, *Journal of Optimization Theory and Applications*, and *International Economic Review*. His research and teaching focus on politics and modeling in macroeconomics and dynamic
theory.

Further Praise for *A Theory of Economic Growth*

"The overlapping generations model and the infinitely lived or dynastic model are the two workhorses of modern macroeconomics. De La Croix and Michel have written a wonderfully accessible graduate textbook on the overlapping generations model. They carefully take students through essentially every variant of the model, prove a large number of known results, and offer a few new ones as well. This book is an essential addition as a teaching tool and an invaluable reference on every economist's shelf."

– V. V. Chari, *University of Minnesota*

"In recent decades overlapping generation models have become a central framework of analysis in the research of economic growth. The authors present a comprehensive and lucid exposition of the dynamic structure of the basic overlapping generation features with production. Highly recommended for researchers and graduate students in the fields of growth theory and dynamic macroeconomics."

– Oded Galor, *Brown University*

"Some of the most hotly debated government policies are those that involve redistribution across generations, such as social security and public education. De la Croix and Michel provide a manual of economic tools for evaluating these sorts of policies based on simple overlapping generations models. Their presentation of these models strives to combine applicability for policy analysis with a solid foundation in dynamic general equilibrium theory. Their book should be of use to economists from the level of advanced undergraduate students to researchers and teachers."

– Timothy J. Kehoe, *University of Minnesota and Federal Reserve Bank of Minneapolis*

A Theory of Economic Growth

Dynamics and Policy in Overlapping Generations

DAVID DE LA CROIX

IRES, Université catholique de Louvain, Belgium

PHILIPPE MICHEL

GREQAM, Université de la Méditerranée, France

PUBLISHED BY THE PRESS SYNDICATE OF THE UNIVERSITY OF CAMBRIDGE
The Pitt Building, Trumpington Street, Cambridge, United Kingdom

CAMBRIDGE UNIVERSITY PRESS
The Edinburgh Building, Cambridge CB2 2RU, UK
40 West 20th Street, New York, NY 10011-4211, USA
477 Williamstown Road, Port Melbourne, VIC 3207, Australia
Ruiz de Alarcón 13, 28014 Madrid, Spain
Dock House, The Waterfront, Cape Town 8001, South Africa

http://www.cambridge.org

First published 2002

Printed in the United Kingdom at the University Press, Cambridge

Typeface Times Ten 9.75/12 pt.   *System* LATEX 2_ε [TB]

A catalog record for this book is available from the British Library.

Library of Congress Cataloging in Publication Data
de la Croix, David
A theory of economic growth : dynamics and policy in overlapping
generations / David de la Croix, Philippe Michel.
p. cm.
Includes bibliographical references and index.
ISBN 0-521-80642-9 (hc.) – ISBN 0-521-00115-3 (pbk.)
1. Macroeconomics.   2. Economic development.   3. Economic policy.
4. Generational accounting.   I. Michel, Philippe.   II. Title.
HB172.5 .L32 2002
339–dc21   2002016579

ISBN 0 521 80642 9 hardback
ISBN 0 521 00115 3 paperback

To Anna, Clémence, Eloïse, Françoise,
Mathieu, Thérèse, Timothée,
and all future, yet unborn, generations.

Contents

Introduction

Inter-generational transfers are today at the center of the economic policy debate. The reduction of public debt, the financing of social security (pensions), the taxation of capital and bequests, and the design of the education system all imply substantial inter-generational transfers.

The tool economists provide to analyze these issues is the overlapping generations model. As it models explicitly the different periods of life – schooling, working, or retirement periods – it is the natural framework to study the allocation of resources across the different generations.

When it includes capital accumulation, this model also allows one to formalize the development of an economy, relating its growth path to the savings behavior of young agents.

The aim of this book is to provide the reader with an in-depth introduction to this model, including its major policy aspects.

OVERLAPPING GENERATIONS AND MACRO-ECONOMICS

Modern macro-economics is generally characterized by four elements: (a) The issues of concern are aggregate in nature. (b) The models in use are derived from optimizing behavior, and, as a consequence, their properties depend essentially on preferences and technologies. (c) Interactions over time are explicitly taken into account, giving therefore an important place to dynamic analysis. (d) The general equilibrium framework is preferred to partial equilibrium setups.

The building blocks of modern macro-economics are taken from two different approaches: The first one considers that agents have an infinite horizon. The second one analyzes the case of an economy in which agents have finite lives. This second approach consists in the so-called overlapping generations models. The central mechanics of this class of model are the decisions of young agents about how much to consume and save for retirement, i.e., the life-cycle hypothesis of savings (see Ando and Modigliani (1963)).

A series of issues are common to both approaches, like the analysis of the factors influencing economic growth. Several issues are, however, specific to the overlapping generations approach. In general they are related to inter-generational redistribution, and hence, e.g., to social security, education policies, and public debt questions. Indeed, even in its simplest version, the overlapping generations model embeds at least two types of agents living at the same time, young and old, which makes possible an analysis of distributional issues.

Moreover, the model with a representative infinite-lived agent can be seen as a special case of the overlapping generations model where households are altruistic and care about their descendants: When altruism is strong enough so that every generation leaves positive bequests, the properties of the two models are the same.

Another domain of research heavily involving the overlapping generations model is the quest for reasonable mechanisms of endogenous fluctuations. Although, as we shall see, the basic model is characterized by monotonic dynamics, various extensions lead to oscillatory dynamics, or even, in extreme cases, permanent endogenous cycles.

When one uses overlapping generations models with two-period-lived agents, the unit of time that one considers is of the order of 20 or 30 years. One could be tempted to think that the results obtained in a simple bench-mark model with this periodicity can be generalized to n-period-lived agents, and the conclusions of the reference model applied to questions relevant at the business cycle frequency.[1] In this case, the model with two-period-lived agents is a metaphor. One should be cautious, however, as all the properties of a model with two-period-lived agents cannot always be extended to n-period-lived agents.

Three important properties of overlapping generations models are the non-neutrality of debt, the possibility of asset bubbles, and the possibility for competitive equilibria to be inefficient. Weil (1989) shows that they do not depend on the horizon (finite or infinite) of the agents. However, the effect of interest rate on saving behavior and the type of dynamics (monotonous, oscillatory, etc.) do depend crucially on the number of periods of life considered. It should then be clear that the overlapping generations model in its standard form[2] has little to say on short-run issues. For this reason, we shall concentrate our attention on long-term problems involving inter-generational transfers.

---

[1] Assuming that workers do not have access to financial markets, Woodford (1986) develops an infinite horizon model with the same structure as an overlapping generations model with two-period-lived agents.

[2] The model of perpetual youth due to Blanchard (1985), which is at the intersection of infinite horizon models and overlapping generations models, can be used to describe phenomena at the business-cycle frequency. This model was further extended by Saint-Paul (1992) to allow for endogenous growth, and by Frenkel and Razin (1986) to an open-economy setup.

Beyond the fact that it is a framework with heterogeneous agents, the overlapping generations model presents two attractive features: First, it focuses on the life-cycle behavior of the agents and hence on their savings behavior as a function of age. Second, it is a model in which the competitive equilibrium is not necessarily Pareto optimal.

OVERLAPPING GENERATIONS IN OTHER FIELDS

There has been an extensive literature in public economics that uses the overlapping generations model. The issues at stake concern the design of optimal tax schemes when the government cannot use non-distortionary lump-sum instruments. The study of bequest taxation and capital taxation has a central role. Education funding through public or private institutions is another typical topic.

Every time policy changes affect different generations in different ways, the overlapping generations model is useful. For example, it is used in environmental economics, as pollution control might harm current generations but promote the welfare of the not yet born generations. Population economics is another example, where authors study the effect of rising longevity, lowered fertility, and population dynamics on human and physical capital accumulation.

Development economics and growth theory also rely on overlapping generations. There are several reasons. First, if one believes that human capital is a relevant factor of development and growth, modeling the education process is important. As education usually takes place at the beginning of the life cycle and involves transfers from one generation to the other, a structure with overlapping generations is appealing. Second, one property of the simplest overlapping generations model is to make long-term growth dependent on initial conditions. In other words, the starting point of the economy is crucial to determining its future. For instance, starting with too low capital might lead the economy into a poverty trap. This dependence on history through initial conditions is important for understanding the different development patterns observed all over the world.

In monetary theory, money has been considered as a medium of exchange between generations and as a store of value. In particular, in the absence of physical capital, money is useful per se, as it allows households to transfer resources across periods.

Finally, mathematical economics have used the overlapping generations model to study under which conditions the equilibrium is indeterminate. Following the logic of Arrow and Debreu, when all markets of all periods clear at once, there is a continuum of equilibria in a context where neither the passage of time nor the formation of expectations is central to the analysis.

OUTLINE OF THE BOOK

Many advanced graduate texts that treat one-sector growth models tackle the basic overlapping generations model. But it is difficult to find, in one single monograph, a survey of the main results, analyzed in detail, as well as extensions of some of the key results in the literature. The extensive analysis of the key models makes this text useful for applied theorists, including researchers in macro-economics, public finance, and development–growth theory, who wish to apply the overlapping generations framework.

The book is also intended for students at the graduate level. True, it is not an easy book for a graduate student to tackle, at least not at the start. In any case, this slot of the textbook market is already well served by general-purpose macro textbooks. But our text adds another dimension: It brings together the standard overlapping generations model with its policy implications (pension funding, debt policy) in one place. It also provides results that have never been demonstrated in the framework considered. We hope that it will be popular with advanced graduate students who have chosen to work in the area of macro dynamics.

This book contains five chapters. The first four chapters cover an analysis of the basic overlapping generations model. One goal that we pursue is to provide the reader with a set of propositions deriving the properties of the overlapping generations model when we make few assumptions on preference and technology. This should help students and researchers in their modeling choices. In chapter 1 we propose an in-depth study of competitive equilibria in the basic overlapping generations model. Chapter 2 is devoted to the analysis of optimality in this setup. Policy issues, including pensions and optimal taxation, are discussed in chapter 3. Public debt is introduced in chapter 4, and its sustainability is analyzed. The last chapter includes various extensions, including altruism, education, and habit formation. The technical points are detailed in the appendix.

Acknowledgments

The various chapters have benefited from comments and suggestions by Steve Ambler, Costas Azariadis, Joel Blot, Raouf Boucekkine, Fabrice Collard, Bertrand Crettez, Antoine d'Autume, Jorge Duran, Roger Farmer, Cecilia Garcia-Peñalosa, Oded Galor, Omar Licandro, Géraldine Mahieu, Pierre Pestieau, Alexandra Rillaers, Emmanuel Thibault, Eric Toulemonde, Alain Venditti, Jean-Pierre Vidal, Claude Wampach, and Bertrand Wigniolle.

We also thank the research centers that have welcomed us during the recent years: CORE and IRES (Université catholique de Louvain), GREQAM (Université de la Méditerranée, CNRS and EHESS), and PRODEC (University of California, Los Angeles).

The first author acknowledges the financial support of the PAI program P5/10 (Belgian Government) and the ARC program "Growth and Incentive Design" (French-speaking community of Belgium).

ONE

Competitive Equilibria

The basic overlapping generations model with capital accumulation is due to Allais (1947)[1] and Diamond (1965).[2] Diamond (1965) considers an economy with physical capital and with or without a public sector. It is a framework in which all goods are real, in the sense that they are consumption goods and/or production factors. In this chapter we describe the framework without a public sector, which is the benchmark model to a wide strand of the literature, and we analyze the properties of the competitive equilibrium.

This chapter is organized as follows. Section 1.1 describes the structure of the model, and section 1.2 discusses the main assumptions. The behavior of the agents is analyzed in section 1.3. The notion of temporary equilibrium is introduced and analyzed in section 1.4. Section 1.5 studies the inter-temporal equilibrium with perfect foresight, its existence and uniqueness. Global dynamics are characterized in section 1.6. In section 1.7 we compare the dynamics under perfect foresight with the dynamics resulting from myopic foresight. Finally, some applications and extensions of the model are presented in section 1.8. Examples are provided throughout the chapter.

1.1 THE MODEL

Time t is discrete and goes from 0 to ∞. t belongs to the set of integer numbers $\mathbb{N}$, $t = 0, 1, 2, \ldots$. All decisions are taken at points in time. The current date is called *period t*, and we study how the economy operates from date $t = 0$ onwards. At the initial date, $t = 0$, there will be initial conditions reflecting the history of the economy.

---

[1] Malinvaud (1987) has stressed the use of the overlapping generations model in the appendix of the book of Allais (1947).

[2] The basic overlapping generations model for an exchange economy is due to Samuelson (1958).

1

At each period t, there exist three goods: capital, labor, and a physical good produced from capital and labor. This physical good is either consumed or invested to build future capital. We take the good produced at each period t as the numeraire. There is thus a different numeraire in each period.

As there are an infinite number of periods, there are an infinite number of goods.

1.1.1 Two-period-lived Individuals

The demographic structure is presented in figure 1.1. In each period t, N_t persons are born, and they live for two periods.[3] From figure 1.1, we understand why this demographic structure is called "overlapping generations": at each point in time, two generations are alive and overlap.

In their first period of life (when *young*), the individuals are endowed with one unit of labor that they supply inelastically to firms. Their income is equal to the real wage w_t. They allocate this income between current consumption c_t and savings s_t, which are invested in the firms. The budget constraint of period t is

$$w_t = c_t + s_t. \tag{1.1}$$

In their second period of life $t + 1$ (when *old*), they are retired. Their income comes from the return on the savings made at time t. As they do not care

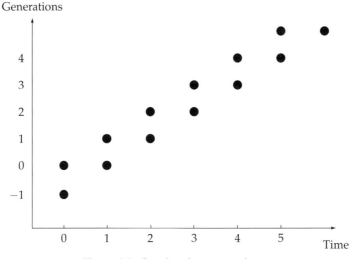

Figure 1.1. Overlapping generations.

---

[3] Alternatively, we may consider that each person lives three periods, is working in the second period, and retires in the third one. During the first period, he does not take any decisions, and his consumption can be thought of as included in that of his parents.

about events occurring after their death (this assumption will be removed in section 5.1), they consume their income entirely. Denoting by $R_{t+1} (= 1 + r_{t+1})$ the return factor on savings from time t to time $t + 1$, the income of an old individual is $R_{t+1}s_t$, and his consumption is

$$d_{t+1} = R_{t+1}s_t. \tag{1.2}$$

The preferences of the households are defined over their consumption bundle (c_t, d_{t+1}). We assume that they can be represented by a life-cycle utility function

$$U(c_t, d_{t+1}).$$

At each period $t \geq 1$, $N_t + N_{t-1}$ individuals are alive, including N_t young households born in t and N_{t-1} old households born in $t - 1$. At the first period $t = 0$, there are, in addition to the N_0 young households, N_{-1} old households.[4] Each of these N_{-1} old persons is the owner of the same fraction s_{-1} of the installed capital stock K_0. Productive capital is the only asset in the economy, so that $s_{-1} = K_0/N_{-1}$. The income of old persons is equal to $R_0 s_{-1}$. These people entirely consume their income:

$$d_0 = R_0 s_{-1} = \frac{R_0 K_0}{N_{-1}}.$$

The number of households of each generation grows at a constant rate $n \in \,]-1, +\infty[$:

$$N_t = (1 + n)N_{t-1}.$$

Consequently, the total population $N_t + N_{t-1}$ grows also at the rate n.[5] Note that, since $n \in \,]-1, +\infty[$, the model may represents economies where population shrinks at a constant rate (negative n).

1.1.2 Neo-classical Technology

The production technology is the same for all periods.[6] It is represented by the neo-classical production function $\bar{F}(K, L)$. The function $\bar{F}$ is homogeneous of degree one (see appendix A.1.1) with respect to its arguments: capital K and labor L.

---

[4] Nothing is said about the past of these households. It is as if they were born old.

[5] Overlapping generations models can be extended to deal with endogenous fertility as in Becker and Barro (1988), with dynastic altruism, or Galor and Weil (1996), with ad hoc altruism.

[6] The generalization of this to include deterministic labor-savings technical progress is performed in section 1.8.6. Notice however that, in standard growth models, technological improvement can coexist with a balance path only with a special type of utility function (see e.g., King, Plosser, and Rebelo (1990)).

During the production process, the capital stock depreciates physically at a rate $\delta \in [0, 1]$.[7]

For simplicity we also assume that, after the production process, the part of capital that is not depreciated is identical to the good produced, so that we may define a total production function:

$$F(K, L) = \bar{F}(K, L) + (1 - \delta)K, \qquad (1.3)$$

which is also homogeneous of the first degree, implying that the technology exhibits constant returns to scale:

$$F(\lambda K, \lambda L) = \lambda F(K, L) \qquad \forall \lambda > 0.$$

1.1.3 Firms

We assume a representative firm producing at period t. This assumption is not restrictive, as, with constant return to scale, the number of firms does not matter and production is independent of the number of firms which use the same technology. At time $t = 0$ the capital stock K_0 is already installed in the firm producing at $t = 0$. For all $t \geq 1$, capital K_t is productive at time t and is built from the savings of time $t - 1$ (there is a one-period time-to-build). The representative firm that produces at time t exists during two periods, $t - 1$ and t.[8] At time $t - 1$ it "receives" the deposits I_{t-1} from the young households. This deposit of goods produced at time $t - 1$ becomes the productive capital used in the production process at time t:

$$K_t = I_{t-1} = N_{t-1}s_{t-1}.$$

The households remain the owners of the stock of capital and will receive the profits of the firm when old.

1.2 MAIN ASSUMPTIONS

1.2.1 The Assumptions on the Utility Function

The life-cycle utility function is assumed to be additively separable:

$$U(c, d) = u(c) + \beta u(d), \qquad (1.4)$$

where β is the psychological discount factor: $\beta = 1/(1 + \varrho)$, where ϱ is the rate of time preference, which varies inversely with β. The non-separable case is treated in section 1.8.3.

---

[7] As one period represents 20 or 30 years, it is often assumed that the depreciation rate is 1.

[8] Alternatively, we may assume that firms live forever. This would not change the results, as the firms' program is in any case a static one.

We assume that the instantaneous utility function u is twice continuously differentiable on the set of strictly positive real numbers $\mathbb{R}_{++}$, strictly increasing (no satiation), and concave (decreasing marginal utility):

Assumption H1.
For all $c > 0$, one has $u'(c) > 0$, $u''(c) < 0$, and $\lim_{c \to 0} u'(c) = +\infty$.

The hypothesis of an infinite marginal utility of zero consumption implies that the household always chooses a positive consumption level c when it maximizes its life-cycle utility (as long as its disposable income is positive).

The two assumptions of additive separability and concavity imply that c and d are normal commodities, i.e., that their demands are non-decreasing in wealth.

Example: The CIES[9] (constant inter-temporal elasticity of substitution) utility function,

$$u(c) = \left[1 - \frac{1}{\sigma}\right]^{-1} c^{1-\frac{1}{\sigma}}, \qquad \sigma > 0, \quad \sigma \neq 1,$$

satisfies the hypothesis **H1**. Indeed,

$$u'(c) = c^{-\frac{1}{\sigma}} > 0, \qquad u''(c) = -\frac{1}{\sigma} c^{-\frac{1}{\sigma}-1} < 0,$$

and

$$\lim_{c \to 0} c^{-1/\sigma} = +\infty.$$

The parameter $-\frac{1}{\sigma}$ is the elasticity of marginal utility:

$$\frac{u''(c)c}{u'(c)} = -\frac{1}{\sigma}.$$

We show below that the elasticity of marginal utility is also the reciprocal of the inter-temporal elasticity of substitution.[10]

The case of a logarithmic utility function,

$$u(c) = \ln(c), \qquad u'(c) = \frac{1}{c}, \qquad u''(c) = \frac{-1}{c^2},$$

gives an elasticity of marginal utility equal to -1. The CIES utility function is plotted in figure 1.2 for the three possible cases: $\sigma > 1, \sigma = 1$ (logarithmic utility), and $\sigma < 1$.

---

[9] The standard name CRRA (for constant relative risk aversion) does not seem suited to a framework in which there is no uncertainty.
[10] In a framework with uncertainty, the coefficient of relative risk aversion is equal to the elasticity of marginal utility.

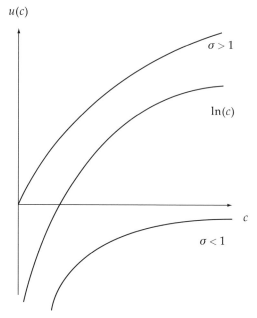

Figure 1.2. The CIES utility function. When $\sigma > 1$, the utility function is positive valued. When $\sigma = 1$, the utility function is simply the ln function. When $\sigma < 1$, the utility function is negative valued.

1.2.2 The Assumptions on the Production Function

As the production function is homogeneous of degree one, it can be expressed by the mean of a function of one variable $k = K/L$:

$$F(K, L) = LF\left(\frac{K}{L}, 1\right) = Lf(k),$$

where $f(k) = F(k, 1)$ is the production function in its intensive form. We make the following hypothesis on the function $f(\cdot)$: it is defined on the set of (strictly) positive real numbers $\mathbb{R}_{++}$ and is twice continuously differentiable. It satisfies:

Assumption H2.
For all $k > 0$, one has $f(k) > 0$, $f'(k) > 0$, and $f''(k) < 0$.

This hypothesis amounts to assuming that the function F is positive valued, increasing, and strictly concave with respect to capital K: indeed, $f'(k) = F'_K(k, 1) = F'_K(K, L)$ because the derivative F'_K is homogeneous of degree 0, and $f''(k) = F''_{KK}(k, 1) = LF''_{KK}(K, L)$ because F''_{KK} is homogeneous of degree -1 (appendix A.1.1).

A consequence of **H2** is the following (appendix A.1.2):

For all $k > 0$, $\qquad \omega(k) = f(k) - kf'(k) = F'_L(K, L) > 0.$

The hypothesis **H2** implies thus that the marginal productivity of labor is strictly positive.

In order to include the popular CES production function, we make no assumption on the limits of the function and its derivatives when $k \to 0$ and $k \to +\infty$. Nevertheless, **H2** implies that the function $f(k)$ and $\omega(k)$ admits non-negative limits when k goes to zero. Thus we may assume that these functions are continuous on the set of non-negative real numbers $\mathbb{R}_+$ with values in $\mathbb{R}_+$.

Notice that additional hypotheses are often made to describe the properties of $f(\cdot)$ on the boundary:

Assumption A1.

$$f(0) = 0.$$

Assumption A2.

$$\lim_{k \to 0} f'(k) = +\infty,$$

$$\lim_{k \to +\infty} f'(k) = 0.$$

Assumption A3.

$$\lim_{k \to 0} f'(k) = +\infty,$$

$$\lim_{k \to +\infty} f'(k) < 1.$$

The assumption **A1** states that capital is essential for production. The assumption **A2** is called the *Inada conditions*. One of these conditions is violated by the CES production function[11] except in the limit case of the Cobb–Douglas function (see appendix A.1.2). The assumption **A3** is less restrictive than **A2**

---

[11] This production function was first introduced by Arrow, Chenery, Minhas, and Solow (1961). The justification given at that time can be used here to avoid imposing Inada conditions: "Two competing alternative [production functions] hold the field at present: the Walras–Leontief–Harrod–Domar of constant input coefficients; and the Cobb–Douglas function, which implies a unitary elasticity of substitution between labor and capital. From a mathematical point of view, zero and one are perhaps the most convenient alternatives for this elasticity. Economic analysis based on these assumptions, however, often leads to conclusions that are unduly restrictive."

and allows us to include the case of a depreciation rate $\delta < 1$. In the sequel of this chapter, we work without making these assumptions.

Example: The CES (constant elasticity of substitution) production function,

$$\bar{F}(K, L) = A[\alpha K^{-\rho} + (1 - \alpha)L^{-\rho}]^{-1/\rho},$$

$$A > 0, \quad 0 < \alpha < 1, \quad \rho > -1, \quad \rho \neq 0,$$

is homogeneous of the first degree. The elasticity of substitution between K and L is equal to

$$\frac{1}{1 + \rho}.$$

In at the limit when ρ tends to -1, the function is linear and the two factors of production are perfect substitutes (the corresponding isoquants are plotted in figure 1.3). This case is excluded by assumption **H2**. They become less and less substitutable as ρ increases. In the limit when $\rho \to +\infty$ the factors of production are perfect complements. The Cobb–Douglas case[12] is obtained as a special

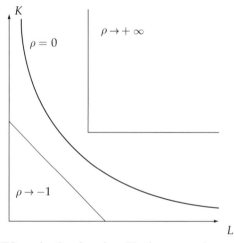

Figure 1.3. The CES production function. The isoquant when $\rho \to +\infty$ shows that capital and labor are complements (no substitution possibilities) in the production process (Leontief technology). For $\rho = 0$ we obtain the isoquant of the Cobb–Douglas function. When $\rho \to -1$, the isoquant becomes linear, and capital and labor can be substituted perfectly.

---

[12] This function was introduced in Douglas (1934) to study American production over the period 1899–1922. The striking agreement between the actual production series and the one generated by the Cobb–Douglas function is at the basis of the success of this production function.

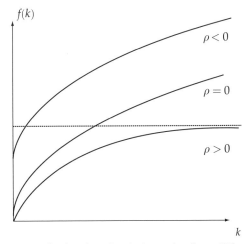

Figure 1.4. The CES production function in intensive form. When $\rho < 0$, each production factor is not essential to production and $f(0) > 0$. When $\rho \geq 0$, $f(0) = 0$. The limit of $f'(k)$ when $k \to 0$ is infinite when $\rho \leq 0$ and finite when $\rho > 0$. The limit of $f'(k)$ when $k \to +\infty$ is positive when $\rho < 0$ and is 0 when $\rho \geq 0$. Only the Cobb–Douglas case $\rho = 0$ satisfies the Inada conditions.

case when $\rho \to 0$ (see appendix A.1.5):

$$\bar{F}(K, L) = A K^{\alpha} L^{1-\alpha}.$$

The three cases are plotted in figure 1.4. With complete depreciation of capital, the function $F = \bar{F}$, and can be written in intensive form:

$$f(k) = A[\alpha k^{-\rho} + (1 - \alpha)]^{-1/\rho}.$$

It is easy to check that $f(k)$ satisfies **H2**:

$$f'(k) = \alpha A[\alpha + (1 - \alpha)k^{\rho}]^{-\frac{1+\rho}{\rho}} = \frac{\alpha}{A^{\rho}} \left(\frac{f(k)}{k} \right)^{1+\rho} > 0,$$

and

$$f''(k) = -\alpha(1 - \alpha)A(1 + \rho)[\alpha + (1 - \alpha)k^{\rho}]^{-\frac{1+2\rho}{\rho}} k^{\rho-1} < 0.$$

Finally, the marginal productivity of labor is

$$\omega(k) = \frac{1 - \alpha}{A^{\rho}} f(k)^{1+\rho} > 0.$$

1.3 THE BEHAVIOR OF THE AGENTS AT PERIOD t

All agents in this economy are price-takers, and all markets are competitive.[13] At a given date, young individuals decide how much to consume and to save, old individuals consume, producing firms hire labor and produce, and investing firms collect the savings from the young and build up the capital stock for the next period. We devote special attention to the savings behavior of the young persons, as it is the engine of capital accumulation.

1.3.1 The Young Individuals

At time t each young individual receives w_t units of the produced good as a wage. He allocates this income between consumption and savings in invested goods (1.1). He anticipates a return R^e_{t+1} for his savings and thus, according to (1.2), a future consumption $d^e_{t+1} = R^e_{t+1}s_t$.

Each young individual maximizes

$$u(c_t) + \beta u\big(d^e_{t+1}\big)$$
$$\text{s.t.} \quad w_t = c_t + s_t, \tag{1.5}$$
$$d^e_{t+1} = R^e_{t+1}s_t,$$
$$c_t \geq 0, \quad d^e_{t+1} \geq 0.$$

There are two ways to solve the problem. We may first substitute c_t and d^e_{t+1} in the objective function, which leads to

$$u(w_t - s_t) + \beta u\big(R^e_{t+1}s_t\big),$$

which is, according to **H1**, strictly concave with respect to s_t. The solution,

$$s_t = s\big(w_t, R^e_{t+1}\big),$$

is interior as a consequence of **H1** and is characterized by the first-order condition

$$u'(w_t - s_t) = \beta R^e_{t+1} u'\big(R^e_{t+1}s_t\big). \tag{1.6}$$

---

[13] Departures from this assumption can be found in the overlapping generations literature. Devereux and Lockwood (1991) and de la Croix and Licandro (1995) analyze capital accumulation under trade-unionism; in such an overlapping generations framework, the wage bargaining process takes place between the young workers and the old capitalists. Weddepohl and Yildirim (1993) study the fixed price temporary equilibria and rationing in an overlapping generations model with capital accumulation. de la Croix and Licandro (2000) also study underemployment of resources, but rationing comes from technological rigidities and idiosyncratic uncertainty instead of fixed prices. Cournot competition on the goods market is introduced in a model with capital by d'Aspremont, Gérard-Varet, and Ferreira (2000), and monopolistic competition is studied in Jacobsen (2000).

The function $s(\cdot)$ is called the *savings function*, and its properties will be analyzed later on.

The second method to solve the problem is to eliminate s_t to obtain the inter-temporal budget constraint of the household:

$$c_t + \frac{1}{R^e_{t+1}} d^e_{t+1} = w_t.$$

We next build the following Lagrangian:

$$u(c_t) + \beta u\big(d^e_{t+1}\big) + \lambda_t \left(w_t - c_t - \frac{d^e_{t+1}}{R^e_{t+1}} \right),$$

where λ_t is a Lagrange multiplier. The first-order conditions for a maximum are

$$u'(c_t) = \lambda_t \quad \text{and} \quad \beta u'\big(d^e_{t+1}\big) = \frac{\lambda_t}{R^e_{t+1}}.$$

Eliminating λ_t, we obtain

$$u'(c_t) = \beta R^e_{t+1} u'\big(d^e_{t+1}\big), \tag{1.7}$$

which is the same as equation (1.6).

Note that the above inter-temporal problem is similar to a static problem where the individual chooses the consumption of two different contemporaneous goods. Here the two goods are distinguished by the date at which they are produced. The price of the good of the second period is the reciprocal of the rate of return, $1/R^e_{t+1}$.

1.3.2 The Inter-temporal Elasticity of Substitution

Equation (1.7) can be used to compute the change in the consumption plan in the face of a shift in the expected rate of return. Indeed, (1.7) can be rewritten

$$\frac{u'(c_t)}{u'(x_{t+1}c_t)} = \beta R^e_{t+1}, \tag{1.8}$$

where $x_{t+1} = d^e_{t+1}/c_t$. The inter-temporal elasticity of substitution measures the effect of a change in R^e_{t+1} on x_{t+1}. We differentiate with respect to R^e_{t+1} and x_{t+1}:

$$u'(c_t) \frac{-1}{[u'(x_{t+1}c_t)]^2} u''(x_{t+1}c_t)c_t \, dx_{t+1} = \beta \, dR^e_{t+1}.$$

Combining this expression with equation (1.8) yields

$$\frac{-1}{u'(x_{t+1}c_t)} u''(x_{t+1}c_t)c_t \, dx_{t+1} = \frac{dR^e_{t+1}}{R^e_{t+1}}.$$

Using the definition of x_{t+1} and rearranging, we have

$$\frac{dx_{t+1}}{x_{t+1}} = \frac{-u'(d_{t+1}^e)}{u''(d_{t+1}^e)d_{t+1}^e} \frac{dR_{t+1}^e}{R_{t+1}^e} = \sigma(d_{t+1}^e)\frac{dR_{t+1}^e}{R_{t+1}^e}.$$

Hence, the size of the effect of dR_{t+1}^e/R_{t+1}^e on dx_{t+1}/x_{t+1} is given by $u'(d_{t+1}^e)/[-u''(d_{t+1}^e)d_{t+1}^e]$.
The quantity

$$-\frac{u'(d)}{du''(d)} \equiv \sigma(d) > 0$$

is the reciprocal of the elasticity of marginal utility evaluated at d in absolute value. The effect of a change in the expected rate of return on consumption is captured by $\sigma(d)$. In the literature, $\sigma(d)$ is referred as the inter-temporal elasticity of substitution.[14] $\sigma(d)$ measures the percentage change in the ratio d_{t+1}/c_t associated with a one percent change in the rate of return. It measures the willingness of the consumer to shift consumption across time in response to changes in the expected rate of return.

Example: With the CIES utility function

$$u(c) = \left(1 - \frac{1}{\sigma}\right)^{-1} c^{1-\frac{1}{\sigma}},$$

the optimality condition (1.7) is

$$\frac{d_{t+1}^e}{c_t} = (\beta R_{t+1}^e)^{\sigma},$$

and the parameter σ is the inter-temporal elasticity of substitution, which is independent of d.

In the logarithmic case, $\sigma = 1$, and

$$\frac{d_{t+1}^e}{c_t} = \beta R_{t+1}^e.$$

1.3.3 The Properties of the Savings Function

The savings function

$$s(w, R) = \arg\max[u(w - s) + \beta u(Rs)]$$

will be central in the subsequent analysis. It is thus useful to analyze its properties. It is characterized by the marginal condition

$$\phi(s, w, R) \equiv -u'(w - s) + \beta R u'(Rs) = 0. \tag{1.9}$$

---

[14] In models with uncertainty this coefficient $\sigma(d)$ has another interpretation. It is the reciprocal of the coefficient of relative risk aversion.

Following the assumptions **H1**, the function $s(w, R)$ is defined and continuously differentiable on the set of pairs $(w, R) \in \mathbb{R}_{++} \times \mathbb{R}_{++}$, i.e. for $w > 0$ and $R > 0$.

To compute its partial derivatives, we use the implicit function theorem (see appendix A.2.2) and differentiate $\phi(s, w, R) = 0$:

$$\phi_s' \, ds + \phi_w' \, dw + \phi_R' \, dR = 0,$$

in which

$$\phi_s' = u''(w - s) + \beta R^2 u''(Rs) < 0,$$

$$\phi_w' = -u''(w - s) > 0,$$

$$\phi_R' = \beta u'(Rs) + \beta Rs \, u''(Rs) = \beta u'(Rs) \left(1 - \frac{1}{\sigma(Rs)}\right),$$

where

$$\sigma(Rs) = \frac{u'(Rs)}{-Rs \, u''(Rs)}$$

is the inter-temporal elasticity of substitution evaluated at $d = Rs$. The partial derivatives of $s(w, R)$ with respect to w and R are

$$s_w'(w, R) = -\frac{\phi_w'}{\phi_s'} = \frac{1}{1 + \frac{\beta R^2 u''(Rs)}{u''(w-s)}},$$

$$s_R'(w, R) = -\frac{\phi_R'}{\phi_s'} = \frac{-\beta u'(Rs)\left(1 - \frac{1}{\sigma(Rs)}\right)}{u''(w - s) + \beta R^2 u''(Rs)}.$$

We thus have that the marginal propensity to save out of income is between 0 and 1:

$$0 < s_w' < 1,$$

which reflects the fact that consumption goods are normal goods. The effect of the rate of return on savings is ambiguous. We have that

$$s_R' \lesseqgtr 0 \quad \text{if} \quad \sigma(Rs) \lesseqgtr 1.$$

A rise in the return on savings has two effects for the consumer: (1) an income effect, as the revenue from savings will be higher, all other things being equal; (2) a substitution effect, making it profitable to substitute consumption today for consumption tomorrow. When the inter-temporal elasticity of substitution is lower than 1, the substitution effect is dominated by the income effect. In that case, a rise in the rate of return has a negative effect on savings. When the inter-temporal elasticity of substitution is higher than 1, the households are ready to exploit the rise in the remuneration of savings by consuming relatively less today. The effect of a rise in the rate of return is in this case to boost savings. When the inter-temporal elasticity of substitution is equal

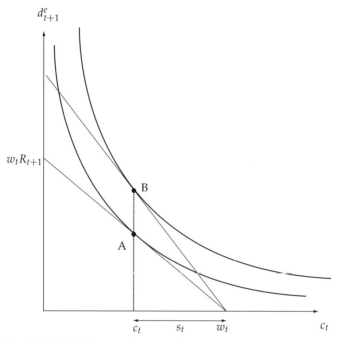

Figure 1.5. A rise in the interest factor. A rise in the interest factor induces a shift in the budget line (whose equation is $d_{t+1}^e = (w_t - c_t)R_{t+1}^e$). The consumer is able to reach a higher indifference curve, from point A to point B. If the inter-temporal elasticity of substitution is equal to one, the income and substitution effects compensate, and c_t and s_t remains unchanged.

to 1, the income effect exactly compensates the substitution effect and there is no effect of the rate of return on savings. This last case is represented in the commodity space in figure 1.5.

Example: In the CIES example, the savings function is

$$s(w, R) = \frac{1}{1 + \beta^{-\sigma}R^{1-\sigma}}w,$$

and the sign of s_R' is the same for all w and R: that is, $s_R' > 0 \iff \sigma > 1$, and $s_R' < 0 \iff \sigma < 1$. The fact that the savings function can be written in the form "savings = propensity to save × wages," with the propensity to consume being independent of wages, is a general property of homothetic preferences (see appendix 1.8.4).

In the logarithmic case,

$$s(w, R) = \frac{\beta}{1 + \beta}w_t$$

is independent of R ($s_R' = 0$, as $\sigma = 1$).

1.3.4 The Old Individuals

At time t, each old individual receives an income from his savings of the previous period and consumes

$$d_t = R_t s_{t-1},$$

where R_t is the return in period t on savings made in period $t-1$. This also applies to the initial date $t = 0$, when $s_{-1} = K_0 / N_{-1}$ is given.

1.3.5 The Firms

The Producing Firm. The representative producing firm has an installed stock of capital K_t. It must only choose the labor input paid at a wage w_t and produces a quantity of output according to its net production function (1.3). This firm maximizes its profits:

$$\pi_t = \max_{L_t} F(K_t, L_t) - w_t L_t.$$

Due to the homogeneity properties of F and to the assumption **H2**, this objective function is strictly concave with respect to L_t (see appendix A.1.2). The labor demand L_t which maximizes this expression is obtained by equalizing the marginal productivity of labor with the wage rate

$$F'_L(K_t, L_t) = w_t.$$

As we have seen in section 1.2.2, $F'_L(K, L) = \omega(k) = f(k) - k f'(k)$, and the above equality can be rewritten

$$\omega \left(\frac{K_t}{L_t} \right) = w_t. \tag{1.10}$$

The profit is distributed to the owners of the capital stock:

$$\pi_t = F(K_t, L_t) - F'_L(K_t, L_t) L_t = F'_K(K_t, L_t) K_t,$$

or

$$\pi_t = f' \left(\frac{K_t}{L_t} \right) K_t.$$

The fact that profits are distributed to the owners of the capital stock is consistent with the idea that the old households are the owners of the firms.

When the production function is Cobb–Douglas, equation (1.10) implies that

$$w_t = A(1 - \alpha) k_t^\alpha,$$

and the labor share in added value,

$$\frac{w_t L_t}{Y_t} = \frac{w_t}{y_t} = 1 - \alpha,$$

is constant, which is one of the empirical regularities of growth processes documented by Kaldor (1963). Moreover, Solow (1957) argues that the particular functional form adopted for the production function is a matter of no great consequence. Almost any function with positive partial derivative and the right curvature will do fairly well in tracking the observed changes in production. As the Cobb–Douglas function is tractable, it can be frankly taken as an approximation, "as long as no deep distributive meaning is read into the results" (Solow (1960)). These two arguments explain why the Cobb–Douglas production function is the preferred functional form in growth models.

The Investing Firm. The firm that invests at time t to produce at time $t + 1$ receives the savings of the young generation born in t:

$$I_t = N_t s_t.$$

1.4 THE TEMPORARY EQUILIBRIUM

To study the equilibrium, we explicitly distinguish the temporary equilibrium and the inter-temporal equilibrium (or equilibrium over time). The concept of temporary equilibrium goes back to Hicks (1939).[15] The articulation of the two is best described by using the words of Hicks: "Temporary equilibrium is such that all are reaching their 'best' positions, subject to the constraints by which they are bound, and with the expectations that they have at the moment. Equilibrium over time, if it is to be defined in a corresponding manner, must be such that it is maintainable over a sequence, the expectations on which it is based, in each single period, being consistent with one another" (Hicks (1965)).

The temporary equilibrium of period t is thus a competitive equilibrium given price expectations. It will give the equilibrium value of the current variables, including current prices, as a function of the past and of the expectations about the future. More precisely, it is defined given the past variables[16]

$$s_{t-1} \quad \text{and} \quad I_{t-1} = N_{t-1} s_{t-1},$$

and given the expectations on the future rate of return,

$$R_{t+1}^e.$$

At time t, two markets are open, the labor market and the goods market. There is no capital market, because the physical capital is already installed and investment I_t results from the decision of the young individuals in t. Nevertheless, the gross rate of return R_t depends on the decisions of the firm

---

[15] See also Grandmont (1983) for a more recent use of the concept.

[16] All variables from time 0 to time $t - 1$ are past data. We only mention those which intervene in the definition of the temporary equilibrium. We do the same for expectations.

that produces at time t, and this decision depends on the equilibrium wage w_t. The equilibrium conditions are thus threefold:

1. **Labor market equilibrium:** At time t the inelastic labor supply is N_t; the labor demand L_t is given by the solution to (1.10). Hence, the equilibrium wage equalizing supply and demand is

$$w_t = \omega \left(\frac{K_t}{N_t} \right) = \omega(k_t). \tag{1.11}$$

   $k_t = K_t/N_t$ is the stock of capital per young person, or the equilibrium capital–labor ratio.

2. **Equality between realized and distributed profits:** By assumption, the effective profits are distributed to the owners of capital. Given the equilibrium on the labor market, we have

$$\pi_t = f'(k_t)K_t.$$

   The old households receive

$$\pi_t = N_{t-1}R_t s_{t-1} = R_t K_t,$$

   as $K_t = N_{t-1}s_{t-1}$. The equality between effective profits and distributed profits implies that the rate of return on the savings made at time $t-1$ is equal to the marginal productivity of capital:

$$R_t = f'(k_t). \tag{1.12}$$

   This equality is obtained from an accounting identity. Suppose now that the young households no longer deposit their savings in an investing firm, but use them to build capital that they sell to the producing firms in the next period (an interpretation often found in the literature). In this case, the interest factor would be a market price equalizing the supply of capital from the old and the demand of capital from the firms.[17]

3. **Good market equilibrium:** The supply of the physical good by the producing firm is

$$Y_t = F(K_t, N_t) = N_t f(k_t).$$

   The demand for the good is the sum of the demand of the old households born in $t-1$ and of the young households that consume and save in the physical good:

$$N_{t-1}d_t + N_t(c_t + s_t).$$

---

[17] The supply from the old is inelastic. At a given wage w, there exists a unique $R(w)$ such that the firms' demand is infinite for $R < R(w)$, nil for $R > R(w)$, and any non-negative value for $R = R(w)$. This demand scheme results from the assumption of constant returns to scale.

The equilibrium on the goods market is

$$Y_t = N_{t-1}d_t + N_t(c_t + s_t). \tag{1.13}$$

It results from the equilibrium in the labor market, from the equality between effective and distributed profits, and from the budget constraint of the households. Indeed, we have

$$N_t(c_t + s_t) = N_t w_t = N_t[f(k_t) - k_t f'(k_t)] = Y_t - K_t f'(k_t),$$
$$N_{t-1}d_t = N_{t-1}R_t s_{t-1} = R_t K_t = K_t f'(k_t).$$

The temporary equilibrium can now be defined as follows.

Definition 1.1 (Temporary equilibrium)
Given the variables from the previous period $\{s_{t-1}, I_{t-1} = N_{t-1}s_{t-1}\}$ and the expected rate of return on savings R_{t+1}^e, the temporary equilibrium of time t is defined by

1. *the wage rate w_t and the gross rate of return R_t,*
2. *the aggregate variables K_t, L_t, Y_t, k_t, and I_t,*
3. *the individual variables c_t, s_t, and d_t*

that satisfy the optimality conditions of the agents and the three equilibrium conditions (1.11), (1.12), and (1.13).

A temporary equilibrium $\{w_t, R_t, K_t, L_t, Y_t, k_t, I_t, c_t, s_t, d_t\}$ can be expressed as a function of $k_t = K_t/N_t = I_{t-1}/N_t$ and R_{t+1}^e. Indeed, we have

$$\begin{aligned}
w_t &= \omega(k_t), \\
R_t &= f'(k_t), \\
L_t &= N_t, \\
Y_t &= N_t f(k_t), \\
I_t &= N_t s_t, \\
c_t &= w_t - s_t, \\
s_t &= s\big(\omega(k_t), R_{t+1}^e\big), \\
d_t &= R_t s_{t-1}.
\end{aligned} \tag{1.14}$$

We next have the following proposition:

Proposition 1.1 (Existence and uniqueness of the temporary equilibrium)
Given $\{s_{t-1}, I_{t-1}, R_{t+1}^e\}$, the temporary equilibrium of period t exists and is unique. This equilibrium can be expressed as a function of

$$k_t = \frac{K_t}{N_t} = \frac{I_{t-1}}{N_t} \quad and \quad R_{t+1}^e.$$

Proof: The system (1.14) defines a unique temporary equilibrium because $\omega(\cdot)$, $f(\cdot)$, and $s(\cdot, R)$ are (single-valued) functions. ∎

Example: When the utility function is logarithmic and the production function is Cobb–Douglas, the temporary equilibrium is given by

$$w_t = A(1 - \alpha)k_t^\alpha,$$

$$R_t = A\alpha k_t^{\alpha - 1},$$

$$Y_t = N_t A k_t^\alpha,$$

$$s_t = \frac{\beta}{1 + \beta} A(1 - \alpha)k_t^\alpha,$$

$$c_t = \frac{1}{1 + \beta} A(1 - \alpha)k_t^\alpha,$$

$$d_t = A\alpha k_t^{\alpha - 1} s_{t-1}.$$

It does not depend on the expectation R_{t+1}^e.

1.5 THE INTER-TEMPORAL EQUILIBRIUM WITH PERFECT FORESIGHT

At equilibrium, the link between two periods t and $t + 1$ is given by the accumulation rule for capital and by the formation of expectations. The accumulation rule for capital states that savings of the young households are transformed into productive capital for the next period:

$$K_{t+1} = I_t = N_t s\big(\omega(k_t), R_{t+1}^e\big),$$

or, in intensive terms,

$$k_{t+1} = \frac{1}{1 + n} s\big(\omega(k_t), R_{t+1}^e\big).$$

We also call this equality the *equilibrium on capital market*, reflecting the idea that the supply of funds by households equals investment by firms.

If expectations on R_{t+1}^e are a function of the past only, the sequence of temporary equilibria is determined uniquely by the initial capital stock. For instance, if expectations are myopic or adaptive and $R_{t+1}^e = R_t = f'(k_t)$, the sequence of temporary equilibria is determined by the following difference equation of the first order:

$$k_{t+1} = \frac{1}{1 + n} s\big(\omega(k_t), f'(k_t)\big), \qquad k_0 = K_0/N_{-1} \text{ given.}$$

We shall study more systematically the equilibrium with perfect foresight:

$$R_{t+1}^e = R_{t+1} = f'(k_{t+1}), \tag{1.15}$$

$$k_{t+1} = \frac{1}{1 + n} s\big(\omega(k_t), R_{t+1}\big). \tag{1.16}$$

Definition 1.2 (Inter-temporal equilibrium)
Given an initial capital stock $k_0 = K_0/N_{-1}$, an inter-temporal equilibrium with perfect foresight is a sequence of temporary equilibria that satisfies for all $t \geq 0$ the conditions (1.15) and (1.16).

The words "perfect foresight" reflect the assumption that there is no uncertainty about the future. Future population, technology, etc. are perfectly forecasted by the agents, and so are the future rates of return.[18]

Hence, at the inter-temporal equilibrium with perfect foresight, the stock of capital of period $t + 1$ should verify the following implicit equation:

$$(1 + n)k_{t+1} - s(\omega(k_t), f'(k_{t+1})) = 0. \tag{1.17}$$

The equilibrium sequence $(k_t)_{t \geq 0}$ is called an *equilibrium trajectory*.

There is a particular difficulty for studying the existence and uniqueness of an equilibrium with perfect foresight, given the initial capital stock. Indeed, k_{t+1} is defined implicitly by (1.17) when k_t is known. At each step, there is an implicit function problem: given k_t, does k_{t+1} exist and is it unique? It is possible to analyze these questions in a simple way, which is the following. Considering a given wage $w > 0$, we look for a capital stock k such that the expectations of the rate of return $R(k) = f'(k)$ will lead to a savings decision $s(w, f'(k))$ corresponding to the level of capital accumulation. In other words, given $w > 0$, we wonder whether it is possible to solve for k the equation[19]

$$\Delta(k, w) \equiv (1 + n)k - s(w, f'(k)) = 0.$$

For the existence, it is enough to prove that the limits of $\Delta(k, w)$ when k goes to 0 and when k goes to $+\infty$ are of opposite sign. Indeed, when this is the case, the continuous function $\Delta(k, w)$ will necessarily take the value 0 at some positive k.

1.5.1 Existence of Equilibria

Proposition 1.2 (Existence of inter-temporal equilibria)
*Under the hypotheses **H1** and **H2**, for any initial capital stock $k_0 > 0$, there exists at least one inter-temporal equilibrium with perfect foresight.*

Proof: We first study the sign of $\Delta(k, w)$ when k tends to $+\infty$. We have the following inequality bearing on the savings function:

$$0 < s(w, f'(k)) < w,$$

---

[18] An extension of the two-period overlapping generations model to uncertain environments is proposed by Demange and Laroque (1999) and (2000).
[19] The method developed here turns out to be simpler than the one consisting in inverting the function (1.17) to find a function $k_t = \Lambda(k_{t+1})$.

i.e., savings are positive and smaller than first-period income. This implies

$$0 < \frac{s(w, f'(k))}{k} < \frac{w}{k}.$$

For a fixed $w > 0$ the limit of w/k when $k \to \infty$ is 0. This implies[20]

$$\lim_{k \to +\infty} \frac{s(w, f'(k))}{k} = 0.$$

As a consequence, for

$$\Delta(k, w) = k\left(1 + n - \frac{s(w, f'(k))}{k}\right),$$

we have

$$\lim_{k \to +\infty} \frac{\Delta(k, w)}{k} = 1 + n > 0.$$

This implies that $\Delta(k, w)$ is positive for large values of k.

We now study the sign of $\Delta(k, w)$ when k goes to 0. The decreasing function $f'(k)$ admits a limit when k goes to 0. We distinguish two cases according to whether this limit is finite (case 1) or infinite (case 2):

- **Case 1:** $\lim_{k \to 0} f'(k) = f'(0)$ is finite. In this case, the savings function $s(w, f'(0))$ is well defined and is positive. Then we have

$$\lim_{k \to 0} \Delta(k, w) = \lim_{k \to 0}[(1 + n)k - s(w, f'(k))] = -s(w, f'(0)) < 0.$$

- **Case 2:** $\lim_{k \to 0} f'(k) = +\infty$. The return on savings becomes infinite as k approaches 0. In this case, savings can remain positive (sub-case 1) or tend to zero (sub-case 2):
  - **Sub-case 1:** $\lim_{k \to 0} s(w, f'(k)) > 0$.[21] This implies that

$$\lim_{k \to 0} \Delta(k, w) = \lim_{k \to 0}[k(1 + n) - s(w, f'(k))] < 0.$$

  - **Sub-case 2:** $\lim_{k \to 0} s(w, f'(k)) = 0$. This is the case when savings go to zero as the interest rate goes to infinity. This property of the savings function implies that the second-period consumption $d = f'(k)s(w, f'(k))$ tends to $+\infty$. Indeed, using equation (1.6) we have

$$\lim_{k \to 0} u'(d) = \lim_{k \to 0} \frac{u'(w - s)}{\beta f'(k)} = 0,$$

---

[20] Any function squeezed between functions that have a common limit necessarily converges toward this limit.

[21] The proof applies to the limit superior (lim sup) when the limit does not exist. The lim sup is an upper bound which always exists, finite or infinite (see appendix A.2.3).

as $\lim_{k \to 0} f'(k) = +\infty$ and $\lim_{k \to 0} u'(w - s) = u'(w) > 0$. The marginal utility of d thus tends to 0, which implies[22]

$$\lim_{k \to 0} f'(k)s(w, f'(k)) = +\infty.$$

We also have $0 < kf'(k) < f(k)$ (as $\omega(k) > 0$), which implies that for k bounded, say $0 < k < 1$, $kf'(k) < f(1)$. Then, for $k < 1$,

$$\frac{s(w, f'(k))}{k} = \frac{f'(k)s(w, f'(k))}{f'(k)k} > \frac{f'(k)s(w, f'(k))}{f(1)}.$$

Hence,

$$\lim_{k \to 0} \frac{s(w, f'(k))}{k} = +\infty,$$

which implies that

$$\frac{\Delta(k, w)}{k} = 1 + n - \frac{s(w, f'(k))}{k}$$

is necessarily negative for small k.

We have shown that, in all cases, $\Delta(k, w)$ takes positive values for large k and negative values for small k. As $\Delta(k, w)$ is continuous with respect to k, there always exists at least one $k > 0$ such that $\Delta(k, w) = 0$. This implies that, given $k_t > 0$, there exists $k_{t+1} > 0$ such that $\Delta(k_{t+1}, \omega(k_t)) = 0$. By induction,[23] given k_0, there exists a sequence (k_t) satisfying (1.17) for all t, i.e., an equilibrium with perfect foresight. ∎

Figure 1.6 illustrates the two cases of proposition 1.2. We have represented a case with three solutions k to $\Delta(k, w) = 0$.

1.5.2 Uniqueness of the Inter-temporal Equilibrium

In order to obtain uniqueness, we need some more assumptions. Typically, when the function $\Delta(k, w)$ is not strictly increasing in k, there may be more than one k which solves $\Delta(k, w) = 0$. In fact, we only need $\Delta(k, w)$ to be strictly increasing at the possible intersection points with the horizontal axis. We shall thus assume that for any (possible) intersection point, i.e., k such that $\Delta(k, w) = 0$, the derivative $\Delta'_k(k, w)$ is positive.[24]

---

[22] This is the case when $\lim_{d \to \infty} u'(d) = 0$. We have not made this assumption, but if this limit is strictly positive, the sub-case is excluded.

[23] Induction relies on a domino effect. If we can prove that a result is true from time t to time $t + 1$, and that it is true for the first case (here, k_0 is given), we can put together a chain of conclusions: Truth for $t = 1$ implies truth for $t = 2$, and so on. Pushing the first domino causes all of the other dominoes to fall in succession.

[24] In fact, we only need the assumption **H3** for the values of w which are equilibrium real wages, i.e., such that there exists $k > 0$ verifying $\omega(k) = w$. Moreover, replacing the assumption

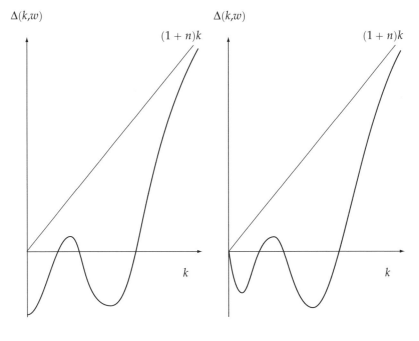

$$\lim_{k \to 0} s(w, f'(k)) > 0 \qquad \lim_{k \to 0} s(w, f'(k)) = 0$$

Figure 1.6. Existence of inter-temporal competitive equilibria. When $\lim_{k \to 0} s(w, f'(k)) > 0$, savings remain positive even when the interest rate goes to infinity. When $\lim_{k \to 0} s(w, f'(k)) = 0$, savings go to zero when the interest rate goes to infinity. In all cases, $\Delta(k, w)$ takes positive values for large k and takes negative values for small k. As $\Delta(k, w)$ is continuous with respect to k, there always exists at least one $k > 0$ such that $\Delta(k, w) = 0$.

Assumption H3.
For all $w > 0$ and all $k > 0$,

$$\Delta(k, w) = 0 \implies \Delta'_k(k, w) > 0,$$

where

$$\Delta(k, w) = (1 + n)k - s(w, f'(k)),$$
$$\Delta'_k(k, w) = 1 + n - s'_R(w, f'(k)) f''(k).$$

The assumption **H3** implies that for any fixed w the curve $\Delta(k, w)$ does not intersect the horizontal axis at more than one point. This is because, if there is

---

$\Delta'_k > 0$ by $\Delta(k, w)$ locally strictly increasing, the condition **H3** is necessary and sufficient for a unique intersection point k solving $\Delta(k, w) = 0$.

a second intersection, the function is necessarily non-increasing, and its derivative is non-positive.

A consequence of this assumption is that the effect of the rate of return on the savings decision should not be too negative at the solution:

$$s'_R(w, f'(k)) > \frac{1+n}{f''(k)}.$$

Hence, the degree of inter-temporal substitution between consumption when young and consumption when old should not be too small, so that the substitution effect will not be dominated too much by the income effect in the face of changes in the rate of return.

Under **H3**, there exists a function h defined on $\mathbb{R}_{++}$ with values in $\mathbb{R}_{++}$ which satisfies, for $w > 0$,

$$k = h(w) \iff \Delta(k, w) = 0. \tag{1.18}$$

In addition, at any point $w > 0$, we have $\Delta'_k(h(w), w) \neq 0$ and we can apply the implicit function theorem: the function $h(w)$ is continuously differentiable at $w > 0$, with derivative

$$h'(w) = -\frac{\Delta'_w(h(w), w)}{\Delta'_k(h(w), w)} = \frac{s'_w(w, f'(h(w)))}{1 + n - s'_R(w, f'(h(w))) f''(h(w))}.$$

As $\Delta'_k(h(w), w) > 0$, $h'(w)$ is positive.

Proposition 1.3 (Uniqueness of the inter-temporal equilibrium)
Under the hypotheses **H1**, **H2**, *and* **H3**, *for any* $k_0 > 0$, *there exists a unique inter-temporal equilibrium with perfect foresight and initial capital stock* k_0. *This equilibrium is characterized by the sequence of capital stocks* k_t *defined by the difference equation*

$$k_{t+1} = g(k_t) = h(\omega(k_t)).$$

The function g is continuously differentiable on $\mathbb{R}_{++}$ *and verifies, for all* $k > 0$,

$$g'(k) > 0 \quad and \quad \Delta(g(k), \omega(k)) = 0.$$

Proof: Proposition 1.3 simply results from proposition 1.2, from the definition of the function $h(w)$ (see equation 1.18), and from the properties of the functions $\omega(k)$ and $h(w)$, both being continuously differentiable and increasing. ∎

Equation (1.17) is then equivalent to $\Delta(k_{t+1}, \omega(k_t)) = 0$, which is equivalent to $k_{t+1} = g(k_t)$. The derivative of g is

$$g'(k) = h'(\omega(k))\omega'(k) = \frac{s'_w(\omega(k), f'(g(k)))\omega'(k)}{1 + n - s'_R(\omega(k), f'(g(k))) f''(g(k))}.$$

One important difficulty for applications is that the hypothesis **H3** is not directly formulated in terms of preferences and technologies and depends on the equilibrium values of k and w. Thus, it is useful to have the following sufficient condition for uniqueness.

Assumption A4.
The utility function verifies $\forall c > 0$, $u'(c) + cu''(c) \geq 0$.

This condition is equivalent to assuming that the inter-temporal elasticity of substitution $\sigma(c)$ is greater or equal to 1. As we have seen, this implies that $s'_R \geq 0$ and hence $\Delta'_k \geq 1 + n$ for all w, $k > 0$: **H3** holds.

Moreover, a more general sufficient condition for **H3** to hold can be drawn in the case of a CIES utility function with inter-temporal elasticity σ and a CES production function with substitution elasticity $1/(1 + \rho)$. In this case,

$$\Delta(k, w) = (1+n)k - \frac{w}{1 + \beta^{-\sigma}[f'(k)]^{1-\sigma}},$$

with

$$f'(k) = \alpha A^{-\rho}\left(\frac{f(k)}{k}\right)^{1+\rho}.$$

The solution k of $\Delta(k, w) = 0$ is obtained by solving for k:

$$\frac{w}{1+n} = \psi(k) \equiv k + k\beta^{-\sigma} f'(k)^{1-\sigma}.$$

The function $\psi(k)$ is bounded above by $k + k\beta^{-\sigma} f'(k) f'(1)^{-\sigma}$ for $k < 1$. The assumption **H2** implies that $\lim_{k \to 0} k f'(k) = 0$ (see appendix A.1.2). Thus, we have $\psi(0+) = 0$. As $\psi(+\infty) = +\infty$, the condition $\psi'(k) > 0$ for all k guarantees the uniqueness of k_{t+1}. Recognizing that $\psi(k)$ can be rewritten as

$$\psi(k) = k + \beta^{-\sigma}(\alpha A^{-\rho})^{1-\sigma} f(k)^{\lambda} k^{1-\lambda} \quad \text{with} \quad \lambda = (1+\rho)(1-\sigma),$$

the condition $\psi'(k) > 0$ holds if $\lambda \leq 1$, i.e., if

$$\sigma \geq 1 - \frac{1}{1+\rho}. \tag{1.19}$$

This condition states that if the inter-temporal elasticity of substitution is larger than 1 minus the elasticity of substitution between production factors, then the inter-temporal equilibrium is unique. Hence, the condition on σ is more restrictive when technological substitution possibilities are small. When $\rho \leq 0$, there is no restriction on σ.

To further illustrate to what extent **H3** is nonrestrictive, we have computed numerically the parameter set where it holds for the CIES–CES case. In figure 1.7 we have plotted this region in the space of the two elasticities $\{\rho, \sigma\}$. The other parameters are $A = 20$, $\alpha = 1/3$, $\beta = 0.3$, $n = 1.097$, which gives reasonable values for the endogenous variables in the case $\sigma = 1$, $\rho = 0$

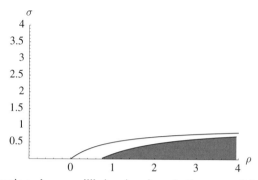

Figure 1.7. The region where equilibrium is unique. In the space of the two elasticities $\{\rho, \sigma\}$, the shaded area represents the region where the equilibrium with perfect foresight is not unique in a CIES–CES example. The solid line represents the sufficient condition (1.19).

(see section A.5.1). The shaded region is the one where the equilibrium is not unique. Non-uniqueness thus arises for low values of both elasticities. To shaded area can also be compared with the sufficient condition (1.19), which is plotted with a solid line. The interest of this latter condition is that it does not depend on the other parameters A, α, β, and n.

We should note that the uniqueness of the equilibrium is a fundamental property for interpreting the perfect foresight assumption in a non-ad-hoc way. Only when the equilibrium is unique can it be analyzed as an equilibrium with rational perfect foresight. In the case of uniqueness, there is no exogenous problem of coordinating expectations, as each agent can solve the model as we did and calculate the next period equilibrium k_{t+1}, which is necessary to obtain the rate of return $R^e_{t+1} = f'(k_{t+1})$. Under the rational perfect foresight hypothesis, the agents use all available information, including the model describing the economy. In the case of multiplicity of equilibria k_{t+1}, as in the left panel of figure 1.8, agents do not know what will be the expectations of the others and thus face non-unique R^e_{t+1}, unless some exogenous coordination device is assumed (e.g., sunspots). In the sequel, we use the following terminology:

Definition 1.3 (Rational inter-temporal equilibrium)
A rational inter-temporal equilibrium is an inter-temporal equilibrium with perfect foresight such that there exists no other inter-temporal equilibrium with perfect foresight having the same initial capital stock.

Note that in the absence of assumption **H3** ensuring the uniqueness of the inter-temporal equilibrium, we end in a logic à la Arrow–Debreu where the way expectations are formed is not treated. This approach will be contrasted with that of this chapter in section 5.4. The literature that models explicitly the formation of expectations is centered around the conditions of uniqueness

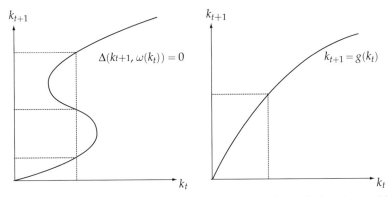

Figure 1.8. Rational inter-temporal equilibrium. In the left panel, there is a multiplicity of solutions k_{t+1}; agents do not know what will be the expectations of the others and thus face non-unique R_{t+1} with perfect foresight. In the right panel, for any level of k_t, there is always a unique solution k_{t+1}, and there is thus a rational inter-temporal equilibrium.

of the equilibrium (see e.g., Blanchard and Kahn (1980)), and would discard models displaying more than one solution.[25]

1.6 CAPITAL DYNAMICS AT A RATIONAL INTER-TEMPORAL EQUILIBRIUM

With the assumptions **H1**, **H2**, and **H3** there exists a unique inter-temporal equilibrium with perfect foresight given the initial capital stock k_0: the *rational inter-temporal equilibrium*. This equilibrium is characterized by the dynamics of the capital stock k_t:

$$k_{t+1} = g(k_t), \qquad (1.20)$$

where $g(k)$ is defined by the implicit function $\Delta(g(k), \omega(k)) = 0$. The function g is continuously differentiable and increasing on $\mathbb{R}_{++}$ with values in $\mathbb{R}_{++}$. This function g is often called the transition function, as it gives k_{t+1} as a function of k_t or the savings locus, as $k_{t+1} = g(k_t)$ gives all the combinations of k_t, k_{t+1} such that savings equal investment.

1.6.1 Steady States and Stability

In this section, we study the properties of the function $g(\cdot)$; this will allow us to characterize the capital accumulation process and discuss growth and convergence issues. We first need to introduce some definitions.

---

[25] In contrast, a recent literature has developed in macroeconomics that exploits the presence of multiple equilibria to understand cycles and growth phenomena. Benhabib and Farmer (1999) survey this approach.

Let us re-define the function g for the dynamics to be defined on $\mathbb{R}_+$. The function $g(k)$ is increasing and non-negative. As a bounded and monotonic function on $\mathbb{R}_{++}$ admits a limit, there exists a limit of $g(k)$ when $k > 0$ goes to 0 and this limit is non-negative:

$$g(0+) = \lim_{k \to 0, \; k>0} g(k) \geq 0.$$

Defining $g(0) = g(0+)$, the function g is defined and continuous on $\mathbb{R}_+$, and the dynamics (1.20) are defined on $\mathbb{R}_+$.

Definition 1.4 (Steady state)
$\bar{k} > 0$ is a steady state of the dynamics described by (1.20) if $g(\bar{k}) = \bar{k}$. For the particular value $\bar{k} = 0$, when $g(0) = 0$, we say that 0 is a corner steady state.

A steady state is thus a point $\bar{k}$ such that the constant sequence $k_t = \bar{k}$ is a solution to equation (1.20). For the corner steady state, we have the following property:

Proposition 1.4 (Corner steady states)
0 is a corner steady state of the dynamics described by (1.20) if and only if $\omega(0) = 0$, or equivalently, if and only if $f(0) = 0$.

Proof: Assume $\omega(0) = 0$. Then, for $k > 0$, the inequality $0 < g(k) < \frac{\omega(k)}{1+n}$ (savings lower than wage) implies $g(0) = 0$.

Assume $\omega(0) > 0$. Then the limit of the continuous function $g(k) = h(\omega(k))$ is $h(\omega(0)) > 0$.

The equivalence between $\omega(0) = 0$ and $f(0) = 0$ is shown in appendix A.1.3. ∎

This proposition says that if $f(0) > 0$ it is possible to produce, and hence accumulate, without capital and 0 is not a steady state. Before analyzing the stability properties of the steady states, we precise two definitions of stability. The standard definition of local stability of a steady state is:[26]

Definition 1.5 (Local stability)
$\bar{k}$ is locally stable if there exists $\varepsilon > 0$ such that for any k_0 in $\mathbb{R}_+$ which verifies $|k_0 - \bar{k}| < \varepsilon$, the dynamics (1.20) with initial capital stock k_0 converge to $\bar{k}$.

This corresponds to two situations:

- If $\bar{k}$ is an interior steady state ($\bar{k} > 0$), there exists $\varepsilon > 0$ such that $\forall k_0 \in [\bar{k} - \varepsilon, \bar{k} + \varepsilon]$ the dynamics converge to $\bar{k}$.

---

[26] A more precise notion of stability (for both local stability and stability in an interval) requires in addition the following condition (Lyapounov stability): $\forall \varepsilon > 0$, $\exists y > 0$ such that $\forall k_0 \in [\bar{k} - y, \bar{k} + y]$, the whole dynamics belong to $[\bar{k} - \varepsilon, \bar{k} + \varepsilon]$.

- If $\bar{k}$ is the corner steady state ($\bar{k} = 0$), there exists $\varepsilon > 0$ such that $\forall k_0 \in [0, \varepsilon]$ the dynamics converge to $\bar{k}$.

A steady state which is not locally stable is unstable.

The definition of stability in a set is:

Definition 1.6 (Stability in an interval)
Let $\mathcal{J}$ be an interval of $\mathbb{R}_+$ and consider $\bar{k}$ a steady state belonging to $\mathcal{J}$. Then $\bar{k}$ is stable in $\mathcal{J}$ if for all $k_0 \in \mathcal{J}$ the dynamics (1.20) with initial capital stock k_0 converges to $\bar{k}$. $\bar{k}$ is globally stable in $\mathbb{R}_+$ ($\mathbb{R}_{++}$) if it is stable in $\mathbb{R}_+$ ($\mathbb{R}_{++}$).

1.6.2 Dynamics

As the function $g(k)$ is non-decreasing, the following result for global dynamics can be obtained (proof in appendix A.3.1):

Proposition 1.5 (Monotonicity of the dynamics)
Any time path of the capital stock satisfying (1.20) is a monotonic sequence. This sequence converges either to a steady state or to a boundary of the interval on which $g(k)$ is defined.

The consequence of this proposition is that the dynamics of k_t converges either to 0, or to $+\infty$, or to a steady state $\bar{k}$. The equilibrium trajectory never goes from one side of a steady state to the other. We shall thus consider the three possible cases ($\infty, \bar{k}, 0$) successively. Let us first show that unlimited growth of capital is excluded, which excludes the convergence of k_t to $+\infty$. Proposition 1.6 is illustrated in figure 1.9.

Proposition 1.6 (Boundedness of the dynamics)
Any time path satisfying (1.20) is bounded. For any $k_0 \geq 0$, the dynamics verify

$$\forall t, \quad k_t \leq \max\{k_0, \bar{k}_{\max}\}.$$

where $\bar{k}_{\max}$ is the upper bound of the set of $k \geq 0$ such that $g(k) \geq k$. It is the largest steady state.

Only in the case where $\forall k > 0$, $g(k) < k$ does one have $\bar{k}_{\max} = 0$, and the dynamics monotonic and convergent to 0, for any $k_0 \geq 0$.

Proof: By definition of g, we have

$$g(k) = \frac{1}{1+n} s(\omega(k), f'(g(k))) < \frac{\omega(k)}{1+n}.$$

Under the assumption **H2**, the ratio $\omega(k)/k$ goes to 0 when k goes to $+\infty$ (see appendix A.1.2). This implies

$$\lim_{k \to +\infty} \frac{g(k)}{k} = 0,$$

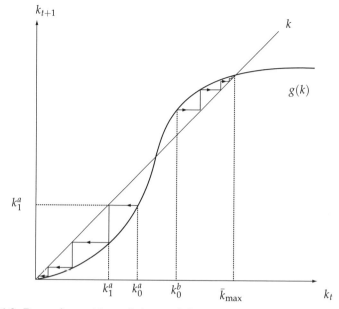

Figure 1.9. Dynamics and boundedness of time paths. We represent in the plane $\{k_t, k_{t+1}\}$ the curve $k_{t+1} = g(k_t)$. The steady states are given by the intersections with the 45° line. As the function $g(k)$ ends below the 45° line when $k \to +\infty$, the dynamics are always bounded. We have represented two different time paths. The first path starts from k_0^a. The value of the capital stock at $t = 1$ is given by $k_1^a = g(k_0^a)$. This value can be reported on the horizontal axis using the 45° line. We see that this trajectory converges to the corner steady state 0. The trajectory starting from k_0^b converges to the steady state $\bar{k}_{\max}$.

and for k large enough, say $k > \hat{k}$, we have $g(k) < k$. This implies that, for any $k_0 \geq \hat{k}$, $g(k_0) < k_0$ and the time path is decreasing and converges to some point $\bar{k} \geq 0$. In the case $\bar{k} > 0$, $\bar{k}$ is the largest steady state (the time path never goes to the other side of a steady state). For such a decreasing trajectory we have:

$$k_t \leq k_0 = \max\{k_0, \bar{k}\}.$$

For all other dynamics, with $k_0 \leq \bar{k}$, we have $\forall t, k_t \leq \bar{k}$, and thus

$$k_t \leq \max\{k_0, \bar{k}\} = \bar{k}.$$

In the case where $\bar{k} = 0$, we have $\forall t > 0$, $g(k) < k$, there is no positive steady state, and $\lim k_t = 0$ for any $k_0 > 0$. By continuity, $g(0) = 0$ and 0 is a corner steady state. In both cases the largest steady state is

$$\bar{k}_{\max} = \bar{k} = \max\{k \geq 0; \ g(k) \geq k\}. \qquad \blacksquare$$

This proposition gives one of the important characteristic of the dynamics in the overlapping generations model. The boundedness of the dynamics results from two properties:

$$(1+n)k_{t+1} = s_t < \omega(k_t) \quad \text{and} \quad \lim_{k_t \to +\infty} \frac{\omega(k_t)}{k_t} = 0,$$

i.e., savings are smaller than wage income and the ratio of wage to capital tends to zero as capital goes to infinity. In other words, as Jones and Manuelli (1992) stress, the young individuals do not have sufficient income to acquire a stock of capital large enough to sustain long-run growth. In section 2.5, we shall see that the allocation chosen by a benevolent planner can display sustained growth. In this case, Jones and Manuelli (1992) argue that income redistribution from the old to the young can fight against the declining wage to capital ratio and achieve sustained growth. Alternatively, if households are altruistic à la Barro (1974) and leave bequests (see section 5.1), growth can also be sustained.[27]

The boundedness of the capital dynamics in the overlapping generations model sharply contrasts with the properties of the standard growth model of Solow (1956). In his model, savings are simply proportional to output: $s_t = af(k_t)$. Moreover, contrary to the wage–capital ratio, the output–capital ratio does not necessarily go to zero as capital increases unboundedly. These two properties make unbounded growth possible (see the original article of Solow (1956) or chapter 1 of Barro and Sala-I-Martin (1995) for a modern presentation). Indeed, we have that the limit of the decreasing function $f(k)/k$ of k, when k goes to infinity, verifies

$$\lim_{k \to +\infty} \frac{f(k)}{k} = \lim_{k \to +\infty} f'(k) = \ell \geq 0.$$

We thus have for all $k_t > 0$, with $k_{t+1} = a\, f(k_t)/(1+n)$,

$$\frac{k_{t+1}}{k_t} = \frac{a\, f(k_t)}{(1+n)k_t} > \frac{a\ell}{1+n}.$$

Thus if $\ell \geq (1+n)/a$, the sequence (k_t) increases and tends to $+\infty$. We can obtain this case, e.g., with a CES production function with $-1 < \rho < 0$ (high substitution), where $\ell = A\alpha^{-1/\rho}$ (see appendix A.1.2).

Example: When the utility function is logarithmic and the production function is Cobb–Douglas, equation (1.20) is

$$k_{t+1} = g(k_t) = \frac{1}{1+n}\frac{\beta}{1+\beta}\omega(k_t) = \frac{1}{1+n}\frac{\beta}{1+\beta}A(1-\alpha)k_t^\alpha.$$

$$(1.21)$$

---

[27] This is also true in the case of the "joy-of-giving" altruism; see Araujo and Martins (1999).

There exists a unique positive steady state,

$$\bar{k} = \left(\frac{1}{1+n} \frac{\beta}{1+\beta} A(1-\alpha) \right)^{\frac{1}{1-\alpha}},$$

which is globally stable in $\mathbb{R}_{++}$, i.e., for all $k_0 > 0$ the trajectory converges to $\bar{k}$. The corner steady state 0 is unstable. This case is illustrated in the left panel of figure 1.10.

When the utility function is logarithmic and the production function is CES, equation (1.20) is

$$k_{t+1} = g(k_t) = \frac{\beta A(1-\alpha) \left(\alpha k_t^{-\rho} + 1 - \alpha \right)^{-(1+\rho)/\rho}}{(1+n)(1+\beta)}.$$

To study the number of steady states we need to discuss the concavity of g:

$$g''(k) = \frac{\beta A(1-\alpha)\alpha(1+\rho)}{(1+n)(1+\beta)} \frac{\rho \alpha k^{-\rho} - (1+\rho)(1-\alpha)}{\left(\alpha k_t^{-\rho} + 1 - \alpha \right)^{(1+3\rho)/\rho} k^{2+\rho}}.$$

- When $\rho < 0$, we have $g''(k) < 0$ and $g(k)$ is strictly concave. Moreover,

$$g(0) = \frac{\beta(1-\alpha)^{-1/\rho} A}{(1+n)(1+\beta)} > 0,$$

and 0 is not a corner steady state. There exists a unique steady state which is globally stable in $\mathbb{R}_+$. This case is illustrated in the right panel of figure 1.10.

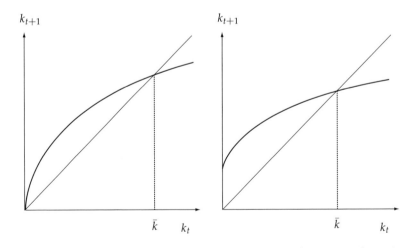

Cobb–Douglas production function   CES production function with $\rho < 0$

Figure 1.10. Examples with a logarithmic utility and $\rho \leq 0$. When factors of production are highly substitutable (CES production function with $\rho \leq 0$), there is always one non-trivial steady state which is globally stable. When $\rho = 0$, 0 is a corner steady state; when $\rho < 0$ there is no corner steady state.

- When $\rho > 0$, we have $g''(k) > 0$ for $k < \hat{k}$ and $g''(k) < 0$ for $k > \hat{k}$, where

$$\hat{k} = \left(\frac{(1+\rho)(1-\alpha)}{\rho\alpha} \right)^{-1/\rho}.$$

The function $g(k)$ is thus convex for $k < \hat{k}$ and concave for $k > \hat{k}$. Moreover, $g(0) = 0$, as $\omega(0) = 0$ (appendix A.1.2). Two cases should be distinguished:

- if

$$\max_k \frac{\omega(k)}{k} < (1+n)\frac{1+\beta}{\beta},$$

which implies that $g(k)$ is always below k, then there is no positive steady state. In this case, the trajectory converges to zero for any k_0. This case is illustrated in the left panel of figure 1.11.

- if

$$\max_k \frac{\omega(k)}{k} > (1+n)\frac{1+\beta}{\beta},$$

there exist two positive steady states $\bar{k}_a < \bar{k}_b$. All trajectories starting from $k_0 < \bar{k}_a$ converge to 0. 0 is locally stable (it is stable in $[0, \bar{k}_a[$). The trajectory starting at $k_0 = \bar{k}_a$ remains at $\bar{k}_a$. $\bar{k}_a$ is unstable. The trajectories starting with $k_0 > \bar{k}_a$ converge to $\bar{k}_b$. $\bar{k}_b$ is locally stable (it is stable in $]\bar{k}_a, +\infty[$). This case is illustrated in the right panel of figure 1.11.

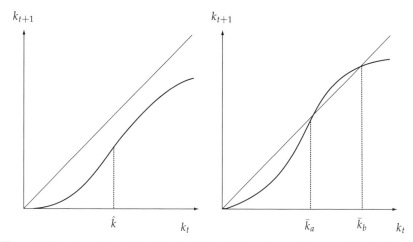

Figure 1.11. Examples with a logarithmic utility and $\rho > 0$. When the factors of production are poorly substitutable (CES production function with $\rho > 0$), there are either no or two non-trivial steady states (plus the case of one steady state when the function is tangent to the 45° line, which is not illustrated). When the corner steady state is the only steady state, it is globally stable. If there are two non-trivial steady states, the higher one is locally stable and so is the corner one.

1.6.3 The Behavior Near 0

We have defined $g(0) = g(0+)$, allowing us to obtain a function $g(k)$ increasing and continuous on $\mathbb{R}_+$ and differentiable on $\mathbb{R}_{++}$. The dynamics are then defined for all $k_0 \geq 0$. We now consider the case where the initial capital stock is $k_0 = 0$:

- At $k_0 = 0$, if $g(0) > 0$, then $\omega(0) > 0$, and the optimal choice of the consumers with perfect foresight is an interior solution with positive consumptions and positive savings $k_1 = s_0/(1+n) = g(0) > 0$. Moreover, for small k, $g(k) > k$ and the dynamics necessarily increase and converge to some steady state $\bar{k}_1 > 0$, which is the lowest positive steady state.
- At $k_0 = 0$ if $g(0) = 0$, then $\omega(0) = 0$. Young households have zero income in period 0, and whatever their expectations R_{t+1}^e may be, their consumptions and savings are zero: $k_1 = g(0) = 0$. Then 0 is a corner steady state for the dynamics defined on $\mathbb{R}_+$. There are two possibilities is general near 0 when $g(0) = 0$ (we consider only the case where $g(k) \neq k$ for small $k \neq 0$):
  - for small $k > 0$, $g(k) > k$, and the dynamics are increasing;
  - for small $k > 0$, $g(k) < k$, and the dynamics are decreasing and converge to 0.

Definition 1.7 (Catching point)
0 is a catching point when for small $k > 0$, $g(k) < k$.

This means that there exists an interval $(0, \underline{k})$, with $\underline{k} > 0$ finite or infinite, such that for all $k_0 \in (0, \underline{k})$ the dynamics with perfect foresight converges to 0. Thus, the capital disappears in the long run. When $\underline{k}$ is finite, $\underline{k}$ is the lowest positive steady state. When $\underline{k} = +\infty$, we say that 0 is a *global* catching point.

A catching point is often called in the literature a *poverty trap*. In figure 1.11, we have in the left panel a case with a global catching point (the poverty trap is said to be *inescapable*). In the right panel, $\underline{k}$ is finite, and the poverty trap can be escaped provided that the initial capital stock is high enough ($k_0 > \underline{k}$).[28] In the latter case, the growth path followed by an economy crucially depends on the initial condition. For low k_0 one can be caught by the trap; for high k_0 one converges to the high steady state. This property of the model is consistent with the stagnation of an important number of countries at low levels of economic development and with the existence of a growing income gap between certain economies that were similar at some points (Lucas (1993)).

We now derive some conditions for such a catching point to arise. A sufficient condition, illustrated in figure 1.12, is the following.

---

[28] Extensive discussions are provided in Galor (1996) and Azariadis (1996).

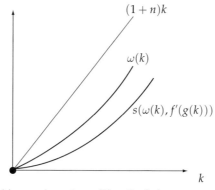

Figure 1.12. A catching point. As $\omega(0) = 0$, 0 is a corner steady state. As $\lim_{k\to 0} \omega(k)/k < (1+n)$, 0 is a catching point.

Lemma 1.1 (Sufficient condition for a catching point)
If we have

$$\lim_{k\to 0} \frac{\omega(k)}{k} < 1 + n,$$

then 0 is a catching point.

Proof: We have for all $k > 0$

$$g(k) = \frac{1}{1+n} s(\omega(k),\, f'(g(k))) < \frac{\omega(k)}{1+n}.$$

The assumption implies that for all small enough k, say $0 < k < \varepsilon$, we have $\frac{\omega(k)}{k} < 1 + n$, and thus $g(k) < k$. ∎

A necessary condition is the following: If 0 is a catching point, then $\omega(0) = 0$. Indeed, if $\omega(0) > 0$, then when $k \to 0$, $g(k) = h(\omega(k))$ converges to $h(\omega(0)) > 0$, and $\omega(0) > 0$ implies that 0 is not an equilibrium.

Another necessary condition is obtained under the assumptions **A4** and $f'(0) > 1/\beta$.

Lemma 1.2 (Necessary condition for a catching point)
*Assume **A4** and $f'(0) > 1/\beta$. Then, if 0 is a catching point,[29] we have*

$$\lim_{k\to 0} \frac{\omega(k)}{k} \le (1+n)\frac{1+\beta}{\beta}.$$

---

[29] As $\frac{\omega(k)}{k}$ is not monotonic, we are not sure that the limit exists. However, the proof applies to the limit superior (lim sup) when the limit does not exist. The lim sup is an upper bound which always exists, finite or infinite (see appendix A.2.3).

Proof: $s(w, 1/\beta)$ is solution of $u'(w - s) = u'(s/\beta)$, which implies $w - s = s/\beta$ and

$$s(w, 1/\beta) = \frac{\beta w}{1 + \beta}.$$

For small $k > 0$, $f'(g(k)) > 1/\beta$ and

$$g(k) = \frac{1}{1 + n} s(\omega(k)), \quad f'(g(k))) \geq \frac{1}{1 + n} s(\omega(k), 1/\beta),$$

as $s'_R \geq 0$ (A4). Hence,

$$g(k) \geq \frac{\beta \omega(k)}{(1 + \beta)(1 + n)},$$

from which we deduce that

$$\frac{g(k)}{k} < 1 \quad \Longrightarrow \quad \frac{\omega(k)}{k} < (1 + n)\frac{1 + \beta}{\beta}. \qquad \blacksquare$$

The necessary condition for 0 to be a catching point can be converted into a sufficient condition for 0 not to be a catching point.

Proposition 1.7 (Absence of catching point)
Assume that $s'_R \geq 0$ and $f'(0) > 1/\beta$. Then 0 is not a catching point if

$$\lim_{k \to 0} \frac{\omega(k)}{k} > (1 + n)\frac{1 + \beta}{\beta}.$$

Intuitively, if the first unit of capital is sufficiently productive in terms of labor productivity, the poverty trap will be avoided.

The above propositions show that the overlapping generations model is an interesting tool to study the conditions under which a poverty trap arises. The example developed above illustrates that CES technologies with low substitution are consistent with catching points and poverty traps. If the initial capital/labor ratio is low enough, the economy will converge to the trivial steady state with zero capital rather than to the one with high capital/labor ratio. The one-sector overlapping generations model is the simplest framework to understand that the path of growth may depend on initial conditions.

A further enrichment of the analysis is to consider a two-sector overlapping generations model, either to make an explicit distinction between investment goods and consumption goods as in Galor (1992), and/or to model explicitly the interactions between two countries (or two part of the world). Such a framework should be able to determine the conditions under which poverty traps persist, although capital can flow from one part of the world to the other, and relieve countries with unfavorable initial conditions. More generally, the two-sector overlapping generations model is an important framework of analysis for issues that require the existence of more than one sector of production. Recently, there have been a large number of applications of this model directed at a more comprehensive study of international trade and growth. Some recent applications of this framework include Mountford (1998) and (1999) and Cremers (2001).

1.6.4 A Quick Look at the Empirics of Growth

A Long-Run Perspective on Savings. One fundamental characteristic of the model developed above is that savings (of the young) drive capital accumulation, and hence medium-run growth. In the standard two-period overlapping generations model, savings are based on wage income. In extended models, capital income (with three-period-lived households; see section 1.8.8) or inherited wealth (with altruistic households; see section 5.1) can be saved.

Maddison (1992) provides historical estimates of long-run gross savings rates for 11 countries. Table 1.1 presents the gross savings as a fraction of GDP, each period corresponding more or less to one generation. Table 1.2 presents the corresponding annual growth rates.

Table 1.1. *Gross Savings as a Fraction of GDP*

Country	1870–1889	1890–1913	1914–1938	1939–1959	1960–1987
Australia	11.2	13.0	12.4	18.5	23.6
Canada	9.1	12.2	14.4	20.3	22.4
India		5.8	7.4	8.7	15.3
Taiwan		9.6	25.5	14.7	27.0
Japan	12.4	12.3	16.7	25.7	35.0
U.K.	13.9	13.6	8.3	8.6	18.8
U.S.	19.1	18.3	17.0	17.4	18.7

Table 1.2. *Growth Rates*

Country	1870–1890	1890–1914	1914–1939	1939–1960	1960–1988
Australia	1.1	0.2	0.5	2.0	2.3
Canada	1.7	2.2	0.7	3.0	3.1
India		0.5	−0.2	0.6	1.9
Taiwan		0.2	2.3	0.0	7.0
Japan	1.4	1.1	3.1	1.7	5.4
U.K.	1.1	0.9	0.7	1.7	2.3
U.S.	1.6	1.5	1.3	2.6	2.4

A first conclusion that we can drawn from these figures is that savings rate of the post-war (World War II) period in most of the countries are well above their pre-war level. Notice that the post-war period is also the period that experienced the highest growth rate in output per head. As stressed by Maddison (1992), "there is a general positive relationship between the faster post-war growth period in output per head and the acceleration in savings rate, and a similar positive relation in the post 1973 slowdown. The U.S.A., which has the smallest post-war acceleration in per capita growth, was also the country with least change in its long run savings habits."

On the one hand, when we consider the countries for which we observe a catching up with the richest, i.e., Taiwan and Japan, they had experienced very high levels of domestic savings. On the other hand, the countries remaining in a sort of poverty trap, like India, remain at very low levels. When there are realistic opportunities for economic catch-up, i.e., when the productivity of capital is high, then the improvement in expected returns induce a rise in savings and investment in the follower countries. This high domestic investment level is the main engine of growth.

Growth in the Very Long Run. When we study growth within an overlapping generations model, we are obviously interested in the dynamics of wealth from one generation to the next, and hence, in growth in the very long run. There is some evidence that economic growth was very slow before 1700. Real wages and per capita GDP were roughly the same in 1700 as they were 2000 years before (see Jones (2001) and the references therein). For the recent past, Maddison (1995) has provided a set of long time series, and this set is helpful in discussing growth in a generational perspective and illustrating some of the theoretical results.

Figure 1.13 presents the GDP per capita of selected years for the whole set of countries for which the data are available (starting in 1820). Each point broadly reflects the standard of living of one generation in one country. The first fact that emerges very clearly from this picture is that growth is a monotonic process at this frequency (the only exception is Mexico, for which the generation living in 1850 had a lower income than the one living in 1820).

An important issue in growth theory is that of *convergence* (see Galor (1996), Quah (1996), Barro and Sala-I-Martin (1995)). Over this very long period of time, there is no single pattern of growth: some (relatively) rich countries remain rich, some poor ones remain poor (Africa, India), some poor ones become rich (Japan), etc. Moreover, there is no clear tendency for the cross-country distribution of income to become more concentrated.

When we consider the most developed countries alone (according to the OECD classification), the pattern of convergence is different. Figure 1.14 presents the same data as figure 1.13, but for the most developed countries only. The absolute convergence of these countries to a single growth path appears clearly.

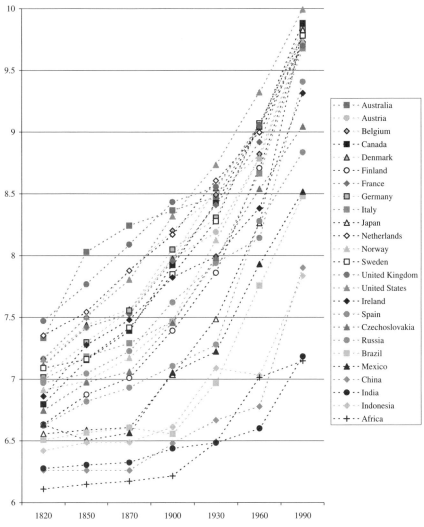

Figure 1.13. GDP per capita in the world. GDP per capita is increasing from one generation to the next in all countries for all periods.

1.7 COMPARISON OF MYOPIC AND PERFECT FORESIGHT

Although the assumption of myopic foresight is no longer used in the literature, it has long been viewed as a useful framework in macro-economics. For example, Lucas and Rapping (1969) see myopic foresight as a good approximation when the growth rates of prices are stable.

In this section, we compare the dynamics occurring under the assumption of perfect foresight with those occurring under myopic foresight (see

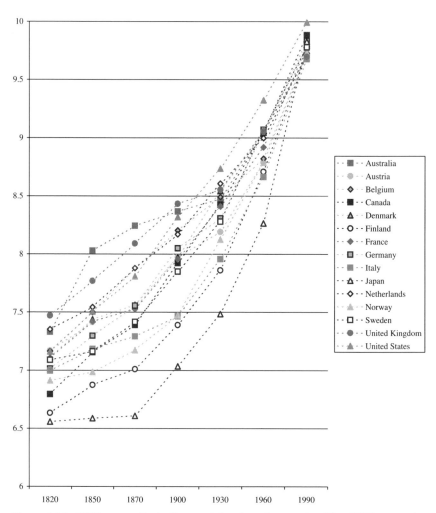

Figure 1.14. GDP per capita in the most developed countries. The GDP per capita in the most developed countries converges to a similar growth path.

Michel and de la Croix (2000)). We shall see that this comparison can be helpful because, under certain conditions, the knowledge of the dynamics under myopic foresight (which are much simpler) allows us to know the dynamics under perfect foresight.

One important difference is that the dynamics of myopic foresight are not monotonic under the assumption **H3**, which will allow us to discuss other types of time paths. With the assumption of myopic foresight,

$$R_{t+1}^e = R_t = f'(k_t).$$

The inter-temporal equilibrium with initial capital stock k_0 is unique, and it is characterized by the dynamics of k_t:

$$k_{t+1} = \frac{1}{1+n} s(\omega(k_t), f'(k_t)) \equiv m(k_t). \tag{1.22}$$

Under the assumptions **H1** and **H2**, $m(k)$ is defined and continuously differentiable on $\mathbb{R}_{++}$ with values in $\mathbb{R}_{++}$. To analyze the myopic dynamics driven by equation (1.22), we can apply the method of the preceding section only when $m(k)$ is increasing. The derivative of $m(k)$ is

$$m'(k) = \frac{1}{1+n}[s'_w(\omega(k), f'(k))\omega'(k) + s'_R(\omega(k), f'(k))]f''(k)). \tag{1.23}$$

As $s'_w, \omega' > 0$ and $f'' < 0$, a sufficient condition for $m'(k) > 0$ is $s'_R \leq 0$. When this is the case, the dynamics with myopic foresight is monotonic, and the study is similar to the one made in the previous section. The inequality $s'_R \leq 0$ is compatible with the assumption **A4** only if $s'_R = 0$. Nevertheless, the positive steady states for the two dynamics are identical.

1.7.1 The Steady States

Proposition 1.8 (Steady states of the dynamics with myopic foresight)
Under the assumptions **H1**, **H2**, *and* **H3**, *the two dynamics with perfect and myopic foresight have the same positive steady states.*

Proof: $\bar{k} > 0$ is a steady state for the dynamics with myopic foresight if and only if

$$\bar{k} = m(\bar{k}) = \frac{1}{1+n} s(\omega(\bar{k}), f'(\bar{k})).$$

For the dynamics with perfect foresight, $\bar{k} > 0$ is a steady state if and only if

$$\bar{k} = g(\bar{k}) = \frac{1}{1+n} s(\omega(\bar{k}), f'(g(\bar{k}))),$$

and the two conditions are equivalent. ∎

When 0 is a *corner* steady state of the dynamics with perfect foresight, we have $\omega(0) = 0$ and $g(0) = 0$ (proposition 1.4). Then it is also a steady state for the dynamics with myopic foresight, as $0 < m(k) < \omega(k)/(1+n)$ and $\lim_{k \to 0} m(k) = 0$. The converse is not necessarily verified (see figure 1.15).

Example: For a CES production function with $\rho < 0$ we have $\omega(0) > 0$ and $f'(0) = +\infty$. For a CIES utility function with $\sigma < 1$ we have $s(\omega(0), f'(0)) = 0$.

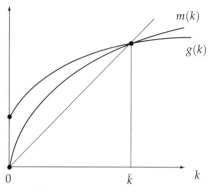

Figure 1.15. Steady states of the dynamics with myopic foresight: The two dynamics with perfect and myopic foresight have the same positive steady state(s). When 0 is a corner steady state of the dynamics with myopic foresight, it is not necessarily a corner steady state of the dynamics with perfect foresight. A case with a CES production function with $\rho < 0$, and a CIES utility function with $\sigma < 1$ is represented.

Hence, $m(0) = 0$, but $g(0) > 0$ and 0 is a corner steady state for the dynamics with myopic foresight only. In this situation, although wages are positive at $k = 0$, savings are zero in the myopic foresight case, because the interest factor forecasted on the basis of the current capital stock is infinite (agents do not forecast that the capital stock can be higher tomorrow). In the perfect foresight case, savings are positive, as the agents expect the interest rate to be finite.

1.7.2 Local Stability

For the myopic dynamics (1.22), the derivative $m'(k)$ is given by (1.23). This derivative is crucial to determine the local stability of the steady state:

Proposition 1.9 (First-order stability condition)
Let $\bar{k}$ be a steady state $\in \mathbb{R}_{++}$. Then for the myopic dynamics:

- *if $|m'(\bar{k})| < 1$, then $\bar{k}$ is locally stable;*
- *if $|m'(\bar{k})| > 1$, then $\bar{k}$ is unstable, i.e., it is not locally stable;*
- *if $|m'(\bar{k})| = 1$, then the stability type of $\bar{k}$ cannot be determined on the basis of the first derivative.*

Proof: We apply the criterion of local stability provided in appendix A.3.2 to the function m. ∎

We say that $\bar{k}$ is *hyperbolic* when $|m'(\bar{k})| \neq 1$.

For the rational dynamics, $k_{t+1} = g(k_t)$, we have at a steady state $\bar{k} > 0$,

$g(\bar{k}) = \bar{k}$, and

$$g'(\bar{k}) = \frac{s'_w(\omega(\bar{k}), \, f'(\bar{k}))\omega'(\bar{k})}{1 + n - s'_R(\omega(\bar{k}), \, f'(\bar{k})) \, f''(\bar{k})}.$$

If $g'(\bar{k}) < 1$, $\bar{k}$ is locally stable. Under the assumption **H3** this is equivalent to $s'_w \omega' < 1 + n - s'_R f''$, or to $m'(\bar{k}) < 1$. If $g'(\bar{k}) > 1$, $\bar{k}$ is unstable. The condition $g'(\bar{k}) > 1$ is equivalent to $m'(\bar{k}) > 1$.

Proposition 1.10 (Stability of monotonic dynamics)
Assume **H1**, **H2**, *and* **H3**, *and consider a steady state* $\bar{k} > 0$.
In the case where $m'(\bar{k}) \geq 0$ *(monotonic dynamics with myopic foresight),* $\bar{k}$ *is respectively stable, unstable, or non-hyperbolic for the two dynamics when* $m'(k)$ *is respectively* <1, >1, *or* $= 1$.
In the case where $m'(\bar{k}) < 0$, $\bar{k}$ *is stable for the rational dynamics, but it may be stable* $(m'(k) > -1)$ *or unstable* $(m'(k) < -1)$ *for the myopic dynamics.*

Proof: When $m'(\bar{k}) \geq 0$, we have $|m'(\bar{k})| = m'(\bar{k})$ and the first-order stability conditions for the two dynamics are identical. When $m'(\bar{k}) < 0$, we have $s'_w \omega' < 1 + n - s'_R f''$, $g'(\bar{k}) < 1$, and $\bar{k}$ is stable for the rational dynamics. ∎

Corollary: *When the rational dynamics are defined and the myopic dynamics are monotonic, then the two dynamics have the same structure in the sense that the positive steady states are the same and the first-order stability conditions are equivalent.*

This is a very useful result in the case of monotonic myopic dynamics: in this case, the study of these dynamics, which are much simpler, allows one to know the dynamics for the perfect foresight situation.

When $m'(\bar{k}) < 0$, the myopic dynamics are non-monotonic and characterized by oscillations. Indeed, if m is decreasing near $\bar{k}$, we have near $\bar{k}$

$$k_t < \bar{k} \quad \Longleftrightarrow \quad m(k_t) > m(\bar{k}) \quad \Longleftrightarrow \quad k_{t+1} > \bar{k}.$$

In section 1.8.1, we further analyze myopic dynamics that are not monotonic.

1.7.3 Uniqueness of the Steady State

We have seen that when the utility function is logarithmic and the production function is CES with $\rho \leq 0$, the positive steady state k is unique and globally stable under perfect foresight. Another example displaying these properties is when the utility function is CIES and the production function is Cobb–Douglas (see section 1.8.1). We have also seen a simple case with either multiple positive steady states or no positive steady states; this case arises when the utility function is logarithmic and the production function is CES with $\rho > 0$. To study the number of steady states we can of course use the results on the myopic dynamics, which are simpler.

The savings function $s(\omega(k), f'(k))$ is defined by

$$u'(\omega(k) - s) = \beta f'(k)u'(f'(k)s).$$

It depends on the first derivatives of u and f. A general condition which is sufficient for uniqueness, like the concavity of g, involves the third derivatives of u and f (see Galor and Ryder (1989)).

To study the number of steady states, however, we can use the results on the myopic dynamics and derive a simpler sufficient condition for uniqueness.

Proposition 1.11 (Uniqueness of the steady state)
There exists no more than one positive steady state $\bar{k}$ of the dynamics with perfect foresight when

$$s'_w(\omega(k), f'(k))\omega'(k) + s'_R(\omega(k), f'(k))f''(k) < \frac{s(\omega(k), f'(k))}{k} \qquad \forall k > 0.$$

Such a steady state exists if and only if

$$\lim_{k \to 0} \frac{s(\omega(k), f'(k))}{k} > 1 + n.$$

Proof: There exists no more than one positive steady state $\bar{k}$ if the function $s(\omega(k), f'(k))/k$ is strictly decreasing:

$$\frac{d}{dk} \frac{s(\omega(k), f'(k))}{k} = \frac{1}{k}\left(s'_w \omega' + s'_R f'' - \frac{s}{k}\right) < 0 \qquad \forall k > 0.$$

This condition can be rewritten

$$m'(k) < \frac{1}{1+n} \frac{s(\omega(k), f'(k))}{k} \qquad \forall k > 0,$$

which leads to the expression in the proposition.

If and only if $\lim_{k \to 0} s(\omega(k), f'(k))/k > 1 + n$ holds, the function $s(\omega(k), f'(k))/k$ starts above $1 + n$, and, as it is decreasing and goes to 0, it takes the value $1 + n$ only once, and the steady state is unique. ∎

As $s(\omega(k), f'(k)) < \omega(k)$, a necessary condition for existence is

$$\lim_{k \to 0} \frac{\omega(k)}{k} > 1 + n$$

(see Galor and Ryder (1989)).

The interest of this proposition is to propose a condition for uniqueness that bears only on the second derivatives of the functions u and f.

For the rational dynamics, the uniqueness of the positive steady state together with the monotonicity implies the global stability of the steady state when it is locally stable.

The aim of this section is to provide some applications and extensions of the competitive overlapping generations model. In the first two subsections we illustrate the basic model with the case of myopic foresight (section 1.8.1) and the study of a demographic shock (section 1.8.2).

The four following subsections should be read one after each other. They present extensions to the model. Section 1.8.3 extends the equilibrium analysis to non-separable utility functions. This allows us to introduce homothetic preferences in section 1.8.4. In section 1.8.5, we show that under the assumption of homothetic preferences, the models with heterogeneous agents can be studied with the same tools as models with representative individuals. Deterministic technical progress is introduced in section 1.8.6.

Section 1.8.7 introduces imperfect credit markets and studies an example with two periods of work. In section 1.8.8, we consider a model with three-period-lived households. Finally, an example with imperfect credit markets in the three-period model is studied in the last section.

1.8.1 Myopic and Perfect Foresight in an Example

We have seen in section 1.7 that the dynamics can be non-monotonic when forecasts are myopic. This exercise illustrates this property and compares the two dynamics (myopic and perfect foresight) in a simple example. We take a Cobb–Douglas production function and a CIES utility function.

Study of the Rational Dynamics. We have

$$\Delta(k, w) = (1+n)k - \frac{w}{1 + \beta^{-\sigma}(\alpha A)^{1-\sigma} k^\gamma},$$

with $\gamma = (\sigma - 1)(1 - \alpha)$. The function

$$\frac{\Delta(k, w)}{k} = (1+n) - \frac{w}{k + \beta^{-\sigma}(\alpha A)^{1-\sigma} k^{1+\gamma}}$$

is strictly increasing in k, since $\gamma + 1 = \sigma(1 - \alpha) + \alpha > 0$. It increases from $-\infty$ to $1 + n$ as k increases from 0 to $+\infty$. Hence, there exists a unique $k > 0$, $k = h(w)$, such that $\Delta(k, w) = 0$. The derivative of $h(w)$, $h'(w) = dk/dw$, is equal to the reciprocal of

$$\frac{dw}{dk} = (1+n)[1 + \beta^{-\sigma}(\alpha A)^{1-\sigma}(1 + \gamma)k^\gamma] > 0.$$

For any values of the parameters $\beta > 0, 0 < \alpha < 1, A > 0, \sigma > 0$, the rational dynamics are defined on $\mathbb{R}_{++}$ and are monotonic:

$$g'(k) = h'(\omega(k))\omega'(k)$$

$$= \frac{\alpha(1-\alpha)Ak^{\alpha-1}}{(1+n)[1+\beta^{-\sigma}(\alpha A)^{1-\sigma}(1+\gamma)k^{\gamma}]}$$

$$= \frac{\alpha(1-\alpha)A}{(1+n)\left[k^{1-\alpha} + \beta^{-\sigma}(\alpha A)^{1-\sigma}(1+\gamma)k^{\sigma(1-\alpha)}\right]}.$$

The denominator increases with k from 0 to $+\infty$. Consequently $g'(k)$ decreases from $+\infty$ to 0. Moreover, g is concave, so that there exists a unique steady state $k^* > 0$ which is globally stable in $\mathbb{R}_{++}$.

Study of the Myopic Dynamics. We have

$$m(k) = \frac{k^{\alpha}}{u + bk^{\gamma}},$$

with

$$a = \frac{1+n}{A(1-\alpha)} > 0 \quad \text{and} \quad b = \frac{(1+n)\beta^{-\sigma}(\alpha A)^{1-\sigma}}{A(1-\alpha)} > 0.$$

The elasticity of m with respect to k is

$$k\frac{m'(k)}{m(k)} = \alpha - \frac{b\gamma k^{\gamma}}{a + bk^{\gamma}} = \frac{\alpha a + b(\alpha - \gamma)k^{\gamma}}{a + bk^{\gamma}}.$$

Hence, for $\gamma \leq \alpha$, we have $m'(k) > 0$ for all $k > 0$, and, according to proposition 1.10, the two dynamics have the same structure: they are monotonic and the steady state k^* is globally stable in $\mathbb{R}_{++}$. Notice that the condition $\gamma \leq \alpha$ is equivalent to

$$\sigma \leq \frac{1}{1-\alpha},$$

requiring a not too large value of the inter-temporal elasticity of substitution.

When $\gamma > \alpha$, i.e., $\sigma > \frac{1}{1-\alpha}$, $m'(k)$ is positive for $k < \hat{k}$ and negative for $k > \hat{k}$ with

$$\hat{k} = \left(\frac{\alpha a}{(\gamma - \alpha)b}\right)^{\frac{1}{\gamma}}.$$

At the steady state k^*, we have $m(k^*) = k^*$, and k^* should solve

$$a + bk^{*\gamma} = k^{*\alpha - 1}.$$

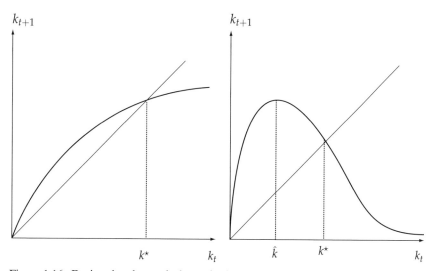

Figure 1.16. Rational and myopic dynamics for $\gamma > \alpha$. The two dynamics with perfect and myopic foresight have the same positive steady state k^* (which is unique with a Cobb–Douglas production function and a CIES utility function). k^* is stable for the rational dynamics, and the trajectory is monotonic. $k^* > \hat{k}$ can be stable or unstable for the myopic dynamics, and the trajectory is oscillating near k^*.

The evaluation of m' at this steady state gives

$$\frac{k^* m'(k^*)}{m(k^*)} = \alpha - \frac{b\gamma\, k^{*\gamma}}{a + b k^{*\gamma}} = \alpha - \gamma(1 - a k^{*1-\alpha}).$$

When $k^* > \hat{k}$, we obtain the chart presented in the second panel of figure 1.16.

When $m'(k^*) < 0$ and the dynamics are oscillating near k^*, then k^* is stable as long as $m'(k^*) > -1$. When $m'(k^*) < -1$, k^* is unstable for the myopic dynamics. In this case, the two steady states k^* and 0 are unstable, but the dynamics are bounded, as the function m has a finite maximum. It can be shown that, in this case, there exist cycles.

To analyze the effect of the inter-temporal elasticity of substitution on the nature of the dynamics, we present the bifurcation diagram (figure 1.17) for the parameter σ given the other parameters ($A = 20, n = 1.025^{30} - 1, \beta = 0.3$, and $\alpha = 1/3$).[30] σ lies on the horizontal axis, and we plot vertically the limit values of the equilibrium sequences (k_t) (computed numerically). When there is only one point k for a given σ, it means that the sequence (k_t) converges to a steady state. For sufficiently low σ, we observe a unique limit point which is a stable steady state. After some *bifurcation* value (called a *flip bifurcation* in the literature) for σ, two points appear. It means that the sequence (k_t)

---

[30] These figures are realized with the tools provided by Holmgren (1996).

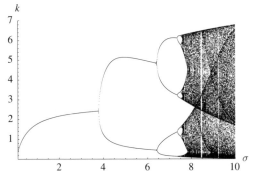

Figure 1.17. Bifurcation diagram for σ. We represents the set of limit points as a function of σ.

has two limit points (appendix A.2.4), i.e., there exist sub-sequences of (k_t) tending to these points. This corresponds to a 2-cycle which is stable, for the following two sub-sequences converge to two different limits: $\lim k_{2t+1} = \ell_1$ and $\lim k_{2t} = \ell_2$. The number of limit points is thus multiplied by 2 when σ increases and crosses the critical value. Figure 1.18 represent the dynamics of k_t in this circumstance. We have computed a series of 100 points starting from an arbitrary k_0, and we clearly distinguished the two limit points. The capital stock follows then a cycle of period 2, switching from one limit point to the other every period. There is then an interval of values of σ for which we have two limit points.

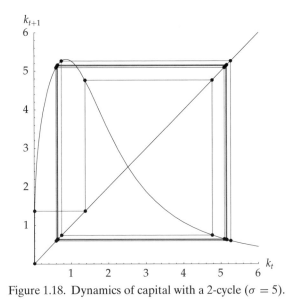

Figure 1.18. Dynamics of capital with a 2-cycle ($\sigma = 5$).

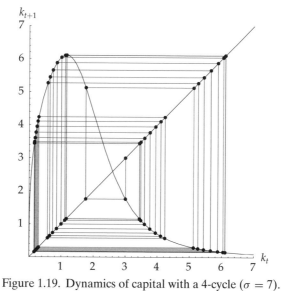

Figure 1.19. Dynamics of capital with a 4-cycle ($\sigma = 7$).

If σ rises further, the number of limit points increases. Figure 1.19 illustrates the dynamics of capital when $\sigma = 7$, and we observe a cycle of period 4. Beyond a certain value of σ, one enters the *chaotic region*, in which case there are an infinite number of limit points.[31] This is illustrated in figure 1.20.

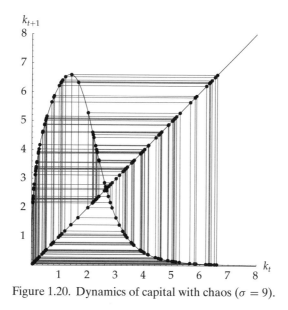

Figure 1.20. Dynamics of capital with chaos ($\sigma = 9$).

---

[31] See Michel and Wigniolle (1993) for a simple presentation of complex dynamics.

1.8.2 A Demographic Shock

Many large overlapping generations models (with more than two generations living at the same date) are now developed to analyze policy issues.[32] In particular, an impressive amount of work has been devoted to studying the effect of the lower rates of fertility on the economy in the twenty-first century. These models extend the basic Diamond framework to allow for elastic labor supply and include many features of real economies such as taxes, transfers, etc. However, it is already possible to capture some insights of these studies with the very simple two-period Diamond model.

To illustrate this, let us assume a logarithmic utility function and a Cobb–Douglas production function. We take the parameters values from appendix A.5.1: $\alpha = 1/3$ (one minus the share of labor in added value with a Cobb–Douglas function), $A = 20$ (simply a scale parameter when the production function is Cobb–Douglas and the utility is log-linear), $\delta = 1$ (full depreciation of capital), $\beta = 0.3$ (implying a quarterly discount factor of 0.99, assuming that one period equals 30 years). At time 0, the economy is assumed to be at an initial steady state with $1 + n = 2.097$, reflecting a long-run growth of total GDP of 2.5% per year. At time 1, n falls permanently by 0.5% per year. The fall is of the order of magnitude of the fall in population growth in OECD countries.

Table 1.3 presents the main results of the simulation. Before the shock, we assume that the capital stock is at its steady state level:

$$k = \left(\frac{1}{1+n} \frac{\beta}{1+\beta} A(1-\alpha) \right)^{\frac{1}{1-\alpha}}.$$

Table 1.3. *A Demographic Shock in a Simple Overlapping Generations Model*

Time	Capital per young person	Interest rate (%)	Life-cycle utility
0	1.78	5.2	0.13
1	1.78	5.2	0.10
2	2.06	4.8	0.16
3	2.16	4.7	0.18
4	2.20	4.7	0.18
5	2.21	4.7	0.19
∞	2.21	4.7	0.19

[32] Auerbach and Kotlikoff (1987) use simulations to investigate such issues in a much more realistic framework with households living 75 periods and endogenous labor supply decision. The deterministic framework of Auerbach and Kotlikoff (1987) is extended to a stochastic world by Rios-Rull (1996) in order to compare the implications for business cycle issues of a model with infinite-lived agents with an overlapping generations model.

At $t = 2$ the drop in the fertility rate implies a drop in the supply of labor. The wage increases and the labor demand decreases, implying that the capital stock per young person, k_t, increases. As a consequence, the rate of return on savings decreases as

$$R_t = A\alpha k_t^{\alpha-1}.$$

In the table, the rate of return and the rate of growth of the population are converted to an annual basis. The last columns gives the life-cycle utility of the generation born in t. This life-cycle utility is given by

$$\ln\left(\underbrace{\frac{1}{1+\beta}A(1-\alpha)k_t^{\alpha}}_{\frac{1}{1+\beta}\omega(k_t)}\right) + \beta \ln\left(\underbrace{A\alpha k_{t+1}^{\alpha-1}}_{R_{t+1}}\underbrace{\frac{\beta}{1+\beta}A(1-\alpha)k_t^{\alpha}}_{s_t}\right)$$

$$= (1+\beta)\alpha \ln(k_t) - (1-\alpha)\beta \ln(k_{t+1}) + \text{constant}.$$

The life-cycle utility of generation t depends positively on k_t through the first-period income, and negatively on k_{t+1} through the rate of return on savings. This explains why the utility of generation $t = 1$ is lower than that of generations $t = 0$ and $t = 2, 3, \ldots$: the income of generation $t = 1$ still depends on the stock of capital installed before the demographic shock, but its interest payments are decreased by the reduction of the interest rate at $t = 2$.

The conclusion of this exercise is twofold: (a) a permanent drop in the fertility rate lowers the rate of return on savings permanently; (b) the losers are the persons which are old at the time of the shock, i.e., the first parents who have a lower fertility rate.

1.8.3 Non-separable Utility Function

The properties of the overlapping generation models rest on the properties of the savings function, which is directly related to the preferences of the households. For simplicity we have assumed that these preference are represented by an additively separable utility function (1.4). With a general utility function[33]

$$U(c, d),$$

we define the savings function

$$s(w, R) = \arg\max U(w - s, Rs).$$

The function $s(\cdot, \cdot)$ is continuously differentiable on $\mathbb{R}_{++} \times \mathbb{R}_{++}$ and takes values on $\mathbb{R}_{++}$ if the function $U(\cdot, \cdot)$ is twice continuously differentiable, strictly

---

[33] The savings function only depends on households preferences. If ϕ is a strictly increasing function, we obtain the same savings function with the utility function $\phi(U(c, d))$.

quasi-concave, strictly increasing, and such that $\forall \bar{c} > 0, \forall \bar{d} > 0$,

$$\lim_{c \to 0} U_c'(c, \bar{d}) = +\infty \quad \text{and} \quad \lim_{d \to 0} U_d'(\bar{c}, d) = +\infty.$$

The consumption levels are given by $c(w, R) = w - s(w, R)$ and $d(w, R) = Rs(w, R)$. Under the assumption of normal goods ($c_w' > 0$ and $d_w' > 0$), we have $1 - s_w' > 0$ and $Rs_w' > 0$, which implies $0 < s_w' < 1$.

Under the assumption that the consumption goods are gross substitutes, $c(w, R)$ is a non-decreasing function of the price $1/R$ of the good d in the inter-temporal budget constraint: $c + d/R = w$. Under this assumption we have $c_R' \leq 0$ and $s_R' = -c_R' \geq 0$, which implies that the assumption **H3** holds. Indeed, the function

$$\Delta(k, w) = (1 + n)k - s(w, f'(k))$$

verifies, $\forall k > 0, \forall w > 0$,

$$\Delta_k'(k, w) = 1 + n - s_R' f'' > 0.$$

To prove the existence of an inter-temporal equilibrium with perfect fore-sight, we study the sign of $\Delta(k, w)$ near $k = 0$ and $k = +\infty$, as in the proof of proposition 1.2. Here we also have

$$\lim_{k \to +\infty} \Delta(k, w) = +\infty,$$

and $\Delta(k, w)$ is positive for k large enough. We also have

$$\frac{s(w, f'(k))}{k} = \frac{f'(k)s(w, f'(k))}{f'(k)k} = \frac{d(w, f'(k))}{f'(k)k}.$$

If d is a non-Giffen good, the demand for it does not increase with its price. Then $d(w, R)$ is non-decreasing in R, and $d(w, f'(k))$ is non-increasing in k. We deduce that its limit when k goes to 0, $d(w, f'(0+))$, is strictly positive (finite or infinite). As $\lim_{k \to 0} kf'(k) = 0$ (see appendix A.1.2), we have

$$\lim_{k \to 0} \frac{d(w, f'(k))}{f'(k)k} = +\infty,$$

which implies

$$\lim_{k \to 0} \frac{\Delta(k, w)}{k} = -\infty.$$

Then $\Delta(k, w)$ is negative for k small enough. We conclude that the existence of the inter-temporal equilibrium with perfect foresight (proposition 1.2) holds for a non-separable utility function where the good d is not a Giffen good. The study of the dynamics (section 1.6) can then be applied to a non-separable utility function.

1.8.4 Homothetic Preferences

When the indifference curves are homothetic with respect to the origin, we say that the preferences are homothetic. Such preferences can be represented by a utility function $U(c, d)$, which is homogeneous of degree 1,[34] or equivalently by the composition of such a function with an increasing function g, i.e.,

$$g(U(c, d)).$$

Any homogeneous function of positive degree λ (i.e., when $g(x) = x^\lambda$) represents homothetic preferences.

Example: Preferences represented by a CIES utility function are homothetic. Indeed,

$$\frac{1}{1 - \frac{1}{\sigma}} \left(c^{1-\frac{1}{\sigma}} + \beta d^{1-\frac{1}{\sigma}} \right) = \frac{1}{1 - \frac{1}{\sigma}} U(c, d)^{1-\frac{1}{\sigma}}$$

$$= g(U(c, d)),$$

where $U(c, d)$ is homogeneous of degree one:

$$U(c, d) = \left(c^{1-\frac{1}{\sigma}} + \beta d^{1-\frac{1}{\sigma}} \right)^{\frac{1}{1-\frac{1}{\sigma}}},$$

and

$$g(x) = \frac{1}{1 - \frac{1}{\sigma}} x^{1-\frac{1}{\sigma}}$$

is increasing ($\sigma \neq 1$).

For the logarithmic utility, we have

$$\ln c + \beta \ln d = (1 + \beta) \ln U(c, d),$$

with

$$U(c, d) = (c \, d^\beta)^{\frac{1}{1+\beta}},$$

and

$$g(x) = (1 + \beta) \ln x.$$

---

[34] This is a necessary and sufficient condition when preferences are homothetic and continuous; see Mas-Colell, Whinston, and Green (1995), p. 50.

Proposition 1.12 (Homothetic preferences)
When preferences are homothetic, the savings function $s(w, R)$ is linear with respect to w and verifies

$$s(w, R) = \zeta(R)w \quad and \quad \zeta(R) = \arg\max_{0<\zeta<1} U(1 - \zeta, R\zeta).$$

The propensity to consume, $1 - \zeta(R)$, does not depend on income.

Proof: With U homogeneous of degree 1, we have

$$U(c, d) = wU\left(\frac{c}{w}, \frac{d}{w}\right).$$

Denoting $\zeta = s/w$, we have

$$\max_s U\left(\frac{w - s}{w}, \frac{Rs}{w}\right) = \max_\zeta U(1 - \zeta, R\zeta).$$

Thus, the solution $\zeta(R)$ coincides with $s(w, R)/w$. ∎

The dynamic equation for an inter-temporal equilibrium with perfect foresight is in this case (from (1.17))

$$k_{t+1} = \frac{1}{1+n}\zeta(f'(k_{t+1}))\omega(k_t).$$

Uniqueness of the inter-temporal equilibrium and monotonicity of the dynamics are equivalent to the condition that $k/\zeta(f'(k))$ is an increasing function of $k > 0$.

1.8.5 Heterogeneous Agents

In this book, we study an economy in which all persons born at the same time are exactly alike. In the introduction, we have already stressed that the simplest overlapping generations model allows already for heterogeneous agents in the sense that young and old individuals coexist at each point in time. A further step in introducing heterogeneity is to allow for idiosyncratic characteristics. These characteristics can be related either to preferences that vary across individuals or to different innate abilities to work. We show that, as long as preferences are homothetic,[35] the model of chapter 1 can be extended easily to allow for heterogenous agents. Of course, the issues of optimality and the design of policies become much more complicated to analyze. The study of the latter is beyond the scope of this work.

---

[35] The assumption of homothetic preferences of section 1.8.4 is particularly useful in the case of heterogeneous agents, since it will allow us to aggregate easily the savings functions.

We assume that households are split into sub-groups, each group containing homogeneous agents in terms of characteristics. i is the index associated to a group. This is modeled by assuming that there is a given constant distribution of different types of agents $i \in I$, which is defined by a probability μ on the set I. Across groups, the individuals differ by their utility function $U_i(c, d)$, which is assumed homothetic, and by their ability to work. We denote h_i for the efficient labor supplied by each of the individual of type i. The aggregate labor supply is given by

$$\int_I N_t h_i \, d\mu(i) \equiv N_t \bar{h},$$

where we define $\bar{h}$ as the average efficient labor endowment, which is constant through time. Total young population N_t grows at rate n. The young population in each group i is $N_t \, d\mu(i)$.

Consumers. The problem of an individual of type i born in t is to maximize

$$U_i(c_{i,t}, d_{i,t+1})$$

with respect to

$$c_{i,t} = h_i w_t - s_{i,t},$$
$$d_{i,t+1} = R^e_{t+1} s_{i,t}$$
$$c_{i,t} \geq 0, \qquad d_{i,t+1} \geq 0.$$

w_t is the wage per unit of efficient labor. Notice that by writing R^e_{t+1} we assume that expectations on macro-economic variables are the same for all agents. We have seen that, in the case of homothetic preferences, savings are given by (see proposition 1.12)

$$s_{i,t} = \zeta_i \left(R^e_{t+1} \right) h_i w_t.$$

An important property of this savings function is that the propensity to save is independent of wage incomes. This property is very useful in aggregating over individuals. Aggregate savings are given by $N_t \bar{s}_t$ with

$$\bar{s}_t = \xi \left(R^e_{t+1} \right) w_t,$$

where

$$\xi(R) = \int_I \zeta_i(R) h_i \, d\mu(i).$$

The wage per unit of efficient labor is thus outside the integral.

Firms. The production function $F(K, H)$ depends on the capital K and the total efficient labor H. F is homogeneous of degree one. We define

$$\kappa = \frac{K}{H}$$

as the ratio of capital to efficient labor. The function $f(\kappa) = F(\kappa, 1)$ verifies the assumption **H2**. The gross rate of return on capital is $f'(\kappa)$. The wage per unit of efficient labor is $\omega(\kappa) = f(\kappa) - \kappa f'(\kappa)$.

Equilibrium. At equilibrium, the labor market clears:

$$H_t = N_t \bar{h},$$

and thus $w_t = \omega(\kappa_t)$ with $\kappa_t = K_t / H_t$. Equilibrium on the goods market is equivalent to the equality between savings and investment:

$$K_{t+1} = N_t \bar{s}_t.$$

With the new savings function, the existence of inter-temporal equilibria can be proved exactly the same way we did before. Under the assumption of perfect foresight, $R_{t+1}^e = f'(\kappa_{t+1})$, and we have

$$(1 + n)\kappa_{t+1} = \frac{\bar{s}_t}{\bar{h}} = \frac{\xi(f'(\kappa_{t+1}))}{\bar{h}} \omega(\kappa_t).$$

An interesting difference arises when we consider the assumption **H3**. In the framework with representative agents, the requirement of **H3** is that the effect of the rate of return on savings should not be too negative (at the solution). The condition is now that the effect of the rate of return on savings should not be too negative *on average*, which implies that it can be negative for some individuals, as long as that is compensated by positive effect from other individuals.

It appears that, conditionally on this, the rest of the analysis can be conducted as before, and the representative agent is a good approximation of the "average" agent of a framework with heterogeneity, provided that preferences are homothetic and that we are not interested in intra-generational distributional issues.

1.8.6 Technical Progress

Assume that the distribution μ on I remains constant but that the efficient labor $h_{i,t}$ increases with exogenous technical progress:

$$h_{i,t} = (1 + \lambda)h_{i,t-1} = (1 + \lambda)^t h_{i,0}.$$

λ is the rate of technical progress, and $h_{i,0}$ is given by the initial conditions. This technical progress is called *labor-augmenting*, because it increases the efficient labor input in the production function.[36] All workers benefit from the technical progress. It can reflect for example the economy-wide improvement in the quality of labor.

We can then apply the same analysis as in the previous section. We obtain the following individual saving function:

$$s_{i,t} = \zeta_i\left(R^e_{t+1}\right)h_{i,t}\omega(\kappa_t).$$

At the aggregate level we have

$$\bar{s}_t = \xi_t\left(R^e_{t+1}\right)\omega(\kappa_t),$$

where

$$\xi_t(R) = \int_I \zeta_i(R)h_{i,t}\,d\mu(i) = (1+\lambda)^t\xi_0(R).$$

The efficient labor at equilibrium is

$$H_t = N_t\bar{h}_t = N_t(1+\lambda)^t\bar{h}_0,$$

and the perfect foresight dynamics can be written

$$(1+n)(1+\lambda)\kappa_{t+1} = \frac{1}{\bar{h}_0}\xi_0(f'(\kappa_{t+1}))\omega(\kappa_t).$$

The dynamics in κ are those studied without technical progress, where $1+n$ has to be replaced by

$$1+\tilde{n} = (1+n)(1+\lambda).$$

Although κ and k have the same dynamics, the interpretation is different in that κ does not represents capital per household. The introduction of technical progress breaks the equivalence between the capital–labor ratio and capital per person. Moreover, individual consumption are affected by technical progress. We have

$$c_t = h_t[\omega(\kappa_t) - s(\omega(\kappa_t), f'(\kappa_{t+1}))].$$

With a constant κ, consumption grows at a rate λ.

1.8.7 Imperfect Credit Market

In the basic overlapping generations model, one representative household lives for two periods and supplies labor only when young. It is optimal in this context to save when young in order to be able to consume when old. The households never borrow. On the contrary, when households live for more than two periods, or when heterogeneous households work in their second period of life, some agents might wish to borrow. In a three-period life context, the

---

[36] Following Harrod (1942), it is also called Harrod neutral.

borrowers are typically the young households. In the two-period life context with labor supply when old, the borrowers are the young households that are going to earn a high wage when old.

When some households borrow, one should assume that the loan contract is enforceable. This requires that agents can seize the labor income of borrowers. In order to capture the idea that credit markets are imperfect and that that labor income – though common knowledge – is partly inalienable, some authors assume a exogenous borrowing limit of the form that one can only borrow at most a fraction of one's life-cycle income. This modeling strategy is pursued by Jappelli and Pagano (1994) and (1999) in a three-period overlapping generations model.[37]

Clearly, this approach to borrowing limits is unsatisfactory. In particular, it is hard to believe that borrowing limits do not depend on prices. Using the concepts developed in Kehoe and Levine (1993), Azariadis and Lambertini (2000) study an overlapping generations model in which endowments (say labor income) are inalienable; enforcement of loan contracts is left to the self-interest of borrowers and will depend on the penalty associated with default. If a household defaults on a contract, it can be excluded from future credit markets, and its potential assets can be seized. In this setup, endogenous borrowing limits arises as the outcome of individual rationality constraints which prevent individuals from defaulting at equilibrium.

A Simple Example with Logarithmic Utility and Cobb–Douglas Production.
To illustrate in the most simple way the effect of borrowing constraints on capital accumulation and inequality, we build an overlapping generations model with heterogeneous two-period-lived households. The size of the successive generations is constant through time and is normalized to 1. We assume that households work in both periods. There is one dimension of heterogeneity, which lies in the ability to work when old. All households supply one unit of labor when young. The endowment of efficient labor when old, denoted h, is distributed according to a probability distribution function on $[h_L, h_H]$, with density function $g(h)$. Thus, we have

$$\int_{h_L}^{h_H} g(h)\, dh = 1, \quad \int_{h_L}^{h_H} h g(h)\, dh = \bar{h}.$$

When young, the highly productive workers would like to borrow from the less productive ones, since they need to transfer resources from the future to the present.

---

[37] Such an assumption has also been made by De Gregorio (1996), Buiter and Kletzer (1995), and De Gregorio and Kim (2000) to study the effect of borrowing limits in models where households have to finance their education (as in section 5.2.3).

The budget constraints of an individual are

$$c_t = w_t - s_t,$$
$$d_{t+1} = R_{t+1}s_t + hw_{t+1}.$$

With a logarithmic utility function $\ln c_t + \beta \ln d_{t+1}$, optimal savings are given by

$$s_t^\star(h) = \frac{1}{1+\beta}\left(\beta w_t - h\frac{w_{t+1}}{R_{t+1}}\right).$$

With imperfect markets, future labor income cannot be a collateral[38] and the young are not able to borrow, because it is never in their interest to reimburse their debt when old. Effective savings are thus

$$s_t(h) = \max(0, s_t^\star(h)).$$

We can define a threshold $\hat{h}_t$ such that individuals with $h > \hat{h}_t$ are constrained. This threshold is

$$\hat{h}_t = \frac{\beta w_t R_{t+1}}{w_{t+1}}.$$

Assuming a Cobb–Douglas production function and total depreciation of capital, we have $y_t = A\kappa_t^\alpha$, with

$$\kappa_t = \frac{K_t}{1+\bar{h}}.$$

Equilibrium prices are given by

$$w_t = A(1-\alpha)\kappa_t^\alpha \quad \text{and} \quad R_t = A\alpha\kappa_t^{\alpha-1}.$$

In the perfect market case, the equilibrium on the capital market implies

$$K_{t+1} = \int_{h_L}^{h_H} s_t^\star(h)g(h)\,\mathrm{d}h.$$

In the imperfect market case, with rationed households ($\hat{h}_t < h_L$), we have

$$K_{t+1} = \int_{h_L}^{h_H} s_t(h)g(h)\,\mathrm{d}h = \int_{h_L}^{\hat{h}_t} s_t^\star(h)g(h)\,\mathrm{d}h.$$

The Effect of Constraints on Capital. To study the effect of borrowing constraints on capital and inequality, it is convenient to define the discounted

---

[38] This assumption is defended, a.o., by Ljungqvist (1993).

growth rate of wages:

$$x_{t+1} = \frac{w_{t+1}}{R_{t+1}w_t}. \qquad (1.24)$$

Savings of an individual with efficient labor h can be rewritten

$$s_t^\star(h) = \frac{w_t}{1+\beta}(\beta - hx_{t+1}),$$

and the threshold is $\hat{h}_t = \beta/x_{t+1}$. Total capital K_{t+1} can be expressed as a function of x_{t+1} and w_t:

$$K_{t+1} = \kappa_{t+1}(1+\bar{h}) = \frac{\alpha w_{t+1}(1+\bar{h})}{(1-\alpha)R_{t+1}} = \frac{\alpha(1+\bar{h})}{1-\alpha}w_t x_{t+1}.$$

We can now compare the equilibrium in the economy with perfect market to the one in the economy with borrowing constraint.

- In the perfect market economy, we have

$$\frac{\alpha(1+\bar{h})}{1-\alpha}w_t x_{t+1} = \frac{w_t}{1+\beta}\int_{h_L}^{h_H}(\beta - hx_{t+1})\,g(h)\,dh.$$

Dividing by $x_{t+1}w_t$, we obtain

$$\frac{\alpha(1+\bar{h})}{1-\alpha} = \frac{1}{1+\beta}\int_{h_L}^{h_H}\left(\frac{\beta}{x_{t+1}} - h\right)g(h)\,dh \equiv \varphi_{NC}(x_{t+1}).$$

When x increases from 0 to $+\infty$, the function $\varphi_{NC}(x)$ decreases from $+\infty$ to a negative value and thus takes the value $\alpha(1+\bar{h})/(1-\alpha)$ for a unique $x_{NC}^\star > 0$. The dynamics of capital are obtained replacing the equilibrium prices in the definition of x (1.24):

$$\kappa_{t+1} = \alpha A \kappa_t^\alpha x_{NC}^\star.$$

- Similarly, the equilibrium in the economy with imperfect markets is (assuming that some households are constrained, i.e., $\hat{h}_t = \beta/x_{t+1} < h_H$)

$$\frac{\alpha(1+\bar{h})}{1-\alpha}w_t x_{t+1} = \frac{w_t}{1+\beta}\int_{h_L}^{\beta/x_{t+1}}(\beta - hx_{t+1})\,g(h)\,dh,$$

which yields to an expression where the left-hand side is the same constant as in the perfect market case:

$$\frac{\alpha(1+\bar{h})}{1-\alpha} = \frac{1}{1+\beta}\int_{h_L}^{\beta/x_{t+1}}\left(\frac{\beta}{x_{t+1}} - h\right)g(h)\,dh \equiv \varphi_C(x_{t+1}).$$

When x increases from β/h_H to β/h_L, $\varphi_C(x)$ decreases from $\varphi_C(\beta/h_H) = \varphi_{NC}(\beta/h_H)$ to zero. Thus, there exists an equilibrium at which some households are constrained if and only if

$$\frac{1}{1+\beta}(h_H - \bar{h}) = \phi_C\left(\frac{\beta}{h_H}\right) > \frac{\alpha(1+\bar{h})}{1-\alpha}. \tag{1.25}$$

The interpretation of this condition is as follows. For an equilibrium with constrained households to exist, it is sufficient that the distance between the highest endowment in efficient labor and the mean endowment $h_H - \bar{h}$ be large enough. This guarantees that the threshold $\hat{h}$ above which people are constrained takes a value inside the interval $[h_H, h_L]$. When the opposite inequality holds, even the household with h_H does not want to borrow, and the equilibrium is then the same as in the economy with perfect market. Assuming that the inequality (1.25) holds, we have a unique constant value solution $x_C^\star$ to $\varphi_C(x_C^\star) = \alpha(1+\bar{h})/(1-\alpha)$. Capital accumulation follows:

$$\kappa_{t+1} = \alpha A \kappa_t^\alpha x_C^\star.$$

- To compare the two economies and study the effect of imperfect credit markets, we compare the two functions $\varphi(\cdot)$. The functions are drawn in figure 1.21. We find that

$$\varphi_{NC}(x) = \varphi_C(x) + \int_{\beta/x}^{h_H} \left(\frac{\beta}{x} - h\right) g(h)\, dh.$$

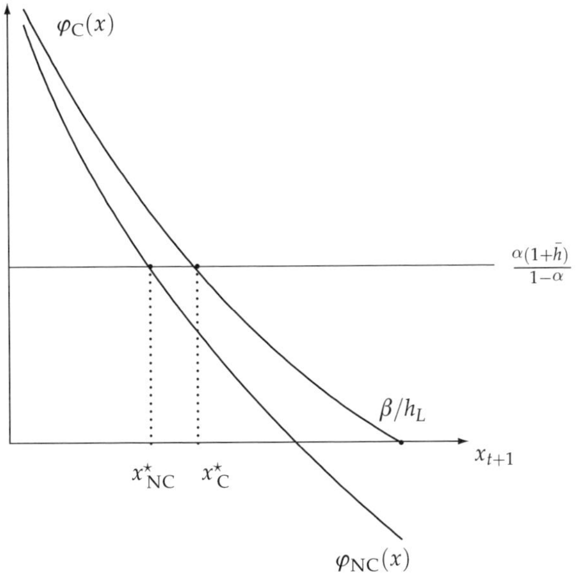

Figure 1.21. Equilibrium in the economies with perfect (NC) and imperfect (C) credit markets.

As the last term, which represents the loans of the skilled persons, is negative, we have

$$\varphi_{NC}(x) > \varphi_C(x).$$

Since both functions are decreasing functions of x and should equal the same constant term, we have at equilibrium

$$x_C^\star > x_{NC}^\star. \tag{1.26}$$

Hence, starting from the same initial condition $k_0^{NC} = k_0^C$, the inequality (1.26) and the law of motion of capital $\kappa_{t+1} = \alpha A \kappa_t^\alpha x$ imply by induction

$$k_{t+1}^C > k_{t+1}^{NC}. \tag{1.27}$$

As a consequence, credit market imperfections foster capital accumulation, because they prevent some individuals from borrowing. This is the main argument of Jappelli and Pagano (1994): the financial market liberalization of the seventies has lowered savings in the OECD countries, which has led to worse growth performance in the 1980s. This view is supported by recent empirical studies by Norman, Schmidt-Hebbel, and Serven (2000) and Bandiera, Caprio, Honohan, and Schiantarelli (2000) showing that liberalization, and in particular the elements that relax liquidity constraints, are associated with a fall in savings.

The Effect of Constraints on Inequality. Borrowing constraints affect skilled and unskilled people differently. The direct effect only bears on skilled people who are prevented from borrowing from financial markets. The indirect effect through prices (higher capital, higher wages, lower interest factor) affects everybody.

To study the effect of market imperfection on inequality, we consider how credit market imperfections change the gap between the consumptions of the most skilled and the least skilled persons. We first compute the individual consumptions at time t:

- In the perfect market case, individual consumptions are

$$c_t^{NC}(h) = w_t^{NC} - s_t^\star = \frac{w_t^{NC}}{1+\beta}(1 + hx_{NC}^\star).$$

Using $w_t^{NC}x_{NC}^\star = w_{t+1}^{NC}/R_{t+1}^{NC} = \omega(k_{t+1}^{NC})/R(k_{t+1}^{NC})$, we have

$$c_t^{NC}(h) = \frac{1}{1+\beta}\frac{\omega(k_{t+1}^{NC})}{R(k_{t+1}^{NC})}\left(\frac{1}{x_{NC}^\star}+h\right).$$

For the old households at time t, we simply use the life-cycle arbitrage condition:

$$d_t^{NC}(h) = \beta R(k_t^{NC})c_{t-1}^{NC}(h) = \frac{\beta}{1+\beta}\omega(k_t^{NC})\left(\frac{1}{x_{NC}^\star}+h\right).$$

- In the imperfect market case, the consumption of an unconstrained household, say h_L, is obtained by replacing $x_{NC}^\star$ and k^{NC} by $x_C^\star$ and k^C in the above equations. For a constrained household, say h_H, the first-period consumption is the current wage:

$$c_t^C(h) = w_t^C.$$

The second-period consumption for a constrained old household is

$$d_t^C(h) = w_t^C h.$$

The consumption gap for young households in the perfect market economy is

$$c_t^{NC}(h_H) - c_t^{NC}(h_L) = \frac{\omega(k_{t+1}^{NC})/R(k_{t+1}^{NC})}{1+\beta}(h_H - h_L).$$

In the imperfect market case,

$$c_t^C(h_H) - c_t^C(h_L) = \omega(k_t^C) - \frac{\omega(k_{t+1}^C)/R(k_{t+1}^C)}{1+\beta}\left(\frac{1}{x_C^\star} + h_L\right)$$

$$= \frac{\omega(k_{t+1}^C)/R(k_{t+1}^C)}{1+\beta}\left(\frac{1+\beta}{x_C^\star} - \frac{1}{x_C^\star} - h_L\right)$$

$$= \frac{\omega(k_{t+1}^C)/R(k_{t+1}^C)}{1+\beta}\left(\frac{\beta}{x_C^\star} - h_L\right).$$

Taking the ratio of the two gaps leads to

$$\frac{c_t^{NC}(h_H) - c_t^{NC}(h_L)}{c_t^C(h_H) - c_t^C(h_L)} = \frac{\omega(k_{t+1}^{NC})/R(k_{t+1}^{NC})}{\omega(k_{t+1}^C)/R(k_{t+1}^C)}\left(\frac{h_H - h_L}{\beta/x_C^\star - h_L}\right) \gtrless 1.$$

The two different effects of borrowing constraint appear distinctly. First, the most skilled persons are prevented from borrowing and consuming when young, which reduces inequality: $h_H - h_L > \beta/x_C^\star - h_L$. Second, discounted wages per unit of efficient labor are higher in the economy with imperfect markets, which enlarges the consumption gap between high and low skilled persons; this increases inequality.

Turning our attention to the old persons, we have

$$d_t^{NC}(h_H) - d_t^{NC}(h_L) = \frac{\beta\omega(k_t^{NC})}{1+\beta}(h_H - h_L)$$

$$d_t^C(h_H) - d_t^C(h_L) = \omega(k_t^C)h_H - \frac{\beta\omega(k_t^C)}{1+\beta}\left(\frac{1}{x_C^\star} + h_L\right)$$

$$= \frac{\beta\omega(k_t^C)}{1+\beta}\left(h_H\frac{1+\beta}{\beta} - \frac{1}{x_C^\star} - h_L\right).$$

The consumption gap is

$$\frac{d_t^{NC}(h_H) - d_t^{NC}(h_H)}{d_t^C(h_H) - d_t^C(h_H)} = \frac{\omega(k_t^{NC})}{\omega(k_t^C)} \left(\frac{h_H - h_L}{h_H - h_L + \frac{1}{\beta}\left(h_H - \frac{\beta}{x_C^*}\right)} \right) < 1.$$

Here, the effect of borrowing constraints is unambiguous. Borrowing constraints increase the consumption of old skilled households and raise the wage per unit of efficient labor. The dispersion of consumption of old people is wider with imperfect markets.

The total effect on inequality depends on the relative importance of these factors. Azariadis and de la Croix (2001) study the effect of liberalization, seen as a move from the imperfect market economy to the perfect market, on inequality. In a calibrated overlapping generations model similar to the one above, but with education choice in the first period, they show that inequality is increased by liberalization. This result explains why a majority of people might object to reform of financial markets.

1.8.8 Three-period-lived Households

The overlapping generations model with two-period-lived households is the most widespread, because it is relatively simple to study. We have seen that it is possible to characterize the accumulation dynamics with perfect foresight. As the agents' expectations bear only on the interest factor of the next period, the dynamics are of order one: The expected return determines the saving decision, the savings decision determines the future stock of capital, and this stock of capital determines the expected return.

A model where households live for three periods and work during the first two periods is however closer to the actual timing of life. It allows one to study savings behavior in a richer way, since it opens the possibility of borrowing in the first period against future wage income; moreover, savings do not bear exclusively on labor income, since part of capital income in the middle period (if any) can be saved for retirement. Unfortunately, the cost in terms of additional difficulties is high. Dynamics will in general be described by a difference equation of order 3, with one forward dimension. To compute the perfect foresight equilibrium, agents thus need to forecast the whole future. Only in the particular case with a logarithmic utility, does the forward dimension disappear, and then the dynamics can be studied globally when the production function is Cobb–Douglas.

Let us first consider the general model, before specializing to the logarithmic example in the next subsection. Households live for three periods and supply one unit of labor in the first period and h units in the second period. $h > 1$ can be interpreted as learning by doing. $h < 1$ can be interpreted as part time work or early retirement. The present value life-cycle income of households born in t is given by

$$\Omega_t = w_t + \frac{w_{t+1}}{R_{t+1}}h.$$

Their preferences are homothetic and can be represented by a utility function

$$U(c_t, d_{t+1}, e_{t+2}),$$

defined over the consumptions levels in the three periods of life c_t, d_{t+1}, and e_{t+2}. The function $U(\cdot)$ is homogeneous of degree 1. Following the argument developed in section 1.8.4, the solution for the maximum of utility subject to the inter-temporal budget constraint

$$c_t + \frac{d_{t+1}}{R_{t+1}} + \frac{e_{t+2}}{R_{t+1}R_{t+2}} = \Omega_t$$

verifies

$$c_t = \zeta_1(R_{t+1}, R_{t+2})\Omega_t, \qquad d_{t+1} = \zeta_2(R_{t+1}, R_{t+2})\Omega_t,$$
$$e_{t+2} = \zeta_3(R_{t+1}, R_{t+2})\Omega_t.$$

The functions ζ_1, ζ_2, and ζ_3 of R_{t+1} and R_{t+2} are the solution to

$$\max U(\zeta_1, \zeta_2, \zeta_3) \qquad \text{subject to} \quad \zeta_1 + \frac{\zeta_2}{R_{t+1}} + \frac{\zeta_3}{R_{t+1}R_{t+2}} = 1.$$

Let us denote by s_t the first-period savings and by z_{t+1} the second-period savings. Then, s_t and z_{t+1} verify

$$c_t = w_t - s_t,$$
$$d_{t+1} = R_{t+1}s_t + w_{t+1}h - z_{t+1},$$
$$e_{t+2} = R_{t+2}z_{t+1}.$$

From these intra-period budget constraints, we deduce that

$$s_t = w_t - \zeta_1(R_{t+1}, R_{t+2})\Omega_t,$$
$$z_{t+1} = \frac{\zeta_3(R_{t+1}, R_{t+2})}{R_{t+2}}\Omega_t.$$

Example: With a CIES utility function $u(c_t) + \beta u(d_{t+1}) + \beta^2 u(e_{t+2})$ and $u(x) = x^{1-1/\sigma}/(1 - 1/\sigma)$, we have

$$\zeta_1(R_{t+1}, R_{t+2}) = (\beta R_{t+1})^{-\sigma}\zeta_2(R_{t+1}, R_{t+2}) = (\beta^2 R_{t+1}R_{t+2})^{-\sigma}\zeta_3(R_{t+1}, R_{t+2}),$$

and

$$\zeta_1(R_{t+1}, R_{t+2}) = \frac{1}{1 + \beta^\sigma R_{t+1}^{\sigma-1} + \beta^{2\sigma} R_{t+1}^{\sigma-1} R_{t+2}^{\sigma-1}}.$$

The production function $F(K, L)$ has the same properties as before. The intertemporal equilibrium with perfect foresight is characterized by

- the equilibrium on the labor market:

$$L_t = N_t + hN_{t-1} = (1 + h + n)N_{t-1},$$

- the equalities between factor prices and marginal productivities:

$$w_t = \omega(\kappa_t), \quad R_t = f'(\kappa_t), \quad \text{where} \quad \kappa_t = \frac{K_t}{N_t + hN_{t-1}},$$

- the equality between the stock of capital and the total savings of the previous period:

$$K_{t+1} = N_t s_t + N_{t-1} z_t.$$

The dynamics of capital are thus given by

$$(1 + h + n)\kappa_{t+1} = [w_t - \zeta_1(R_{t+1}, R_{t+2})\Omega_t] + \frac{\zeta_3(R_t, R_{t+1})}{(1+n)R_{t+1}}\Omega_{t-1}.$$

The dynamics of κ are described by a difference equation of order 3. The highest-order term κ_{t+2} comes from R_{t+2}, and the lowest-order term κ_{t-1} comes from Ω_{t-1}. There are two initial conditions, corresponding to the initial stock of capital and its re-partition between the first old generation and the first middle-aged generation. There is thus one forward dimension. Indeed, the savings of the young in t depend not only on the forecasted variables w_{t+1} and R_{t+1} but also on their anticipation of R_{t+2}.

Beyond the specific logarithmic utility case studied in the next subsection, the dynamics of capital include two predetermined variables and one forward-looking variable.

1.8.9 Borrowing Constraints in the Three-period Model

We shall introduce a simple non-negativity constraint on savings in the model with three-period-lived households. We consider the simple case of a logarithmic utility and a Cobb–Douglas production function. This exercise illustrates the three-period model of section 1.8.8. It will also allow us to compare the role of imperfect credit market in the two-period (section 1.8.7) and the three-period model.

The Perfect Market Case. With the logarithmic utility

$$\ln c_t + \beta \ln d_{t+1} + \beta^2 \ln e_{t+2},$$

the first-period propensity to consume out of life-cycle income is constant:

$$\zeta_1 = \frac{1}{1 + \beta + \beta^2}.$$

In this model with homogeneous agents, we define the growth factor of the discounted wage over the life cycle as

$$x_{t+1} = \frac{hw_{t+1}/R_{t+1}}{w_t}.$$

We have

$$\Omega_t = w_t + \frac{hw_{t+1}}{R_{t+1}} = w_t(1 + x_{t+1}),$$

$$s_t = w_t - \zeta_1\Omega_t = w_t - \zeta_1 w_t(1 + x_{t+1}),$$

$$z_t = \zeta_1\beta^2 R_t\Omega_{t-1} = \zeta_1\beta^2 R_t w_{t-1}(1 + x_t).$$

Since $R_t w_{t-1}/w_t = h/x_t$, we have

$$z_t = \zeta_1\beta^2 w_t h\left(\frac{1 + x_t}{x_t}\right).$$

The rule for accumulation of capital is

$$(1 + h + n)k_{t+1} = s_t + \frac{1}{1+n}z_t,$$

which implies, after replacing s_t and z_t by their optimal values and dividing by w_t,

$$(1 + h + n)\frac{\kappa_{t+1}}{w_t} = 1 - \zeta_1(1 + x_{t+1}) + \frac{1}{1+n}\zeta_1\beta^2 h\left(\frac{1 + x_t}{x_t}\right). \quad (1.28)$$

We shall study these dynamics in the case of a Cobb–Douglas production function. With $f(\kappa) = A\kappa^\alpha$, the equilibrium wage is

$$w_t = (1 - \alpha)A\kappa_t^\alpha,$$

and the return on savings is

$$R_t = \alpha A\kappa_t^{\alpha-1}.$$

We also have

$$x_{t+1} = \frac{hw_{t+1}}{R_{t+1}w_t} = h\left(\frac{1 - \alpha}{\alpha}\right)\frac{\kappa_{t+1}}{w_t} = \frac{h\kappa_{t+1}}{A\alpha\kappa_t^\alpha}.$$

By substitution in equation (1.28), the dynamics of the wage growth factor are

$$\left(\frac{(1+h+n)\alpha}{h(1-\alpha)} + \zeta_1\right) x_{t+1} = 1 - \zeta_1 + \frac{\zeta_1 \beta^2 h}{1+n}\left(1 + \frac{1}{x_t}\right). \qquad (1.29)$$

Hence, the assumption of a Cobb–Douglas production function makes the dynamic system recursive:

$$x_{t+1} = a + \frac{b}{x_t},$$

$$\kappa_{t+1} = x_{t+1}\frac{\alpha A}{h}\kappa_t^\alpha,$$

with $a, b > 0$. The dynamics of x_t are oscillatory and converge to the steady state $x^\star$, which is globally stable in $\mathbb{R}_{++}$, as shown by the following proposition.

Proposition 1.13 (Dynamics $x_{t+1} = a + b/x_t$)
The dynamics in $\mathbb{R}_{++}$,

$$x_{t+1} = a + \frac{b}{x_t}, \qquad a, b > 0,$$

admit a unique steady state $x^\star$ which is globally stable in $\mathbb{R}_{++}$. The steady state $x^\star$ is the positive root of the equation $x^2 - ax - b = 0$.

Proof: Let $x^\star$ be the positive solution to $x^\star = a + b/x^\star$. We have

$$x_{t+2} - x^\star = \frac{b}{x_{t+1}} - \frac{b}{x^\star} = \frac{bx_t}{ax_t + b} - \frac{bx^\star}{ax^\star + b},$$

$$|x_{t+2} - x^\star| = \frac{b^2|x_t - x^\star|}{(ax_t + b)(ax^\star + b)} < \left(\frac{b}{ax^\star + b}\right)|x_t - x^\star|,$$

since $b/(ax_t + b) < 1$. Also since $b/(ax^\star + b) < 1$, the sequence (x_t) converges to $x^\star$. ∎

This proposition is illustration in figure 1.22. Since (x_t) converges to $x^\star$, the dynamics of the capital–labor ratio, which verify

$$\kappa_{t+1} = x_{t+1}\frac{\alpha A}{h}\kappa_t^\alpha,$$

converges to

$$\kappa^\star = \left(\frac{\alpha A}{h}x^\star\right)^{\frac{1}{1-\alpha}}.$$

The oscillations of the wage growth factor x_t induce oscillations in the

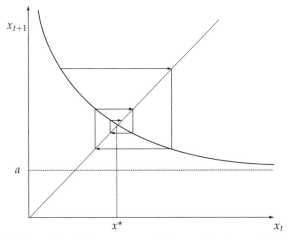

Figure 1.22. The dynamics of the wage growth factor when households live for three periods in the Cobb–Douglas case. The slope of the transition function $x_{t+1} = a + b/x_t$ is always negative. Moreover, $\lim_{x_t \to 0} x_{t+1} = +\infty$ and $\lim_{x_t \to +\infty} x_{t+1} = a$. The dynamics are oscillatory and converge towards the unique steady state equilibrium x^*, which is globally stable.

investment rate:

$$\frac{K_{t+1}}{Y_t} = \frac{(1 + h + n)\kappa_{t+1}}{A\kappa_t^\alpha} = \frac{\alpha(1 + n + h)}{h} x_{t+1}.$$

Moreover, for some parameter values and initial conditions, these oscillations might induce non-monotonicity in capital dynamics. The oscillations result from the aggregation of savings of two different generations; they contrast with the monotonic dynamics of the two-period model.[39]

Borrowing Constraints. Let us now introduce a constraint of non-negative savings, i.e., the saving s_t is the maximum of 0 and the desired savings $w_t - \zeta_1 w_t(1 + x_{t+1})$:

$$s_t = \max[0, w_t - \zeta_1 w_t(1 + x_{t+1})] = -\zeta_1 w_t \min[0, x_{t+1} - \bar{x}],$$

where

$$\bar{x} = \frac{1 - \zeta_1}{\zeta_1}$$

is the threshold of the wage growth factor above which the young households are willing to borrow. Indeed, as in the model of section 1.8.7, a high wage

---

[39] In fact, monotonic dynamics rarely apply to overlapping generations models in which persons live for more than two periods, i.e., where the unit of time considered is smaller. See Azariadis, Bullard, and Ohanian (2001).

growth factor is an incentive to transfer resources from the future. The dynamics of x_t are now given by

$$\left(\frac{(1+h+n)\alpha}{h(1-\alpha)} + \zeta_1\right) x_{t+1} + \zeta_1 \min[0, x_{t+1} - \bar{x}] = \frac{\zeta_1 \beta^2 h}{1+n}\left(1 + \frac{1}{x_t}\right), \quad (1.30)$$

to be compared with equation (1.29). Since the right-hand side is a function of x_{t+1} increasing from 0 to $+\infty$ as x_{t+1} increases from 0 to $+\infty$, these dynamics are well defined in $\mathbb{R}_{++}$ and admit a unique positive steady state $\hat{x}$. This steady state is in the constrained regime, $\hat{x} > \bar{x}$, if and only if $x^\star > \bar{x}$ (i.e., first-period savings are negative in the perfect market case). Since $x^\star$ is the positive root of $x^2 - ax - b = 0$, the condition $x^\star > \bar{x}$ is equivalent to $\bar{x}^2 - a\bar{x} - b < 0$, i.e., using (1.29),

$$\left(\frac{(1+h+n)\alpha}{h(1-\alpha)} + \zeta_1\right)\bar{x} < (1 - \zeta_1)\bar{x} + \frac{\zeta_1 \beta^2 h}{1+n}(1 + \bar{x}_t).$$

With $\bar{x} = (1 - \zeta_1)/\zeta_1$, this condition becomes

$$\frac{h^2}{1+h+n} > \frac{\alpha(1+n)}{(1-\alpha)\beta^2}\left(\frac{1 - \zeta_1}{\zeta_1}\right)^2 = \frac{\alpha(1+n)}{(1-\alpha)}(1 + \beta)^2.$$

Since $h^2/(1 + h + n)$ is increasing in h, this condition defines a lower bound $\bar{h}$ on h. As a consequence, the steady state displays credit rationing if the endowment in efficient labor of middle-age households is sufficiently high. Note that the lower bound $\bar{h}$ is an increasing function of β.

In the constrained regime, $x_{t+1} < \bar{x}$, the dynamics (1.30) are also of the type $x_{t+1} = \bar{a} + \bar{b}/x_t$ with $\bar{a} > 0$ and $\bar{b} > 0$. This implies that $\hat{x}$ is locally stable, but a change of regime may occur, for example when starting from $x_0 > \bar{x}$.

1.9 CONCLUSION

In this chapter, we have proposed an in-depth study of competitive equilibria in the basic overlapping generations model. We performed the analysis for general classes of utility and production functions, without assuming that Inada conditions are satisfied; indeed, these conditions seem to us too restrictive, as they allow us to chose only one case among the whole class of CES production functions, namely, the Cobb–Douglas production function.

The existence of both the temporary equilibrium and the inter-temporal equilibrium is guaranteed under fairly weak assumptions on preference and technology. Although we did not study the formation of expectations, we have defined the notion of rational inter-temporal equilibrium, which pertains to inter-temporal equilibria with perfect foresight which are unique, and hence for which there is no problem of coordinating expectations.

Priority has been given to a global analysis of the dynamics rather than to local arguments. We have proved that the dynamics of a rational inter-temporal equilibrium are monotonic and bounded. The notion of catching point as been defined. A catching point arises when zero is a steady state that is locally or globally stable. Conditions for such a point to exist have been analyzed.

We have also shown the usefulness of studying myopic foresight in order to characterize more easily the stability of steady states under perfect foresight. Some extensions are provided in section 1.8. In particular, we show that under the assumption of homothetic preferences, models with heterogeneous agents can be studied with the same tools as models with representative individuals.

TWO

Optimality

In an economy without externality and public goods, the competitive equilibrium is Pareto-optimal, provided that the numbers of goods and agents are finite. It is therefore impossible to improve the welfare of one agent without diminishing the welfare of another agent. This result is the First Welfare Theorem (Arrow (1951), Debreu (1954)).

This property is not necessarily verified when there is an infinite number of agents and goods. We shall see that in the standard model of chapter 1, the inter-temporal competitive equilibrium may or may not be Pareto-optimal. In a dynamic economy with an infinity of periods, we may distinguish two aspects of optimality. The dynamic efficiency deals with the issue of the productive efficiency when the production frontier is extended to an infinite horizon set-up. The welfare of the agents depends on their life-cycle utility, and hence on the allocation of total consumption between two generations living at the same time, but also among all generations.

A natural way to study allocations is thus to proceed in three steps: feasibility, (productive) efficiency, optimality.

Another important question will be addressed. How will a central benevolent planner – that can take all the consumption and savings decisions – allocate the resources of the economy between capital accumulation, consumption of the young, and consumption of the old for each generation? After the resolution of this problem, we shall be able, in chapter 3, to characterize feasible allocations which can be decentralized by means of lump-sum transfers between generations. In particular, any Pareto-optimal allocation can be decentralized with such transfers (Second Welfare Theorem).

The chapter is organized as follows. The optimality of stationary paths is studied in section 2.1. The optimality of dynamics is analyzed in section 2.2, in which we introduce the concept of dynamic inefficiency and Pareto optimality. Section 2.3 proposes a global analysis of the problem of the planner, and shows the existence, uniqueness, and monotonicity of optimal paths. Section 2.4 further characterizes the optimal solutions with the standard marginal analysis.

Finally, section 2.5 uses the results derived so far to characterize the optimal paths when the optimal growth is unbounded. Some applications and extensions are provided in section 2.6.

2.1 OPTIMALITY OF STATIONARY PATHS

We start the study of the optimality problem by specifying the resource constraint of the economy. We have seen in the previous chapter that the dynamics of the capital stock corresponding to an inter-temporal equilibrium with rational foresight are monotonic and converge to a steady state $\bar{k}$. These dynamics satisfy the following conditions for all $t \geq 0$:

$$(1+n)k_{t+1} = s_t = s(\omega(k_t), f'(k_{t+1})),$$

$$c_t = \omega(k_t) - s_t,$$

$$d_{t+1} = f'(k_{t+1})s_t.$$

They also satisfy the resource constraint:

$$F(K_t, N_t) = I_t + N_t c_t + N_{t-1} d_t.$$

The total available production is allocated between investment, consumption of the N_t young agents, and consumption of the N_{t-1} old agents alive in period t. Investment determines the capital stock of the next period:

$$K_{t+1} = I_t.$$

Dividing by N_t, we obtain the resource constraint in intensive form, with $k_t = K_t/N_t$, $f(k_t) = F(k_t, 1)$, and $K_{t+1}/N_t = (1+n)k_{t+1}$:

$$f(k_t) = (1+n)k_{t+1} + c_t + \frac{1}{1+n}d_t. \tag{2.1}$$

If the steady state $\bar{k}$ is strictly positive, savings and consumption converge respectively to

$$\bar{s} = s(\omega(\bar{k}), f'(\bar{k})),$$

$$\bar{c} = \omega(\bar{k}) - \bar{s},$$

$$\bar{d} = f'(\bar{k})\bar{s},$$

and these limits satisfy the resource constraint at steady state:

$$f(\bar{k}) = (1+n)\bar{k} + \bar{c} + \frac{1}{1+n}\bar{d}. \tag{2.2}$$

If $\bar{k}=0$ is a corner steady state, then we have $\omega(0) = f(0) = 0$ (see proposition 1.4) and the variables k_t, s_t, c_t, and d_t converge to zero. Indeed, we have

$$0 < s_t < \omega(k_t), \qquad 0 < c_t < \omega(k_t), \qquad 0 < d_t < (1+n)f(k_t).$$

Thus, the limits also satisfy the resource constraint (2.2). Before analyzing the optimality of stationary paths, we first study the set of feasible long-run capital stock.

All our definitions concerning feasibility are stated in per capita terms, assuming therefore that there is no under-employment ($L_t = N_t$). Indeed, as the production function and the utility function are monotonic, any efficient trajectory should obviously satisfy the full-employment condition.

2.1.1 Feasible Long-run Capital Stock

Definition 2.1 (Long-run feasibility)
A capital stock $k \geq 0$ is feasible in the long run if the corresponding production $f(k)$ is at least large enough to allow for replacement investment, i.e., $f(k) \geq (1+n)k$.

Stated otherwise, for a capital stock to be feasible in the long run, the production net of investment, henceforth the *net production*, should be non-negative:

$$\phi(k) = f(k) - (1+n)k \geq 0.$$

By the assumption **H2**, the function ϕ is strictly concave:

$$\phi'(k) = f'(k) - (1+n), \qquad \phi''(k) = f''(k) < 0,$$

and satisfies the following limit conditions:

$$\phi(0) = f(0) \geq 0,$$
$$\phi'(0+) = f'(0+) - (1+n),$$
$$\phi'(+\infty) = f'(+\infty) - (1+n).$$

Three different cases should be considered. These three cases are represented in figure 2.1.

Case (a). Increasing Net Production. In this case $\phi'(k)$ is always positive and the net production is increasing for all k. The largest net production is obtained with k infinite. We have the following necessary and sufficient condition: $f'(+\infty) \geq 1+n$, or equivalently, $\phi'(+\infty) > 0$.

Proposition 2.1 (Feasibility of all capital stocks)
All capital stocks are feasible in the long run if and only if the net production $\phi(k)$ is increasing for all k, i.e., if and only if $f'(+\infty) \geq (1+n)$.

Proof: The sufficient condition is straightforward: as $\phi(0) \geq 0$, the property that $\phi'(k) > 0$ for all k implies that $\phi(k) > 0$ for all k.

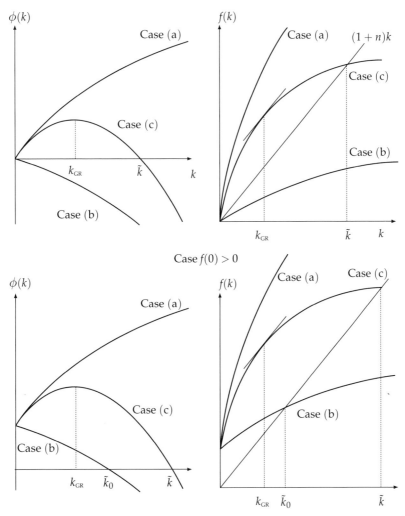

Figure 2.1. The golden rule. In case (a) all $k \geq 0$ are feasible in the long run and the largest net production is obtained with k infinite. In case (b) the largest net production is obtained for $k = 0$. In case (c) the net production is increasing in $(0, k_{\mathrm{GR}})$, attains a maximum at k_{GR}, and is decreasing in $(k_{\mathrm{GR}}, +\infty)$.

To prove the necessary condition, we start from the assumption $\phi(k) > 0$ for all k. We next have

$$\forall k > 0, \qquad \frac{f(k)}{k} > 1 + n.$$

From the previous chapter, we know that the limits of the average and the marginal productivity are equal when $k \to +\infty$. We deduce

$$f'(+\infty) = \lim_{k \to +\infty} \frac{f(k)}{k} \geq 1 + n,$$

and ϕ is increasing in all k.   ∎

Example: For a CES production function with high substitution possibilities ($\rho < 0$), we have

$$\phi(k) = A(\alpha k^{-\rho} + 1 - \alpha)^{-1/\rho} - (1+n)k,$$

and $\rho < 0$. We also have

$$\phi'(+\infty) = A\alpha^{-1/\rho} - (1+n),$$

which is non-negative for $A \geq (1+n)\alpha^{1/\rho}$.

Case (b). Decreasing Net Production. In this case, $\phi'(k)$ is decreasing for all k ($\phi'(k) < 0 \ \forall k$), and thus $f'(0) \leq 1 + n$. The largest net production is obtained for $k = 0$. There are two possibilities:

1. $f(0) = 0$, and 0 is the only capital stock feasible in the long run, as $\phi(k) < \phi(0) = 0$ for all $k > 0$. The technology does not allow one to sustain a positive level of net production, whatever the level of investment.
2. $f(0) > 0$, and there exists a largest capital stock $\tilde{k}_0$ which is feasible in the long run. This capital stock is finite and satisfies $\phi(\tilde{k}_0) = 0$. Indeed, it results from proposition 2.1 that the largest capital stock feasible in the long run is infinite only when $f'(+\infty) \geq 1 + n$.

Example: For a CES production function with low substitution ability ($\rho > 0$), we have

$$f(0) = 0,$$
$$f'(0) = A\alpha^{-1/\rho},$$

and

$$1 + n \geq A\alpha^{-1/\rho} \implies \phi'(k) < 0 \ \forall k.$$

Then, 0 is the only feasible capital stock.

Case (c). Non-monotonic Net Production. Only in the case where

$$f'(+\infty) < 1 + n < f'(0)$$

is the net production non-monotonic. In this case, there exists a unique positive $k = k_{GR}$, called the *golden rule* capital stock, such that $f'(k_{GR}) = 1 + n$. At this level k_{GR}, the net production is maximized. The concave function $\phi(k)$ is thus increasing in $(0, k_{GR})$, attains a maximum at k_{GR}, and is decreasing in

$(k_{GR}, +\infty)$. Moreover (from proposition 2.1) it becomes negative after some finite level $\tilde{k}$ of the capital stock. The set of capital stocks which are feasible in the long run is the interval $(0, \tilde{k})$.

2.1.2 The Optimal Stationary Path: The Golden Age

The life-cycle welfare of the young generation in t is given by

$$U(c_t, d_{t+1}) = u(c_t) + \beta u(d_{t+1}).$$

The consumption levels of a given agent, c_t and d_{t+1}, appear in two resource constraints, in period t and period $t + 1$. Along a stationary path with constant values $\bar{k}, \bar{c}$, and $\bar{d}$ the two resource constraints coincide; the life-cycle welfare is $U(\bar{c}, \bar{d})$, and equation (2.2) holds for all periods. The highest stationary utility is thus defined by[1]

$$\max u(c) + \beta u(d) \quad \text{subject to} \quad f(k) = (1+n)k + c + \frac{d}{1+n}. \quad (2.3)$$

There is no other restriction than the non-negativity of the quantities k, c, and d. The set of possible consumptions is defined by

$$c \geq 0, \qquad d \geq 0, \qquad c + \frac{d}{1+n} = \phi(k),$$

and the maximum of utility implies the maximum of net production $\phi(k)$. The maximum of net production is a recurrent theme in economic growth theory. As we have seen in the preceding subsection, it is obtained with $k = +\infty$ is case (a), $k = 0$ in case (b), and finite positive $k = k_{GR}$ in case (c).

The golden rule capital stock k_{GR} was studied by many authors in the 1960s.[2] To define it formally we need to make the following assumption:

Assumption A5.

$$f'(0) > 1 + n > f'(+\infty).$$

Definition 2.2 (Golden rule)
Under the assumption **A5**, *there exists a unique positive stock of capital such that*

$$f'(k_{GR}) = 1 + n, \quad (2.4)$$

which is the golden rule *capital stock.*

---

[1] This question should not be seen as a problem of allocating resources between young and old who are alive at the same time, but it is a dynamic problem of allocating consumption across periods of life.

[2] The term "golden rule" was introduced by Phelps (1961).

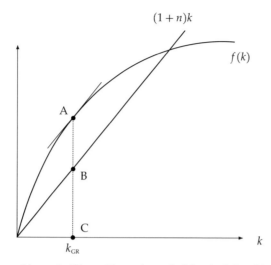

Figure 2.2. The golden rule. The golden rule capital k_{GR} is defined by the equality of the growth of the population $1 + n$ with the marginal productivity of capital, $f'(k_{GR})$. It is the level of the capital stock that maximizes available consumption, represented by the distance A–B.

The golden rule is represented in figure 2.2. The classical interpretation of the golden rule is the following: The golden rule capital k_{GR}, if it exists, is defined by the equality of the growth rate of the population n with the marginal productivity of capital net of depreciation, $f'(k_{GR}) - 1$. Indeed, considering the production function $F(K, L) = \bar{F}(K, L) + (1 - \delta)K$, the marginal productivity net of depreciation is

$$\bar{F}'_K(K, L) - \delta = F'(K, L) - 1 = f'(k) - 1.$$

Alternatively, we can say that the golden rule is characterized by the equality between the gross marginal productivity of capital and the sum $\delta + n$:

$$\bar{F}'_K(K, L) = \delta + n.$$

The condition for the existence of the golden rule is given by **A5**. Notice that the Inada conditions **A2** imply that **A5** holds, as $n > -1$.

Example: With the CES production function, we should distinguish the different cases depending on ρ:

- Only in the Cobb–Douglas case ($\rho = 0$) does the assumption A5 fail to impose any condition, as $f'(0) = +\infty$ and $f'(+\infty) = 0$.
- When factors of production are weak substitutes ($\rho > 0$), one has $f'(0) = A\alpha^{-1/\rho}$ and $f'(+\infty) = 0$. **A5** thus imposes a condition on the parameters stating that the productivity parameter A should be large enough: $A > (1 + n)\alpha^{1/\rho}$.

- When factors of production are highly substitutable ($\rho < 0$), one has $f'(0) = +\infty$ and $f'(+\infty) = A\alpha^{-1/\rho}$. **A5** thus imposes a condition on the parameters stating that the productivity parameter A should be small enough: $A < (1+n)\alpha^{1/\rho}$.

We now characterize the golden age (Diamond (1965), pp. 1128–1129), which is the solution to problem (2.3):

Proposition 2.2 (Existence and uniqueness of the golden age)
*Under the assumptions **H1**, **H2**, and **A5** there exists a unique optimal stationary path, the golden age, which is characterized by the following conditions: $k = k_{GR}$, and c_{GR} and d_{GR} satisfy*

$$c_{GR} + \frac{1}{1+n}d_{GR} = \phi(k_{GR}),$$

$$u'(c_{GR}) = (1+n)\beta u'(d_{GR}).$$

Proof: The maximum of ϕ is attained at k_{GR}, and the maximum of $u(c) + \beta u(d)$ under the constraint $c + \frac{d}{1+n} = \phi(k)$ is characterized by the first-order necessary condition $u'(c_{GR}) = (1+n)\beta u'(d_{GR})$. ∎

Proposition 2.3 (Optimal allocation and life-cycle arbitrage)
The optimal stationary path satisfies the decentralized arbitrage condition of a consumer over his life cycle when the return on savings is $f'(k_{GR}) = 1 + n$, and his life-cycle income is $\omega(k_{GR}) = f(k_{GR}) - k_{GR}f'(k_{GR})$. But his choice of savings is generally different from the optimal investment $(1+n)k_{GR}$.

Proof: The optimal choice of a consumer satisfies (see equation (1.6))

$$u'(c_t) = \beta R_{t+1}u'(d_{t+1}).$$

When the return on savings in $1+n$ (the biological interest rate of Samuelson (1958)), we have $R_{t+1} = 1 + n$; this is the optimal arbitrage condition between c_t and d_{t+1}. Moreover, the actual value of the lifetime spending on consumption is

$$c_{GR} + \frac{1}{1+n}d_{GR} = \phi(k_{GR}) = f(k_{GR}) - (1+n)k_{GR}$$

$$= f(k_{GR}) - f'(k_{GR})k_{GR} = \omega(k_{GR}),$$

which is the wage corresponding to the stock of capital of the golden rule. However, our optimal path is not the decentralized equilibrium of the competitive economy because, in general,

$$s(\omega(k_{GR}), 1+n) \neq (1+n)k_{GR},$$

i.e., savings differ from the replacement investment. ∎

This appears clearly in the following simple example considered by Diamond.

Example: Let us take a logarithmic utility and a Cobb–Douglas production function. We find that the capital stock satisfying the golden rule is

$$k_{\text{GR}} = \left(\frac{\alpha A}{1+n} \right)^{\frac{1}{1-\alpha}},$$

and

$$\phi(k_{\text{GR}}) = (1-\alpha)Ak_{\text{GR}}^{\alpha}, \qquad c_{\text{GR}} = \frac{1}{1+\beta}\phi(k_{\text{GR}}), \qquad d_{\text{GR}} = \frac{(1+n)\beta}{1+\beta}\phi(k_{\text{GR}}).$$

Savings are given by

$$s(\omega(k_{\text{GR}}), 1+n) = \phi(k_{\text{GR}}) - c_{\text{GR}} = \frac{\beta}{1+\beta}\phi(k_{\text{GR}}),$$

as $\omega(k_{\text{GR}}) = \phi(k_{\text{GR}})$. The comparison between savings and optimal capital is given by the following condition:

$$s(\omega(k_{\text{GR}}), 1+n) \gtreqless (1+n)k_{\text{GR}}$$

$$\Longleftrightarrow \quad \frac{\beta}{1+\beta}(1-\alpha)Ak_{\text{GR}}^{\alpha} \lesseqgtr (1+n)k_{\text{GR}} = \alpha Ak_{\text{GR}}^{\alpha}$$

$$\Longleftrightarrow \quad \frac{\beta}{1+\beta} \lesseqgtr \frac{\alpha}{1-\alpha}.$$

Only in the special case $\frac{\beta}{1+\beta} = \frac{\alpha}{1-\alpha}$ is there equality between savings and replacement investment. If, for a given α, time preference is such that $\frac{\beta}{1+\beta} > \frac{\alpha}{1-\alpha}$, i.e., β is "large," then savings exceed the golden rule capital stock.

We should thus study the consequence of the absence of coincidence between the golden age and the competitive equilibrium.

2.1.3 Under- and Over-accumulation of Capital

Let us consider a stationary capital stock which is feasible in the long run: $\phi(k) \geq 0$.

Definition 2.3 (Under- and over-accumulation of capital)
If an increase in k implies an increase in net production, i.e. $f'(k) > 1+n$, we say that there is under-accumulation of capital at k. If an increase in k implies a decrease in net production, i.e., $f'(k) < 1+n$, we say that there is over-accumulation of capital at k.

Notice that if there exists a golden rule level of the capital stock k_{GR} (i.e., if **A5** holds), these conditions are respectively equivalent to $k < k_{GR}$ and $k > k_{GR}$.

At a steady state $\bar{k}$ of an inter-temporal equilibrium, there is under-accumulation of capital when $f'(\bar{k}) > 1 + n$, and there is over-accumulation of capital when $f'(\bar{k}) < 1 + n$. Equivalently, there is under-accumulation (or over-accumulation) when the long-run rate of return $f'(\bar{k}) - 1$ is higher (or lower) than the growth rate of the population. In both cases, for a given $\bar{k}$, the maximum of utility is different from the utility at the competitive steady state. Indeed, the latter satisfies $u'(\bar{c}) = \beta f'(\bar{k}) u'(\bar{d})$ and the maximum utility with fixed net production $\phi(\bar{k})$ satisfies $u'(c) = \beta(1 + n) u'(d)$.

A standard implication of the optimality condition is that a stationary path with over-accumulation of capital is not Pareto-optimal in terms of consumption levels, implying that we can increase the total consumption at (at least) one date without reducing it at any other date. In particular, we can show that it is possible to increase total consumption by reducing k in a discretionary manner. The total net production is $\phi(k)$ for all periods. If we reduce the capital stock to the golden rule level k_{GR} at some period, the total consumption will be $\phi(k) + (k - k_{GR})(1 + n)$, the first part being the standard surplus obtained with the old level of k, and the second being the surplus obtained by the reduction in the stock of capital. We have thus increased total consumption for that period. For the following periods, the surplus is $\phi(k_{GR})$, which is also superior to $\phi(k)$ by definition of the golden rule. Hence, total consumption can be increased at all dates by moving the capital stock towards the golden rule k_{GR}.

It was initially thought that the breakdown of the first welfare theorem in overlapping generations economies was due to the fact that all generations do not meet in a single market (see, e.g., Stein (1969)). This is not true, however, and Shell (1971) pointed out that the infinity of agents and goods in these models breaks the proof of the First Welfare Theorem under certain circumstances. There is a sense in which the economy has infinite resources, and one may no longer conclude that a proposed Pareto-dominating allocation cannot be reached. In the above reasoning, if we assume that the horizon is not infinite but finite, say T, the surplus to be consumed during the last period will have been k_{GR} instead of k, and in this case the increase in consumption for all $t < T$ will be at the expense of the last period. The infinite number of periods is thus a crucial assumption.

Notice also that the time horizon of the agents is not a crucial element as long as the number of agents is infinite. Indeed, Weil (1989) proposes an overlapping generations model with infinite-lived agents in which competitive equilibria can be inefficient. The crucial point in this case is the birth of agents who have no parents to take care of them, i.e., of "unloved children."

The problem of the golden age illustrates the two aspects of optimality in overlapping generations models: the maximum of productive efficiency when we choose the stock of capital, and the maximum of life-cycle utility when we choose the allocation of net production between consumptions. We shall consider these two issues separately for the optimality problem of non-stationary paths that we study in the next section.

2.2 OPTIMALITY OF THE DYNAMICS

In this section we first address the issue of productive efficiency, called, in a dynamic setup, dynamic efficiency. We next consider the problem of the Pareto-optimal allocation of resources between the different generations and individuals.

2.2.1 Dynamic Efficiency

The first studies of inefficient capital accumulation are due to Phelps (1965) and Koopmans (1965) in a setup where the distributional issue was not addressed. We consider a production function $f(k)$ satisfying **H2**, and we give the following definitions from Cass (1972):

Definition 2.4 (Feasible path of capital)
A sequence of capital stock $(k_t)_{t \geq 0}$ is a feasible path if, for all $t \geq 0$, the net production is non-negative:

$$\phi(k_t, k_{t+1}) = f(k_t) - (1+n)k_{t+1} \geq 0.$$

Definition 2.5 (Efficiency and inefficiency)
A feasible sequence of capital stock $(k_t)_{t \geq 0}$ is inefficient if there exists another feasible path $(k_t^1)_{t \geq 0}$ such that:

1. *$k_0^1 = k_0$ and $\forall t \geq 0$, $\phi(k_t^1, k_{t+1}^1) \geq \phi(k_t, k_{t+1})$;*
2. *there exists at least one $t \geq 0$ such that $\phi(k_t^1, k_{t+1}^1) > \phi(k_t, k_{t+1})$.*

A feasible path is efficient if it is not inefficient.

The rationale for these definitions is simple. The net production $\phi(k_t, k_{t+1})$ is the total level of consumption (in intensive form) which is available when the capital stock is k_t at t and k_{t+1} at $t+1$. Feasibility means that total consumption is non-negative; efficiency means that it is not possible to increase total consumption at one date without decreasing total consumption at another date. This is a property of Pareto optimality for the sequence $\phi(k_t, k_{t+1})$ of feasible consumption.

Dynamic efficiency is the same as Pareto optimality in terms of aggregate consumptions. It is also a necessary condition for Pareto optimality in terms of the amount of consumption by young and old agents.

Let us consider a feasible growth path characterized by k_t, which converges to the steady state $k^* > 0$. We have the following proposition:

Proposition 2.4 (Efficiency)
Under the assumption H2, a feasible path which converges to a limit $k^* > 0$ is inefficient when there is over-accumulation at k^*; it is efficient when there is under-accumulation at k^*.

Proof:
- **Over-accumulation:** $f'(k^*) < 1 + n$. To demonstrate inefficiency in this case, we show that we can lower the stock of capital and increase consumption at one date without reducing consumption at another date. The argument developed for steady state allocation is now applied to a feasible trajectory converging to a steady state. In a neighborhood $(k^* - 2\varepsilon, k^* + 2\varepsilon)$ of k^*, we have $f'(k) < 1 + n$. After some date t_0, we have $k_t \in (k^* - \varepsilon, k^* + \varepsilon)$, $f'(k_t) < 1 + n$, and $f'(k_t - \varepsilon) < 1 + n$. The concavity of $f(\cdot)$ implies

$$f(k - \varepsilon) - f(k) \geq -f'(k - \varepsilon)\varepsilon.$$

  Let us diminish the capital stock by ε after date t_0 and forever. Investment k_{t_0+1} is reduced by ε and consumption $\phi(k_{t_0}, k_{t_0+1})$ is increased by $\varepsilon(1 + n)$. At $t > t_0$, the new consumption level is

$$\begin{aligned}
\phi(k_t - \varepsilon, k_{t+1} - \varepsilon) &= f(k_t - \varepsilon) - (1 + n)(k_{t+1} - \varepsilon) \\
&\geq f(k_t) - f'(k_t - \varepsilon)\varepsilon - (1 + n)(k_{t+1} - \varepsilon) \\
&\geq f(k_t) - (1 + n)k_{t+1} + (\varepsilon(1 + n) - f'(k_t - \varepsilon)\varepsilon) \\
&> f(k_t) - (1 + n)k_{t+1} = \phi(k_t, k_{t+1}).
\end{aligned}$$

  Consumption can thus be increased for all periods, and the path is dynamically inefficient.
- **Under-accumulation:** Case $f'(k^*) > 1 + n$. To assess efficiency in this case, we show that an increase in consumption for one period t_1 without reducing it in any other period would lead to an impossibility. $f'(k^*) > 1 + n$ implies that we have $f'(k^*) > b(1 + n)$, with some $b > 1$. For t large enough, say $t \geq t_0$, we have $f'(k_t) > b(1 + n)$. At any date t, the difference from another feasible path $\tilde{k}_t$ satisfies

$$\begin{aligned}
(1 + n)(\tilde{k}_{t+1} - k_{t+1}) &= f(\tilde{k}_t) - f(k_t) - \Delta c_t \\
&\leq f'(k_t)(\tilde{k}_t - k_t) - \Delta c_t,
\end{aligned} \tag{2.5}$$

where Δc_t is the difference of total consumptions:

$$\Delta c_t = \tilde{c}_t - c_t = f(\tilde{k}_t) - (1 + n)\tilde{k}_{t+1} - [f(k_t) - (1 + n)k_{t+1}].$$

Assume that consumption never decreases. In this case, capital never increases. Indeed, by induction, if $\tilde{k}_t - k_t \leq 0$, which is true at $t = 0$, and if

$\Delta c_t \geq 0$, then (2.5) implies $\tilde{k}_{t+1} - k_{t+1} \leq 0$. Assume, moreover, that consumption increases at some date t_1: $\Delta c_{t_1} > 0$. Then the preceding argument implies $\tilde{k}_t - k_t < 0 \; \forall t > t_1$. Moreover, it implies, for $t > t_2 = \max\{t_0, t_1\}$,

$$(1+n)(\tilde{k}_{t+1} - k_{t+1}) \leq f'(k_t)(\tilde{k}_t - k_t) \qquad \text{by (2.5) with } \Delta c_t \geq 0$$
$$< b(1+n)(\tilde{k}_t - k_t),$$

since $\tilde{k}_t - k_t < 0$ and $f'(k_t) > b(1+n)$. Hence,

$$\tilde{k}_{t+1} - k_{t+1} < b(\tilde{k}_t - k_t),$$

and

$$\tilde{k}_{t+1} - k_{t+1} < b^{t-t_2}(\tilde{k}_{t_2} - k_{t_2}).$$

As $b > 1$ and k_{t+1} converges, we have that $\tilde{k}_t - k_t$ converges to $-\infty$ and $\tilde{k}_{t+1}$ becomes negative, which is excluded. ∎

Proposition 2.4 allows us to determine whether any given feasible path is efficient or not. We can now apply this result to inter-temporal competitive equilibria.

Corollary: *Under the assumptions* **H1**, **H2**, *and* **H3**, *a rational inter-temporal competitive equilibrium converging towards a positive steady state $\bar{k}$ is dynamically efficient if $f'(\bar{k}) > 1 + n$ and dynamically inefficient if $f'(\bar{k}) < 1 + n$.*

Considering again figure 2.2, the intuition is the following: When we have over-accumulation, the capital stock converges to some point at the right of the golden rule. We can thus increase all future consumptions by diminishing the capital after the date at which k_t becomes larger than k_{GR} (the slope of the $f(k)$ line is smaller than that of the $(1+n)k$ line). When we have under-accumulation, the capital stock converges to some point at the left of the golden rule. We should thus increase capital to increase the production and hence all future consumptions, but this requires an initial drop in consumption.

A natural question arising from these theoretical results is whether actual economies are dynamically inefficient. Historically, risk-free interest rates have been far below the rate of economic growth of developed economies. However, the rate of return on capital has generally been above the growth rate, which might suggest dynamic efficiency. This illustrates that interest rate comparisons do not provide a unequivocal answer to the question of dynamic efficiency, essentially because the real world is stochastic and includes more sources of growth than the model. An alterative test is proposed by Abel, Mankiw, Summers, and Zeckhauser (1989); they compare gross profits with gross investment in different countries and conclude in favor of dynamic efficiency. Other authors have addressed the issue by calibrating realistic overlapping generations economies and studying the efficiency properties of the steady state(s) (see Bullard and Russell (1999)).

Example: Let us consider an economy with a CES production function with $\rho = 1$ and $\alpha = 1/2$, and a logarithmic utility $U(c, d) = \ln c + \beta \ln d$.[3] In this case,

$$f(k) = \frac{2Ak}{1+k}, \qquad \omega(k) = \frac{2Ak^2}{(1+k)^2}.$$

The steady state levels of k are given by

$$(1+n)k = \frac{\beta}{1+\beta} \frac{2Ak^2}{(1+k)^2}.$$

If $f'(0) = 2A > 1+n$, then 0 is a corner steady state and the inter-temporal competitive equilibria converging towards 0 are dynamically efficient.

The positive steady states are the roots of $P(k)$ with

$$P(k) = k^2 + 2\left(1 - \frac{A\beta}{(1+n)(1+\beta)}\right)k + 1.$$

We have two positive steady states $k_a < k_b$ if and only if the discriminant of $P(k)$ is greater than 0. This condition can be written

$$\left(1 - \frac{A\beta}{(1+n)(1+\beta)}\right)^2 > 1,$$

requiring either

$$\left(1 - \frac{A\beta}{(1+n)(1+\beta)}\right) > 1 \quad \text{or} \quad \left(1 - \frac{A\beta}{(1+n)(1+\beta)}\right) < -1.$$

As $\frac{A\beta}{(1+n)(1+\beta)}$ is always positive, this requires

$$\frac{A\beta}{(1+n)(1+\beta)} > 2,$$

which is the same as $A > 2(1+n)(1+\beta)/\beta$. It can be checked that k_a is unstable, and k_b is stable.

The golden rule capital stock exists if and only if $2A > 1+n$, and then

$$k_{GR} = \sqrt{\frac{2A}{1+n}} - 1.$$

In the case $2A \leq 1+n$, we have $f'(k) < 1+n$ for all k, and all equilibria are inefficient. When $2A > 1+n$ we distinguish the following cases:

If $P(k_{GR}) < 0$, then $k_a < k_{GR} < k_b$, k_a is dynamically efficient, k_b is dynamically inefficient, and the inter-temporal competitive equilibria converging toward k_b are dynamically inefficient.

If $P(k_{GR}) > 0$, then either $k_a < k_b < k_{GR}$, and both steady states are dynamically efficient, or $k_{GR} < k_a < k_b$, and both steady states are dynamically inefficient.

---

[3] A numerical example of such an economy is provided in section A.5.2.

The Inefficiency Criterion Due to Cass. With some additional assumptions, Cass (1972), building on previous work by Malinvaud (1953), establishes a necessary and sufficient condition for inefficiency. An allocation is inefficient if the infinite sum of the numbers $1/N_t P_t$ converges, where P_t is the discount factor defined by induction in the following way:

$$P_{t+1} = \frac{1}{f'(k_{t+1})} P_t \quad \text{and} \quad P_0 = 1. \tag{2.6}$$

2.2.2 Pareto Optimality of Dynamics

We now consider the optimality of an allocation across the different genera-tions. For simplicity, we only consider the case where all agents of the same generation consume the same quantities[4] and all quantities are positive.[5]

Definition 2.6 (Feasible allocation)
Given k_0, a feasible allocation is a sequence of positive quantities $(c_t, d_t, k_{t+1})_{t \geq 0}$, which satisfies the resource constraint

$$f(k_t) = c_t + \frac{d_t}{1+n} + (1+n)k_{t+1}$$

for all $t \geq 0$.

Definition 2.7 (Pareto optimality)
An allocation $(\check{c}_t, \check{d}_t, \check{k}_{t+1})$ is Pareto-optimal if it is feasible and if there is no other feasible allocation, which increases the utility of at least one household of one generation without diminishing the utility of any other household.

Proposition 2.5 (Efficiency and Pareto optimality)
A Pareto-optimal allocation is efficient and satisfies, for all $t \geq 0$,

$$u'(\check{c}_t) = \beta f'(\check{k}_{t+1}) u'(\check{d}_{t+1}). \tag{2.7}$$

Proof: The efficiency property results from the assumption **H1** (the utility function is increasing). Indeed, if a feasible trajectory is inefficient, it is possible to increase total consumption at least in one period without decreasing it in any other period. It is therefore possible to increase the utility of one generation (in fact two) without decreasing the utility of any other, showing that this feasible trajectory is not Pareto-optimal.

---

[4] The extension to heterogeneous agents inside the same generation is a standard static problem.
[5] Positive consumptions allow us to define the life-cycle utilities without making an additional assumption on the utility of zero consumption.

To prove that equation (2.7) is a necessary condition for Pareto optimality, let us take the consumptions of all generations except generation t as constant, and fix $\check{k}_t$ and $\check{k}_{t+2}$. Then, we have the two following resource constraints involving c_t and d_{t+1}:

$$f(\check{k}_t) = (1+n)k_{t+1} + c_t + \frac{1}{1+n}\check{d}_t,$$

$$f(k_{t+1}) = (1+n)\check{k}_{t+2} + \check{c}_{t+1} + \frac{1}{1+n}d_{t+1}.$$

Any change in k_{t+1} implies a change in the utility of generation t. The derivative with respect to k_{t+1} is

$$\frac{\partial U_t}{\partial k_{t+1}} = u'(c_t)\frac{\partial c_t}{\partial k_{t+1}} + \beta u'(d_{t+1})\frac{\partial d_{t+1}}{\partial k_{t+1}}$$

$$= -u'(c_t)(1+n) + \beta u'(d_{t+1})(1+n)f'(k_{t+1}).$$

The maximum of utility keeping the utility of all other generations unchanged is obtained by equating the above derivative to zero. Hence, applying the same reasoning to all generations, we deduce that a Pareto-optimal trajectory verifies equation (2.7) $\forall t$. ∎

Notice that any competitive equilibrium with perfect foresight satisfies

$$u'(c) = \beta R^e_{t+1}u'(d_{t+1}),$$

and

$$R^e_{t+1} = R_{t+1} = f'(k_{t+1}).$$

It also satisfies equation (2.7). However, an inter-temporal competitive equilibrium such that the corresponding path of the capital stock is inefficient is not Pareto-optimal. As it is possible to increase total consumption at one period without decreasing it at any other period, it is possible to increase the utility of one generation (in fact two) without decreasing the utility of any other generation.

Moreover, efficiency of the path of the capital stock does not guarantee by itself the Pareto optimality. In order to study this problem, we use the standard method of the First Welfare Theorem (which says that a competitive equilibrium is Pareto-optimal); we show that there is, in addition to the standard proof in a static environment, a limit condition coming from the infinite horizon of the equilibrium in the overlapping generations model. We first prove a lemma corresponding to theorem 1 of Homburg (1992), which says basically that, if an equilibrium is not Pareto-optimal, there remains something valuable at the end of time that has not been distributed.

Lemma 2.1 (non-Pareto-optimality)
If an inter-temporal equilibrium with perfect foresight $(\bar{c}_t, \bar{d}_t, \bar{k}_{t+1})_{t\geq 0}$ is not Pareto-optimal, then the limit inferior[6] of the discounted value of the wage bill, $P_t \omega(\bar{k}_t) N_t$, is strictly positive when t tends to infinity, where P_t is defined following (2.6):

$$P_{t+1} = \frac{1}{f'(\bar{k}_{t+1})} P_t \quad and \quad P_0 = 1.$$

Proof: Let $(\bar{c}_t, \bar{d}_t, \bar{k}_{t+1})_{t\geq 0}$ be an inter-temporal equilibrium starting at k_0 which is not Pareto-optimal. Thus, there exists a feasible trajectory $(c_t, d_t, k_{t+1})_{t\geq 0}$ starting at k_0, such that $d_0 \geq \bar{d}_0$ and for all $t \geq 0$, $U(c_t, d_{t+1}) \geq U(\bar{c}_t, \bar{d}_{t+1})$, and the strict inequality holds for some t_0.

• **First step:** We show that all the quantities $A_0 = N_{-1} P_0 (d_0 - \bar{d}_0)$, and

$$A_t = N_t P_t (c_t - \bar{c}_t) + N_t P_{t+1}(d_{t+1} - \bar{d}_{t+1})$$

are non-negative and there is at least one date t_0 for which A_{t_0} is positive. The condition $d_0 \geq \bar{d}_0$ implies $A_0 \geq 0$. To show that $A_t \geq 0$ for all $t > 0$ we use a reductio ad absurdum. Assume $A_t < 0$. This implies, after division by $N_t P_t$,

$$c_t + \frac{1}{\bar{R}_{t+1}} d_{t+1} < \bar{c}_t + \frac{1}{\bar{R}_{t+1}} \bar{d}_{t+1} = \bar{w}_t,$$

where $\bar{R}_{t+1} = f'(\bar{k}_{t+1}) = P_t / P_{t+1}$ and $\bar{w}_t = \omega(\bar{k}_t)$. Thus, there exists $v_t > 0$ such that $(c_t + v_t, d_{t+1})$ belongs to the budget set

$$\mathcal{B}_t = \left\{ (c_t, d_{t+1}) \in \mathbb{R}_+^2; \ c_t + \frac{1}{\bar{R}_{t+1}} d_{t+1} \leq \bar{w}_t \right\}.$$

This implies

$$U(\bar{c}_t, \bar{d}_{t+1}) = \max_{\mathcal{B}_t} U(c, d) \geq U(c_t + v_t, d_{t+1}) > U(c_t, d_{t+1}).$$

This is excluded by assumption, and thus $A_t \geq 0$. Moreover, $A_t \leq 0$ implies (with a similar proof and $v_t = 0$) $U(\bar{c}_t, \bar{d}_{t+1}) \geq U(c_t, d_{t+1})$. From the strict inequality that holds for t_0, we have $A_{t_0} > 0$.

• **Second step:** We show that all the quantities

$$B_t = N_{t+1} P_{t+1} [f(\bar{k}_{t+1}) - f(k_{t+1})] - N_{t+1} P_t (\bar{k}_{t+1} - k_{t+1})$$

are non-negative. The maximum of the concave function $f(k) - \bar{R}_{t+1} k$ is attained at $\bar{k}_{t+1}$, verifying $f'(\bar{k}_{t+1}) = \bar{R}_{t+1}$. Hence we have that $f(\bar{k}_{t+1}) - \bar{R}_{t+1} \bar{k}_{t+1} \geq f(k_{t+1}) - \bar{R}_{t+1} k_{t+1}$. As $P_{t+1} \bar{R}_{t+1} = P_t$, we have that $B_t \geq 0$.

---

[6] See appendix A.2.3 for a definition.

- **Third step:** We compute the sum $\sum_{t=0}^{T-1}(A_t + B_t)$ and show that this sum is less or equal to $P_T N_T \bar{w}_T$. The sum can be rearranged as

$$\sum_{t=0}^{T-1}(A_t + B_t) = [N_{-1}(d_0 - \bar{d}_0) + N_0(c_0 - \bar{c}_0) - N_1(\bar{k}_1 - k_1)]P_0$$

$$+ \sum_{t=1}^{T-1}\{N_{t-1}(d_t - \bar{d}_t) + N_t[c_t - \bar{c}_t + f(\bar{k}_t) - f(k_t)]$$

$$- N_{t+1}(\bar{k}_{t+1} - k_{t+1})\}P_t$$

$$+ \{N_{T-1}(d_T - \bar{d}_T) + N_T[f(\bar{k}_T) - f(k_T)]\}P_T.$$

The factor multiplying P_0 is nil, as

$$\frac{d_0}{1+n} + c_0 + (1+n)k_1 = f(k_0) = \frac{\bar{d}_0}{1+n} + \bar{c}_0 + (1+n)\bar{k}_1.$$

Using the resource constraint,

$$f(k_t) = (1+n)k_{t+1} + c_t + \frac{d_t}{1+n},$$

the factor multiplying P_t is nil too. Following again the resource constraint, the factor multiplying P_T is

$$N_{T-1}(d_T - \bar{d}_T) + N_T[f(\bar{k}_T) - f(k_T)] = N_T(\bar{c}_T - c_T) + N_{T+1}(\bar{k}_{T+1} - k_{T+1}).$$

As c_T and k_{T+1} are non-negative, this expression is bounded above by

$$N_T\bar{c}_T + N_{T+1}\bar{k}_{T+1} = N_T\bar{w}_T,$$

since at the competitive equilibrium, $\bar{w}_T = \bar{c}_T + \bar{s}_T = \bar{c}_T + (1+n)\bar{k}_{T+1}$.

- **Last step:** We conclude that for $T > t_0$ the sum of the $A_t + B_t$ is larger or equal to $A_{t_0} > 0$, and this sum is bounded above by $P_T N_T \bar{w}_T$. Hence we deduce that

$$\liminf_{T \to +\infty} P_T N_T \bar{w}_T \geq A_{t_0} > 0. \qquad \blacksquare$$

Proposition 2.6 (Pareto optimality)
*Under the assumptions **H1** and **H2**, let us consider an inter-temporal competitive equilibrium such that the sequence $(\bar{k}_t)$ converges towards a limit $\bar{k} > 0$. Then this equilibrium is Pareto-optimal if there is under-accumulation at $\bar{k}$. It is not Pareto-optimal if there is over-accumulation at $\bar{k}$.*

Proof: When there is over-accumulation at $\bar{k}$, then the path of the capital stock $(\bar{k}_t)$ is inefficient; it is possible to increase the consumption of one generation, and hence its utility, without decreasing the consumption and utility of the other generations.

When there is under-accumulation at $\bar{k}$, we have $f'(\bar{k}) > 1 + n$ and the sequence $x_t = N_t P_t$ satisfies

$$x_{t+1} = \frac{1+n}{f'(\bar{k}_{t+1})} x_t.$$

As the limit of $(1 + n)/f'(\bar{k}_{t+1})$ is less than one, the limit of $x_t = N_t P_t$ is zero. As the equilibrium wage $\bar{w}_t$ converges, it is bounded, and the limit of the discounted wage bill $P_t N_t \bar{w}_t$ is zero. Then the lemma implies that the equilibrium is necessarily Pareto-optimal.   ∎

Notice that under the assumptions **H1**, **H2**, and **H3**, for any rational inter-temporal competitive equilibrium, the sequence (k_t) converges towards a steady state $\bar{k}$. The rational inter-temporal competitive equilibrium is Pareto-optimal if there is under-accumulation at $\bar{k}$. It is not Pareto-optimal if there is over-accumulation at $\bar{k}$. Two special cases ($\bar{k} = 0$ and $\bar{k} = k_{\text{GR}}$) are not covered by the above results.

2.3 THE PLANNING PROBLEM

Having analyzed the conditions under which a given allocation is or is not Pareto-optimal, we now consider the problem of the benevolent planner who can allocate the resources of the economy between capital accumulation, consumption of the young, and consumption of the old for each generation.

We first define the objective function of the planner in section 2.3.1, and next characterize the optimal solution. Two methods are possible. The most widespread is the marginal approach developed in section 2.4. It introduces a shadow price for capital (as a co-state variable like in the Pontryagin (1966) principle in continuous time). The advantage of this method for economists is that the shadow price gives an evaluation of the stock of capital in terms of future welfare, along the optimal path. However, the marginal conditions do not allow one, except in very special cases (see the example at the end of section 2.4.1), to establish the existence of the solution from a global point of view. The other approach involves the value function proposed by Bellman (1957).[7] The value function gives the maximum welfare for any initial stock of capital. As it solves the optimization problems parametrized by k_0 (i.e. for all possible k_0) and studies the effect of k_0 on the solution, it requires additional specific assumptions.[8] In section 2.3.2 we introduce the specific assumptions which ensure the existence of the value function and study its properties. Section 2.3.3

---

[7] See also Stokey and Lucas (1989). We are almost forced to use this approach in a stochastic environment.

[8] Note that, when the value function is differentiable, the shadow price of the marginal approach is equal to its derivative taken along the optimal path.

applies these results to derive the policy functions which describe the global dynamics of capital.

The interest of the approach with the value function is to establish the existence and the monotonicity of the solution, and to study its limit. In particular we show that when the modified golden rule defined below exists, the optimal path converges to it. When the marginal productivity of capital at 0 is so weak that the modified golden rule does not exists, the optimal path converges to 0. When the marginal productivity of capital at infinity remains so high that the modified golden rule does not exist, the optimal path goes to infinity and optimal growth is unbounded (this case will be studied further in section 2.5).

2.3.1 The Objective Function

The objective of the social planner is to maximize a discounted sum of the life-cycle utility of all current and future generations,

$$\sum_{t=-1}^{\infty} \gamma^t U(c_t, d_{t+1}),$$

under the resource constraint (2.1):

$$f(k_t) = (1+n)k_{t+1} + c_t + \frac{1}{1+n}d_t,$$

with k_0 and c_{-1} given. c_{-1} is the hypothetical young-age consumption of the first old generation. γ is the planner's discount factor, or social discount factor. The planner's objective function is often called a social welfare function.

When the utilities are bounded, the assumption that γ is smaller than 1 ensures that the objective function is finite. More generally, it is sufficient that the actual values of utilities $\gamma_0^t U_t$ are bounded for some discount factor $\gamma_0 > \gamma$ (see the assumption **A6** below).

As the life-cycle utility function is separable,[9] $U_t = u(c_t) + \beta u(d_{t+1})$, we can rearrange the objective function in the following way (grouping the contemporaneous terms together and ignoring the constant term $u(c_{-1})$):

$$W = \sum_{t=0}^{\infty} \gamma^t \left(u(c_t) + \frac{\beta}{\gamma} u(d_t) \right). \tag{2.8}$$

The Ramsey Optimal Growth Problem. For Ramsey (1928), the optimal growth problem should not be discounted. With $\gamma = 1$ the social welfare

---

[9] Michel and Venditti (1997) solve the planning problem when the utility function is non-separable. They show that the properties of optimal paths may be altered substantially.

objective is not necessarily defined, but, as Ramsey did, it is possible to consider

$$\sum_{t=-1}^{\infty} [U(c_t, d_{t+1}) - \hat{U}],$$

where $\hat{U} = \sup\{U(c, d)$ under the resource constraint} is the maximum stationary utility level.[10] For a global analysis, we should use a general definition of the value function along the lines of Michel (1990a). For a marginal analysis of this problem, we can apply the same methods as below (substitution, Lagrangian, local dynamics), replacing γ by 1 and modifying the transversality condition.[11] In general, this solution is obtained as the limit when $\gamma \to 1$ of the optimal growth path with the discounted objective function. It will also be studied in the case $\hat{U} = 0$ (see section 2.5).

The choice of the planner's discount factor is an old debate. We shall see in the sequel (under some assumptions; see **A9** below) that the ex ante choice of a constant discount factor γ is equivalent to an ex post choice of the long-run stationary state. Michel (1990b) argues that, within a utilitarian setup, one should choose the discount rate which allows the economy to converge to the golden rule. This discount rate is equal to the growth rate of population, and the corresponding social objective function is the un-discounted sum of Ramsey.

2.3.2 Properties of the Value Function

The value function is the upper bound of the objective of the benevolent planner, taken on all possible allocations starting from $\bar{k}_0$:

$$\mathcal{V}(\bar{k}_0) = \sup\{\mathcal{W}; \text{ all feasible allocations starting from } \bar{k}_0\}.$$

To be allowed to define this function, two conditions should be met. The first condition is that the objective function of the planner should be defined for all feasible allocations, that is, the infinite sums should have a limit for all feasible allocations, finite or infinite. The second condition is that the upper bound of the infinite sums should be finite.

Assumption H4.
All the infinite sums $\mathcal{W}$ corresponding to all feasible allocations $(c_t, d_t, k_{t+1})_{t \geq 0}$ starting from k_0 converge in $\mathbb{R} \cup \{-\infty\}$ and admit a finite upper bound. This holds for all $k_0 > 0$.

---

[10] Ramsey assumes that this maximum utility is finite, as "economic causes alone could never give us more than a certain finite rate of enjoyment."

[11] If k_{GR} exists, the transversality condition becomes (see Michel (1990a)): the limit of the capital stock is the golden rule capital stock.

This assumption guarantees that the value function is defined. It is necessarily verified if the usual optimal solution exists for all k_0.[12] We shall study whether it is also sufficient.

We now introduce two sufficient assumptions bearing more directly on preferences and technology, and we show below that they imply **H4**.

Assumption A6.
For all $\bar{k}_0 > 0$, the sequence of highest feasible capital $(\bar{k}_t)_{t>0}$ defined by

$$\bar{k}_{t+1} = \frac{1}{1+n} f(\bar{k}_t),$$

is such that $\exists b_0 \in \mathbb{R}$ and $\exists \gamma_0 > \gamma$ such that $\forall t \geq 0$,

$$\gamma_0^t u(f(\bar{k}_t)) \leq b_0,$$
$$\gamma_0^t u((1+n)f(\bar{k}_t)) \leq b_0. \tag{2.9}$$

Note that the two conditions (2.9) are both useful, as $n \in]-1, +\infty[$. Depending on the case ($n \geq 0$ or $0 \geq n > -1$), (2.9) bears on $u((1+n)f(\bar{k}_t))$ or on $u(f(\bar{k}_t))$.

Assumption A7.
For all $\bar{k}_0 > 0$, there exists a feasible path $(c_t, d_t, k_{t+1})_{t\geq0}$ starting at $\bar{k}_0$ such that the sequence

$$\sum_{t=0}^{T} \gamma^t \left(u(c_t) + \frac{\beta}{\gamma} u(d_t) \right),$$

is bounded from below in $\mathbb{R}$ when $T \to +\infty$.

The assumption **A6** applies the assumption **B1** of appendix A.4.1 to the optimal growth problem. It holds if the sequence $(\bar{k}_t)$ is bounded and $\gamma < 1$. This is the case, for instance, when $f(k) = Ak^\alpha + (1-\mu)k$, with $0 < \alpha < 1$ and $1 - \mu < 1 + n$. Indeed, in this case, the sequence $\bar{k}_t$ converges to the steady state $\bar{k} = [A/(\mu+n)]^{\frac{1}{1-\alpha}}$, which implies that it is bounded. More generally, this assumption requires that the highest possible growth factor of the objective $u(c_t) + (\beta/\gamma)u(d_t)$ be lower than $1/\gamma$. Indeed, we have, for any feasible

---

[12] More general notions of optimality are considered in the literature, mainly those of Brock (1970) and Gale (1967). These definitions are respectively based on the lower and upper limits of the difference between feasible and optimal allocation. See Michel (1990a) for an in-depth study.

allocation (under assumption **A6**),

$$u(c_t) + \frac{\beta}{\gamma} u(d_t) \le u(f(\bar{k}_t)) + \frac{\beta}{\gamma} u((1+n)f(\bar{k}_t))$$

$$\le \frac{1}{\gamma_0^t} b_0 \left(1 + \frac{\beta}{\gamma}\right) < \frac{1}{\gamma^t} b_0 \left(1 + \frac{\beta}{\gamma}\right).$$

If **A6** does not hold, this means that the resources of the economy are so abundant that the planner has to distribute an "infinite amount of utility" between generations and a more general notion of optimality should be used.

The assumption **A7** applies the assumption **B2** of appendix A.4.1. It means that there exists at least one feasible trajectory such that the discounted sum of the utilities is different from $-\infty$. This is obviously verified if $u(0+)$ is non-negative. With $\gamma < 1$, it is sufficient that $u(0+)$ be bounded from below. An evident sufficient condition often found in the literature is $u(0) = 0$. When $u(0+) = -\infty$ (e.g. with a logarithmic utility function), it suffices to have $f(k) > (1+n)k$ for $k > 0$ small enough (this is a sort of weak Inada condition). It is then possible to follow, a.o., the feasible trajectory $c = d/(1+n) = [f(k) - (1+n)k]/2$ for which the objective is finite. If **A7** does not hold, this means that the production possibilities are so weak that the discounted sum of payoffs is inevitably $-\infty$.

Proposition 2.7 (Existence of the value function)
*Under **H1**, **H2**, **A6**, and **A7**, the assumption **H4** holds and the value function of the planner is defined for all $\bar{k}_0 > 0$.*

Proof: For the convergence of the infinite sum in $\mathbb{R} \cup \{-\infty\}$, we can apply proposition A.11 of appendix A.4.1. Indeed, the assumption **B0** holds under **H2**, and **B1** results from **A6**. For the objective function to have a finite upper bound, we use proposition A.12 of appendix A.4.1, which requires **A7** in addition. ∎

Proposition 2.8 (Properties of the value function)
*Under the assumptions **H1**, **H2**, and **H4**, the function $\mathcal{V}$ is continuous, concave, and non-decreasing on $\mathbb{R}_{++}$ and verifies, for all $k > 0$,*

$$\mathcal{V}(k) = \sup \left\{ u(c) + \frac{\beta}{\gamma} u(d) + \gamma \mathcal{V} \left(\frac{f(k) - c - d/(1+n)}{1+n} \right); \right.$$

$$\left. c > 0, d > 0, c + \frac{d}{1+n} < f(k) \right\}. \quad (2.10)$$

Equation (2.10) is the Bellman equation. The intuition behind it is the following: Starting from $k_0 > 0$ with $c_0 > 0$, $d_0 > 0$, and

$$k_1 = \frac{1}{1+n}\left(f(k_0) - c_0 - \frac{d_0}{1+n}\right) > 0,$$

the maximum of feasible inter-temporal utility starting from k_1 is, by definition, $V(k_1)$, and its discounted value at time 0 is $\gamma V(k_1)$. The corresponding value of the objective function starting at time 0 with the initial capital stock k_0 and the choice of consumptions levels is then

$$u(c_0) + \frac{\beta}{\gamma}u(d_0) + \gamma V(k_1). \tag{2.11}$$

As $V(k_1)$ is the maximum of the objective starting at time $t = 1$ with k_1, the maximum starting at time 0 with k_0 is simply obtained by maximizing equation (2.11) with respect to c_0, d_0, and k_1.

The proof of this proposition in a more general setup is given in appendix A.4.1.

2.3.3 Existence and Monotonicity of Optimal Paths

One important result is that, if the optimal path exists, it is unique. This results from the strict concavity of the utility function u and of the convexity of the set of feasible production $\{(k, y) \in \mathbb{R}_+ \times \mathbb{R}_+; y \leq f(k)\}$. This uniqueness can be shown directly. We shall obtain it through the uniqueness of the solution to the Bellman equation.

We show in appendix A.4.1 that, with the assumptions **A6** and **A7**, if the bound of the Bellman equation (2.10) is reached for all $k > 0$, then the optimal path exists and can be characterized by $c^*(k), d^*(k)$, i.e., the trajectory for which the bound is reached. $c^*(k)$ and $d^*(k)$ are called *policy functions*.

There is however a difficulty: we have to demonstrate that the maximum of the Bellman equation is reached (i.e., we can replace the sup in (2.10) by max). This should be proven in the case where the solution is interior, but also when there is a corner solution, i.e., the optimal investment is zero after some point in time. We first show that the maximum of the Bellman equation is interior if $f(0) = 0$.

Lemma 2.2
Assume that **H1, H2, H4,** *and* $f(0) = 0$ *hold. The maximum of the Bellman equation (2.10) with* $k_0 > 0$,

$$V(k_0) = \sup\left\{u(c_0) + \frac{\beta}{\gamma}u(d_0) + \gamma V(k_1)\right\},$$

subject to the constraints

$$c_0 > 0, \qquad d_0 > 0, \qquad k_1 = \frac{1}{1+n}\left(f(k_0) - c_0 - \frac{d_0}{1+n} \right) > 0,$$

is obtained with an interior solution: $c^\star(k_0) > 0, d^\star(k_0) > 0,$ *and* $k_1^\star = x^\star(k_0) > 0.$

Proof: Take any $k_0 > 0$. Applying the Bellman equation twice at k_0 and $k_1 > 0$, we get

$$V(k_0) = \sup \left\{ u(c_0) + \frac{\beta}{\gamma} u(d_0) + \gamma \left(u(c_1) + \frac{\beta}{\gamma} u(d_1) \right) + \gamma^2 V(k_2) \right\}. \quad (2.12)$$

The upper bound is taken on the set of positive quantities $c_0, d_0, c_1, d_1, k_1,$ and k_2, which satisfy

$$(1+n)k_1 = f(k_0) - c_0 - \frac{d_0}{1+n} \quad \text{and} \quad (1+n)k_2 = f(k_1) - c_1 - \frac{d_1}{1+n}.$$

Now consider k_2 such that

$$0 < k_2 < \frac{1}{1+n} f\left(\frac{f(k_0)}{1+n} \right).$$

When k_2 is fixed, the upper bound is reached with positive quantities for the other variables. For the consumptions, this results from **H1**: $u'(0) = +\infty$, and for k_1 it results from the assumption $f(0) = 0$, which implies that c_1 and d_1 are nil if $k_1 = 0$. Now take the upper bound of (2.12) also with respect to k_2. The property $k_1 > 0$ holds with the limit of k_2 even if the upper bound is obtained with $k_2 = 0$. Hence, the maximum with respect to $(c_0, d_0, c_1, d_1, k_1, k_2)$ is reached with positive values for the four consumptions, which implies $k_1 > 0$. This maximum thus satisfies

$$V(k_0) = u(c^\star(k_0)) + \frac{\beta}{\gamma} u(d^\star(k_0)) + \gamma V(x^\star(k_0)),$$

with

$$x^\star(k_0) = \frac{1}{1+n}\left(f(k_0) - c^\star(k_0) - \frac{d^\star(k_0)}{1+n} \right) > 0. \qquad \blacksquare$$

In the case $f(0) > 0$ (positive production with zero capital) it is possible that the maximum of the Bellman equation is reached with $k_1^\star = 0$. This extreme case will happen only if the marginal productivity $f'(0)$ is low. As we refrain from imposing conditions on the production function at 0 (in order to include the interesting CES case), we shall also study this case. However, in order to make this section more readable, that study is proposed as an extension in section 2.6.1. We use here the following assumption.

Assumption A8.
For all $k > 0$, the maximum of the Bellman equation is interior: $c^\star(k) > 0$, $d^\star(k) > 0$, and

$$x^\star(k) = \frac{1}{1+n}\left(f(k) - c^\star(k) - \frac{d^\star(k)}{1+n}\right) > 0.$$

Lemma 2.2 shows that if $f(0) = 0$, the assumption **A8** holds.

We now study the properties of the value function and the policy functions, solution to the Bellman equation. This analysis is done without having proven the existence of the optimal path, which requires the additional assumption **A6** and is shown in proposition 2.10.

Proposition 2.9 (Properties of the policy functions)
*Under the assumptions **H1**, **H2**, **H4**, and **A8**, the value function V is strictly increasing and differentiable in $\mathbb{R}_{++}$. The consumption and investment functions $c^\star(k)$, $d^\star(k)$ and $x^\star(k)$ solving the Bellman equation (2.10) are continuous and increasing, defined in $\mathbb{R}_{++}$ and have values in $\mathbb{R}_{++}$. These policy functions are characterized by, $\forall k > 0$,*

$$V(k) = u(c^\star(k)) + \frac{\beta}{\gamma}u(d^\star(k)) + \gamma V^\star(x^\star(k)),$$

$$(1+n)x^\star(k) = f(k) - c^\star(k) - \frac{d^\star(k)}{1+n}.$$

Proof: We consider $k_0 > 0$. The proof follows two steps.

1. We apply proposition A.16 of appendix A.4.1. The function $\tilde{C}$ considered in assumption **B3** can be $\tilde{c}(k) = f(k) - f(k_0) + c^\star(k_0)$ and $\tilde{d}(k) = d^\star(k_0)$. It satisfies $\tilde{c}(k_0) = c^\star(k_0)$, and leaves $\tilde{k}_1 = x^\star(k_0)$ unchanged:

$$V(k_0) = u(c^\star(k_0)) + \frac{\beta}{\gamma}u(d^\star(k_0)) + \gamma V^\star(x^\star(k_0)),$$

$$V(k) \geq u(\tilde{c}(k)) + \frac{\beta}{\gamma}u(\tilde{d}(k)) + \gamma V^\star(x^\star(k_0)),$$

$$V(k) - V(k_0) \geq u(\tilde{c}(k)) - u(\tilde{c}(k_0)).$$

This implies that the function V is differentiable[13] at $k_0 > 0$ and its derivative is

$$V'(k_0) = u'(c^\star(k_0))f'(k_0).$$

We deduce that $V'(k_0) > 0$, and the function V is strictly increasing.

---

[13] Since the function V is concave and is bounded below by the differentiable function $u(\cdot)$; see proposition A.16 in appendix A.4.1.

2. We now show that the policy functions are increasing. The function

$$(c, d) \rightarrow u(c) + \frac{\beta}{\gamma} u(d) + \gamma V \left(\frac{1}{1+n} \left(f(k) - c - \frac{d}{1+n} \right) \right) \quad (2.13)$$

is strictly concave, because u is strictly concave (assumption **H1**). Its maximum $V(k)$ is thus obtained at a single point $(c^*(k), d^*(k))$, which depends continuously on k. The first-order conditions

$$u'(c^*(k)) = \frac{\gamma}{1+n} V'(x^*(k)),$$

$$\frac{\beta}{\gamma} u'(d^*(k)) = \frac{\gamma}{(1+n)^2} V'(x^*(k))$$

imply that the three functions $c^*(\cdot)$, $d^*(\cdot)$, and $x^*(\cdot)$ vary in the same direction when k increases (V' is decreasing, as V is concave). Moreover, their sum,

$$c^*(k) + \frac{d^*(k)}{1+n} + (1+n)x^*(k) = f(k),$$

is an increasing function of k. Hence, the three functions $c^*(\cdot)$, $d^*(\cdot)$, and $x^*(\cdot)$ are increasing. ∎

The policy functions are useful to define the following monotonic dynamics. Starting from k_0, we can define by induction $k_0^* = k_0$ and

$$c_t^* = c^*(k_t^*), \qquad d_t^* = d^*(k_t^*), \quad \text{and} \quad k_{t+1}^* = x^*(k_t^*).$$

This path is feasible and satisfies, $\forall t$,

$$V(k_t^*) = u(c_t^*) + \frac{\beta}{\gamma} u(d_t^*) + \gamma V(k_{t+1}^*).$$

These monotonic dynamics obtained from the Bellman equation are those of the optimal path when an optimal path exists. More precisely, the existence is guaranteed under the assumption **A6**, as is shown in the next proposition.

Proposition 2.10 (Existence of the optimal path)
*Under the assumptions **H1**, **H2**, **A6**, **A7**, and **A8**, there exists an optimal solution to the planning problem for all $k_0 > 0$. This optimal path is unique and monotonic and is defined by the policy functions*

$$c_t^* = c^*(k_t^*), \qquad d_t^* = d^*(k_t^*), \qquad k_{t+1}^* = x^*(k_t^*), \qquad k_0^* = k_0.$$

Proof: From **A8** we may define by induction the paths $c_t^\star = c^\star(k_t^\star)$, $d_t^\star = d^\star(k_t^\star)$, and $k_{t+1}^\star = x^\star(k_t^\star)$ which are the solution to the Bellman equation. Following proposition A.13 of appendix A.4.1, under **A6** and **A7**, this path is optimal. ∎

2.3.4 Limit of the Optimal Path and Optimal Steady State

We have seen that, under the assumptions **H1, H2, A6, A7**, and **A8**, the optimal trajectory $(c_t^\star, d_t^\star, k_{t+1}^\star)_{t \geq 0}$ exists, is unique, and is monotonic. There are thus three possibilities:

1. convergence of $k_t^\star$ towards a steady state $\bar{k} > 0$ such that $x^\star(\bar{k}) = \bar{k}$;
2. convergence towards 0;
3. convergence toward $+\infty$.

The following proposition gives the conditions under which each case arises.

Proposition 2.11 (Limit of the optimal trajectory)
Assume that the assumptions **H1, H2, A6, A7,** *and* **A8** *hold. Then the optimal trajectory starting from* $\bar{k}_0 > 0$ *satisfies:*

- *if* $f'(0) \leq \frac{1+n}{\gamma}$, $\lim k_t^\star = 0$;
- *if* $f'(+\infty) \geq \frac{1+n}{\gamma}$, $\lim k_t^\star = +\infty$;
- *if* $f'(0+) > \frac{1+n}{\gamma} > f'(+\infty)$, $\lim k_t^\star = f'^{-1}\left(\frac{1+n}{\gamma}\right) \equiv k_\gamma$.

Proof: Following proposition 2.9, the value function is differentiable and we have

$$V'(k) = u'(c^\star(k)) f'(k).$$

We also have, with the first-order conditions (see the proof of proposition 2.9),

$$u'(c^\star(k)) = \frac{\gamma}{1+n} V'(x^\star(k)).$$

We deduce that, along the optimal path, we have

$$\frac{\gamma}{1+n} V'(k_{t+1}^\star) = u'(c^\star(k_t^\star)),$$

$$V'(k_{t+1}^\star) = u'(c^\star(k_{t+1}^\star)) f'(k_{t+1}^\star),$$

and therefore

$$\frac{u'(c^\star(k_t^\star))}{u'(c^\star(k_{t+1}^\star))} = \frac{\gamma f'(k_{t+1}^\star)}{1+n}. \tag{2.14}$$

- In the case $f'(0+) \leq \frac{1+n}{\gamma}$, the ratio (2.14) is smaller than 1 for all t which implies $k_t^* > k_{t+1}^*$ as the function $k \to u'(c^*(k))$ is decreasing (c^* is increasing and u' decreasing). Then the sequence (k_t^*) is decreasing. We show by a reductio ad absurdum that its only possible limit is 0. Assume it admits a limit $\bar{k} > 0$. Then $\bar{k}$ is a stationary optimum, and $\gamma f'(\bar{k}) = 1 + n$ holds. This is excluded because $f'(0) \leq (1+n)/\gamma$ and $f'(\cdot)$ is a decreasing function. Hence $\lim k_t^* = 0$.
- In a similar fashion, in the case $f'(+\infty) \geq \frac{1+n}{\gamma}$, the ratio (2.14) is larger than 1 and the sequence (k_t^*) is increasing. As it cannot have a finite limit, $\lim k_t^* = +\infty$.
- Finally, in the case $f'(0+) > \frac{1+n}{\gamma} > f'(+\infty)$, let $k_\gamma = f'^{-1}\left(\frac{1+n}{\gamma}\right)$. There are three possibilities:
  - if $k_{t+1}^* < k_\gamma$, the ratio (2.14) is larger than 1, and we have $k_t^* < k_{t+1}^* < k_\gamma$.
  - if $k_{t+1}^* = k_\gamma$, the ratio (2.14) is equal to 1, and we have $k_t^* = k_{t+1}^* = k_\gamma$.
  - if $k_{t+1}^* > k_\gamma$, the ratio (2.14) is smaller than 1, and we have $k_\gamma < k_{t+1}^* < k_t^*$.

This implies that the optimal path k_t^* converges to k_γ. ∎

We have seen that k_γ is the limit of the optimal path if and only if the following assumption holds:

Assumption A9.

$$f'(0+) > \frac{1+n}{\gamma} > f'(+\infty).$$

We also conclude that, starting with $k_0 = k_\gamma$, the optimal path is $k_t = k_\gamma$ for all t. Indeed, it is the only monotonic path starting from k_γ and ending at k_γ. k_γ is thus an optimal steady state of the planner's problem, which is called the *modified golden rule*.

Definition 2.8 (Modified golden rule)
Under the assumption **A9** *there exists a unique positive capital stock* k_γ *such that*

$$f'(k_\gamma) = \frac{1+n}{\gamma},$$

which is the modified golden rule capital stock.

Let us now comment on some of the assumptions used so far.

First, note that we have not explicitly assumed that the social discount factor γ is smaller than one. However, $\gamma < 1$ results from **H4** when **A9** holds. Indeed, with **A9**, there exists a constant optimal path starting at $k_0 = k_\gamma$; together with **H4**, it implies that the sum $\mathcal{W}$ with constant utilities converges, which in turn implies $\gamma < 1$.

When the golden rule exists, the assumption **A5** is satisfied, and by continuity **A9** is also satisfied for γ sufficiently close to 1. In that case, **A9** can be thought as an assumption on the parameter γ.

With $\gamma < 1$, when k_{GR} exists (assumption **A5**) and k_γ exists (assumption **A9**), the modified golden rule k_γ verifies

$$0 < k_\gamma < k_{\mathrm{GR}},$$

as we have $f'(k_\gamma) = f'(k_{\mathrm{GR}})/\gamma > f'(k_{\mathrm{GR}})$. The unique steady state capital stock of the planning problem is thus between 0 and the golden rule level, and there is under-accumulation at k_γ. Notice also that $\lim_{\gamma \to 1} k_\gamma = k_{\mathrm{GR}}$ and that k_γ is increasing in γ: the more the planner cares about future generations, the higher the steady state capital stock should be.

Example: With the CES production function, we should distinguish the different cases depending on ρ:

- Only in the Cobb–Douglas case ($\rho = 0$) does the assumption **A9** fail to impose any condition, as $f'(0) = +\infty$ and $f'(+\infty) = 0$.
- When factors of production are weak substitutes ($\rho > 0$), we have $f'(0) = A\alpha^{-1/\rho}$ and $f'(+\infty) = 0$. The assumption **A9** imposes a lower bound on the planner's discount factor. **A9** is indeed equivalent to $\gamma > (1 + n)\alpha^{1/\rho}/A$.
- When factors of production are highly substitutable, ($\rho < 0$), we have $f'(0) = +\infty$ and $f'(+\infty) = A\alpha^{-1/\rho}$. The assumption **A9** imposes $\gamma < (1 + n)/A\alpha^{1/\rho}$.

When **A8** does not hold, the maximum of the Bellman equation (2.10) is obtained with $k_1 = x^\star(k_0) = 0$, $c_0 = c^\star(k_0) > 0$, and $d_0 = d^\star(k_0) > 0$ for some $k_0 > 0$. This case can only occur when production is possible without capital ($f(0) > 0$), and it is optimal not to invest for some $k_0 > 0$. The case $f(0) > 0$ is studied in section 2.6.1. We show that all preceding results hold without the assumption **A8**, except that the policy function $x^\star$ is non-decreasing (instead of increasing), as we may have $x^\star(k) = 0$ on some interval $[0, \underline{k}]$.

In the very particular case when **A8** does not hold, 0 is an optimum steady state. This last situation can arise when the production function displays high substitutability for low levels of capital. An example with such a production function is provided in section 2.6.4.

2.4 MARGINAL ANALYSIS OF OPTIMAL SOLUTIONS

In this section, we characterize the optimal solutions further, using the standard marginal analysis (Euler equations), and propose a local analysis around the steady state. This local analysis requires a different set of assumptions from the global approach of the preceding section. In particular, three assumptions play a central role. First, **A9** has to hold for the existence of the modified golden rule. Second, we assume $\gamma < 1$, which guarantees the convergence of the infinite sum with constant utilities. Third, we only need **H4** for one value of the initial capital stock instead of for the whole range of possible values. We make these three assumptions in this section.

2.4.1 The Optimality Conditions

The planner thus maximizes $\mathcal{W}$ given an initial capital stock k_0 and given the resource constraint. One simple method for obtaining the first-order optimality conditions is to make the substitution of the resource constraint in the objective function; substituting d_t, the planner's problem can then be rewritten

$$\max \sum_{t=0}^{\infty} \gamma^t \left(u(c_t) + \frac{\beta}{\gamma} u\left((1+n)[f(k_t) - (1+n)k_{t+1} - c_t] \right) \right).$$

For an interior optimal solution the first-order necessary conditions are obtained by differentiating with respect to c_t and k_{t+1}:

$$u'(c_t) = \frac{(1+n)\beta}{\gamma} u'(d_t), \tag{2.15}$$

$$u'(d_t) = \frac{f'(k_{t+1})\gamma}{1+n} u'(d_{t+1}). \tag{2.16}$$

Equation (2.15) describes the optimal allocation between old and young who are alive at the same time. Equation (2.16) describes the optimal inter-temporal allocation. Combining the two conditions leads to

$$u'(c_t) = \beta f'(k_{t+1}) u'(d_{t+1}),$$

which is the same as equation (1.7) of the previous chapter, showing that, within an individual lifetime, the planner allocates resources in the same way as the individual would allocate them when the expected gross return on savings is equal to $f'(k_{t+1})$.

Another interesting (and equivalent) method consists in using the shadow price q_t of the capital stock. McKenzie (1986) uses the Lagrangian $\mathcal{L}_t$ of period t in his study of optimal growth in discrete time. The Lagrangian $\mathcal{L}_t$ of period t (times γ^t) is composed of the terms of the infinite Lagrangian

$$\sum_{t=0}^{\infty} \gamma^t \left\{ u(c_t) + \beta u(d_{t+1}) + \gamma q_{t+1} \left[\frac{1}{1+n} \left(f(k_t) - c_t - \frac{d_t}{1+n} \right) - k_{t+1} \right] \right\},$$

which depend on c_t, d_t, and k_t. Thus $\mathcal{L}_t$ is equal to the sum of the current utilities and the increase in the shadow value of the capital stock: $\gamma q_{t+1} k_{t+1} - q_t k_t$,[14]

---

[14] The current shadow price q_{t+1} of the capital stock k_{t+1} in period $t+1$ is discounted by the factor γ in order to define the increase of shadow value in t.

i.e.,

$$\mathcal{L}_t = u(c_t) + \frac{\beta}{\gamma}u(d_t) + \frac{\gamma q_{t+1}}{1+n}\left(f(k_t) - c_t - \frac{d_t}{1+n}\right) - q_t k_t.$$

The use of the Lagrangian of period t does not need any condition on differentiability of the infinite sum.

Optimality leads to the maximum of $\mathcal{L}_t$ with respect to c_t, d_t, and k_t (see appendix A.4.2). For an interior optimal solution, the derivatives of $\mathcal{L}_t$ with respect to c_t, d_t, and k_t are zero:

$$u'(c_t) = \frac{\gamma q_{t+1}}{1+n}, \tag{2.17}$$

$$u'(d_t) = \frac{\gamma^2 q_{t+1}}{\beta(1+n)^2}, \tag{2.18}$$

$$\frac{\gamma q_{t+1}}{1+n} = \frac{q_t}{f'(k_t)}. \tag{2.19}$$

Defining $q_t = u'(c_t)f'(k_t)$, these conditions are equivalent to (2.15) and (2.16) and the interpretation is straightforward: q_t is the marginal value of an additional unit of capital k_t in period t for the social welfare from t onward; with the assumptions **A6** and **A7** it is equal to $\mathcal{V}'(k_t)$.

From appendix A.4.2, a sufficient condition for optimality of a feasible path $(c_t, d_t, k_{t+1})_{t\geq 0}$ with positive quantities and starting at $\bar{k}_0$ is the following: there exists a sequence $(q_t)_{t\geq 0}$ verifying (2.17), (2.18), (2.19), and the following limit condition:

$$\lim_{t\to+\infty} \gamma^t q_t k_t = 0. \tag{2.20}$$

The transversality condition states that the limit of the actual shadow value of the capital stock is equal to zero, i.e., the actual value of the capital in terms of welfare is exhausted.[15] This sufficient condition is also necessary when for all feasible paths the objective of the planner is finite. If not, more sophisticated transversality conditions should be used (appendix A.4.2, proposition A.17).

Proposition 2.12 (Necessary condition for the planner's optimum)
Given an initial capital stock $k_0 > 0$, an interior planner's optimum, if it exists, is a sequence of strictly positive quantities $(c_t, d_t, q_t, k_{t+1})_{t\geq 0}$, which verifies the

---

[15] The transversality condition could also be rewritten as

$$\lim_{t\to\infty} \gamma^t u'(c_{t-1})k_t = 0.$$

It imposes that the limit of the marginal utility of capital in terms of consumption be nil.

two dynamic equations

$$k_{t+1} = \frac{1}{1+n}\left[f(k_t) - C\left(\frac{q_t}{f'(k_t)}\right)\right] \equiv \Phi(k_t, q_t), \tag{2.21}$$

$$q_{t+1} = \frac{(1+n)q_t}{\gamma f'(k_t)} \equiv \Psi(k_t, q_t), \tag{2.22}$$

where

$$C\left(\frac{q_t}{f'(k_t)}\right) = u'^{-1}\left(\frac{q_t}{f'(k_t)}\right) + \frac{1}{1+n}u'^{-1}\left(\frac{\gamma q_t}{\beta(1+n)f'(k_t)}\right),$$

The consumptions are then given by (2.17) and (2.18).

Proof: Together with the dynamics (2.22), the conditions (2.17)–(2.18) are equivalent to

$$c_t = u'^{-1}\left(\frac{q_t}{f'(k_t)}\right) \quad \text{and} \quad d_t = u'^{-1}\left(\frac{\gamma q_t}{\beta(1+n)f'(k_t)}\right). \tag{2.23}$$

These conditions imply $c_t + d_t/(1+n) = C(q_t/f'(k_t))$, and (2.21) is the resource constraint. ∎

Notice that the function $C(\cdot)$ is the total consumption per young person. It is decreasing in its arguments and when $u'(+\infty) = 0$, it is a bijection from $\mathbb{R}_{++}$ to $\mathbb{R}_{++}$.[16] This property will be used in the graphical exposition.

Proposition 2.13 (Sufficient condition for the planner's optimum)
A positive sequence $(c_t, d_t, q_t, k_{t+1})_{t\geq 0}$ satisfying (2.22), (2.21), (2.23), and the transversality condition (2.20) is an optimal solution to the planner's problem.

Proof: This is a standard result. See section A.4.2. ∎

The dynamic system (2.21)–(2.22) cannot in general be solved explicitly, as the planner's chosen allocation is described by a set of non-linear difference equations. An exception is when the production function is Cobb–Douglas, the utility function is logarithmic and the depreciation of capital is total[17] (see McCallum (1989)). This case is developed in the example below. In the general case, further insights into the properties of the solutions can be drawn

---

[16] u' is a decreasing function from $\mathbb{R}_{++}$ to $(u'(+\infty), +\infty)$. As a consequence, $C(\cdot)$ is decreasing from $(\underline{x}, +\infty)$ to $\mathbb{R}_{++}$, where $\underline{x} = \max\{1, \gamma/\beta(1+n)\}u'(+\infty)$.

[17] Instead of assuming a total depreciation, it is possible to use an accumulation rule for capital of the form $K_{t+1} = K_t^{1-\delta}I_t^{\delta}$ and find an explicit solution; see, e.g., Hercowitz and Sampson (1991) in a setup with infinite-lived agents.

by first considering the steady state and then the local dynamics. This analysis is done in the next two subsections. To draw quantitative implications we have to rely on numerical methods. One of the best methods is the one proposed by Laffargue (1990) and Boucekkine (1995), which is suited to simulate deterministic non-linear forward-looking models. The method is described in appendix A.5.4.

Example: With a Cobb–Douglas production function, total depreciation of capital, and a logarithmic utility function, an explicit analytical solution to the planning problem can be found. In this case, $u'(c) = 1/c$, $f(k) = Ak^\alpha$, $u'^{-1}(x) = 1/x$, and

$$c\left(\frac{q_t}{f'(k_t)}\right) = \left(1 + \frac{\beta}{\gamma}\right)\frac{f'(k_t)}{q_t}.$$

By multiplying the two equations (2.22) and (2.21) term by term, we obtain

$$q_{t+1}k_{t+1} = q_t\frac{f(k_t)}{\gamma f'(k_t)} - \frac{q_t}{\gamma f'(k_t)}c\left(\frac{q_t}{f'(k_t)}\right) = \frac{q_t k_t}{\alpha\gamma} - \frac{1}{\gamma}\left(1 + \frac{\beta}{\gamma}\right),$$

since $f'(k_t) = \alpha f(k_t)/k_t$. Thus, $q_t k_t$ is solution to a linear dynamic equation, and the general solution of this equation is

$$q_t k_t = \frac{\alpha(1 + \beta/\gamma)}{1 - \alpha\gamma} + \varrho\left(\frac{1}{\alpha\gamma}\right)^t,$$

with ϱ a real constant. There is a unique solution that verifies the transversality condition (2.20): the constant solution

$$q_t k_t = \frac{\alpha(1 + \beta/\gamma)}{1 - \alpha\gamma},$$

with $\varrho = 0$ (if $\varrho \neq 0$, $q_t k_t$ would grow faster than γ). By substitution we obtain

$$c_t = \frac{f'(k_t)}{q_t} = \frac{k_t f'(k_t)}{k_t q_t} = \frac{1 - \alpha\gamma}{1 + \beta/\gamma}Ak_t^\alpha,$$

$$d_t = \frac{\beta(1 + n)k_t f'(k_t)}{\gamma q_t k_t} = \frac{\beta(1 + n)}{\gamma}\frac{1 - \alpha\gamma}{1 + \beta/\gamma}Ak_t^\alpha,$$

$$k_{t+1} = \frac{\alpha\gamma}{1 + n}Ak_t^\alpha.$$

The dynamics of the optimal capital stock converge to

$$\left(\frac{\alpha\gamma}{1 + n}A\right)^{\frac{1}{1-\alpha}}.$$

2.4.2 The Planner's Stationary Solution

Looking for a stationary path $(c_t, d_t, q_t, k_{t+1}) = (c, d, q, k)$ with positive quantities that verifies the optimality conditions, we obtain

$$\gamma f'(k) = 1 + n,$$

$$c\left(\frac{\gamma q}{1+n}\right) = f(k) - (1+n)k,$$

$$c = u'^{-1}\left(\frac{\gamma q}{1+n}\right),$$

$$d = u'^{-1}\left(\frac{\gamma^2 q}{\beta(1+n)^2}\right).$$

These conditions are necessary and sufficient for optimality of the constant path starting at k, as this path satisfies the transversality condition. This condition is indeed verified with constant quantities, since we have assumed $\gamma < 1$.

The stationary level of k given by $f'^{-1}((1+n)/\gamma)$ is the modified golden rule k_γ defined previously. The pair (k_γ, q_γ) with

$$q_\gamma = \frac{1+n}{\gamma} c^{-1}\left(f(k_\gamma) - (1+n)k_\gamma\right)$$

is a steady state of the dynamics (2.21)–(2.22) characterizing the optimal solution.

The optimal allocation of consumption between young and old satisfies

$$u'(c) = \frac{(1+n)\beta}{\gamma} u'(d).$$

At the planner's stationary solution, the inter-temporal rate of substitution $\beta u'(d)/u'(c)$ should be equal to the planner's discount factor divided by the factor of population growth. It coincides with the optimal arbitrage of a consumer when the rate of return is equal to $(1+n)/\gamma$, i.e., when the capital stock is at the modified golden rule level.

2.4.3 Local Dynamics

It is important to notice that the two endogenous variables of the system (2.22)–(2.21) are not of the same nature. The variable k_t is predetermined at time t (it has been chosen at time $t - 1$) and there is an initial condition for capital, k_0. The variable q_t is a non-predetermined variable (forward-looking variable). There is no initial condition q_0: the planner chooses the entire optimal trajectory $(q_t)_{t \geq 0}$. The proper choice of q_0 will determine this path.

To study the characteristics of the dynamics, we take a first-order Taylor expansion of the system around its unique steady state (k_γ, q_γ) to study the local dynamics. This leads to the linear dynamics:

$$\begin{bmatrix} k_{t+1} - k_\gamma \\ q_{t+1} - q_\gamma \end{bmatrix} = \begin{bmatrix} a_1 & a_2 \\ b_1 & b_2 \end{bmatrix} \begin{bmatrix} k_t - k_\gamma \\ q_t - q_\gamma \end{bmatrix}, \tag{2.24}$$

with the partial derivatives taken at the steady state (k_γ, q_γ):

$$a_1 = \frac{\partial \Phi}{\partial k_t} = \frac{f'(k_\gamma)}{1+n} + \frac{q_\gamma f''(k_\gamma)}{(1+n) f'(k_\gamma)^2} C' \left(\frac{q_\gamma}{f'(k_\gamma)} \right)$$

$$= \frac{1}{\gamma} + \frac{q_\gamma f''(k_\gamma)}{(1+n) f'(k_\gamma)^2} C' \left(\frac{q_\gamma}{f'(k_\gamma)} \right),$$

$$a_2 = \frac{\partial \Phi}{\partial q_t} = -\frac{1}{(1+n) f'(k_\gamma)} C' \left(\frac{q_\gamma}{f'(k_\gamma)} \right),$$

$$b_1 = \frac{\partial \Psi}{\partial k_t} = -\frac{(1+n) q_\gamma f''(k_\gamma)}{\gamma f'(k_\gamma)^2}$$

$$= -\frac{q_\gamma f''(k_\gamma)}{f'(k_\gamma)},$$

$$b_2 = \frac{\partial \Psi}{\partial q_t} = \frac{1+n}{\gamma f'(k_\gamma)}$$

$$= 1.$$

Proposition 2.14 (Saddle-point property of the optimal path)
The characteristic polynomial of the linear approximation (2.24) admits two positive roots of which only one is stable. Given $\bar{k}_0$, there exists a unique solution to (2.24) that converges to (k_γ, q_γ), and the convergence is monotonic. The steady state (k_γ, q_γ) is thus a saddle point.

Proof: The characteristic polynomial (see appendix A.3.4) of the matrix defining the linear dynamics (2.24) is

$$P(\lambda) = \begin{vmatrix} a_1 - \lambda & a_2 \\ b_1 & b_2 - \lambda \end{vmatrix}$$

$$= \lambda^2 - (a_1 + b_2)\lambda + a_1 b_2 - a_2 b_1$$

$$= \lambda^2 - (a_1 + 1)\lambda + \frac{1}{\gamma},$$

and we have $a_1 > 1/\gamma$ as $f''C' > 0$. The properties of $P(\lambda)$ are illustrated in figure 2.3: $P(0) = 1/\gamma > 0$ and $P(1) = 1/\gamma - a_1 < 0$. This implies that there exists only one root λ_1 such that $0 < \lambda_1 < 1$. Moreover, the product of the two real roots is equal to $1/\gamma$ (the determinant of the matrix); thus the second root verifies $\lambda_2 = 1/(\gamma \lambda_1) > 1/\gamma$. Given $\bar{k}_0$, there exists a unique solution of the linear dynamics (2.24) for k_t which converges to k_γ:

$$k_t - k_\gamma = \lambda_1^t (\bar{k}_0 - k_\gamma),$$

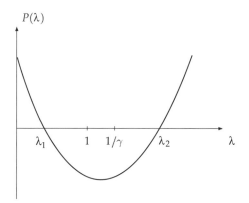

Figure 2.3. The characteristic polynomial. The characteristic polynomial of the linear approximation (2.24) admits two positive roots, of which only one is stable.

and there is a unique corresponding solution for q_t, which is obtained with the dynamics of k_t. Using

$$k_{t+1} - k_\gamma = a_1(k_t - k_\gamma) + a_2(q_t - q_\gamma),$$

one obtains

$$q_t - q_\gamma = \frac{1}{a_2}(\lambda_1 - a_1)\lambda_1^t(\bar{k}_0 - k_\gamma). \qquad \blacksquare$$

As the steady state is a saddle point, for a given $\bar{k}_0$ there is only one value of q_0 such that the trajectory converges to the steady state:

$$q_0 = q_\gamma + \frac{1}{a_2}(\lambda_1 - a_1)(\bar{k}_0 - k_\gamma).$$

Any other value of q_0 would lead the trajectory of the linear system to explode.

Note that the diverging trajectories with a non-zero coefficient of λ_2^t do not verify the transversality condition, as $\lambda_2 > 1/\gamma$.

These properties apply locally to the non-linear dynamics near the steady state: given $\bar{k}_0$, there exists a unique solution for these dynamics which converges to the steady state, and this solution is the optimal path. We have established this result globally in the study of the value function.

2.4.4 A Graphical Exposition

To describe the dynamics of a system of order two, it is convenient to use a phase diagram. We should keep in mind, however, that in discrete time the phase diagram is not sufficient to characterize the dynamics. Indeed, the trajectories are collections of points rather than continuous lines, and the variables can therefore jump during the adjustment process.

To build this diagram we use the two equations of the dynamical system (2.21)–(2.22):

$$k_{t+1} = \Phi(k_t, q_t),$$

$$q_{t+1} = \Psi(k_t, q_t),$$

so that we can describe the direction of motion of the variables as a function of their current values. For the graphical exposition we assume $u'(+\infty) = 0$, which implies that $\mathcal{C}$ is decreasing from $\mathbb{R}_{++}$ with values in $\mathbb{R}_{++}$ (like u'^{-1}).

We should first characterize the set of points (k_t, q_t) for which there is no change in k_t, i.e., for which $\Phi(k_t, q_t) = k_t$. Solving $\Phi(k_t, q_t) = k_t$ for q_t, we obtain

$$q_t = f'(k_t)\mathcal{C}^{-1}(f(k_t) - (1+n)k_t).$$

This function $q_t = q_\Phi(k_t)$ is defined on the set of feasible capital stocks $(0, \tilde{k})$.[18] Differentiating $q_\Phi(k_t)$ leads to

$$q'_\Phi(k_t) = f''(k_t)\mathcal{C}^{-1}(\cdot) + f'(k_t)(\mathcal{C}^{-1})'(\cdot)[f'(k_t) - (1+n)].$$

Hence, the function $q_t = q_\Phi(k_t)$ is decreasing when $f'(k_t) > 1 + n$, i.e., when $k_t < k_{\mathrm{GR}}$. As $\mathcal{C}'(\cdot) < 0$, the function can attain a minimum only for capital above the golden rule level. An example of this function is plotted in the left panel of figure 2.4. To describe the direction of change in k_t, we remark that $\Phi(k_t, q_t)$ increases unambiguously with q_t as $\mathcal{C}' < 0$. Hence, $k_{t+1} > k_t$ above the curve and $k_{t+1} < k_t$ below. The corresponding direction of motion are also plotted in the figure.

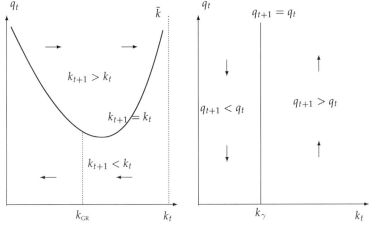

Figure 2.4. The two phase lines. The function $k_{t+1} = \Phi(k_t, q_t) = k_t$ plotted in the left panel is negatively sloped at the left of the golden rule level. The function $q_{t+1} = \Psi(k_t, q_t) = q_t$ plotted in the right panel is a vertical line crossing the horizontal axis at the modified golden rule level. The arrows indicates the direction of motion.

[18] Remember that the concave function $\phi(k) = f(k) - (1+n)k$ becomes negative when $k > \tilde{k}$; see section 2.1.1.

The set of points (k_t, q_t) for which there is no change in q_t, i.e., for which $\Psi(k_t, q_t) = q_t$, is easy to characterize. Indeed,

$$\Psi(k_t, q_t) = q_t \iff \frac{1+n}{f'(k_t)\gamma} = 1 \iff k_t = k_\gamma.$$

Hence, the phase line $\Psi(k_t, q_t) = 0$ is a vertical line in the space (q_t, k_t) that crosses the horizontal axis at $k_t = k_\gamma$. The function is plotted in the right panel of figure 2.4. To describe the direction of change in q_t, we remark that $\Psi(k_t, q_t)$ increases strictly with k_t. Hence, $q_{t+1} < q_t$ on the left of the line and $q_{t+1} > q_t$ on the right of the line. The corresponding direction of motion are also plotted in the figure.

We now gather the information on a single diagram, tracing various possible time paths for the dynamics (2.21)–(2.22). The intersection of the two phase lines represents the steady state. Notice that the two phase lines intersect at the modified golden rule level, which lies to the left of the golden rule level. Figure 2.5 illustrates that there is only one trajectory converging to (k_γ, q_γ), which is the optimal solution. All other trajectories lead to a zero level

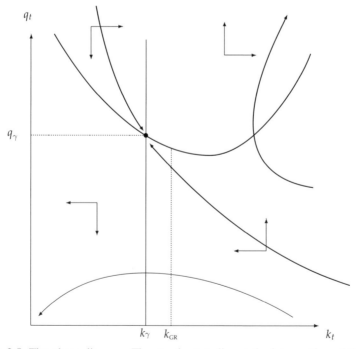

Figure 2.5. The phase diagram. The steady state lies at the intersection of the two phase lines. There is only one trajectory that converges to the steady state, which is the optimal one. All other trajectories lead to a zero level of capital or an infinite level of its shadow price.

of consumption or of capital. It also shows that for a given initial condition k_0 there is only one value for q_0 on the saddle path converging to the steady state. The use of the phase diagram is illustrated in an application in section 2.6.3.

Let us finally show what the phase diagram looks like in discrete time and consider an economy with a CES production function with $\rho = 1$, $\alpha = 1/2$, and a logarithmic utility. Let us take the numerical values presented in section A.5.2: $A = 20$, $\beta = 0.3$, $n = 1.025^{30} - 1$. Assuming further that $\gamma = 0.99$, the dynamical system is (2.21)–(2.22):

$$k_{t+1} = \frac{-24.8 + 19.1(1 + k_t)k_t q_t}{(1 + k_t)^2 q_t},$$

$$q_{t+1} = 0.053(1 + k_t)^2 q_t.$$

The steady state is at $q = 0.116$, $k = 3.345$. The phase diagram is represented in figure 2.6 in the space $(k_t, \ln q_t)$. The phase lines are represented by bold lines. A series of diverging trajectories have been computed by fixing different initial conditions q_0, k_0. The optimal trajectories (squares + dashed lines) have been computed by finding the appropriate level of $(q_t)_{t \geq 0}$ using the method presented in appendix A.5.4.

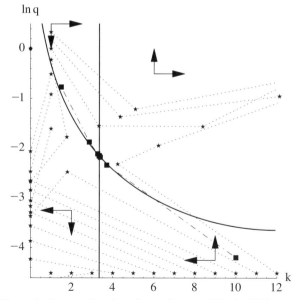

Figure 2.6. Numerical example of a phase diagram. The bold lines represent the phase lines. The dotted lines represent the exploding trajectories. The dashed lines represent the converging trajectories (saddle path).

2.5 UNBOUNDED OPTIMAL GROWTH

Assuming **A9**, we have proposed in the previous section a local stability analysis of stationary optimal allocations. In the case where **A9** is not verified, there exists no interior optimal steady state. In this case, as shown in section 2.3.3, under the assumptions **A6** and **A7**, the optimal solution exists and the capital stock dynamics are monotonic and converge to a limit which is either 0 or $+\infty$. We study in this section particular cases in which the assumption **A9** is violated and capital grows unboundedly. We still use **A6** and **A7** as sufficient conditions for the existence of the optimal path. More precisely, we shall use **A6** and **A7** to derive conditions on the parameters under which there is an optimal solution displaying unbounded growth.

We shall show that unbounded growth is possible if and only if $A_\infty = f'(+\infty) \geq 1 + n$. To this end, we study the sequence of the maximum feasible capital $\bar{k}_t$.

As shown in appendix A.1.2, the marginal productivity of capital and the average productivity $f(k)/k$ are decreasing functions which have the same limit when k tends to $+\infty$:

$$A_\infty = f'(+\infty) = \lim_{k \to +\infty} \frac{f(k)}{k}.$$

The highest possible growth of the maximum feasible capital is obtained with no consumption and satisfies, given $\bar{k}_0$:

$$\bar{k}_{t+1} = \frac{1}{1+n} f(\bar{k}_t),$$

$$\frac{\bar{k}_{t+1}}{\bar{k}_t} = \frac{1}{1+n} \frac{f(\bar{k}_t)}{\bar{k}_t} > \frac{A_\infty}{1+n}.$$

Then, when $A_\infty \geq 1 + n$, $\bar{k}_t$ is increasing and tends to $+\infty$. When the maximum feasible capital grows without limit, optimal unbounded growth is made possible. Conversely, when $A_\infty < 1 + n$, then for $\bar{k}_t$ large enough, we have $f(\bar{k}_t)/\bar{k}_t < 1 + n$ and $\bar{k}_{t+1} < \bar{k}_t$.

Assuming that unbounded growth is possible, i.e., $A_\infty \geq 1 + n$, we look for the conditions under which **A6** and **A7** hold, guaranteeing the existence of an optimal planner's solution. We assume a CIES utility function:

$$u(c) = \frac{c^{1-\frac{1}{\sigma}}}{1 - \frac{1}{\sigma}}, \qquad \sigma > 0,$$

and for $\sigma = 1, u(c) = \ln c$.

2.5.1 Existence of Optimal Paths When $\sigma > 1$

When the inter-temporal elasticity of substitution is larger than one, the CIES utility is positive for all consumption levels and **A7** holds. To study **A6**, we look for $\gamma_0 > 0$ verifying **A6** and analyze the sequence of discounted utilities evaluated at the maximum possible consumption:

$$\bar{h}_t = \gamma_0^t u(f(\bar{k}_t)) = \gamma_0^t \frac{[(1+n)\bar{k}_{t+1}]^{1-\frac{1}{\sigma}}}{1-\frac{1}{\sigma}}.$$

We have then

$$\frac{\bar{h}_{t+1}}{\bar{h}_t} = \gamma_0 \left(\frac{f(\bar{k}_{t+1})}{(1+n)\bar{k}_{t+1}} \right)^{1-\frac{1}{\sigma}},$$

which implies

$$\lim_{t\to+\infty} \frac{\bar{h}_{t+1}}{\bar{h}_t} = \gamma_0 \left(\frac{A_\infty}{1+n} \right)^{1-\frac{1}{\sigma}},$$

i.e., $\bar{h}_{t+1}/\bar{h}_t$ converges. Thus, for $\bar{h}_t$ to be bounded, it is sufficient that

$$\gamma_0 \left(\frac{A_\infty}{1+n} \right)^{1-\frac{1}{\sigma}} < 1.$$

To have this with $\gamma_0 > \gamma$, it is sufficient to have

$$\gamma \left(\frac{A_\infty}{1+n} \right)^{1-\frac{1}{\sigma}} < 1 \quad \Leftrightarrow \quad \gamma < \left(\frac{1+n}{A_\infty} \right)^{1-\frac{1}{\sigma}}. \tag{2.25}$$

This condition is in fact also necessary for the existence of $\gamma_0 > \gamma$ such that **A6** holds. The same condition holds for $\gamma_0^t u((1+n)f(\bar{k}_t))$, as the ratio $\bar{h}_{t+1}/\bar{h}_t$ will remain the same.

From the study made in section 2.3.3, the optimal growth path exists if (2.25) holds together with $\sigma > 1$.

This optimal path displays unbounded growth if and only if

$$\frac{1+n}{A_\infty} \leq \gamma < \left(\frac{1+n}{A_\infty} \right)^{1-\frac{1}{\sigma}}.$$

This condition determines an interval of γ when $A_\infty > 1+n$. In the other cases, i.e., when growth is bounded, k_t^* converges to k_γ when

$$\frac{1+n}{f'(0)} < \gamma < \frac{1+n}{A_\infty},$$

and k_t^* converges to 0 when

$$\gamma \leq \frac{1+n}{f'(0)}.$$

The different types of solutions are represented as a function of γ in figure 2.7 (assuming $f'(0)$ finite). The interpretation of this picture is straightforward: if the planner puts little weight on future generations (and $f'(0)$ is finite), it is optimal to consume the production almost entirely, and let the capital

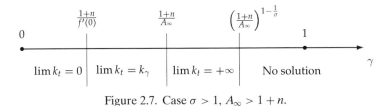

Figure 2.7. Case $\sigma > 1$, $A_\infty > 1 + n$.

tend to zero in the future. On the contrary, when future generations have a large weight in the objective and when technology in favorable ($A_\infty > 1 + n$), optimal growth is unbounded. Convergence to the modified golden rule arises in the intermediate cases.

2.5.2 Existence of Optimal Paths When $\sigma < 1$ (and $\gamma \geq 1$)

When $\sigma < 1$, the CIES utility is negative for all consumption levels and condition **A6** holds. As $f(\bar{k}_0) > (1 + n)\bar{k}_0$ (since $A_\infty \geq 1 + n$ and $f(k)/k$ is decreasing), a constant path is feasible with $c_0 = d_0/(1 + n) = \frac{1}{2}[f(\bar{k}_0) - (1 + n)\bar{k}_0]$. Thus, for $\gamma < 1$, **A7** holds.

We want to investigate the scope of the assumption **A7** when $\gamma \geq 1$. For example, $\gamma = 1$ in the Ramsey problem, or $\gamma = 1 + n$ if the planner puts equal weight on each individual (utilitarian objective function). This eventuality makes sense in that infinite levels of capital and consumption are possible. We thus consider the feasibility of some paths with a finite value of the planner's objective (i.e., in this case, different from $-\infty$).

Assume $A_\infty > 1 + n$, and let us build the following feasible path. There exists ϵ such that $1/2 > \epsilon > 0$ and $(1 - 2\epsilon)A_\infty > 1 + n$, and thus

$$k_{t+1} = \frac{1 - 2\epsilon}{1 + n} f(k_t), \qquad k_0 = \bar{k}_0,$$

is increasing and tends to $+\infty$. The consumptions:

$$c_t = \epsilon f(k_t) \quad \text{and} \quad d_t = (1 + n)\epsilon\, f(k_t),$$

together with k_t, are a feasible path $(c_t, d_t, k_{t+1})_{t \geq 0}$ starting at $\bar{k}_0$. The sequence of discounted utilities $l_t = \gamma^t u(c_t)$ and $\gamma^t u(d_t)$ satisfy

$$\frac{l_{t+1}}{l_t} = \gamma \left(\frac{f(k_{t+1})}{f(k_t)} \right)^{1 - \frac{1}{\sigma}} = \gamma \left(\frac{f(k_{t+1})(1 - 2\epsilon)}{(1 + n)k_{t+1}} \right)^{1 - \frac{1}{\sigma}},$$

and

$$\lim \frac{l_{t+1}}{l_t} = \gamma \left(\frac{A_\infty(1 - 2\epsilon)}{1 + n} \right)^{1 - \frac{1}{\sigma}}.$$

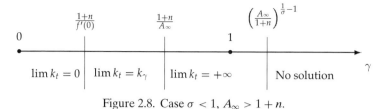

Figure 2.8. Case $\sigma < 1$, $A_\infty > 1 + n$.

The convergence of the infinite sum of utilities is equivalent to

$$\gamma \left(\frac{A_\infty(1 - 2\epsilon)}{(1 + n)} \right)^{1 - \frac{1}{\sigma}} < 1 \quad \Leftrightarrow \quad \gamma < \left(\frac{A_\infty(1 - 2\epsilon)}{1 + n} \right)^{\frac{1}{\sigma} - 1},$$

and the condition of existence of such a path with $\epsilon > 0$ is equivalent to

$$\gamma < \left(\frac{A_\infty}{1 + n} \right)^{\frac{1}{\sigma} - 1}.$$

This condition, which is the same as in the case $\sigma > 1$, is sufficient for the existence of an optimal solution. It allows in the case $\sigma < 1$ for discount factors that are larger than one when $A_\infty > 1 + n$, i.e., when the long-run marginal productivity of capital net of depreciation is larger than the growth rate of the population. A sufficient condition of existence for $\gamma = 1 + n$ (utilitarian planner) is

$$A_\infty > (1 + n)^{\frac{1}{\sigma - 1}}.$$

The optimal growth path is unbounded under the same conditions:

$$\frac{1 + n}{A_\infty} \leq \gamma < \left(\frac{A_\infty}{1 + n} \right)^{\frac{1}{\sigma} - 1}.$$

These results are summarized in figure 2.8.

2.5.3 Existence of Optimal Paths When $\sigma = 1$

In this case, $u(c) = \ln c$. The two conditions **A6** and **A7** should be analyzed.

Consider **A6**. As we have seen before, when $A_\infty > 1 + n$, the sequence $(\bar{k}_t)$ defined by $\bar{k}_{t+1} = f(\bar{k}_t)/(1 + n)$ is increasing and tends to $+\infty$. The highest possible discounted utility of first-period consumption is then

$$\bar{h}_t = \gamma_0^t \ln f(\bar{k}_t) = \gamma_0^t \ln[(1 + n)\bar{k}_{t+1}],$$

and we have

$$\frac{\bar{h}_{t+1}}{\bar{h}_t} - \gamma_0 = \gamma_0 \left(\frac{\ln[f(\bar{k}_{t+1})]}{\ln[(1 + n)\bar{k}_{t+1}]} - 1 \right) = \gamma_0 \frac{\ln\left(\frac{f(\bar{k}_{t+1})}{(1+n)\bar{k}_{t+1}} \right)}{\ln[(1 + n)\bar{k}_{t+1}]}.$$

The numerator tends to the finite limit $\ln[A_\infty/(1+n)] > 0$, and the denominator tends to $+\infty$. Hence,

$$\lim_{t \to +\infty} \frac{\bar{h}_{t+1}}{\bar{h}_t} = \gamma_0,$$

and the condition "$\exists \gamma_0 > \gamma$ such that $\bar{h}_t$ is bounded" is equivalent to $\gamma < 1$.

A similar reasoning applies to the upper bound of the discounted utility of second-period consumption,

$$\gamma_0^t \ln[(1+n) f(\bar{k}_t)],$$

which gives the same conclusion.

Consider **A7**. As $f(\bar{k}_0) > (1+n)\bar{k}_0$ when $A_\infty > 1+n$, there exists a constant path starting from $\bar{k}_0 > 0$:

$$c_0 = \frac{d_0}{1+n} = \frac{1}{2}[f(\bar{k}_0) - (1+n)\bar{k}_0].$$

With this path, utilities are constant and **A7** holds when $\gamma < 1$.

Hence, with a logarithmic utility function, the usual restriction $\gamma < 1$ is sufficient to guarantee the boundedness of the objective function. This property is widely used in the literature.

2.5.4 General Result

We have thus a general conclusion for the CIES utility function, with $A_\infty = f'(+\infty) > 1+n$, which is summarized in the following proposition.

Proposition 2.15 (Unbounded optimal growth)
Assume $A_\infty = f'(+\infty) > 1+n$. There exists an optimal planner's solution for the CIES utility function with elasticity σ if

$$\gamma < \left(\frac{1+n}{A_\infty}\right)^{1-\frac{1}{\sigma}}. \tag{2.26}$$

This solution exhibits unbounded growth when

$$\frac{1+n}{A} \leq \gamma < \left(\frac{1+n}{A}\right)^{1-\frac{1}{\sigma}}.$$

There are thus some cases for which optimal growth is unbounded although the competitive equilibrium leads to bounded dynamics.

2.5.5 The Long-run Growth Rate

When the conditions are met for unbounded optimal growth, the optimal allocation tends to a balanced growth path, i.e., a situation where quantities grow at a constant rate. We now compute the value of the long-run optimal growth rate.

Following (2.15) and (2.16), the optimal path satisfies, for a CIES utility function,

$$\left(\frac{c_{t+1}^\star}{c_t^\star}\right)^{\frac{1}{\sigma}} = \left(\frac{d_{t+1}^\star}{d_t^\star}\right)^{\frac{1}{\sigma}} = \frac{u'(d_t^\star)}{u'(d_{t+1}^\star)} = \frac{\gamma f'(k_{t+1}^\star)}{1+n}.$$

In the case, $A_\infty = f'(+\infty) \geq \frac{1+n}{\gamma}$, $k_{t+1}^\star$ tends to $+\infty$, and

$$\lim_{t\to+\infty} \frac{c_{t+1}^\star}{c_t^\star} = \lim_{t\to+\infty} \frac{d_{t+1}^\star}{d_t^\star} = \left(\frac{\gamma A_\infty}{1+n}\right)^\sigma.$$

Then the long-run growth rate of consumption levels and output is given by

$$\left(\frac{\gamma A_\infty}{1+n}\right)^\sigma - 1.$$

Example: Let $f'(+\infty) > 1 + n$ be the following: $f(k) = Ak + Bk^\alpha$, with $0 < \alpha < 1$ and $A > 1 + n$ (from Jones and Manuelli (1990)).

We first notice that

$$f'(0) = +\infty \quad \text{and} \quad f'(+\infty) = A.$$

If the condition

$$\gamma < \left(\frac{1+n}{A}\right)^{1-\frac{1}{\sigma}}$$

holds, we know from propositions 2.11 and 2.15 that the optimal solution exists, is monotone, and satisfies

$$\lim k_t^\star = \begin{cases} \left(\dfrac{\alpha \gamma B}{1+n-\gamma A}\right)^{\frac{1}{1-\alpha}} & \text{if } \dfrac{1+n}{\gamma} > A, \\[2ex] +\infty & \text{if } A \geq \dfrac{1+n}{\gamma}. \end{cases}$$

We cannot solve the planner's problem explicitly in the case of the example, but we can do it with the linear production function $f(k) = Ak$ and a CIES utility function. The production function $f(k) = Ak$ is a standard assumption in endogenous growth theory, in which the social return to capital (or more generally to the reproducible factors) is constant. This line is pursued in section 2.6.5.

2.6 APPLICATIONS AND EXTENSIONS

In this section, we first extend the analysis of section 2.3.3 in order to include all cases where **A8** is not verified. Two applications follow: We illustrate the effect of the inter-temporal elasticity of substitution on the speed of convergence in section 2.6.2. We next illustrate the use of the phase diagram in section 2.6.3. Competitive equilibria and the optimal path are then characterized with a specific production function in section 2.6.4. Finally, optimal growth in the model with a linear technology is studied in section 2.6.5.

2.6.1 Properties of the Policy Functions When $f(0) > 0$

Following Lemma 2.2, $f(0) = 0$ implies the assumption **A8**. When $f(0) > 0$, **A8** may or may not be verified. We list here the main differences from the case $f(0) = 0$:

- The planning problem is defined when the initial condition is $k_0 = 0$.
- The assumption **A7** holds when $\gamma < 1$: with $c = d/(1+n) = f(0)/2$ and $k = 0$, we obtain a feasible trajectory such that the objective function is finite.
- With the assumption **A6**, the value function is defined on $\mathbb{R}_+$, concave, and non-decreasing. It is continuous on $\mathbb{R}_{++}$ (but not necessarily at 0), and it satisfies the Bellman equation (2.10). The upper bound is taken on the set of pairs (c, d) which satisfies $c > 0$, $d > 0$, and $c + d/(1+n) \leq f(k)$. We need the continuity of V at zero to be sure that the upper bound (2.10) is reached.

In the following proposition, it appears that main difference from the case $f(0) = 0$ is the eventuality of zero optimal investment. When investment is 0, the economy reaches 0 in a finite time, remains there, and produces. This is why we have only weak monotonicity of the investment policy function.

Proposition 2.16 (Properties of the policy function when $f(0) > 0$)
Under the assumptions **H1**, **H2**, **H4**, *and* $f(0) > 0$, *the value function V is continuous, concave, and increasing in $\mathbb{R}_+$. The consumption functions $c^\star$ and $d^\star$ are continuous and increasing in $\mathbb{R}_+$, and the investment function $x^\star$ is continuous and non-decreasing in $\mathbb{R}_+$.*

Proof: The proof follows three steps.
1. We should first show that V is continuous at 0. As V is non-decreasing, there exists a limit $V(0+)$ with $V(0+) \geq V(0)$. The function $\bar{V}(\cdot)$ defined on $\mathbb{R}_+$ by $\bar{V}(k) = V(k)$ if $k > 0$ and $\bar{V}(0) = V(0+)$ is continuous. Then the continuous function

$$u(c) + \frac{\beta}{\gamma} u(d) + \gamma \bar{V} \left(\frac{f(k) - c - d/(1+n)}{1+n} \right)$$

attains its upper bound. Taking a limit point[19] $(\bar{c}, \bar{d})$ of the sequences that maximize our objective for a sequence $k > 0$ tending to 0, we obtain

$$\mathcal{V}(0+) = u(\bar{c}) + \frac{\beta}{\gamma} u(\bar{d}) + \gamma \bar{\mathcal{V}}(\bar{x}), \qquad \bar{x} = \frac{f(0) - \bar{c} - \bar{d}/(1+n)}{1+n}.$$

- If $\bar{x} > 0$, then $\bar{\mathcal{V}}(\bar{x}) = \mathcal{V}(\bar{x})$ and $\mathcal{V}(0+) = u(\bar{c}) + \frac{\beta}{\gamma} u(\bar{d}) + \gamma \mathcal{V}(\bar{x}) \leq \mathcal{V}(0)$.
- If $\bar{x} = 0$, then $\bar{\mathcal{V}}(\bar{x}) = \mathcal{V}(0+)$ and thus $\mathcal{V}(0+)(1 - \gamma) = u(\bar{c}) + \frac{\beta}{\gamma} u(\bar{d})$. As the constant trajectory $(\bar{c}, \bar{d})$ and $k = 0$ is feasible from $k = 0$, we have

$$\mathcal{V}(0) \geq \sum_{t=0}^{\infty} \gamma^t \left(u(\bar{c}) + \frac{\beta}{\gamma} u(\bar{d}) \right) = \frac{1}{1 - \gamma} \left(u(\bar{c}) + \frac{\beta}{\gamma} u(\bar{d}) \right) = \mathcal{V}(0+).$$

We thus obtain, in the two cases, $\mathcal{V}(0+) \leq \mathcal{V}(0)$, which implies the continuity of $\mathcal{V}$ at 0: $\mathcal{V}(0+) = \mathcal{V}(0)$.

2. The maximum of the continuous and strictly concave function (2.13) is attained at a unique point $(c^\star(k), d^\star(k)) \in \mathbb{R}^2_{++}$. Let us show that

$$x^\star(k) = \frac{1}{1+n} \left(f(k) - c^\star(k) - \frac{d^\star(k)}{1+n} \right)$$

is monotonic:

- If $x^\star(k) > 0$, the maximum is attained at an interior point and the function $\mathcal{V}$ is differentiable at $x^\star(k)$. As in proposition 2.9, we deduce that $x^\star(k)$ is increasing, as well as $c^\star(k)$ and $d^\star(k)$. It results that $x^\star(k')$ is positive for all $k' > k$.
- If $x^\star(k) = 0$, we have, for all $k' > k$, $x^\star(k') \geq 0$, and thus $x^\star(k') \geq x^\star(k)$. The function $x^\star$ is thus non-decreasing: It could be nil on an interval that contains 0. As $c^\star(k) + \frac{1}{1+n} d^\star(k) = f(k)$ on the interval where $x^\star(k) = 0$, and as the maximization of the objective at given $x^\star$ gives

$$u'(c^\star(k)) = \frac{\beta(1+n)}{\gamma} u'(d^\star(k)),$$

$c^\star$ and $d^\star$ are increasing functions of k.

3. The last step is to show that $\mathcal{V}(k)$ is strictly increasing. We have

$$\mathcal{V}(k) = u(c^\star(k)) + \frac{\beta}{\gamma} u(d^\star(k)) + \gamma \mathcal{V}(x^\star(k)).$$

For $k' > k$, $c' = c^\star(k) + f(k') - f(k)$ is feasible with $d' = d^\star(k)$ and

$$x' = \frac{1}{1+n} \left(f(k') - c' - \frac{d'}{1+n} \right) = x^\star(k).$$

---

[19] For a definition of limit points, see appendix A.2.4.

We thus have

$$V(k') \geq u(c') + \frac{\beta}{\gamma} u(d') + \gamma V(x') > V(k),$$

as $u(c') > u(c^*(k))$.   ∎

As in section 2.3.3, the monotonic dynamics obtained from the Bellman equation are the ones of the optimal path when an optimal path exists. The existence is guaranteed under the assumption **A6**.

Proposition 2.17 (Existence of the optimal path when $f(0) > 0$)
*Under the assumptions **H1**, **H2**, **A6**, and **A7**, the path starting from k_0 defined by the policy functions defined in proposition 2.16 is the optimal solution to the planning problem.*

Proof: The proof also results from proposition A.13 of appendix A.4.1.   ∎

2.6.2 Application: The Optimal Speed of Convergence

When the capital stock is far below its long-run level, should the economy invest massively by refraining consumption in order to grow quickly or, on the contrary, should the pace of convergence be slow? The answer depends crucially on household preferences. Let us consider an economy with a CIES utility function and a CES production function with the numerical values of section A.5.2: $\rho = 1$, $\alpha = 1/2$, $A = 20$ (i.e., $f(k) = 40k/(1 + k)$), $\beta = 0.3$, $n = 1.025^{30} - 1$. Assuming further that $\gamma = 0.99$.

We now investigate the effect of different inter-temporal elasticities of substitution on the dynamics. Notice that σ does not affect k_y, which depends only on demographics and technology.

From the simulation results presented in table 2.1, it appears that σ is related to the speed of convergence. For a very high σ ($\sigma = 10$), the stock of capital quickly comes very close to its stationary state. On the contrary, for low σ ($\sigma = 0.2$), convergence is quite slower. The rationale for this is the following: To converge optimally, the planner lowers the first-period consumption for the

Table 2.1. *Convergence of k_t*

Time	k_t		
t	$\sigma = 0.2$	$\sigma = 1$	$\sigma = 10$
0	3.000	3.000	3.000
1	3.205	3.291	3.338
2	3.291	3.337	3.345
3	3.324	3.344	3.345
∞	3.345	3.345	3.345

benefit of investment, compensating each generation with a higher consumption when old (made possible by more capital and hence production). When σ is low, households lose utility from this postponement of consumption, and it is expensive in terms of welfare for the planner to foster capital accumulation at a high rate.

2.6.3 Application: Rise in β

To illustrate the use of the phase diagram we consider the effect of a rise in the individual discount factor, reflecting the fact that agents put more weight on the utility when old.[20] We compare, using the phase diagrams, the response of the competitive economy with that of the central planner in the face of such a shock.

Assuming a unique positive steady state in the competitive economy (left panel of figure 2.9), it is straightforward to show, using equation (1.9), that the increase in β raises the savings rate; this shifts the transition function $g(k_t)$, reflecting the fact that the propensity to save out of income has increased. The rise in savings lead to a rise in investment, and the capital stock increases during the following periods, converging to a new, higher steady state. The increase in the stock of capital hurts the first generation after the shock, who

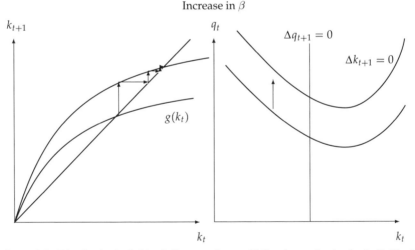

Figure 2.9. Rise in the individual discount factor. Following a rise in the individual discount factor, the steady state capital stock increases in the competitive economy, but not in the planned economy.

---

[20] This could, under several assumptions, reflect an increase in life expectancy; see Ehrlich and Lui (1991). For a treatment of life expectancy in a discrete time overlapping generations model, see Chakraborty (1999), Blackburn and Cipriani (2002), and Zhang, Zhang, and Lee (2001).

suffer a lower return on savings; if the economy is characterized by under-accumulation of capital, the rise in capital benefits to all future generations through an increase in net production. Contrarily, if there is over-accumulation, the rise in the capital stock decreases net production in the future.

In the optimal economy (right panel of figure 2.9) we have seen that the planner allocates consumption between the two periods of life as a given individual would. All things being equal, the shift in β should lead to a rise in consumption when old at the expense of consumption when young. This effect is graphically reflected by an upward shift in the $k_{t+1} = k_t$ locus.[21] Moreover, the $q_{t+1} = q_t$ locus remains unchanged. As a consequence, starting from the modified golden rule, the dynamic effect of the rise in β is a sudden, once for all increase in q and no change in k. As $q_t = u'(c_t) f'(k_t)$, there is a once for all decrease in c_t and a corresponding increase in d_t. The new steady state displays a higher level of consumption when old and the same level of the capital stock. The adjustment to this new steady state is instantaneous. This shows that the planner does not modify the tradeoff between the welfare of the different generations. He will thus leave the stock of capital unchanged and simply reallocate production between the young and the old households.

2.6.4 A Mixed CES–Linear Production Function

We take the standard two-period model with a logarithmic utility function $\ln c_t + \beta \ln d_{t+1}$ and a production function which consists of a sum of a linear production function that does not use capital, $F(K, L) = bL$, and a CES production function. This production function is rich enough to illustrate many results derived in this chapter.

We chose the following particular values for the parameters: $A = a/2, \alpha = 1/2, \rho = 1$, which leads to the production function

$$f(k) = b + \frac{ak}{1 + k}.$$

The returns on capital and labor are given by

$$f'(k) = \frac{a}{(1 + k)^2}, \qquad \omega(k) = b + \frac{ak^2}{(1 + k)^2}.$$

This production function has the following properties:

$$\lim_{k \to 0} f(k) = b, \qquad \lim_{k \to 0} f'(k) = a, \qquad \lim_{k \to +\infty} f'(k) = 0.$$

As in the case of a simple CES production function with high substitutability, production is possible without capital; in contrast, however, the marginal productivity of capital tends to 0 when capital tends to infinity.

---

[21] This is an unambiguous effect, given the definition of the $k_{t+1} = k_t$ locus.

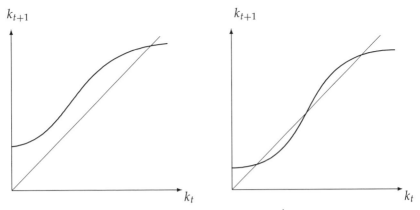

Figure 2.10. Competitive dynamics with $f(k) = b + \frac{ak}{1+k}$. Examples with one and three steady states.

In a competitive equilibrium, the dynamics are characterized by

$$k_{t+1} = \frac{\beta}{(1+n)(1+\beta)} \left(b + \frac{a k_t^2}{(1+k_t)^2} \right).$$

Steady state equilibria can be obtained by finding the roots of a cubic equation. Depending on the values of the different parameters, we can have one, two, or three positive steady states (see figure 2.10). There exists at least one steady state because $\omega(0) > 0$, and the curve starts above the 45° line.

Let us now consider optimal paths with this production function. The assumption **A6** hold for $\gamma < 1$, as k_t is bounded by $\bar{k}_t$ s.t. $(1+n)\bar{k}_{t+1} = f(\bar{k}_t)$:

$$\bar{k}_{t+1} = \frac{1}{1+n} \left(b + \frac{a \bar{k}_t}{1 + \bar{k}_t} \right) < \frac{b+a}{1+n}.$$

The assumption **A7** also holds, as $c = d/(1+n) = b/2$ is feasible. Then, from proposition 2.17, for any $k_0 > 0$, there exists an optimal solution (c_t^*, d_t^*, k_t^*) which is monotonic. Moreover, since $f'(+\infty) = 0$, there are two possibilities for the limit of the optimal trajectory:[22]

- if $\frac{1+n}{\gamma} < f'(0) = a$, then k_t^* converges to the modified golden rule:

$$k_\gamma = f'^{-1} \left(\frac{1+n}{\gamma} \right) = \sqrt{\frac{\gamma a}{1+n}} - 1;$$

- if $\gamma < \frac{1+n}{a}$, then k_t^* converges to 0, and then necessarily the investment policy function is such that $x^*(0) = 0$.

Let us show by a reductio ad absurdum that k_t^* reaches 0 after a finite number of steps when $\gamma \le \frac{1+n}{a}$. Assume that $k_t^* > 0$ for all t, i.e., the optimal solution

---

[22] In the knife edge case $\frac{1+n}{\gamma} = a$, the modified golden rule coincides with the corner steady state. The optimal capital is positive at all dates and converges to 0.

is interior. Note that

$$u'^{-1}\left(\frac{q_t}{f'(k_t)}\right) = \left(1 + \frac{\beta}{\gamma}\right)\frac{f'(k_t)}{q_t}.$$

According to (2.21) and (2.22), the optimal solution, if it is interior, is characterized by

$$k_{t+1}^{\star} = \frac{1}{1+n}\left[b + \frac{ak_t^{\star}}{1+k_t^{\star}} - \left(1 + \frac{\beta}{\gamma}\right)\frac{a}{q_t(1+k_t^{\star})^2}\right],$$

$$q_{t+1} = \frac{1+n}{\gamma}\frac{q_t}{a}(1+k_t^{\star})^2.$$

The following inequality holds:

$$q_{t+1} = \frac{1+n}{\gamma}\frac{q_t}{a}(1+k_t^{\star})^2 > \frac{1+n}{\gamma a}q_t.$$

As $1 + n > a\gamma$, we have that $\lim q_t = +\infty$. Using the first dynamical equation, $k_t^{\star}$ has a limit $\bar{k}^{\star}$ such that

$$a\bar{k}^{\star} = [(1+n)\bar{k}^{\star} - b](1 + \bar{k}^{\star}),$$

which contradicts $\lim k_t^{\star} = 0$. This implies that the optimal capital stock should be nil after a finite number of periods.

2.6.5 Optimal Growth in the Ak Model

The Ak model is a model with the linear aggregate production function $f(k) = Ak$.[23] As stressed before, $f(k) = Ak$ is a good approximation of a function $f(k)$ such that $f'(+\infty) = A$ for large value of k, and it gives the optimal long-run growth rate of the economy. Moreover, the production function $f(k) = Ak$ is a standard assumption in endogenous growth theory, in which the social marginal return of capital (or more generally of the reproducible factors) is constant.

There are two different interpretations of this model in the endogenous growth literature. The simplest one is due to Rebelo (1991): the variable k represents all production factors, which are assumed to be reproducible (like physical capital and human capital). Another interpretation, proposed by Romer (1989), relies on the idea of Frankel (1962). He assumes a standard Cobb–Douglas production function for firm j:

$$Y_j = \tilde{A}K_j^{\alpha}L_j^{1-\alpha},$$

---

[23] The Ak production function does not satisfy the assumption **H2**. Notice, moreover, that we do not need strict concavity to study the sufficient and necessary conditions for optimality (see appendix A.4.2, assumption **B3**).

in which the productivity parameter depends on the overall capital–labor ratio:

$$\tilde{A} = A(K/L)^a,$$

i.e., the stock of knowledge depends on the amount of capital per capita in the economy (through, e.g., learning-by-doing). When $\alpha + a = 1$ and when the labor supply is constant and normalized to 1, we obtain the so-called *AK* production function, in which the social return that takes into account the external effects of the total capital stock is constant, but the private return is decreasing.[24] The *AK* model stricto sensu with externalities is presented in Romer (1989).

The following proposition characterizes the optimal solution when the utility function is CIES.

Proposition 2.18 (Optimal solution with linear production)
In the case of a linear production function $f(k) = Ak$ *and a CIES utility function with elasticity* σ, *assuming that the planner's discount factor verifies*

$$\gamma < \left(\frac{A}{1+n} \right)^{\frac{1}{\sigma}-1},$$

the optimal solution given an initial level of capital k_0 *is the path* $(c_t^\star, d_t^\star, k_{t+1}^\star)_{t \geq 0}$ *growing at the constant rate*

$$g = \left(\frac{A\gamma}{1+n} \right)^{\sigma} - 1,$$

with

$$c_0^\star = \frac{A - (1+n)(1+g)}{1 + \frac{1}{1+n} \left(\frac{(1+n)\beta}{\gamma} \right)^{\sigma}} k_0 \quad \text{and} \quad d_0^\star = \left(\frac{(1+n)\beta}{\gamma} \right)^{\sigma} c_0^\star.$$

Proof: We first consider the necessary first-order conditions for optimality. Next we check the transversality condition and compute the initial value of optimal consumption.

- **Necessary conditions:** With the linear production function, the Lagrangian in period t is

$$\mathcal{L}_t = u(c_t) + \frac{\beta}{\gamma} u(d_t) + \frac{\gamma q_{t+1}}{1+n} \left(Ak_t - c_t - \frac{d_t}{1+n} \right) - q_t k_t,$$

---

[24] Frankel's idea of the externality was first exploited in a dynamic general equilibrium model by Romer (1986) (with increasing returns) and further popularized by Lucas (1988) (increasing returns for the human capital).

and the optimality conditions are

$$u'(c_t^\star) = \frac{\gamma q_{t+1}}{1+n},$$

$$\frac{\beta}{\gamma} u'(d_t^\star) = \frac{\gamma q_{t+1}}{(1+n)^2},$$ (2.27)

$$\frac{\gamma q_{t+1} A}{1+n} = q_t.$$

From (2.27), the shadow price q_t admits a constant growth rate

$$\frac{1+n}{A\gamma} - 1,$$

which is negative if $A < (1+n)/\gamma$, positive if $A > (1+n)/\gamma$, or nil if $A = (1+n)/\gamma$. In the case of a CIES utility function,[25] $u'(c) = c^{-1/\sigma}$, it is possible to obtain an explicit solution. With this utility function, the two consumptions c_t and d_t grow at a rate g defined by

$$1+g = \left(\frac{A\gamma}{1+n}\right)^\sigma,$$ (2.28)

and we have

$$c_t^\star = c_0^\star(1+g)^t \quad \text{and} \quad d_t^\star = \left(\frac{(1+n)\beta}{\gamma}\right)^\sigma c_t^\star.$$

Thus, total consumption per young person is

$$c_t^\star + \frac{1}{1+n} d_t^\star = v c_0^\star (1+g)^t, \quad \text{with} \quad v = 1 + \frac{1}{1+n}\left(\frac{(1+n)\beta}{\gamma}\right)^\sigma,$$

and the dynamics of the capital stock are

$$k_{t+1}^\star = \frac{1}{1+n}[Ak_t^\star - v c_0^\star(1+g)^t].$$ (2.29)

- **Sufficient condition:** There exists a unique value of $c_0^\star$ such that the capital stock $k_t^\star$ in the solution to (2.29) grows at the same rate g as the consumptions:

$$k_t^\star = k_0(1+g)^t \iff v c_0^\star = [A - (1+n)(1+g)]k_0,$$

---

[25] As is known, long-run growth with a balanced growth path can coexist with a special type of utility function, namely the CIES type, for which marginal utility grows at a constant rate (see, e.g., King, Plosser, and Rebelo (1990)).

and thus this value of $c_0^\star$ is positive if and only if

$$A > (1+n)(1+g). \tag{2.30}$$

In addition, the condition (2.30) implies that the transversality condition holds. Indeed,

$$\gamma^t q_t k_t^\star = \gamma^t q_0 \left(\frac{1+n}{A\gamma}\right)^t k_0(1+g)^t,$$

and the limit of $\gamma^t q_t k_t$ is equal to 0 when $(1+n)(1+g) < A$. Thus the path under consideration is the planner solution if (2.30) holds. ∎

Unbounded growths prevail if and only if $\gamma > \frac{1+n}{A}$. In the case $\gamma < \frac{1+n}{A}$, which corresponds to the case $f'(0) = A < \frac{1+n}{\gamma}$, capital and consumptions decrease along the optimal path at a constant rate $g < 0$ and converge to 0. Only in the case $\gamma = \frac{1+n}{A}$ does there exist a stationary solution: this is the case where $g = 0$ in the preceding study, and for all k_0, the constant solution defined in the proposition is the optimal path.

Notice finally that the condition (2.30) is also equivalent to the convergence of the objective function. Indeed, the growth factor of the discounted utility is

$$\gamma(1+g)^{1-1/\sigma} = \gamma(1+g)\frac{1+n}{A\gamma} \qquad \text{by (2.28)}$$

$$= \frac{(1+g)(1+n)}{A},$$

which is smaller than 1 if and only if $(1+n)(1+g) < A$.

Intuitively it is clear that the growth rate of capital, if it is constant, is necessarily equal to the growth rate of consumptions. If it is larger, there is a loss of feasible consumptions. If it is smaller, then the capital stock would become negative.

2.7 CONCLUSION

In this chapter, we have first analyzed one of the main issues of overlapping generations models, namely, the possibility for competitive equilibria to be suboptimal. The specificity of our approach was first to carefully distinguish efficiency issues (extending the production frontier to an infinite horizon setup) from welfare issues (discussing the allocation of total consumption among all generations). Second, all the propositions, including the first welfare theorem, are provided for inter-temporal equilibria, not only for stationary state equilibria.

The problem of the planner is a problem of optimal control in which the existence, uniqueness, and characterization (monotonicity and convergence) of the solution do not rely on the study of the local dynamics, but on the very nature of the optimal growth problem itself (concavity and boundedness of the objective). Moreover, the dynamical properties arising from the saddle-point local property are consequences of the existence and uniqueness of the optimal path.[26]

We have studied the value function associated to the problem of the planner and its properties. We have also provided a local analysis when there exists a stationary state, and a characterization of the optimal solution when growth is unbounded.

---

[26] More generally, the uniqueness of the solution, which results from the strict concavity of the problem, implies that the stationary state is either a saddle or a source.

THREE

Policy

The overlapping generations model provides an interesting toolkit to analyze various types of policies. In particular, it is the requisite tool for studying intergenerational distribution issues, such as the design of pension schemes. In this chapter, we devote our attention to different balanced budget policies for which an overlapping generations setup is of significant interest. Policies associated with public debt will be considered in chapter 4.

In a first section, we introduce lump-sum transfers in the competitive model of chapter 1 and study the policies designed to decentralize the allocation chosen by the benevolent planner. We show that any Pareto-optimal allocation can be decentralized with lump-sum transfers (Second Welfare Theorem). In the second section, the equilibrium with lump-sum transfers is used to study pension systems. The fact that transfers to the old are positive in a pension system allows us to further characterize the equilibrium and discuss the effect of pensions on capital accumulation. The third section is devoted to the study the role of government spending. We analyze, in section 4, the problem of financing such spending when the government cannot use lump-sum taxes (second-best policies). In section 5, we provide some applications and extensions.

3.1 LUMP-SUM TRANSFERS AND THE SECOND WELFARE THEOREM

3.1.1 Equilibrium with Lump-sum Transfers

We extend the model of chapter 1 and assume that there is a transfer system. There are lump-sum taxes a_t bearing on the young generation, and $-z_t$ bearing on the old generation. The tax a_t can be either positive or negative, but should remain smaller that the income of the young. For the generation born at time t, the first-period budget constraint is

$$w_t - a_t = c_t + s_t, \tag{3.1}$$

and the second-period budget constraint is

$$d_{t+1}^e = R_{t+1}^e s_t + z_{t+1}^e,$$

in which z_{t+1}^e is the expected lump-sum transfer when old, and R_{t+1}^e is the expected interest factor.

The budget of the system that organizes the transfers should remain balanced:

$$N_t a_t = N_{t-1} z_t \iff z_t = (1+n)a_t.$$

The optimal savings of the representative individual are

$$s_t = \arg\max_s u(w_t - a_t - s) + \beta u\big(R_{t+1}^e s + z_{t+1}^e\big),$$

and thus, for an interior solution,

$$u'(w_t - a_t - s_t) = \beta R_{t+1}^e u'\big(R_{t+1}^e s_t + z_{t+1}^e\big).$$

The Savings Function. We define

$$\tilde{s}(\omega_1, \omega_2, R) = \arg\max u(\omega_1 - s) + \beta u(\omega_2 + Rs), \tag{3.2}$$

which are the optimal savings of a household receiving a first-period income ω_1 and a second-period income ω_2. The function $\tilde{s}$ is defined for positive interest factor and life-cycle income (i.e., $R > 0$ and $\omega_1 + \omega_2/R > 0$) and satisfies

$$\frac{-\omega_2}{R} < \tilde{s} < \omega_1.$$

This inequality ensures that both consumption levels are positive:

$$c_t > 0 \quad \text{and} \quad d_{t+1}^e > 0.$$

There is a simple relation linking savings with first- and second-period income ($\tilde{s}$) and savings with first-period income only (s). Indeed, the expression

$$u(\omega_1 - s) + \beta u(\omega_2 + R s)$$

is equivalent to

$$u\left(\omega_1 + \frac{\omega_2}{R} - \left(s + \frac{\omega_2}{R}\right)\right) + \beta u\left(R\left(s + \frac{\omega_2}{R}\right)\right),$$

from which we deduce that

$$s\left(\omega_1 + \frac{\omega_2}{R}, R\right) = \tilde{s}(\omega_1, \omega_2, R) + \frac{\omega_2}{R}. \tag{3.3}$$

Hence, to compute the savings with a second-period income, $\tilde{s}(\omega_1, \omega_2, R)$, we can take the standard savings function of chapter 1 defined over the life-cycle income $s(\omega_1 + \omega_2/R, R)$ from which we subtract the discounted second-period income ω_2/R. This allows us to characterize easily the properties of

$\tilde{s}(\cdot)$. Indeed,

$$\tilde{s}'_{\omega_1} = s'_w > 0,$$

$$\tilde{s}'_{\omega_2} = \frac{1}{R}(s'_w - 1) < 0,$$

$$\tilde{s}'_R = s'_R + \frac{\omega_2}{R^2}(1 - s'_w).$$

The effect of the first-period income on savings is positive, as in the basic model of chapter 1. As expected, the effect of the second-period income on savings is unambiguously negative. Indeed, the need of savings is reduced by an increase in the second-period income. The effect of the interest factor is more complex to study. In particular, if the second-period income is positive (negative), then $\tilde{s}'_R > s'_R$ ($\tilde{s}'_R < s'_R$), and savings react more positively (more negatively) than in the standard model.

The Temporary Equilibrium. The temporary equilibrium can now be defined as:

Definition 3.1 (Temporary equilibrium with lump-sum transfers)
Given the variables $\{s_{t-1}, I_{t-1} = N_{t-1}s_{t-1}\}$ from the previous period, the current transfer a_t, the expected rate of return on savings R^e_{t+1}, and the expected future transfer z^e_{t+1}, the temporary equilibrium at period t with lump-sum transfers is defined by

1. *the wage rate w_t and the gross rate of return R_t, satisfying*

$$w_t = \omega(k_t),$$
$$R_t = f'(k_t),$$

2. *the aggregate variables K_t, L_t, Y_t, k_t, and I_t, satisfying*

$$k_t = K_t/N_t = I_{t-1}/N_t,$$
$$L_t = N_t,$$
$$Y_t = N_t f(k_t),$$
$$I_t = N_t s_t,$$

3. *the individual variables c_t, s_t, and d_t, satisfying*

$$c_t = w_t - a_t - s_t,$$
$$s_t = \tilde{s}(\omega(k_t) - a_t, z^e_{t+1}, R^e_{t+1}),$$
$$d_t = R_t s_{t-1} + z_t,$$

4. *and the lump-sum transfers z_t, satisfying*

$$z_t = (1+n)a_t.$$

The temporary equilibrium with lump-sum transfers exists and is unique if the following two conditions are met:

- The consumption of the old is positive:

$$f'(k_t)s_{t-1} + (1+n)a_t > 0,$$

which imposes a condition on a_t (lower bound).
- Savings are defined if the life-cycle income is positive:

$$\omega(k_t) - a_t + \frac{z_{t+1}^e}{R_{t+1}^e} > 0,$$

which imposes a condition on expectations.

At this temporary equilibrium, investment is positive if and only if $s_t > 0$, which imposes another necessary condition on the tax level a_t (upper bound):

$$a_t < \omega(k_t).$$

Moreover, there is one additional condition on expectations to guarantee the positivity of savings:

$$\tilde{s}\left(\omega(k_t) - a_t, z_{t+1}^e, R_{t+1}^e\right) > 0.$$

The Inter-temporal Equilibrium. The inter-temporal equilibrium with perfect foresight is obtained as a sequence of temporary equilibria with positive investment by imposing the equality between savings and investment and between expectations and realization.

Definition 3.2 (Inter-temporal equilibrium with lump-sum transfers)
Given an initial capital stock $k_0 = K_0/N_0$ and a sequence of lump-sum transfers $(a_t)_{t \geq 0}$, an inter-temporal equilibrium with perfect foresight and lump-sum transfers is a sequence of temporary equilibria that satisfies, for all $t \geq 0$,

$$(1+n)k_{t+1} = \tilde{s}\left(\omega(k_t) - a_t, z_{t+1}^e, R_{t+1}^e\right) > 0,$$

$$R_{t+1}^e = R_{t+1} = f'(k_{t+1}),$$

$$z_{t+1}^e = (1+n)a_{t+1}.$$

Hence, at the inter-temporal equilibrium with perfect foresight, the stock of capital of period $t+1$ should verify the following implicit equation:

$$(1+n)k_{t+1} - \tilde{s}(\omega(k_t) - a_t, (1+n)a_{t+1}, f'(k_{t+1})) = 0.$$

To analyze the existence of such an equilibrium, we follow the same strategy as in chapter 1. However, compared to chapter 1, there are restrictions on taxes for the net wage to be positive and for savings with perfect foresight to be defined and positive.[1]

Considering a given net wage $w > 0$ and a transfer z, we look for a capital stock k such that the expectations of the rate of return $R(k) = f'(k)$ will lead to a savings decision $\tilde{s}(w, z, f'(k))$ corresponding to the level of capital accumulation. In other words, given $w > 0$ and $z \in \mathbb{R}$, we wonder whether it is possible to solve for k, the equation

$$\Delta(k, w, z) \equiv (1 + n)k - \tilde{s}(w, z, f'(k)) = 0.$$

It is enough to prove that $\Delta(k, w, z)$ takes values of opposite sign on one interval of k's for which it is defined. Indeed, when this is the case, the continuous function $\Delta(k, w, z)$ will necessarily take the value 0 at some positive k.

We look for a $k > 0$ such that $\Delta(k, w, z) = 0$. For such a k, we clearly have $\tilde{s} > 0$. The function Δ is defined only if k satisfies

$$w + \frac{z}{f'(k)} > 0,$$

i.e., if the life-cycle income is positive. Let us now consider the two possible cases depending upon the sign of z

- **Case $z \le 0$**: Since $\tilde{s} < w$, $\Delta(k, w, z) > 0$ for $(1 + n)k \ge w$. Values of k larger than $w/(1 + n)$ cannot be solution to $\Delta(k, w, z) = 0$. On the one hand, $\Delta(k, w, z)$ is defined for $0 < k \le w/(1 + n)$ if and only if

$$z > -wf'\left(\frac{w}{1 + n}\right).$$

On this set savings are positive (case of negative transfer to the old). We next study the value of Δ at the bounds of the interval $(0, w/(1 + n)]$. We have for $k = w/(1 + n)$

$$\Delta\left(\frac{w}{1 + n}, w, z\right) = w - \tilde{s}\left(w, z, f'\left(\frac{w}{1 + n}\right)\right) > 0.$$

On the other hand, $\tilde{s}(w, z, f'(k)) \ge s(w, f'(k))$ as $z \le 0$. Hence, we have for $k \in (0, \frac{w}{1+n})$

$$\Delta(k, w, z) \le (1 + n)k - s(w, f'(k)).$$

As we have seen in chapter 1, the right-hand side becomes negative when k approaches zero. Consequently, as $0 \ge z > -wf'(w/(1 + n))$, $\Delta(k, w, z)$ is equal to zero for some $k > 0$ such that $0 < k < w/(1 + n)$.
- **Case $z \ge 0$**: The functions $\tilde{s}$ and $\Delta(k, w, z)$ are defined for all $k > 0$. On the one hand, considering $k = w/(1 + n)$, we deduce from $\tilde{s}(w, z, f'(k)) < w$ that $\Delta(k, w, z) > (1 + n)k - w = 0$. On the other hand, there exists $k > 0$ sufficiently close to 0 such that $s(w, f'(k)) > (1 + n)k$. Fixing such

---

[1] With perfect foresight, there is no longer a condition for the positivity of the consumption of old people, except for the first period.

a value of k, denoted k^0, the same inequality holds with the function $\tilde{s}$: $\tilde{s}(w, z, f'(k^0)) > (1 + n)k^0$ for small z, i.e., $z < \bar{z}^0$. Hence, $\Delta(k^0, w, z) < 0$, and there exists, for $0 \leq z < \bar{z}^0$, a $k > 0$ such that $\Delta(k, w, z) = 0$.

This proof simply reflects the fact that we cannot make any transfer. When z is too large, the transfer to the old is so large that it could lead to $\tilde{s} < 0$. When z is too negative, the life-cycle income becomes negative, and savings are no longer defined.

The difficulty of the preceding approach with lump-sum transfers is that, in the analysis of existence, a conclusion can be reached only for small values of z. A more general study will be provided with z constant and positive in the next section. A more complete study is possible in the following example.

Example: With a logarithmic utility function, $\ln c_t + \beta \ln d_{t+1}$, the savings are given by

$$s_t = \frac{\beta}{1 + \beta}(w_t - a_t) - \frac{1}{1 + \beta}\frac{z_{t+1}}{R_{t+1}}.$$

We assume a Cobb–Douglas production function $f(k_t) = Ak_t^{\alpha}$. At the intertemporal equilibrium with perfect foresight, the sequence (k_t) should satisfy

$$(1 + n)k_{t+1} = \frac{\beta}{1 + \beta}\left(A(1 - \alpha)k_t^{\alpha} - \frac{z_t}{1 + n}\right) - \frac{z_{t+1}}{A(1 + \beta)\alpha k_{t+1}^{\alpha-1}} > 0. \quad (3.4)$$

Equation (3.4) always admits a solution $k_{t+1} > 0$ for all z_{t+1} if the net wage is positive. Indeed, for all $z \in \mathbb{R}$, the function

$$(1 + n)k + \frac{zk^{1-\alpha}}{A(1 + \beta)\alpha}$$

tends to 0 $(+\infty)$ when k tends to 0 $(+\infty)$. More precisely, when $z \geq 0$, this function is increasing; when $z < 0$, it is first negative and decreasing for

$$k^{\alpha} < -\frac{(1 - \alpha)z}{(1 + n)A(1 + \beta)\alpha},$$

attains a minimum, and is then increasing. In all cases, it takes the positive value $\beta w/(1 + \beta)$ for a unique value $k > 0$. But given a sequence of transfers (z_t), it is necessary to solve equation (3.4) in order to check at each step that the conditions on transfers are verified. These conditions require a net positive wage and a positive life-cycle income:

$$\omega(k_t) > \frac{z_t}{1 + n} \quad \Longleftrightarrow \quad z_t < (1 + n)A(1 - \alpha)k_t^{\alpha},$$

$$\omega(k_t) - \frac{z_t}{1 + n} + \frac{z_{t+1}}{f'(k_{t+1})} > 0.$$

The solution $k_{t+1} > 0$ automatically implies positive savings.

It is much simpler to analyze proportional taxes or transfers, with $a_t = \lambda_t w_t$ or $z_t = (1+n)\lambda_t w_t$. Equation (3.4) then becomes

$$(1+n)k_{t+1} = \frac{\beta}{1+\beta}(1-\lambda_t)w_t - \frac{(1+n)\lambda_{t+1}w_{t+1}}{(1+\beta)R_{t+1}},$$

$$(1+n)k_{t+1}\left(1 + \frac{(1-\alpha)\lambda_{t+1}}{(1+\beta)\alpha}\right) = \frac{\beta A(1-\alpha)(1-\lambda_t)}{1+\beta}k_t^\alpha.$$

The condition for a positive net wage is

$$\lambda_t < 1 \qquad \forall t.$$

For the sequence k_{t+1} to be defined and positive (positive savings), one needs

$$\lambda_{t+1} > -\frac{\alpha(1+\beta)}{1-\alpha}. \tag{3.5}$$

But, for savings to be defined, the life-cycle income should be positive, which implies

$$A(1-\alpha)k_t^\alpha(1-\lambda_t) + \frac{(1+n)\lambda_{t+1}(1-\alpha)}{\alpha}k_{t+1} > 0.$$

Substituting k_{t+1} and simplifying, one obtains

$$1 + (1-\alpha)\lambda_{t+1}\frac{\beta}{\alpha(1+\beta) + (1-\alpha)\lambda_{t+1}} > 0.$$

The condition (3.5) implies that the denominator is positive, and the last condition becomes[2]

$$\lambda_{t+1} > -\frac{\alpha}{1-\alpha}.$$

We note that this condition is more restrictive than (3.5), showing well the importance of taking into account the theoretical restrictions on individual behavior in addition to the existence of the solution of the dynamic equation of k.

The final conditions on transfers proportions do not depend on k_t:

$$-\frac{\alpha}{1-\alpha} < \lambda_t < 1 \qquad \forall t.$$

---

[2] This condition is equivalent in this model to imposing the positivity of $d_{t+1} = A\alpha k_{t+1}^\alpha(1+n) + z_{t+1} > 0$. This equivalence results from the relation $d_{t+1} = \frac{\beta}{1+\beta}R_{t+1}\Omega_t$ linking d_{t+1} and the life-cycle income Ω_t.

3.1.2 The Second Welfare Theorem

After having studied the inter-temporal equilibria when the households are subject to lump-sum transfers in the previous section, we analyze the decentralization of an optimal path by means of such transfers. Assuming both that an optimum policy exists and that it converges to a steady state, Atkinson and Sandmo (1980) show that a first-best allocation can be achieved if the government can use lump-sum taxes. We now express a proposition stating that any feasible trajectory that satisfies (2.7) can be decentralized as a competitive equilibrium. Applying this proposition to a Pareto-optimal trajectory leads to the Second Welfare Theorem.

Proposition 3.1 (Decentralization of feasible trajectories)
For any feasible allocation with positive quantities $(\check{c}_t, \check{d}_t, \check{k}_{t+1})_{t \geq 0}$ starting at $\check{k}_0 = k_0$, which satisfies for all $t \geq 0$

$$u'(\check{c}_t) = \beta f'(\check{k}_{t+1}) u'(\check{d}_{t+1}), \tag{3.6}$$

there exists a sequence of lump-sum transfers $(a_t)_{t \geq 0}$ such that this trajectory is an inter-temporal equilibrium with perfect foresight.

Proof: Let us define our transfers in the following way, for all $t \geq 0$:

$$\check{a}_t = \frac{\check{z}_t}{1+n} = \frac{\check{d}_t - f'(\check{k}_t)(1+n)\check{k}_t}{1+n},$$

which are the levels that allow the old people to consume $\check{d}_t$ at equilibrium. Using the resource constraint, this implies

$$\check{a}_t = f(\check{k}_t) - \check{c}_t - (1+n)\check{k}_{t+1} - f'(\check{k}_t)\check{k}_t,$$

and, with $\omega(k) = f(k) - k f'(k)$,

$$\check{a}_t = \omega(\check{k}_t) - \check{c}_t - (1+n)\check{k}_{t+1}.$$

Consider any date $t \geq 0$. At the given capital stock $\check{k}_t$, assume that the forecasts are $R^e_{t+1} = f'(\check{k}_{t+1})$ and $z^e_{t+1} = \check{z}_{t+1}$. The optimal choices c_t, d^e_{t+1}, and s_t of the households for period t are characterized by $\arg\max u(\omega(\check{k}_t) - \check{a}_t - s_t) + \beta u(\check{z}^e_{t+1} + R^e_{t+1} s_t)$, i.e.,

$$u'(c_t) = f'(\check{k}_{t+1}) \beta u'(d_{t+1}),$$

$$c_t = \omega(\check{k}_t) - \check{a}_t - s_t = \check{c}_t + (1+n)\check{k}_{t+1} - s_t,$$

$$d^e_{t+1} = \check{z}_{t+1} + f'(\check{k}_{t+1}) s_t = \check{d}_{t+1} + f'(\check{k}_{t+1})[s_t - (1+n)\check{k}_{t+1}].$$

The unique solution of the above system is $s_t = (1+n)\check{k}_{t+1}, c_t = \check{c}_t$, and $d_{t+1} = \check{d}_{t+1}$. The assumed forecasts are thus perfect. Since this holds for all dates, the given path is an inter-temporal equilibrium with perfect foresight. For the first old generation, $d_0 = (1+n)R_0 k_0 + \check{z}_0 = \check{d}_0$ by definition of $\check{z}_0$. ∎

Although section 3.1.1 showed that not every transfer is necessarily compatible with the existence of an inter-temporal equilibrium, the above proposition states that there always exist transfers to decentralize a feasible allocation that satisfy the arbitrage condition (3.6).

All Pareto-optimal trajectories are feasible and satisfy equation (3.6). As a consequence of the above proposition, any Pareto-optimal trajectory can be decentralized by the means of lump-sum taxes. As a particular case, the planner's problem can be decentralized.

Example: Let us compute the optimal transfer in the case of a log-linear utility function and a Cobb–Douglas production function. From chapter 2 (section 2.4.1), we know that the optimal path is characterized by

$$\check{d}_t = \frac{\beta(1+n)}{\gamma} \frac{1-\alpha\gamma}{1+\beta/\gamma} A\check{k}_t^\alpha,$$

$$\check{k}_{t+1} = \frac{\alpha\gamma}{1+n} A\check{k}_t^\alpha.$$

The transfer that ensures that the competitive d_t is equal to $\check{d}_t$ satisfies

$$d_t = (1+n)\check{R}_t\check{k}_t + \check{z}_t = \check{d}_t$$

with

$$\check{R}_t = \alpha A\check{k}_t^{\alpha-1}.$$

Hence, we have

$$\check{z}_t = \check{d}_t - (1+n)\check{R}_t\check{k}_t = A(1+n)\left(\frac{\beta(1-\alpha\gamma)}{\gamma+\beta} - \alpha\right)\check{k}_t^\alpha,$$

which gives the optimal transfer as a function of the installed capital stock. This transfer to the old is positive if and only if

$$\frac{\beta(1-\alpha\gamma)}{\gamma+\beta} > \alpha,$$

which is equivalent to

$$\gamma < \left(\frac{\beta}{1+\beta}\right)\left(\frac{1-\alpha}{\alpha}\right).$$

On the contrary, if γ is above this threshold, the optimal modified golden rule level is relatively high and requires positive transfers to the young to be implemented. To interpret this condition further, we consider the gross rate of return at the competitive steady-state without transfer (see section 1.6.2):

$$R = \alpha A k^{\alpha-1} = (1+n)\frac{\alpha(1+\beta)}{(1-\alpha)\beta}.$$

Thus transfers to the old are positive when the interest rate in the competitive economy without transfer is smaller than the modified golden rule interest factor:

$$R < R_\gamma = \frac{1+n}{\gamma},$$

or when $k > k_\gamma$, i.e., when the steady state capital of the competitive economy without transfer is larger than the modified golden rule level. Notice that, when there is over-accumulation of capital in the competitive economy (i.e., $R < 1 + n$), the transfers to the old are positive for all $\gamma \leq 1$.

In this example, the long-term condition gives the direction of transfers at every point along the trajectory. Indeed, the transfers are a constant proportion of income given by

$$\lambda_t = \frac{\tilde{z}_t}{(1+n)w_t} = \left(\frac{\beta(1-\alpha\gamma)}{\gamma + \beta} - \alpha \right) \frac{1}{1-\alpha}.$$

3.1.3 The Direction of Optimal Transfers in the Long Run

In general we can have more than one steady state in the competitive economy, and the direction of transfers can change along the trajectory. We study this issue in the case where the optimal steady state k_γ exists (assumption **A9**).

At steady state, we first notice that optimal transfers are nil if the private savings evaluated at the optimal wage $\omega(k_\gamma)$, and at the optimal interest rate $(1+n)/\gamma$ are equal to optimal investment $k_\gamma(1+n)$:

$$\check{a} = 0 \quad \Leftrightarrow \quad \tilde{s}\left(\omega(k_\gamma), 0, \frac{1+n}{\gamma} \right) = (1+n)k_\gamma.$$

The difference

$$\tilde{s}\left(\omega(k_\gamma) - a, (1+n)a, \frac{1+n}{\gamma} \right) - (1+n)k_\gamma$$

is decreasing in a. It is thus positive for $a < \check{a}$. Hence, $\check{a}$ is positive if and only if the function $\tilde{s} - (1+n)k$ evaluated at $a = 0$ is positive:

$$\check{a} > 0 \quad \Leftrightarrow \quad \tilde{s}\left(\omega(k_\gamma), 0, \frac{1+n}{\gamma} \right) = s\left(\omega(k_\gamma), \frac{1+n}{\gamma} \right) > (1+n)k_\gamma.$$

Hence, in the case of positive optimal transfer to the old at steady state ($\check{a} > 0$), we have $s(\cdot) > (1+n)k_\gamma$, which implies there exists a steady state in the competitive economy without transfer that is larger than the modified golden rule. Indeed, $s(\omega(k), f'(k)) - (1+n)k$ is positive for $k = k_\gamma$ and becomes negative for large k. As a consequence of the preceding property, if there is no steady state in the competitive economy larger than the modified golden

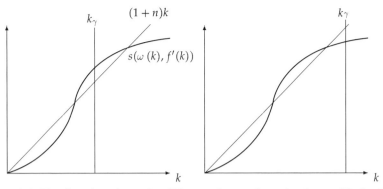

Figure 3.1. The direction of transfers. When savings evaluated at the modified golden rule are greater than $(1 + n)k$, the optimal transfers to the old are positive (left panel). When savings evaluated at the modified golden rule are smaller than $(1 + n)k$, the optimal transfers to the old are negative (right panel).

rule, the optimal transfer to the old should be negative. This is illustrated in figure 3.1.

3.1.4 Reversal of Optimal Transfers Over Time: An Example

We have seen in the previous section that in the example with Cobb–Douglas production, logarithmic utility, and full depreciation of capital, the optimal transfer is a constant proportion λ of wages. This implies that the direction of transfer is always the same along a trajectory. If we depart from these assumptions, however, the direction of transfer can change along the trajectory.

To illustrate this point in a numerical example, we assume that the depreciation rate of capital is no longer equal to one, but we keep the Cobb–Douglas production and the logarithmic utility. We rely on the numerical method of appendix A.5.4 to compute the optimal path. We take the following parameters: $\alpha = 1/3, \gamma = 0.43, \beta = 0.3, n = 1.025^{30} - 1, A = 20$. The value for γ has been chosen to have small transfers at steady state. Setting the initial capital stock equal to $k_0 = 1/3$, the optimal path is presented in table 3.1 for two different values of δ. Both the optimal stock of capital and the optimal transfer as a percentage of income of the young are presented. For $\delta = 1$, transfers are a constant proportion of income, in conformity with the result derived above. For $\delta = 0.5$, the optimal transfers are in favor of the old in the beginning of the growth process and are in favor of the young at the end.

The rationality behind the reversion of optimal transfers is as follows. At the competitive equilibrium, a lower depreciation rate increases the return from capital and leaves the wage income unchanged. Since the utility function is logarithmic, savings do not depend on the interest factor. Thus, a lower depreciation rate, which increases the return from capital, only affects positively the consumptions of the old households. The competitive path of capital without

Table 3.1. *Reversion in the Direction of Transfers*

Time	$\delta = 0.5$		$\delta = 1$	
t	Capital	Transfer rate λ_t	Capital	Transfer rate λ_t
0	0.33		0.33	
1	1.01	1.1%	0.95	2.8%
2	1.50	0.0%	1.34	2.8%
3	1.73	−1.0%	1.51	2.8%
4	1.82	−1.3%	1.57	2.8%
5	1.86	−1.5%	1.59	2.8%
∞	1.88	−1.6%	1.60	2.8%

transfer is not affected. For the optimal solution, this implies a direct effect on redistribution which decreases the optimal transfer to the old. In addition to this redistribution effect, there is a production effect modifying the whole optimal growth path; the higher level of gross production $\bar{F}(k_t, 1) + (1 - \delta)k_t$ leads to an increase of all consumptions and savings. In our example, the redistribution effect dominates with a significant drop in the transfer rate. Moreover, with a depreciation rate lower than one, the weight of profits relative to labor income increases with the capital stock. Indeed, we have

$$\frac{\mathrm{d}(Rk)}{\mathrm{d}k} = \alpha^2 Ak^{\alpha-1} + 1 - \delta, \qquad \frac{\mathrm{d}w}{\mathrm{d}k} = \alpha(1 - \alpha)Ak^{\alpha-1},$$

and

$$\frac{\mathrm{d}(Rk)}{\mathrm{d}w} = \frac{\alpha^2 A + (1 - \delta)k^{1-\alpha}}{\alpha(1 - \alpha)A}$$

increases with k for $\delta < 1$. Hence, in the long run, the low δ essentially benefits the old households in the future, which can consume the part of capital that is not depreciated. For the planner it is optimal to decrease the transfer rate as time passes. In our example, this implies that the direction of the transfer is reversed after some date.

3.2 PENSIONS

Overlapping generations models are an obviously appropriate setup to discuss the effect of the pension system on the accumulation of capital. Two different pension systems should be distinguished: in the fully funded system, the contributions paid by the young individual at time t are invested and returned with interest at time $t + 1$ to the same agent. In the pay-as-you-go system, the contributions paid by the young individual at time t are used to pay pensions to the contemporaneous old agents.

In his influential article, Samuelson (1975a) views pay-as-you-go pensions as lump-sum transfers that can lead a stationary economy to the golden rule.

Indeed, we have seen in the preceding section that if there is a steady state in the competitive economy larger than the golden rule (over-accumulation), the optimal transfer is a positive transfer to the old household. Interpreting this transfer as a pension, Samuelson's paper can be viewed as a positive theory of pensions. However, the empirical evidence in favor of the existence of over-accumulation is rather weak and controversial, which gives Samuelson's argument little weight.[3] This explains why many economists now argue against the existing pay-as-you-go pensions scheme and in favor of a transition towards fully funded systems.

In this section, we review the two main pension systems and provide analytical tools to study economic dynamics under pay-as-you-go pensions.

3.2.1 Fully Funded System

In the model of chapter 1, assume that there are lump-sum taxes a_t bearing on the young generation, and that these taxes are invested and returned with interest the next period. As a consequence, the capital stock of the economy consists in private savings plus the reserves of the pension system:

$$K_{t+1} = N_t s_t + N_t a_t.$$

For the generation born at time t, the first-period budget constraint is given by (3.1), and the second period budget constraint is

$$d_{t+1} = R^e_{t+1} s_t + R^e_{t+1} a_t.$$

The optimal savings of the representative individual are

$$s_t = \arg\max u(w_t - a_t - s_t) + \beta u\big(R^e_{t+1}(s_t + a_t)\big),$$

and thus verify for an interior solution

$$u'(w_t - a_t - s_t) = \beta R^e_{t+1} u'\big(R^e_{t+1}(s_t + a_t)\big).$$

The expression $s_t + a_t$ plays the same role as s_t in chapter 1, and optimal savings are given by

$$s_t = s\big(w_t, R^e_{t+1}\big) - a_t.$$

This equation shows that, at given capital stock, any increase in the contributions to the pension system is exactly offset by a decrease of the same amount in private savings, as long as expectations remain unaffected. The consumptions c_t and d^e_{t+1} are unchanged.

---

[3] In the presence of externalities, some authors have provided other mechanisms through which pensions can still be Pareto-improving. These mechanisms rely on the existence of negative externalities exerted by the old workers as in Sala-I-Martin (1996) or on financial market imcompleteness as in Diamond (1977).

Thus, as in the model of chapter 1, the temporary equilibrium with fully funded pensions exists and is unique. Notice that the first-period income $\omega(k_t) - a_t$ need not be positive as long as capital markets are perfect, allowing individuals to borrow against their pension rights, which would then entail negative private savings.

Investment $a_t + s_t$ is unchanged from chapter 1; likewise the next-period capital stock and the perfect foresight of the interest factor. The inter-temporal equilibrium with perfect foresight is obtained as a sequence of temporary equilibria by imposing the equality between savings and investment:

$$(1 + n)k_{t+1} = s_t + a_t,$$
$$= s(\omega(k_t), f'(k_{t+1})) > 0.$$

Hence, at the inter-temporal equilibrium with perfect foresight, the stock of capital of period $t + 1$ should verify the same implicit equation as in chapter 1, and the two equilibria are equivalent (Samuelson (1975a)).

Proposition 3.2 (Fully funded pensions)
Provided that capital markets are perfect, the fully funded pension system affects neither capital accumulation nor consumptions and welfare.

As the rate of return provided by the pension funds is equal to the one provided by private savings, the two forms of savings are perfect substitutes. Any change in contributions is perfectly offset by a change in private savings, and the aggregate capital stock is left unaffected.

In the above model, private savings $s_t = s(w_t, R_{t+1}) - a_t$ are negative if the pension rights are very high. In this case, the young individual borrows against his pension rights. If credit markets are imperfect (see section 1.8.7), future pension rights cannot be used as collateral. In this case, young individuals will not be able to borrow, and we should impose the additional constraint

$$s_t \geq 0.$$

In this case, the neutrality result can obviously break down. In a model with heterogeneous households, neutrality is obviously broken if at least one agent is constrained on capital markets (see Belan (1997)).

Let us finally remark that a fully funded system with perfect capital markets does not imply any transfer between individuals. In the case of heterogeneous households, we can introduce intra-generational transfers by breaking the link between individual contributions and pensions, in which case the fully funded system will no longer be neutral.

3.2.2 Pay-as-you-go System: Existence of Equilibrium

The equilibrium with a pay-as-you-go pension system is equivalent to the economy with positive lump-sum transfers. We consider a sequence of transfers to the old households $(a_t)_{t \geq 0}$ such that

$$z_t = (1+n)a_t \geq 0 \qquad \forall t.$$

An inter-temporal equilibrium with perfect foresight starting at k_0 is characterized by a sequence $(k_t)_{t \geq 0}$, which verifies, for all t, $k_t > 0$ and

$$\tilde{\Delta}_t(k_t, k_{t+1}) = (1+n)k_{t+1} - \tilde{s}(\omega(k_t) - a_t, (1+n)a_{t+1}, f'(k_{t+1})) = 0. \quad (3.7)$$

At such an equilibrium, savings are necessarily positive and hence the first-period income is positive:

$$\forall t, \qquad \omega(k_t) > a_t. \quad (3.8)$$

Equation (3.8) is thus a necessary condition for the existence of the inter-temporal equilibrium k_t.

Contrary to the general case of lump-sum transfers studied in the previous section, the function $\tilde{\Delta}_t(k_t, k_{t+1})$ is necessarily defined for a sequence $k_t > 0$ that verifies (3.8), as the life-cycle income

$$\omega(k_t) - a_t + \frac{(1+n)a_{t+1}}{f'(k_{t+1})}$$

is positive. This results from equation (3.8) and from the hypothesis of positive transfers to the old, $a_{t+1} \geq 0$.

The central issue is now to study the sustainability of a given pension policy. A policy (a_t) is said to be *sustainable* if the corresponding inter-temporal equilibrium exists. A policy which leads to a point in time where the income of the workers is negative is not sustainable. We shall associate to a given policy a threshold $\underline{k}(a)$ on the initial capital stock above which the policy is sustainable. We will call it the smallest sustainable initial capital. If the economy has $k_t < \underline{k}(a)$, it is led to a situation where taxes will become larger than the income of the young households.

To analyze the issue of sustainability, we first introduce a lemma stating that if, for an arbitrary path of capital, savings are always higher than or equal to the investment needed to sustain this path, then there necessarily exists an intertemporal equilibrium with a trajectory of capital higher than the arbitrary path.

Lemma 3.1
We $(k_t)_{t \geq 0}$ be a sequence with $\tilde{\Delta}_t(k_t, k_{t+1}) \leq 0$ and $\omega(k_t) > a_t$, $\forall t \geq 0$. Taking $k'_0 \geq k_0$, there exists an inter-temporal equilibrium $(k'_t)_{t \geq 0}$, such that $k'_t \geq k_t$ holds $\forall t$.

Proof: The proof is by induction. Assume $k'_t \geq k_t$ (which holds at $t = 0$). As $\tilde{\Delta}_t(k_t, k_{t+1}) \leq 0$ and $\tilde{\Delta}_t$ is decreasing with respect to its first argument (the derivative is $-\tilde{s}'_{\omega_1}\omega' < 0$), we have $\tilde{\Delta}_t(k'_t, k_{t+1}) \leq 0$. Moreover, $\tilde{\Delta}_t(k'_t, k)$, which is defined for $k > 0$, verifies

$$\lim_{k \to +\infty} \tilde{\Delta}_t(k'_t, k) = +\infty,$$

as $\tilde{s}$ is bounded above by $\omega(k'_t) - a_t$. We deduce by continuity that there exists $k'_{t+1} \geq k_{t+1}$ such that $\tilde{\Delta}_t(k'_t, k'_{t+1}) = 0$. This argument can be applied by induction for all $t \geq 0$. ∎

We now define the lowest sustainable initial capital and show in the next proposition that it determines a threshold above which an inter-temporal equilibrium exists.

Definition 3.3 (Lowest sustainable initial capital)
Given $(a_t)_{t \geq 0}$, the lowest sustainable initial capital stock $\underline{k}$ is the lower bound of the set of initial capital stock such that there exists an inter-temporal equilibrium:

$$\underline{k} = \inf\{k_0 > 0; \text{ there exists } (k_t)_{t \geq 0} \text{ solution to (3.7)}\}.$$

When for all $k_0 > 0$ there exists no solution $(k_t)_{t \geq 0}$ to (3.7), we define $\underline{k} = +\infty$.

Proposition 3.3 (Existence of inter-temporal equilibrium with pensions)
For all $k_0 > \underline{k}$, there exists an inter-temporal equilibrium with initial capital stock k_0. For all $k_0 > 0$ such that $k_0 < \underline{k}$, there exists no inter-temporal equilibrium with initial capital stock k_0.

Proof: The non-existence for $k_0 < \underline{k}$ results from the definition of $\underline{k}$.

Let us take $k'_0 > \underline{k}$. We show that there always exists an inter-temporal equilibrium starting at k'_0. Indeed, by definition[4] of $\underline{k}$ there exists another k_0 such that $\underline{k} \leq k_0 < k'_0$, and there exists $(k_t)_{t \geq 0}$ starting from k_0 solution to (3.7): $\tilde{\Delta}_t(k_t, k_{t+1}) = 0 \; \forall t$. Then, following Lemma 3.1, there exists an inter-temporal equilibrium $(k'_t)_{t \geq 0}$ starting at k'_0 for which $k'_t \geq k_t \; \forall t$. ∎

3.2.3 Pay-as-you-go Systems with Constant Pensions

To obtain further results on competitive equilibria with pensions, we consider the case of a constant transfer $z = (1 + n)a > 0$ and study its effect on the lowest sustainable capital. We look at the inter-temporal equilibrium with perfect foresight starting at k_0, i.e., the solution to

$$\Delta_a(k_t, k_{t+1}) = (1+n)k_{t+1} - \tilde{s}(\omega(k_t) - a, (1+n)a, f'(k_{t+1})) = 0. \quad (3.9)$$

---

[4] Given that $\underline{k}$ is the lower bound of a set, there exists $k_0 < k'_0$ belonging to this set.

We denote by $\underline{k}(a)$ the lower bound of the set of sustainable initial capital stocks. With constant transfers, we have the additional property that the equilibrium trajectory will remain above $\underline{k}(a)$: $\forall t, k_t \geq \underline{k}(a)$. Indeed, if $k_t < \underline{k}(a)$ for some t, then the sequence starting from t is a solution to (3.9), which is excluded by the definition of $\underline{k}(a)$. Let us now characterize the function $\underline{k}(a)$.

Proposition 3.4 (Lowest sustainable initial capital and pensions)
The lowest sustainable initial capital $\underline{k}(a)$ is non-decreasing with respect to a.

Proof: Let $a_1 < a_2$. If $\underline{k}(a_2) = +\infty$, we obviously have $\underline{k}(a_1) \leq \underline{k}(a_2)$.

If $\underline{k}(a_2)$ is finite, let us consider $k > \underline{k}(a_2)$. Then there exists an inter-temporal equilibrium $(k_t)_{t \geq 0}$ with $\Delta_{a_2}(k_t, k_{t+1}) = 0$ and $k_0 = k$. As $\Delta_a(k_t, k_{t+1})$ is an increasing function of a (its derivative is $\tilde{s}'_{\omega_1} - (1+n)\tilde{s}'_{\omega_2} > 0$), we have $\forall t \geq 0$

$$\Delta_{a_1}(k_t, k_{t+1}) < 0.$$

We can apply Lemma 3.1 at $k'_0 = k_0 = k$: there exists an inter-temporal equilibrium with $\Delta_{a_1}(k'_t, k'_{t+1}) = 0$ $\forall t$. Hence, we deduce that $\underline{k}(a_1) \leq k$. We have shown $k > \underline{k}(a_2) \Rightarrow k \geq \underline{k}(a_1)$, which implies $\underline{k}(a_2) \geq \underline{k}(a_1)$. ∎

Notice that, as we shall see in the next example, the function $\underline{k}(a)$ is not necessarily continuous. The function $\underline{k}(a)$ can now be used to prove that there is a highest sustainable transfer above which no equilibrium exists.

Proposition 3.5 (Highest sustainable transfer)
There exists a finite threshold $\bar{a} \geq 0$,

$$\bar{a} = \sup\{a \geq 0; \ \underline{k}(a) \text{ is finite}\},$$

such that for $a < \bar{a}$, $\underline{k}(a)$ is finite, and for $a > \bar{a}$, $\underline{k}(a)$ is equal to $+\infty$, i.e., no inter-temporal equilibrium exists.

Proof: We first prove that $\underline{k}(a)$ is $+\infty$ for large a. There exists $\bar{k}$ such that $\forall k \geq \bar{k}$, $\omega(k) \leq (1+n)k$, since $\lim_{k \to +\infty} \omega(k)/k = 0$. We shall show that for $a = \omega(\bar{k})$ we have $\underline{k}(a) = +\infty$. We use a reductio ad absurdum: assume that there exists an inter-temporal equilibrium (k_t) with transfer $a = \omega(\bar{k})$ $(\omega(\bar{k})$ is the maximum long-run feasible wage, i.e., when wage income is entirely invested):

$$(1+n)k_{t+1} = \tilde{s}(\omega(k_t) - a, (1+n)a, f'(k_{t+1})).$$

We have then $\omega(k_t) > a = \omega(\bar{k})$, $k_t > \bar{k}$, and $\omega(k_t) < (1+n)k_t$ by definition of $\bar{k}$. Thus, we have

$$(1+n)k_{t+1} < \omega(k_t) - a < \omega(k_t) < (1+n)k_t,$$

which implies $k_{t+1} < k_t$. The sequence k_t is decreasing and admits a limit $k_\infty \geq \bar{k}$, since $\forall t, \ k_t > \bar{k}$. This limit verifies $\omega(k_\infty) \leq (1+n)k_\infty$, and

$$(1+n)k_\infty = \tilde{s}(\omega(k_\infty) - a, (1+n)a, f'(k_\infty)) < \omega(k_\infty) - a$$
$$\leq (1+n)k_\infty - a,$$

which is impossible. Thus, $\underline{k}(a) = +\infty$ for $a = \omega(\bar{k})$ and for $a \geq \omega(\bar{k})$. As a consequence, $\bar{a} < \omega(\bar{k})$.

By definition of the bound $\bar{a}$, we have for $a > \bar{a}$, $\underline{k}(a) = +\infty$. For $a < \bar{a}$, $\exists a', \ a < a' \leq \bar{a}$, such that $\underline{k}(a')$ is finite. Then, as $\underline{k}(a)$ is non-decreasing, $\underline{k}(a) \leq \underline{k}(a') < +\infty$, and $\underline{k}(a)$ is finite. ∎

We now introduce assumption **H3a**, which corresponds to **H3** without transfers and ensures that the inter-temporal equilibrium is unique. This assumption is made for a given $a > 0$, such that $\underline{k}(a)$ is finite.

Assumption H3a.
For all $k, \ k' > 0$ such that $k \geq \underline{k}(a)$ and $k' \geq \underline{k}(a)$,

$$\Delta_a(k, k') = 0 \quad \Longrightarrow \quad \frac{\partial \Delta_a(k, k')}{\partial k'} > 0,$$

with

$$\Delta_a(k, k') = (1+n)k' - \tilde{s}(\omega(k) - a, (1+n)a, f'(k')).$$

Notice that **H3a** holds under the assumption **A4**:

$$\frac{\partial \Delta_a(k, k')}{\partial k'} = 1 + n - \tilde{s}'_R f'' > 1 + n - s'_R f'' = \Delta'_k > 0 \qquad \text{for} \quad s'_R \geq 0.$$

By definition, we know that there is no trajectory starting to the left of $\underline{k}(a)$. Under **H3a** it is moreover possible to show that $\underline{k}(a)$ is the smallest positive steady state (see figure 3.2).

Proposition 3.6 (Smallest steady state)
*Under assumption **H3a**, when $\underline{k}(a)$ is positive and finite, it is the smallest positive steady state of the dynamics (3.9).*

Proof: Every positive steady state $k^\star$ verifies $\Delta_a(k^\star, k^\star) = 0$. Then there exists an inter-temporal equilibrium $k_t = k^\star$ for all $t \geq 0$, and thus $k^\star \geq \underline{k}(a)$.

Let us consider a sequence of initial conditions $k_{0i} > \underline{k}(a)$ which converges to the lowest sustainable initial capital: $\lim_{i \to \infty} k_{0i} = \underline{k}(a)$. For each of these initial conditions, there exists an equilibrium $(k_{ti})_{t \geq 0}$, and thus $\Delta_a(k_{0i}, k_{1i}) = 0$ with $k_{1i} \geq \underline{k}(a)$. To show that $\underline{k}(a)$ is a steady state it is sufficient to show that the sequence $(k_{1i})_{t \geq 0}$ converges to $\underline{k}(a)$ when i goes to infinity. This sequence

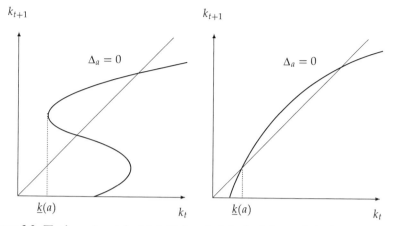

Figure 3.2. The lowest sustainable initial capital: In the left panel, the lowest sustainable initial capital is represented in a case where **H3a** does not hold. In the right panel, **H3a** holds and the lowest sustainable initial capital is the smallest steady state.

is bounded because $(1 + n)k_{1i} < \omega(k_{0i}) - a$ and admits a limit point k_1 which verifies $\Delta_a(\underline{k}(a), k_1) = 0$.

We next show by a reductio ad absurdum that $k_1 > \underline{k}(a)$ is not possible. If $k_1 > \underline{k}(a)$, then the assumption **H3a** implies that there exists k_1', $\underline{k}(a) < k_1' < k_1$, such that $\Delta_a(\underline{k}(a), k_1') < 0$, because Δ_a is increasing near k_1 in its second argument. By continuity we have $\Delta_a(k_0', k_1') < 0$ for $k_0' < \underline{k}(a)$, k_0' near enough $\underline{k}(a)$. Moreover, there exists $k_1'' > k_1' > \underline{k}(a)$ such that $\Delta(k_0', k_1'') = 0$. As $k_1'' > \underline{k}(a)$, there exists an inter-temporal equilibrium starting from k_1'', and, as $\Delta(k_0', k_1'') = 0$, there exists also an inter-temporal equilibrium starting from k_0', which contradicts $k_0' < \underline{k}(a)$. Hence,

$$\Delta_a(\underline{k}(a), \underline{k}(a)) = 0,$$

and $\underline{k}(a)$ is the smallest positive steady state. ∎

Concerning the local stability of the smallest steady state we have the following result: as there exists no inter-temporal path starting from $k_0 < \underline{k}(a)$, the steady state $\underline{k}(a)$ is necessarily unstable from the left. But it may happen, when $\underline{k}(a)$ is non-hyperbolic, that the steady state is stable from the right. $\underline{k}(a)$ is thus either unstable (right panel of figure 3.2) or non-hyperbolic with stability on the right-hand side (figure 3.3).

We illustrate the above results in the following example.

Example: Let us take a logarithmic utility function and a Cobb–Douglas production function. The dynamics are given by equation (3.4):

$$\Delta_a(k_t, k_{t+1}) = (1 + n)k_{t+1} - \frac{\beta}{1 + \beta}\left[(1 - \alpha)Ak_t^\alpha - a\right] + \frac{(1 + n)a}{(1 + \beta)\alpha A}k_{t+1}^{1-\alpha}.$$

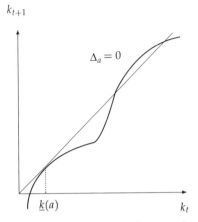

Figure 3.3. Non-hyperbolic smallest steady state.

For $a > 0$ we have $a > \omega(0) = 0$, and the lowest sustainable initial capital $\underline{k}(a) > 0$ is finite or equal to $+\infty$. Either there exists at least one steady state and $\underline{k}(a)$ is the smallest one, or there does not exist a steady state and there is no inter-temporal equilibrium with pension a. The steady states are solutions to $\Delta_a(k, k) = 0$:

$$a = \frac{\beta(1 - \alpha)Ak^\alpha - (1 + \beta)(1 + n)k}{\beta + \frac{1+n}{\alpha A}k^{1-\alpha}} \equiv \tilde{a}(k).$$

The function $\tilde{a}(k)$ is defined and continuous on $\mathbb{R}_+$, and $\tilde{a}(k) > 0$ for

$$0 < k < \left(\frac{\beta(1 - \alpha)A}{(1 + \beta)(1 + n)}\right)^{\frac{1}{1-\alpha}}.$$

Its derivative $\tilde{a}'(k)$ has the sign of

$$\alpha\beta^2(1 - \alpha)Ak^{\alpha-1} - \beta(1 + n)\left(\alpha + \beta + \frac{(1 - \alpha)^2}{\alpha}\right) - \frac{(1 + \beta)(1 + n)^2}{A}k^{1-\alpha},$$

which is decreasing in k from $+\infty$ to $-\infty$. Hence the derivative of $\tilde{a}(k)$ is equal to zero for some $\bar{k} > 0$, and $\tilde{a}(k)$ attains there a maximum $\bar{a}$. Given these elements, we deduce that for $0 < a < \bar{a}$ there are two steady states $\underline{k}(a)$ and $\bar{k}(a)$, which are solutions to $\tilde{a}(k) = a$ and, which verify $0 < \underline{k}(a) < \bar{k}(a)$. For $a = \bar{a}$ there exists a unique steady state $\bar{k}$, and we have $\underline{k}(\bar{a}) = \bar{k}$. For $a > \bar{a}$ there is no steady state and hence no inter-temporal equilibrium. The point $\bar{a}$ is called a tangent bifurcation (see appendix A.3.5). Figure 3.4 presents the bifurcation diagram for the parameter a.

The interpretation of the tangent bifurcation point in terms of sustainability is clear: pensions greater than $\bar{a}$ are never sustainable, whatever the initial stock of capital. Pensions a smaller than $\bar{a}$ are sustainable provided that the

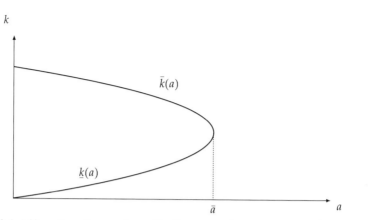

Figure 3.4. Bifurcation diagram for a: For $0 < a < \bar{a}$ there are two steady states $\underline{k}(a)$ and $\bar{k}(a)$. For $a = \bar{a}$ there exists a unique steady state $\bar{k}$. For $a > \bar{a}$ there is no steady state. The point $\bar{a}$ is called a tangent bifurcation.

economy is endowed with an initial capital larger than $\underline{k}(a)$. A numerical example is provided in appendix A.5.3.

To be able to further analyze the effect of pensions on equilibrium we introduce the following definition.

Definition 3.4 (Pension–capital compatibility set)
The compatibility set $\mathcal{D}_p$ is the set of pairs (k, a) such that there exists an inter-temporal equilibrium with transfer a and initial capital k.

In formal terms, the set $\mathcal{D}_p$ is such that $a \geq 0$, $\underline{k}(a)$ is finite, $k > 0$, and $k \geq \underline{k}(a)$:

$$\mathcal{D}_p = \{(k, a) \in \mathbb{R}_+^2; \ k > 0 \text{ and } k \geq \underline{k}(a)\}.$$

For $k > \underline{k}(a)$, this results from proposition 3.3. Assuming **H3a**, for $k = \underline{k}(a) > 0$, $\underline{k}(a)$ is the smallest positive steady state (proposition 3.6), and this implies that there exists an inter-temporal equilibrium with initial stock $\underline{k}(a)$.

A property of $\mathcal{D}_p$ is the following one: for a pair (k, a) belonging to $\mathcal{D}_p$, we have that any pair (k', a') with higher capital and/or lower transfer, i.e. $k' \geq k$ and $a' \leq a$, also belongs to $\mathcal{D}_p$. Indeed, according to proposition 3.4, $\underline{k}(a') \leq \underline{k}(a)$ and thus $k' \geq k \geq \underline{k}(a) \geq \underline{k}(a')$.

Proposition 3.7 (Uniqueness of trajectories)
*Assume **H1**, **H2**, and **H3a** for all a such that $\underline{k}(a)$ is finite. Then, for any (k_0, a) belonging to the compatibility set $\mathcal{D}_p$, there exists a unique inter-temporal equilibrium with pension a and initial capital stock k_0. This equilibrium is characterized*

by the sequence of capital stocks k_t defined by the difference equation

$$\Delta_a(k_t, k_{t+1}) = 0 \quad \Leftrightarrow \quad k_{t+1} = g(k_t, a).$$

The function g is defined in $\mathcal{D}_p$ and is increasing with respect to k_t and decreasing with respect to a. It is continuously differentiable at any interior point of $\mathcal{D}_p$, and its partial derivatives verify $g'_k > 0$ and $g'_a < 0$.

Proof: g is defined: By definition, for $(k_0, a) \in \mathcal{D}_p$, there exists one inter-temporal equilibrium with transfers, $(k_t)_{t \geq 0}$, with initial stock k_0. We thus have $\Delta_a(k_0, k_1) = 0$, and the solution $k_1 = g(k_0, a)$ of $\Delta_a(k_0, k_1) = 0$ is unique fol-lowing assumption **H3a**.

g is increasing in k: For $k'_0 > k_0$, we have $\Delta_a(k'_0, k_1) < 0$, as Δ_a is decreas-ing with respect to its first argument. Moreover, as $\lim_{k \to +\infty} \Delta_a(k'_0, k) = +\infty$, there exists $k'_1 > k_1$ such that $\Delta_a(k'_0, k'_1) = 0$. The uniqueness of this solution (assumption **H3a**) implies $g(k'_0, a) = k'_1 > k_1 = g(k_0, a)$.

g is decreasing in a: Similarly, for $a' < a$ we have $\Delta_{a'}(k_0, k_1) < 0$, as Δ_a is increasing with respect to a, and we deduce that $g(k_0, a') > k_1 = g(k_0, a)$.

g is differentiable: Finally, at the interior of $\mathcal{D}_p$ we may apply the implicit function theorem to equation $\Delta_a(k_t, k_{t+1}) = 0$ and deduce by differentiation the sign of the partial derivatives of $g(k_t, a)$.   ∎

The function g allows to characterize the inter-temporal equilibrium with transfer a. The dynamics of k_t are monotone and bounded. They converge either to 0, which is possible only if $\underline{k}(a) = 0$, or to a steady state.

3.2.4 Capital Accumulation and Pay-as-you-go Pensions

As already stressed in Feldstein (1974), the most obvious effect of the pay-as-you-go pension system is to reduce the amount of savings during the working years by providing income during retirement. This standard partial equilib-rium result at given prices is derived at the temporary equilibrium by com-puting a simultaneous shift in current taxes and in the expected future pen-sion, $dz^e_{t+1} = (1 + n) da_t$, but with fixed expectations on the interest factor $dR^e_{t+1} = 0$.

Proposition 3.8 (Individual savings and pay-as-you-go pensions)
Consider a temporary equilibrium with a pay-as-you-go pension system and fixed expectations of R^e_{t+1}. A simultaneous drop in the expected future pension z^e_{t+1} and in contributions a_t, with $dz^e_{t+1} = (1 + n) da_t$, increases private savings. It increases private savings more (less) than proportionally if the expected interest factor is smaller (larger) than the growth factor of the population.

Proof: Savings are given by

$$s_t = \tilde{s}\left(w_t - a_t, z^e_{t+1}, R^e_{t+1}\right),$$

and we have

$$ds_t = -\tilde{s}'_{\omega_1}\, da_t + \tilde{s}'_{\omega_2}\, dz^e_{t+1},$$

$$ds_t = -\tilde{s}'_{\omega_1}\, da_t + \tilde{s}'_{\omega_2}(1+n)\, da_t,$$

$$\frac{ds_t}{da_t} = -s'_w + (s'_w - 1)\frac{1+n}{R^e_{t+1}} < 0.$$

Moreover,

$$\frac{ds_t}{da} < -1 \quad \Longleftrightarrow \quad (1-s'_w)\frac{1+n}{R^e_{t+1}} > 1 - s'_w \quad \Longleftrightarrow \quad R^e_{t+1} < 1+n. \qquad \blacksquare$$

The above result concerns the partial equilibrium effect of pensions on savings. It is consistent with the empirical finding that countries that operate unfunded pay-as-you-go systems tend to have lower savings rates, the magnitude of the effect increasing with the degree of coverage for the system (see Samwick (2000)). To analyze the general equilibrium effect on capital accumulation, we have the following proposition, illustrated in figure 3.5:

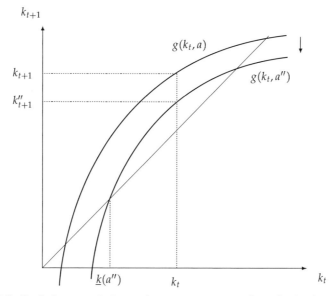

Figure 3.5. Capital accumulation and pay-as-you-go pensions: In the face of a permanent increase in pensions at time t, the new equilibrium path, if it exists, displays lower capital than the previous one.

Proposition 3.9 (Capital accumulation and pay-as-you-go pensions)
Assume that **H1**, **H2**, *and* **H3a** *hold for all a. For* (k_0, a) *belonging to the compatibility set* $\mathcal{D}_p$, *there exists a unique inter-temporal equilibrium* $(k_t)_{t \geq 0}$ *starting at* k_0 *with constant pensions a and with long-run capital stock* $\lim k_t = k$.

- *Following a drop in a, with* $a' < a$, *the inter-temporal equilibrium* $(k'_t)_{t \geq 0}$ *starting at* k_0 *verifies* $k'_t > k_t \; \forall t \geq 1$. *Moreover, provided that* $k > 0$, *long-run capital stocks are such that* $k' > k$.
- *Following a rise in a,* $a'' > a$, *either there is an inter-temporal equilibrium* $(k''_t)_{t \geq 0}$ *starting at* k_0 *which verifies* $k''_t < k_t \; \forall t \geq 1$ *(case* $(k_0, a'') \in \mathcal{D}_p$*), or there no longer exists an inter-temporal equilibrium with initial capital stock* k_0 *(case* $(k_0, a'') \notin \mathcal{D}_p$*).*

Proof: For $a' < a$, one has $(k_0, a') \in \mathcal{D}_g$ and the sequence (k'_t) with initial capital $k'_0 = k_0$ verifies $k'_{t+1} = g(k'_t, a'_t) \geq g(k_t, a'_t) > g(k_t, a_t) = k_{t+1}$.

Moreover, if the limit of (k_t) is positive ($\lim k_t = k > 0$), then k is a steady state of the dynamics with a: $\Delta_a(k, k) = 0$. As $\lim k'_t = k' \geq k$, we have $\Delta_{a'}(k', k') = 0$. The equality $k = k'$ is excluded, as $\Delta_{a'}(k, k) < 0$.

The same argument applies to a'' if $(k_0, a'') \in \mathcal{D}_g$. But if $\underline{k}(a'') > k_0$, there exists no inter-temporal equilibrium with a''. ∎

The effect of pensions on welfare is an interesting issue for economic policy. The negative effect of pensions on capital plays a different role depending on whether there is over- or under-accumulation. On the one hand, consider a steady state equilibrium that is characterized by over-accumulation of capital. Following a small rise in a, the new steady state equilibrium, provided that it exists and that it is still characterized by over-accumulation, will display a higher welfare. The increase in the pensions reduces the stock of capital, which is beneficial when the equilibrium is inefficient. On the other hand, when the equilibrium is efficient, the introduction of pensions always benefits the first old generations at the expense of subsequent generations.

3.2.5 Further Comments

We mention in this subsection some relevant debates on pensions and possible extensions.

A Quick Look at the Empirical Literature. From the empirical side, two findings are in line with theoretical results.

First, in his positive theory of social security, Sala-I-Martin (1996) stresses that retirement programs are introduced only after a certain level of development has been reached. This appears clearly in figure 3.6, where we show the GDP per capita at the time of the introduction of the first pension system for selected countries (viz. those for which the GDP is available in Maddison (1992) and for which retirement is necessary according to Sala-I-Martin (1996)).

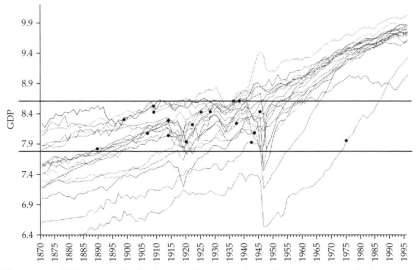

Figure 3.6. GDP per capita in the world and pensions. Dots represents the introduction of pension systems. Retirement programs are introduced only after a certain level of development has been reached.

Second, the literature suggests that the effect of social security transfers on capital accumulation is negative. Indeed, by providing income during retirement, they reduce private savings. In addition to the *saving replacement effect* of pension systems inducing a reduction in personal savings, some authors (e.g., Feldstein (1974)) emphasize a second effect that tends to increase savings: the *induced retirement effect*. Social security may lead individuals to retire earlier and to increase savings during working life to finance the longer retirement period. This could offset the negative effect of social security on private savings. The evidence shows however that capital accumulation is still reduced by social security. Feldstein (1996) estimates that the social security programs in the U.S. reduce overall savings by nearly 60% of their potential.

Pensions with Endogenous Growth. In models where externalities and growth come from physical capital accumulation, pensions reduce savings, whereas the contrary would be needed to correct the externality.

In endogenous growth models with constant social returns to capital (as in section 2.6.5) and externalities, Saint-Paul (1992) shows that it is no longer possible to make a case for public pensions as a Pareto-improving policy. This is because an increase in pensions has no effect on the gap between private and social interest rates. Instead, it reduces the growth rate and, hence, hurts future generations. As long as a pension affects savings negatively, an increase in it has a negative effect on growth and on the welfare of some future generations. This result will remain true even if the pension affects the interest rate. In a very particular case, external effects are so strong that the social marginal productivity is increasing (see Weil (1994)).

The Transition to a Fully Funded System. The transition from a pay-as-you-go pension system to a fully funded system is a widely debated issue. The central point of the debate is how to compensate the last generation that paid the contributions to finance the pension of the previous generation for the fact that they will not receive a pension in exchange.

Clearly, if under-accumulation of capital prevails, the competitive equilibrium with lump-sum transfer (pensions) is Pareto-optimal. Indeed, starting from a Pareto-optimal situation, any lump-sum redistribution of incomes entails an allocation which is different but also Pareto-efficient as long as we remain in the under-accumulation regime. It is thus not possible to set up a Pareto-improving transition to a fully funded system (see Breyer (1989)).

Some authors have analyzed this issue introducing a source of inefficiency. In this case, if the transition to a fully funded system is accompanied by other measures that correct the inefficiency, it is possible to build Pareto-improving transitions. This can be done in a framework with endogenous labor supply and proportional income taxation, in which case pension systems introduce a distortion (see Homburg (1990)). This can also be done in a setup with endogenous growth, as in Belan, Michel, and Pestieau (1998). Notice however that in this case the pension problem is artificially connected to the existence of some inefficiencies (externalities in the case of endogenous growth). These imperfections should be corrected in any case, whether there is a transition or not.

Application: Rise in β. In the application of section 2.6.3 we have seen that, in face of a rise in the individual discount factor, the planner has no reason to modify the tradeoff between the welfare of the different generations. He will thus leave the stock of capital unchanged, but simply reallocate production between the young and the old households. As the capital stock of the competitive economy is increased by the rise in β, the optimal policy will consist in increasing the tax on young households immediately after the shock and redistributing the product to the old generation. This permits increasing the consumption of the old generation instantaneously. Furthermore, this optimal tax level is kept constant in the future, and there is no additional dynamic effect. This example shows that the optimal policy in the face of a rise in the discount factor is to increase the pensions paid to the old individuals. This illustrates again how the debate on pensions can be related to the decentralization of the optimal allocation.

Proportional Payroll Taxes. In the previous section, we have followed the usual approach of macroeconomic textbooks, which treats pensions as lump-sum transfers (Blanchard and Fischer (1989), McCandless and Wallace (1991),

Azariadis (1993), Auerbach and Kotlikoff (1995)). In the literature on pensions in public finance it is often (realistically) assumed that payroll taxes are proportional to the wage income (see, e.g., Feldstein (1985)). This amounts to imposing

$$a_t = \lambda_t w_t,$$

where λ_t is the social security contribution rate. It is often thought than the two formulations are equivalent as long as there is no endogenous labor supply, in which case proportional taxation does not introduce any distortion. However, from the standpoint of inter-temporal equilibrium, the two formulations are not equivalent when the path of taxes λ_t or a_t has been fixed, as the transfer payments under proportional taxation become endogenous. Nevertheless, once the equilibrium with λ_t has been computed, it is always possible to compute the a_t, which would give the same equilibrium.

The Optimal Retirement Age. A further extension of the model is to allow for endogenous retirement decision. In this case, the households optimally select the share of their time in the second period of life that is devoted to retirement. Hu (1979) shows that if the transfers are tied to the individual retirement decision, the pension system introduces some distortions into the labor supply choice. Michel and Pestieau (1999) compare the decentralized equilibrium with the golden rule and show that in order to achieve the steady state first-best optimum, one needs to control both an unrestricted pay-as-you-go transfer and the retirement age. This analysis is generalized to a wider class of utility functions and to transitional dynamics by de la Croix, Mahieu, and Rillaers (2001).

3.3 PUBLIC SPENDING

Governments, through the importance of their spending, play a significant role in the economic activity. The twentieth century has experienced a massive increase in the government's role in the economy (see the data in Maddison (1992)). The effect of public spending on growth is thus a natural question to address. In this chapter, we limit our investigation to balanced budget policies. Debt financing will be analyzed in the next chapter.

3.3.1 Public Spending in the Competitive Economy

We extend the model of chapter 1 and assume that there are lump-sum taxes a_t bearing on the young generation, and that these taxes are used to finance an amount g_t of public spending per young individual. Such public spending is unproductive, so that it does not affect the production function. Moreover, it does not affect the marginal utility of consumptions. As in the lump-sum transfer case, a_t should remain smaller that the income of the young. For the generation born at time t, the first-period budget constraint is given by (3.1). The second-period budget constraint is not affected.

The budget of the government should remain balanced:

$$N_t a_t = N_t g_t \iff g_t = a_t.$$

Thus, the optimal savings of the representative individual are given by

$$s_t = \arg \max u(w_t - g_t - s_t) + \beta u(R^e_{t+1} s_t).$$

This leads to

$$s_t = s(w_t - g_t, R^e_{t+1}).$$

The effect of the tax on savings is negative, and is given by

$$\frac{\partial s_t}{\partial g_t} = -s'_w, \quad \text{with} \quad 0 < s'_w < 1.$$

The temporary equilibrium with government spending exists and is unique if the first-period income is positive:

$$\omega(k_t) - g_t > 0,$$

which can be read as a condition on g_t. The inter-temporal equilibrium with perfect foresight is obtained as a sequence of temporary equilibria by imposing the equality between R^e_{t+1} and $f'(k_{t+1})$ and between savings and next-period capital.

Definition 3.5 (Inter-temporal equilibrium with public spending)
Given an initial capital stock K_0 and a sequence of public spending $(g_t)_{t \geq 0}$, an intertemporal equilibrium with perfect foresight and public spending is a sequence of temporary equilibria that satisfies, for all $t \geq 0$,

$$(1 + n)k_{t+1} = s\left(\omega(k_t) - g_t, R^e_{t+1}\right) > 0,$$

$$k_0 = K_0/N_{-1},$$

$$R^e_{t+1} = R_{t+1} = f'(k_{t+1}).$$

We limit our analysis to constant public spending policies $g_t = g \; \forall t$. At the inter-temporal equilibrium with perfect foresight, the stock of capital of period $t + 1$ should verify the implicit equation $\Delta_g(k_t, k_{t+1}) = 0$ with

$$\Delta_g(k_t, k_{t+1}) = (1 + n)k_{t+1} - s(\omega(k_t) - g, f'(k_{t+1})),$$

which is defined for $\omega(k_t) > g$.

To analyze the existence of such inter-temporal equilibrium we can use the same method as the one presented in the analysis of pay-as-you-go pensions. We define a lowest sustainable initial capital stock $\underline{k}(g)$ that is non-decreasing in g. Then we assume **H3**, which guarantees that, if it exists, the inter-temporal equilibrium is unique and the dynamics are monotonic.[5] This assumption also implies that when $\underline{k}(g)$ is positive it is the smallest positive steady state capital stock.

It is useful to define a set of compatible capital–government-spending pairs as we did for pensions.

Definition 3.6 (Public-spending–capital compatibility set)
The compatibility set $\mathcal{D}_g$ is the set of pairs (k, g) such that there exists an inter-temporal equilibrium with public spending g and initial capital k.

In formal terms, it is the set $\mathcal{D}_g$ of pairs (k, g) such that $g \geq 0$, $\underline{k}(g)$ is finite, $k > 0$, and $k \geq \underline{k}(g)$:

$$\mathcal{D}_g = \{(k, g) \in \mathbb{R}_+^2; \ k > 0 \text{ and } k \geq \underline{k}(g)\}.$$

Under the assumptions **H1**, **H2**, and **H3**, for any $(k_0, g) \in \mathcal{D}_g$, we can apply the same reasoning as with pensions: there exists a unique inter-temporal equilibrium with government spending g and initial capital stock k_0. This equilibrium is characterized by the sequence of capital stocks k_t defined by the difference equation

$$\Delta_g(k_t, k_{t+1}) = 0 \quad \Leftrightarrow \quad k_{t+1} = h(k_t, g).$$

The function h is defined in $\mathcal{D}_g$, and is increasing with respect to k_t and decreasing with respect to g. It is continuously differentiable at any interior point of $\mathcal{D}_g$, and its partial derivatives verify $h'_k > 0$ and $h'_g < 0$. We now have the following proposition:

Proposition 3.10 (Capital accumulation and government spending)
*Assume that **H1**, **H2**, and **H3** hold. For $(k_0, g) \in \mathcal{D}_g$, there exists a unique inter-temporal equilibrium $(k_t)_{t \geq 0}$ starting at k_0 with constant g.*

- *Following a drop in g, $g' < g$, there is an inter-temporal equilibrium $(k'_t)_{t \geq 0}$ starting at k_0, which verifies $k'_t > k_t \ \forall t \geq 1$. Moreover, if positive, the long-run capital stocks are such that $k' > k$.*
- *Following a rise in g, $g'' > g$, either there is an inter-temporal equilibrium (k''), which verifies $k''_t < k_t \ \forall t \geq 1$ or there no longer exists an inter-temporal equilibrium with initial capital stock k_0.*

Proof: The proof follows the same steps as in proposition 3.9. ∎

Hence, as the two-period lived individuals do not compensate an increase in taxes by an equivalent decrease in consumption, savings drop in the face of

---

[5] Notice that **H3** (and not **H3a**) is the relevant hypothesis, as public spending modifies the first-period but not the second-period income.

a rise in government spending (at given interest rate). This pushes the interest rate up, and, as long as there is a rational inter-temporal equilibrium, the stock of capital of the period after is diminished. This drop in capital persists in the long run: if $k > 0$, we have that $dk/dg < 0$. Contrary to what happens in an infinite horizon model (see, e.g., Blanchard and Fischer (1989), p. 54), an increase in taxes is not fully offset by a proportional decrease in consumption in the long run, and savings are decreased.

Notice that this holds for stable steady state equilibria. The effect is reversed for unstable steady state equilibria. Indeed, differentiating $\Delta_g(k, k) = 0$, we have

$$\frac{dk}{dg} = \frac{-s'_w}{1 + n - s'_w \omega'(k) - s'_R f''(k)},$$

which is negative (positive) if $1 + n - s'_w \omega'(k) - s'_R f''(k)$ is positive (negative). In particular, an increase in g raises the lowest sustainable initial capital stock, which is unstable when it is hyperbolic.

3.3.2 Public Spending: Optimal Financing

The study of first-best – optimal – financing of constant public expenditure is straightforward given the tools developed in chapter 2. We define a production function net of government spending:

$$f_g(k_t) = f(k_t) - g,$$

and the sequence of maximum possible production is given by

$$\bar{k}_{t+1} = f_g(\bar{k}_t),$$

with $\bar{k}_0 = k_0$. Provided that this sequence is defined with positive $\bar{k}_t$ $\forall t$, the rest of the analysis of chapter 2 applies with the modified production function. In particular, one obtains the two following results.

First, under the assumption that it exists, the modified golden rule level of capital is unaffected by the presence of public spending. This holds because public spending does not modify the marginal productivity of capital. Hence, the optimal level of capital remains unchanged, and optimal aggregate private consumption should then be lower.

Second, the first-best solution can still be decentralized by means of lump-sum transfers. In general, the financing of public spending will be supported by the young and the old households. The budget constraint of the transfer system is

$$N_t g_t = N_t a_t - N_{t-1} z_t. \tag{3.10}$$

The capital market equilibrium at the steady state requires

$$(1 + n)k_y = \tilde{s}(\omega(k_y) - a, (a - g)(1 + n), f'(k_y)). \tag{3.11}$$

To determine which generation (young vs old) bears the majority of the government spending burden, we compute

$$\frac{da/dg}{|dz/dg|}.$$

We first study da/dg. Differentiating equation (3.11), we obtain

$$\frac{da}{dg} = \frac{-\tilde{s}'_{\omega_2}(1+n)}{\tilde{s}'_{\omega_1} - \tilde{s}'_{\omega_2}(1+n)} = \frac{1 - s'_w}{1 - s'_w + s'_w/\gamma},$$

using that $\tilde{s}'_{\omega_1} = s'_w$ and $\tilde{s}'_{\omega_2} = -(1 - s'_w)/R$. From equation (3.10), we have that

$$\frac{dz}{dg} = (1+n)\left(\frac{da}{dg} - 1\right) = \frac{-(1+n)s'_w/\gamma}{1 - s'_w + s'_w/\gamma}.$$

We find that

$$\frac{da/dg}{|dz/dg|} = \frac{1 - s'_w}{(1+n)s'_w/\gamma}.$$

Hence, if the propensity to save out of income is high, the young generation is less solicited to finance public spending than the old generation.

Example: With a logarithmic utility $\ln c + \beta \ln d$, the condition becomes

$$\frac{da/dg}{|dz/dg|} = \frac{1 - s'_w}{(1+n)s'_w/\gamma} = \frac{\gamma}{(1+n)\beta},$$

which can be read as a condition on β: if $\beta > \frac{\gamma}{1+n}$, the old generation pays marginally more for public spending than the young one.

3.3.3 Second-best Policies

A classical problem in public finance deals with the optimal way to finance a given path of government expenditures in the absence of lump-sum taxation, using only distorting fiscal instruments. This so-called *Ramsey problem* (from Ramsey (1927)) leads, in a representative agent model with infinite horizon, to the conclusion that income from capital should not be taxed in the long run[6] and that, under certain conditions, the different consumption goods should be taxed at the same rate (see the survey of Chari and Kehoe (1999)). There is also a significant literature on the overlapping generations setup (see the contributions of Atkinson (1971), Pestieau (1974), Atkinson and Sandmo (1980), and Erosa and Gervais (1998)) that challenges the result of optimal zero taxation for capital.

---

[6] And, under some conditions, even after a finite number of periods; see Chamley (1986).

We now address the issue of optimal fiscal policy, i.e., the determination of optimal proportional taxes on labor and capital income, using the framework developed in the previous chapters. As there is no utility drawn from leisure and there is no public debt in our setup, this amounts to simplifying the traditional problem, as for instance presented in Chari and Kehoe (1999), pp. 71–74, in order to obtain more precise results.

The resource constraint of the economy is given by

$$c_t + \frac{d_t}{1+n} + (1+n)k_{t+1} + g_t = f(k_t), \tag{3.12}$$

where g_t denotes government consumption per young household. Each young household in t solves

$$\max u(c_t) + \beta u(d_{t+1})$$

subject to

$$c_t + s_t = (1 - \tau_t)w_t,$$

$$d_{t+1} = R_{t+1}(1 - \theta_{t+1})s_t,$$

where τ_t is the tax rate on labor income, and θ_{t+1} is the tax rate on capital income.[7] The first-order condition of this problem is

$$u'(c_t) = \beta R_{t+1}(1 - \theta_{t+1})u'(d_{t+1}). \tag{3.13}$$

The government budget constraint is

$$\tau_t w_t + \frac{1}{1+n}\theta_t R_t s_{t-1} = g_t.$$

The equilibrium on the labor market and the equality between effective and distributed profits imply $w_t = \omega(k_t)$ and $R_t = f'(k_t)$. The equality between savings and investment, $(1+n)k_{t+1} = s_t$, is obtained by combining the resource constraint with the individuals and government budget constraints.

In the sequel, it is convenient to use what is called in the literature the implementability constraint. This constraint is derived from the first-order-condition (3.13) in which we have substituted out prices and taxes using the budget constraints of the household. This constraint is thus

$$u'(c_t) = \beta R_{t+1}(1 - \theta_{t+1})u'(d_{t+1}) = \beta \frac{d_{t+1}}{s_t}u'(d_{t+1}),$$

which, together with $s_t = (1+n)k_{t+1}$, gives

$$(1+n)k_{t+1}u'(c_t) = \beta d_{t+1}u'(d_{t+1}). \tag{3.14}$$

---

[7] The usual formulation in public economics is to tax the interest income from capital at a rate τ_k. This is equivalent to our formulation with $\tau_k r = \theta(1+r)$.

For a given path $(g_t)_{t\geq0}$ and an initial condition k_0, the solution to the second-best problem is a path $(c_t, d_t, k_{t+1})_{t\geq0}$ that maximizes

$$\sum_{t=0}^{\infty} \gamma^t \left(u(c_t) + \frac{\beta}{\gamma} u(d_t) \right)$$

subject to the resource constraint (3.12) and the implementability constraint (3.14).

Once the path $(c_t, d_t, k_{t+1})_{t\geq0}$ is obtained, we can compute the optimal taxes using the budget constraints of the household:

$$\tau_t = 1 - \frac{c_t + (1+n)k_{t+1}}{\omega(k_t)},$$

$$\theta_t = 1 - \frac{d_t}{f'(k_t)(1+n)k_t}.$$

3.4 STUDY OF THE SECOND-BEST PROBLEM

We propose in this section an in-depth study of the simplified second-best problem in the standard model of chapter 1, i.e., with inelastic labor supply. We start by rewriting the problem in a more convenient way.

3.4.1 Restating the Problem

As d_{t+1} intervenes in (3.14), we use the following change of variables (as in Michel and Venditti (1997)):

$$x_t = f(k_t) - \frac{d_t}{1+n} - g_t.$$

x_t is the production net of the consumption of the old individuals and of government spending. Then the resource constraint (3.12) implies

$$(1+n)k_{t+1} = f(k_t) - c_t - \frac{d_t}{1+n} - g_t = x_t - c_t,$$

and the law of motion of x_t is

$$x_{t+1} = f\left(\frac{x_t - c_t}{1+n}\right) - \frac{d_{t+1}}{1+n} - g_{t+1}. \tag{3.15}$$

This equation is equivalent to the resource constraint, except that x_0 is not given; it depends on the choice

$$d_0 = (1 - \theta_0) f'(k_0)(1+n)k_0,$$

and hence on θ_0:

$$x_0 = f(k_0) - \frac{d_0}{1+n} - g_0. \tag{3.16}$$

We restate the implementability constraint (3.14) by defining:

Definition 3.7 (Implementability set)
The implementability set $Q(x)$ is the set of consumption pairs (c, d) such that the implementability constraint (3.14) holds for a given level of x.

Formally, $Q(x)$ is defined as

$$Q(x) = \{(c, d) \in \mathbb{R}_{++}^2;\ \beta d u'(d) = u'(c)(x - c)\},$$

and the implementability constraint is equivalent to

$$(c_t, d_{t+1}) \in Q(x_t). \tag{3.17}$$

We can then rewrite the objective in its original form:[8]

$$\max \frac{\beta}{\gamma} u(d_0) + \sum_{t=0}^{\infty} \gamma^t [u(c_t) + \beta u(d_{t+1})]$$

under the constraints (3.15), (3.16), and (3.17).

3.4.2 Three Issues

At this stage, we face three main problems.

The Non-Convexity of the Optimization Problem. First, nothing guarantees that the optimization problem is convex. Indeed, compared to the optimal growth problem, there is an additional constraint, the implementability constraint, that is in general non-convex. For example, with a CIES utility function, the set $Q(x)$ is

$$Q(x) = \{(c, d) \in \mathbb{R}_{++}^2;\ \beta d^{1-\frac{1}{\sigma}} = c^{-\frac{1}{\sigma}}(x - c)\},$$

and the set is convex only for the specific value $\sigma = 1$ (see figure 3.7).
    Because the implementability constraint imposes conditions on the first-order derivatives of the utility function, the second-best problem can be non-convex. This difficulty is neglected in the literature, and one generally assumes that the optimal solution exists and that it is interior. However, the first-order conditions are only necessary conditions for optimality, and they can correspond to a local minimum. The second-order conditions are often

---

[8] One additional interest of the change of variables is that the new maximization problem can also be applied to non-separable utility functions $u(c_t, d_{t+1})$ with c_{-1} given.

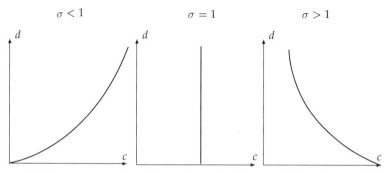

Figure 3.7. The non-convexity of the implementability set: The implementability set consists of the points (c, d) such that the implementability constraint holds for a given level of x. It takes the form of a smooth curve. With a CIES utility function, this set is convex only for $\sigma = 1$.

not tractable (they bear on the third-order derivatives of utility and production functions) and can only be used to establish the existence of a local maximum.

In a first step, we shall present the standard approach, which gives the necessary first-order conditions, ignoring all these difficulties. To tackle the problem in a more rigorous way, we shall analyze, in a second step, an auxiliary problem is which the implementability constraint is replaced by an inequality which renders the problem convex. We then study the conditions under which the inequality constraint is binding with equality.

The Time Inconsistency Problem and the Commitment Technology. In the infinite horizon optimization problem, we assume that the decisions are made once for all at the initial date. The problem is time consistent if the optimization at some later date $t > 0$ leads to the same solution as the initial problem. From Kydland and Prescott (1977) we know that this will in general not be the case in the choice of optimal policy: capital taxes θ_t have an effect on savings s_{t-1} and hence on k_t;[9] if we re-optimize one period later, k_t becomes fixed, and another choice of θ_t has no effect on k_t. The optimal choice of θ_t will thus differ depending on when the optimization takes place. This is the time inconsistency property of the second-best policies: It would be optimal to modify the tax rate once it is too late for the agents to revise their investment choice.

As a consequence, agents will believe that the government will apply the time inconsistent policy only if the government effectively has access to a commitment "technology." In the literature, this problem is tackled in three different ways. The first is simply to assume that the government can commit to its future actions by, say, restriction in its constitution. More simply, this

---

[9] An exception is when θ_t has no effect on the savings decision (logarithmic utility).

solution should be considered as a benchmark: It gives what would be optimal for the government if it were able to pre-commit itself. This is the way we shall pursue in this book. A second way is to develop a model in which the commitment outcomes are sustained by reputational mechanisms.[10] A third way is to study the optimal taxation problem without commitment.[11]

The Initial Policy Rule. The fact that the initial capital stock held by the first generation of old persons is supplied inelastically introduces an additional difficulty. The first-period tax rate θ_0 is equivalent to a lump-sum tax on the income of the old people in period 0. Its optimal choice is equivalent to the choice of d_0 and has to be analyzed separately. Of course, if one is interested only in the steady state, the problem can be ignored.

In our two-period OLG setup, the government has an incentive, under certain conditions, to set the initial tax rate on capital relatively high. This is moderated by the fact that the only resource of the first old generation lies in the existing capital stock. As the government cares about this generation, it will not tax the initial capital as highly as in the model with infinite-lived agents who can borrow to finance consumption. Fixing the initial tax rate at some constant[12] θ_0 is equivalent in our setup to fixing an initial value of d_0 as

$$d_0 = R_0(1 - \theta_0)s_{-1} = f'(k_0)(1 - \theta_0)(1 + n)k_0,$$

where k_0 is given.

In our simple model, we have one good reason to fix a specific value of θ_0. Indeed, starting from a steady state situation, if the government re-optimizes, the optimal policy will be different from the steady state. It is however sufficient to fix $\theta_0 = \theta_\infty$ for the optimal policy to be constant. Hence, to study the effects of temporary shocks from a steady state, we shall fix θ_0 at its steady state value.

---

[10] A seminal example of such trigger mechanisms is given in Barro and Gordon (1983) for monetary policy (see Chari and Kehoe (1990) for an example on fiscal policy in a growth model).

[11] Such a study of time consistent fiscal policies is developed in Klein and Rios-Rull (1999).

[12] In models with infinite-lived agents, the government has always an incentive to tax the initial level at a very high rate, as the agents can compensate their initial loss by borrowing on credit markets. In Chamley (1986), where preferences are separable between consumption and leisure and iso-elastic with respect to consumption, the optimal tax rate on capital income (interests) is 100% for a finite length of time and zero thereafter. For other utility specifications it is optimal to adjust the tax gradually towards zero (Renstrom (1999)). Chari, Christiano, and Kehoe (1994) adopt the convention that the initial capital tax rate is fixed. Their motivation is to avoid the rather trivial possibility of lump-sum taxation. This amounts to assuming that the capital income tax rate in inherited from the past at $t = 0$, i.e., θ_0 has been announced at $t = -1$, and for credibility reasons it is applied at $t = 0$.

3.4.3 A Standard Approach to the Problem

The standard approach consists in studying the marginal conditions of optimality that one obtains by maximizing an infinite Lagrangian:

$$\mathcal{L} = \sum_{t=0}^{\infty} \gamma^t [u(c_t) + \beta u(d_{t+1})] + \sum_{t=0}^{\infty} \gamma^t p_t [\psi(c_t, d_{t+1}) + c_t - x_t]$$
$$+ \sum_{t=0}^{\infty} \gamma^{t+1} q_{t+1} \left[f\left(\frac{x_t - c_t}{1+n}\right) - \frac{d_{t+1}}{1+n} - g_{t+1} - x_{t+1} \right],$$

where

$$\psi(c_t, d_{t+1}) = \frac{\beta d_{t+1} u'(d_{t+1})}{u'(c_t)},$$

p_t is the Lagrange multiplier of the constraint, and q_t is the shadow price of x_t. The constraint $\psi(c_t, d_{t+1}) = x_t - c_t$ is obtained from the resource constraint (3.12), where $(1+n)k_{t+1}$ has been replaced by its value from the implementability constraint (3.14). The function ψ is increasing in c_t and, under the assumption **A4**, increasing in d_{t+1}.

When the initial condition x_0 is given (d_0 fixed), after differentiating with respect to c_t and d_{t+1}, we obtain

$$u'(c_t) = \frac{\gamma q_{t+1}}{1+n} f'\left(\frac{x_t - c_t}{1+n}\right) - p_t[1 + \psi'_c(c_t, d_{t+1})], \qquad (3.18)$$

$$\beta u'(d_{t+1}) = \frac{\gamma q_{t+1}}{1+n} - p_t \psi'_d(c_t, d_{t+1}). \qquad (3.19)$$

Differentiating with respect to $x_t, t \geq 1$, we get

$$q_t = \frac{\gamma q_{t+1}}{1+n} f'\left(\frac{x_t - c_t}{1+n}\right) - p_t. \qquad (3.20)$$

Alternatively, if d_0 is not fixed but chosen optimally, one should add to the Lagrangian the following terms, including a constraint specific to the first period:

$$\frac{\beta}{\gamma} u(d_0) + q_0 \left(f(k_0) - \frac{d_0}{1+n} - g_0 - x_0 \right).$$

We then obtain an additional first-order condition:

$$\frac{\beta}{\gamma} u'(d_0) = \frac{q_0}{1+n}, \qquad (3.21)$$

which gives d_0 as a function of q_0. Differentiating $\mathcal{L}$ with respect to x_0 gives the relation (3.20) for $t = 0$. Comparing equations (3.19) and (3.21), it appears clearly that the choice of d_0 for the first old generation (and hence θ_0) is not affected by an implementability constraint at $t = 0$. Such a constraint bears on the following generations (see equation (3.14)). This clearly shows the time inconsistency property of the optimal solution.

The steady state c, d, x, p, q, and $k = (x - c)/(1 + n)$ is obtained after some algebraic manipulations:

$$q = \frac{\gamma q}{1 + n} f'(k) - p,$$

$$u'(c) = q - p\psi'_c(c, d),$$

$$u'(c) - \beta u'(d) f'(k) = -p(1 + \psi'_c(c, d) + f'(k)\psi'_d(c, d)),$$

and the resource and implementability constraints are

$$(1 + n)k = f(k) - c - \frac{d}{1 + n} - g,$$

$$(1 + n)k = \psi(c, d) = \frac{\beta d u'(d)}{u'(c)}.$$

$$(3.22)$$

We can distinguish three types of steady state, depending on the value of p at equilibrium:

- With $p = 0$, the implementability constraint is not binding and the second-best problem leads to the same outcome as the benevolent planner problem (section 2.4). We have

$$q = u'(c) > 0, \qquad f'(k) = \frac{1 + n}{\gamma}, \qquad u'(c) = \beta u'(d) f'(k).$$

Then $k = k_\gamma$, and the modified golden rule holds. The taxation of capital income is zero, for equation (3.13) can be written at steady state as

$$u'(c) = \beta(1 - \theta) f'(k)u'(d).$$

We deduce from the second-period budget constraint that $d = d_\gamma = f'(k_\gamma)$ $(1 + n)k_\gamma = (1 + n)^2 k_\gamma/\gamma$ and $c = c_\gamma$ is solution to $u'(c) = \beta(1 + n) \times u'(d_\gamma)/\gamma$. The first-best solution is obtained. This case arises when g takes a particular value

$$g = \tilde{g} \quad \Rightarrow \quad p = 0$$

with

$$\tilde{g} = f(k_\gamma) - c_\gamma - \frac{d_\gamma}{1 + n} - (1 + n)k_\gamma.$$

$$(3.23)$$

Obviously, $\tilde{g}$ should be positive to make this case possible. We study this issue below. $\tilde{g}$ is the level of tax on wages which leads the competitive economy to the modified golden rule steady state.

- With $p > 0$ we have $u'(c) < q$ (as $\psi'_c > 0$) and

$$f'(k) > \frac{1 + n}{\gamma},$$

and thus $k < k_\gamma$. Moreover, if $1 + \psi_c' + f'(k)\psi_d' > 0$, which holds as long as $\psi'(d)$ is non-negative (which is the case under **A4**) or not too negative, we have $\beta u'(d) f'(k) > u'(c) = \beta(1-\theta) f'(k)u'(d)$, which in turn implies $\theta > 0$.

- With $p < 0$ we have $u'(c) > q$ (as $\psi_c' > 0$) and

$$f'(k) < \frac{1+n}{\gamma},$$

and thus $k > k_\gamma$. Moreover if $1 + \psi_c' + f'(k)\psi_d' > 0$, then θ is negative.

When the shadow price of the implementability constraint is nil, the capital stock is at the modified golden rule level and the first-best solution is reached. In all other situations it is in general optimal to either tax or subsidize capital.

3.4.4 An Auxiliary Problem

To perform a rigorous study of the second-best outcome and take care of the convexity issue, we propose to study a different problem where the implementability constraint is written as an inequality. We consider the constraint

$$\beta du'(d) \geq u'(c)(x - c),$$

leading to the set

$$Q_1(x) = \{(c, d) \in \mathbb{R}_{++}^2; \ c < x \leq c + \psi(c, d)\}.$$

This set is convex if the function ψ is concave. With a CIES utility function, this is the case when $\sigma \geq 1$ as $\psi(c, d) = \beta c^{\frac{1}{\sigma}} d^{1-\frac{1}{\sigma}}$ is concave for $\sigma \geq 1$. This case is illustrated in figure 3.8.

For the auxiliary problem with constant $g_t = g$, one can prove the existence of an optimal solution under the assumptions **B0**, **B1**, **B2**, and **B3** of

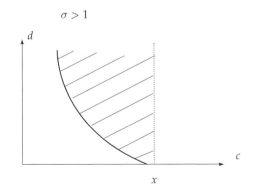

$\sigma > 1$

Figure 3.8. The convexity of the modified implementability set: The modified implementability set also includes points at the right of the standard implementability set, which are such that $c < x$. With a CIES utility function, this set is convex for $\sigma \geq 1$.

appendix A.4.1 and apply the necessary and sufficient conditions for optimality of appendix A.4.2. We can then study the Lagrangian of period t:

$$\mathcal{L}_t = u(c_t) + \beta u(d_{t+1}) + \gamma q_{t+1} \left[f\left(\frac{x_t - c_t}{1+n}\right) - \frac{d_{t+1}}{1+n} - g \right] - q_t x_t,$$

which attains its maximum with respect to (c_t, d_{t+1}, x_t) on the set of triples for which $(c_t, d_{t+1}) \in Q_1(x_t)$ holds. To solve this static problem we introduce the Kuhn–Tucker multiplier p_t for the implementability constraint $c_t + \psi(c_t, d_{t+1}) - x_t \geq 0$. The derivatives of

$$\mathcal{L}_t + p_t[c_t + \psi(c_t, d_{t+1}) - x_t],$$

should be set equal to zero, which leads to

$$q_t = \frac{\gamma q_{t+1}}{1+n} f'\left(\frac{x_t - c_t}{1+n}\right) - p_t, \tag{3.24}$$

$$u'(c_t) = q_t - p_t[1 + \psi_c'(c_t, d_{t+1})], \tag{3.25}$$

$$\beta u'(d_{t+1}) = \frac{\gamma q_{t+1}}{1+n} - p_t \psi_d'(c_t, d_{t+1}). \tag{3.26}$$

But instead of the implementability constraint, we have the Kuhn–Tucker conditions:

$$p_t \geq 0, \qquad c_t + \psi(c_t, d_{t+1}) - x_t \geq 0, \qquad p_t[c_t + \psi(c_t, d_{t+1}) - x_t] = 0.$$

These conditions, together with the transversality condition

$$\lim_{t \to \infty} \gamma^t q_t x_t = 0,$$

are sufficient for optimality in the auxiliary problem.

Moreover, an optimal solution of the auxiliary problem with $Q_1(x)$ for which $p_t > 0$ holds for all t verifies the implementability constraint for all t and is thus an optimal solution to the second-best problem.

We now study the steady state solution to the auxiliary problem, when this solution is obtained with a Kuhn–Tucker multiplier $p = 0$. In this case, the first-order conditions are the same as in the first-best problem, and we obtain the modified golden rule. Only in the very particular case where the implementability constraint is binding at this point does the second-best problem coincide with the first-best outcome. In all other cases, the constraint is not binding and the auxiliary problem is not helpful for studying the second-best problem.

We shall show that there exists a threshold $\tilde{g}$ such that if $g > \tilde{g}$ then $p > 0$ and the second-best steady state can be obtained by solving the auxiliary problem. To do that, it is sufficient to show that $p = 0$ implies $g \leq \tilde{g}$. In the case $p = 0$, we obtain $k = k_\gamma$ and $u'(c) = \beta f'(k_\gamma) u'(d)$. However, the relationship (3.22) of the standard approach becomes an inequality in the auxiliary problem

$$(1+n)k_\gamma \leq \psi(c, d). \tag{3.27}$$

The resource constraint

$$c + \frac{d}{1+n} = f(k_\gamma) - (1+n)k_\gamma - g,$$

and the individual arbitrage condition (which holds with $p = 0$)

$$u'(c) = \beta f'(k_\gamma)u'(d),$$

form a system of two equations that we can solve to obtain two decreasing and continuous functions $c(g)$ and $d(g)$ for government spending $g \in [0, f(k_\gamma) - (1+n)k_\gamma)$. Moreover the implementability constraint can be rewritten

$$\psi(c, d) = \frac{\beta d u'(d)}{u'(c)} = \frac{d}{f'(k_\gamma)}.$$

Hence, the condition (3.27) is equivalent to

$$d(g) \geq (1+n)k_\gamma f'(k_\gamma).$$

Formally, the function $d(g)$ is defined for $g < 0$ and decreases from $+\infty$ to 0 when g rises from $-\infty$ to 0. We thus have a value $\tilde{g}$, positive or negative, for which $d(\tilde{g}) = (1+n)k_\gamma f'(k_\gamma)$, and the condition (3.27) is equivalent to $g \leq \tilde{g}$. Now $d(\tilde{g}) = (1+n)^2 k_\gamma/\gamma = d_\gamma$, so, provided that $\tilde{g}$ is positive, the threshold $\tilde{g}$ is the same as the value of government spending leading to the first best in the standard approach (equation (3.23)):

$$\tilde{g} = f(k_\gamma) - c_\gamma - \frac{d_\gamma}{1+n} - (1+n)k_\gamma.$$

To analyze the sign of $\tilde{g}$ is it sufficient to study $d(0)$, as we have

$$\tilde{g} > 0 \quad \Leftrightarrow \quad d(0) > (1+n)^2 k_\gamma/\gamma.$$

$d(0)$ is the optimum of the planner in the absence of government spending, and we have $d(0) > (1+n)^2 k_\gamma/\gamma$ if and only if the decentralization of the optimum is obtained with a positive transfer to the old at the steady state.

A central result is obtained when $g > \tilde{g}$. Then $p = 0$ is impossible, and the steady state solution of the auxiliary problem verifies $p > 0$: the weak inequality constraint holds with equality. Thus, when $g > \tilde{g}$, the auxiliary problem gives the second-best optimum.

Proposition 3.11 (Solution to the second-best problem)
Assume $\psi(c, d)$ concave. Consider the excess of net production over private consumption at the modified golden rule $\tilde{g}$:

$$\tilde{g} = f(k_\gamma) - c_\gamma - \frac{d_\gamma}{1+n} - (1+n)k_\gamma,$$

where

$$d_\gamma = \frac{k_\gamma}{\gamma}(1+n)^2 \quad and \quad u'(c_\gamma) = \beta\frac{1+n}{\gamma}u'(d_\gamma).$$

The steady state solution to the second-best problem coincides with the first-best optimum when $\tilde{g} \geq 0$ and $g = \tilde{g}$.

*When $g > \tilde{g}$ (positive or negative), the steady state solution of the auxiliary problem with $Q_1(x)$ is also the steady state solution of the second-best problem. At this optimum, $k < k_y$ holds, and if $\psi'_d(c, d) \geq 0$ (assumption **A4**), capital taxes θ are positive.*

Proof: As $g > \tilde{g}$, $p = 0$ is excluded at the steady state solution of the auxiliary problem, which verifies $p > 0$. This implies that the implementability constraint holds with equality, and the solution is thus a fortiori the steady state second-best optimum. Given that $p > 0$, we have $u'(c) < q$, $f'(k) > (1+n)/\gamma$, and thus $k < k_y$. Moreover, we have from equations (3.25)–(3.26)

$$u'(c) - \beta f'(k)u'(d) = -p[1 + \psi'_c + f'(k)\psi'_d],$$

which is negative if $1 + \psi'_c + f'(k)\psi'_d > 0$. Then, using the individual's first-order condition (3.13), we have

$$\beta(1 - \theta) f'(k)u'(d) = u'(c) < \beta f'(k)u'(d),$$

which implies $\theta > 0$. A sufficient condition for $1 + \psi'_c + f'(k)\psi'_d > 0$ is $\psi'_d \geq 0$. ∎

For $g > \tilde{g}$ we have $p_t > 0$ for t large enough when the optimal dynamics of the auxiliary problem converge to the steady state. Our conclusions thus remain valid locally near the steady state.

This method does not allow reaching a conclusion in the case $g < \tilde{g}$, when $\tilde{g} > 0$.

Notice that when the function $\psi(c, d)$ is convex, for example with a CIES utility function and $\sigma \leq 1$, one may consider another auxiliary problem with

$$Q_2(x) = \{(c, d) \in \mathbb{R}^2_{++};\ x \geq c + \psi(c, d)\},$$

which is a convex set. We can then make a similar study with a multiplier $p \leq 0$ and analyze the auxiliary problem. As the first-order conditions when $p = 0$ are the same as above, the threshold $\tilde{g}$ is unchanged, and a solution to the second-best problem is obtained by studying the auxiliary problem when $g < \tilde{g}$ (which makes sense when $\tilde{g} > 0$).

Example: We compute $\tilde{g}$ in the case of a CIES utility function with $\sigma \geq 1$. The optimal allocations of consumptions should satisfy

$$c^{-1/\sigma} = \frac{\beta(1 + n)}{\gamma} d^{-1/\sigma},$$

and hence

$$c = \left(\frac{\gamma}{\beta(1 + n)}\right)^{\sigma} d.$$

Using this result in the resource constraint, we obtain the function $d(g)$:

$$d(g) = \left[\frac{1}{1+n} + \left(\frac{\gamma}{\beta(1+n)}\right)^{\sigma}\right]^{-1} [f(k_\gamma) - (1+n)k_\gamma - g],$$

and $\tilde{g}$ is obtained with

$$d(\tilde{g}) = \frac{(1+n)^2}{\gamma} k_\gamma,$$

leading to

$$\tilde{g} = f(k_\gamma) - (1+n)\left(1 + \frac{1}{\gamma} + \frac{\gamma^{\sigma-1}}{\beta^{\sigma}(1+n)^{\sigma-1}}\right)k_\gamma.$$

In the special case $\sigma = 1$, $\psi(c, d) = \beta c$ is linear and the set

$$Q(x) = \{(c, d) \in \mathbb{R}^2_{++};\ c(1 + \beta) = x\},$$

is convex. We can then apply the standard second-best problem, and

$$\tilde{g} = f(k_\gamma) - (1+n)\left(1 + \frac{1}{\gamma} + \frac{1}{\beta}\right)k_\gamma.$$

For $g > \tilde{g}$ we have $k < k_\gamma$ and $\theta > 0$. For $g < \tilde{g}$ (when $\tilde{g} > 0$), we have $k > k_\gamma$ and $\theta < 0$. This illustrates that, although θ does not affect the choice of savings with a logarithmic utility, it introduces a gap in the condition $u'(c)/u'(d) = \beta(1 - \theta) f'(k)$ which makes the allocation not a first best.

With a Cobb–Douglas production function, the modified golden rule is

$$\alpha A k_\gamma^{\alpha-1} = \frac{1+n}{\gamma},$$

$f(k_\gamma) = A k_\gamma^{\alpha} = \frac{1+n}{\alpha\gamma} k_\gamma$, and the sign of $\tilde{g}$ is the same as the sign of

$$\frac{1}{\alpha\gamma} - \left(1 + \frac{1}{\gamma} + \frac{1}{\beta}\right),$$

which is positive for

$$\gamma < \frac{1-\alpha}{\alpha\left(1 + \frac{1}{\beta}\right)}.$$

The study of the dynamics in the Cobb–Douglas case is made in section 3.5.4, assuming government spending proportional to production: $g_t = \epsilon f(k_t)$.

3.5 APPLICATIONS AND EXTENSIONS

One relevant issue for the policy debate in developing countries is the implementation of a demographic policy designed to monitor the evolution of the population. Behind this political debate we find the idea that there is an optimal level of population growth. This issue is studied in section 3.5.1. It is followed by two applications that illustrate the properties of the second-best problem (sections 3.5.2 and 3.5.3). Finally, we determine the second-best optimal fiscal policy in an example where government spending is proportional to output (section 3.5.4).

3.5.1 Optimal Growth Rate of Population

Samuelson (1975b) (see also Arthur and McNicoll (1978)) studies the optimum rate of population growth that maximizes utility among all the golden ages. Going back to the problem of the optimal stationary path (section 2.1.2), the problem of Samuelson is to maximize

$$u(c) + \beta u(d)$$

subject to

$$f(k) = (1+n)k + c + \frac{d}{1+n} \tag{3.28}$$

with respect to the variables k, c, d, and $1+n$. The first-order necessary conditions for this problem are

$$f'(k) = 1 + n, \tag{3.29}$$

$$u'(c) = (1+n)\beta u'(d), \tag{3.30}$$

$$d = (1+n)^2 k. \tag{3.31}$$

Equation (3.29) is the golden rule (2.4). Equations (3.28) and (3.30) are those describing the golden age (see proposition 2.2). Equation (3.31) is the additional equation related to the optimal choice of $1+n$.

Comparing now these equations with the equations that describe the competitive equilibrium, we observe that just picking the optimal rate of population growth, when it exists, is sufficient for the market conditions to coincide with the optimal conditions, and leads a competitive economy to the goldenest golden age. Indeed, if equation (3.31) holds, we have, from the budget constraint of the old, $d = R(1+n)k$ when $R = 1+n$ holds; the golden rule is verified, and the optimal choice of the consumer, $u'(c) = R\beta u'(d)$, leads to equation (3.30). There is thus no need of transfer. This result is the *serendipity theorem* of Samuelson.

The validity of such a strong result depends of course on the existence of such an interior optimum growth rate of population. This is not granted, however, because the problem is non-convex; in the example with a logarithmic utility function and a Cobb–Douglas production function, Deardorff (1976) shows that the first-order conditions lead to a minimum and not to a maximum (see also the answer by Samuelson (1976)). The discussion is generalized to the CIES utility function and the CES production function by Michel and Pestieau (1993). They show that, for the serendipity theorem to hold, it is sufficient that the factors of production have low substitutability ($\rho > 0$) and the inter-temporal elasticity of substitution be small enough: $\sigma < 2 - 1/(1 + \rho)$.

3.5.2 Application: The Tax on the First Old Generation

In the following applications, we consider an economy with a CES production function with $\rho = 1$ and $\alpha = 1/2$ and a CIES utility. Taking the numerical values proposed in appendix A.5.3, we have $n = 1.025^{30} - 1$, $\beta = 0.3$, $A = 20$. We also choose $g = 6$, implying a share of government spending in GDP of 25% (in the example below with $\sigma = 2$) at the competitive equilibrium.

To illustrate the importance of the time inconsistency problem, we first propose a simulation with optimal θ_0 (assuming furthermore $\gamma = 0.99$). In this case, there is one optimality condition, which is specific to period 0. As we have stressed above, the comparison of equations (3.19) and (3.21) shows clearly that the choice of d_0 for the first old generation (and hence θ_0) is not directly subject to an implementability constraint. Equations (3.19) and (3.21) give the same rule only when $p_0 = 0$, or when $\psi'_d = 0$. This last possibility occurs with a logarithmic utility function. In that case, there is no time consistency problem and the choice of d_t, $t > 0$, will obey the same rule as the choice of d_0.

Starting from a steady state situation, we compute the equilibrium trajectory recognizing the specific nature of period 0.

- With $\sigma = 1$ (logarithmic utility), the economy will remain at the steady state for the reason explained above. The optimal path of taxes is

$$\{0.69895, 0.69895, 0.69895, 0.69895, \ldots, 0.69895\} \quad \text{for} \quad \sigma = 1.$$

The before-tax interest rate affecting old people is 4.58, i.e., 5.20% per year; the after-tax rate is 1.08%.
- For $\sigma \neq 1$, because the first-period optimality rule is different, the planner will not choose to remain at steady state:
- For $\sigma > 1$, The planner implements a solution with a high tax on the first old generation. A negative effect of this tax is to lower the utility of the first old. Moreover, taxes on young people are reduced, and this increases the capital stock in the future. This temporarily higher capital stock gives some additional resources to subsequent generations, which leads to a higher social welfare. The optimal path of taxes for different values of σ is

$$\{0.828650, 0.653712, 0.668855, 0.675271, \ldots, 0.680617\} \quad \text{for} \quad \sigma = 1.25,$$

$$\{0.878292, 0.516106, 0.567345, 0.585429, \ldots, 0.598781\} \quad \text{for} \quad \sigma = 1.50,$$

$$\{0.901269, 0.235558, 0.400403, 0.434292, \ldots, 0.450569\} \quad \text{for} \quad \sigma = 2.00,$$

$$\{0.918837, -0.13809, 0.253517, 0.276748, \ldots, 0.282633\} \quad \text{for} \quad \sigma = 3.00.$$

- For $\sigma < 1$, the inverse result holds: the first old generation will be less taxed than the next ones. The optimal path of taxes is

$$\{0.379923, 0.453591, 0.450169, 0.448001, \ldots, 0.444539\} \quad \text{for} \quad \sigma = 0.50,$$

$$\{0.524408, 0.600673, 0.597757, 0.596238, \ldots, 0.594637\} \quad \text{for} \quad \sigma = 0.75.$$

Note also in these examples that the steady state level of capital taxation depends on σ. For σ higher than 1 (lower than one), capital taxation has a negative (positive) influence on savings and capital. For this reason, steady state capital taxation should be lowered when σ increases above 1; otherwise capital accumulation will be discouraged too strongly.

3.5.3 Application: Financing Future Spending

We now propose another simulation, considering the initial tax rate θ_0 fixed at its steady state value as an initial condition. Assume that government spending are expected to increase by 10% during one given period in the future, say at $t = 3$. This extra spending can be due, for instance, to fighting the consequences of global warming in one century. How should this cost be supported by the different generations? In particular, should the economy accumulate more capital temporarily to face the future shock? In the absence of debt, there are limited possibilities to redistribute the shock among generations. We illustrate this issue by simulating a numerical example of the second-best problem. The given path of government spending is

$$\{6, 6, 6, 6.6, 6, 6, \ldots\}.$$

We assume that the economy is at a stationary equilibrium in period $t = 0$ and that the government should choose labor and capital taxes to finance the given path of spending. We solve the problem for two different values of the inter-temporal elasticity of substitution, $\sigma = 2$ and $\sigma = 3/4$. The results are reported in tables 3.2 and 3.3. Data are reported in terms of deviation from steady state. The last column reports the loss or gain in the life-cycle utility of the generation born in t with respect to steady state life-cycle utility.[13]

When inter-temporal substitution possibilities are high, the strategy of the planner is to play on inter-temporal substitution to compensate the generations alive at $t = 3$. This can be achieved by compensating the old persons at $t = 2$ and $t = 3$ by giving them more consumption when young at $t = 1$ and $t = 2$. In table 3.2, we also observe that the consumption of the old at $t = 4$ is not affected much, illustrating the relative compensation they receive in exchange for higher wage taxation at $t = 3$.

---

[13] The absolute values of these latter deviations would be affected by any monotonic linear transformation of the utility function. However, their ranking would be preserved.

Table 3.2. *Optimal Policy for* $\sigma = 2$

Time t	c_t (%)	d_t (%)	k_t (%)	Labor tax	Capital tax	Utility (%)
1	+0.1	0	0	0	0	−0.0
2	+0.2	−0.4	−0.2	−0.2	+0.3	−0.0
3	−5.3	−1.0	−0.4	+3.9	+0.6	−2.0
4	−2.4	−0.3	−2.8	−0.2	+0.5	−0.6
5	−1.1	−0.1	−1.3	−0.1	+0.2	−0.2
6	−0.5	−0.1	−0.6	−0.0	+0.1	−0.1
∞	0	0	0	0	0	0

θ_0 fixed at its steady state value.
Percentage changes for c_t, d_t, and k_t. Absolute changes for tax rates.

When inter-temporal substitution possibilities are small, it is not optimal for the household to reallocate much consumption across time in response to change in the environment. In this case, we observe in table 3.3 that the cost of the shock is partly supported by the old generation at $t = 2$ through an increase in taxes. This allows redistributing resources to the young in order for the economy to build up its stock of capital in advance, so as to reduce the impact of the shock on production capacities.

3.5.4 Proportional Government Spending

It is possible to explicitly compute the dynamics of the second-best problem when the production function is Cobb–Douglas, $f(k_t) = Ak_t^\alpha$, the utility is logarithmic, the depreciation rate is 1, and government spending is proportional to production:

$$g_t = \epsilon f(k_t).$$

Table 3.3. *Optimal Policy for* $\sigma = 3/4$

Time t	c_t (%)	d_t (%)	k_t (%)	Labor tax	Capital tax	Utility (%)
1	−0.1	0	0	0	0	−0.1
2	−0.0	−1.1	+0.2	−0.1	+0.4	−0.3
3	−2.0	−3.3	+1.1	+2.5	+1.1	−0.8
4	−0.7	−1.5	−2.2	−0.5	+1.0	−0.2
5	−0.2	−0.5	−0.7	−0.2	+0.3	−0.1
6	−0.1	−0.2	−0.2	−0.1	+0.1	−0.0
∞	0	0	0	0	0	0

θ_0 fixed at its steady state value.
Percentage changes for c_t, d_t, and k_t. Absolute changes for tax rates.

This proportionality factor can be interpreted by assuming that government spending is a factor of production which is complementary to the private inputs:

$$Y_t = \min\left\{ F(K_t, N_t), \frac{1}{\epsilon} G_t \right\}.$$

With a logarithmic utility function, the implementability constraint is given by

$$c_t = \frac{x_t}{1+\beta},$$

and the dynamics of x_t are

$$x_{t+1} = (1-\epsilon) f\left(\frac{x_t - c_t}{1+n}\right) - \frac{d_{t+1}}{1+n}.$$

Replacing c_t in the objective and the dynamics, the second-best problem is to maximize

$$\sum_{t=0}^{\infty} \gamma^t \left[\ln\left(\frac{x_t}{1+\beta}\right) + \beta \ln d_{t+1} \right]$$

subject to

$$x_{t+1} = B x_t^\alpha - \frac{d_{t+1}}{1+n},$$

where

$$B = \frac{(1-\epsilon)\beta^\alpha A}{(1+n)^\alpha (1+\beta)^\alpha}.$$

To study the problem, we define the ratio

$$m_t = \frac{d_{t+1}}{(1+n) B x_t^\alpha}.$$

The problem then becomes to maximize

$$\sum_{t=0}^{\infty} \gamma^t \left((1+\beta\alpha) \ln x_t + \beta \ln m_t \right)$$

subject to

$$\ln x_{t+1} = \ln(1 - m_t) + \alpha \ln x_t + \ln B.$$

Denoting $z_t = \ln x_t$, the Lagrangian of period t is

$$\mathcal{L}_t = (1+\beta\alpha) z_t + \beta \ln m_t + \gamma q_{t+1} [\ln(1 - m_t) + \alpha z_t - \ln B] - q_t z_t,$$

and the first-order conditions are

$$\beta(1 - m_t) = \gamma q_{t+1} m_t,$$

$$q_t = \alpha \gamma q_{t+1} + (1+\beta\alpha).$$

The general solution to the dynamic equation in q_t is

$$q_t = \frac{1 + \alpha\beta}{1 - \alpha\gamma} + \varrho \left(\frac{1}{\alpha\gamma}\right)^t,$$

with ϱ a real constant. There is a unique solution that verifies the transversality condition, which is the constant solution

$$q_t = \frac{1 + \alpha\beta}{1 - \alpha\gamma}.$$

The optimal path of m_t is thus constant too:

$$m_t = \frac{\beta}{\beta + \gamma q_t} = \frac{\beta(1 - \alpha\gamma)}{\beta + \gamma}.$$

The dynamics of x_t is given by

$$x_{t+1} = B \frac{(1 + \alpha\beta)\gamma}{\beta + \gamma} x_t^\alpha.$$

Consumptions and capital are functions of x_t:

$$c_t = \frac{x_t}{1 + \beta}, \qquad d_{t+1} = \frac{(1 + n)\beta(1 - \alpha\gamma)}{\beta + \gamma} B x_t^\alpha,$$

$$k_{t+1} = \frac{\beta}{(1 + \beta)(1 + n)} x_t.$$

The tax on labor income is

$$\tau_t = 1 - \frac{c_t + (1 + n)k_{t+1}}{\omega(k_t)} = 1 - \frac{x_t}{(1 - \alpha)A k_t^\alpha}$$

$$= 1 - \frac{(1 - \epsilon)(1 + \alpha\beta)\gamma}{(\beta + \gamma)(1 - \alpha)}.$$

It is constant and increases with ϵ. The tax on capital income is

$$\theta_t = 1 - \frac{d_t}{f'(k_t)(1 + n)k_t}$$

$$= 1 - \frac{(1 - \epsilon)(1 - \alpha\gamma)\beta}{(\beta + \gamma)\alpha}.$$

It is also constant, different from 0 except for a specific ϵ, and increasing with ϵ.

Without government spending ($\epsilon = 0$), distortionary taxes implement intergenerational transfers which verify

$$\tau w_t + \theta R_t s_{t-1} = 0.$$

This amounts to

$$(1 - \alpha)\tau + \theta\alpha = 0.$$

A further study would be to compare these taxes with the optimal lump-sum taxes.

3.6 CONCLUSION

The aim of this chapter was to show that the overlapping generations model provides a useful toolkit to analyze economic policies. In particular, we have provided three key results.

We first studied the Second Welfare Theorem in the context of overlapping generations. We showed that any feasible trajectory that satisfies the optimal individual life-cycle arbitrage can be decentralized as a competitive equilibrium by using lump-sum taxes and transfers. As any Pareto-optimal trajectory respects the optimal individual life-cycle arbitrage, it can be decentralized.

After the study of general lump-sum transfers, we considered lump-sum pensions, i.e., transfers in favor of the old generation. Applying the results of the welfare theorems, we state that, if under-accumulation of capital prevails, the competitive equilibrium with pensions is Pareto-optimal. Indeed, starting from a Pareto-optimal situation, any lump-sum redistribution of incomes entails an allocation, which is different but also Pareto-efficient as long as one remains in the under-accumulation regime. Consequently, it is not possible to set up a Pareto-improving transition to another pension system. In the study on pensions we also devoted particular attention to the sustainability of the system. A policy is called *sustainable* if the corresponding intertemporal equilibrium exists. Because a sustainable pay-as-you-go pension system reduces the amount of saving during the working years by providing income during retirement, the effect of pensions on capital accumulation is negative. In the long run, a decrease in capital reduces (increases) the net production available for consumption when there is under-accumulation (over-accumulation).

We have also analyzed the optimal way to finance a given path of government expenditures in the absence of lump-sum taxation, using only distorting fiscal instruments. A key point is that this second-best problem is in general non-convex. This difficulty is ignored in the literature, and one generally assumes that the optimal solution exists and is interior. For the simple case with inelastic labor supply, we have tackled this problem in a rigorous way, by analyzing a convex auxiliary problem that characterizes the original problem under certain conditions. We concluded that, when government spending are above a certain threshold, the steady state solution of the auxiliary problem is also the steady state solution of the second-best problem. At this optimum, under-accumulation prevails, and optimal capital taxes are likely to be positive.

FOUR

Debt

Government debt allows the financing of public spending or transfer policies. Issuing debt (for one period in our setup) implies that the government has to pay interest and eventually to reimburse the principal. This can be done in two different ways: if one taxes the future generations to reimburse the debt, the policy amounts to performing an inter-generational transfer. If the government issues new debt in order to reimburse the preceding debt, then the question of the sustainability of such a policy becomes central.

The effect of government debt on growth and welfare is an old debate. According to the view of Ricardo (1817), "it is not by the payment of the interest on the national debt that a country is distressed, nor is it by the exoneration from payment that it can be relieved. It is only by saving from income, and retrenching in expenditure, that the national capital can be increased; and neither the income would be increased, nor the expenditure diminished by the annihilation of the national debt." This famous neutrality result holds in the basic neoclassical growth model but breaks down in the overlapping generations model of Diamond (1965), Phelps and Shell (1969), and Blanchard (1985), in which finite-lived agents consider government debt as net wealth (Barro (1974)). As pointed out by Weil (1989), it is not the assumption of a finite horizon which is responsible for the breakdown of the Ricardian equivalence, but the presence of unborn future generations whose interests are not taken into account by present generations. The overlapping generations model thus provides a relevant framework to study the role of public debt.

In his seminal contribution, Diamond (1965) examines the effect of government debt on the long-run competitive equilibrium of an economy with overlapping generations; he shows that positive debt lowers utility when the equilibrium is efficient (under-accumulation case) but may raise utility in the inefficient case (over-accumulation).[1]

---

[1] The contribution of Diamond (1965) often serves as a building block for further studies on debt and related issues. See, for instance, King (1992), Grossman and Yanagawa

Two kind of policy rules are considered in the literature. In one case, the deficit is kept constant, and debt changes over time. In another case, which is the one considered by Diamond (1965), the debt per capita is kept constant, and taxes are adjusted to meet this objective.

In the case where deficit per capita is constant, two different sub-cases should be distinguished. When the budget is balanced, current taxes finance current spending, and the government reimburses the debt plus interest by issuing new debt. There are in this case some similarities with the dynamics of bubbles studied by Tirole (1985), which can eliminate over-accumulation if the initial bubble is at an adequate level. Studying the different steady states and establishing clearly the distinction between bubbles and debt are on the agenda of this chapter. When the deficit is non-zero, the dynamics can take various forms (Azariadis (1993), Farmer (1986)), depending, a.o., on the value of the deficit. To perform a more complete study than the mentioned authors one should relate each possible steady state with a value of the deficit and study the corresponding local dynamics. This should inform us on the desirability of different deficit policies.

Even in the case where debt per capita is constant, as it is considered by Diamond, the dynamic effects of debt on capital accumulation are complex. Indeed, although debt can be beneficial in a long-run equilibrium, nothing guarantees that, given its initial endowment in capital, the economy will converge to this equilibrium rather than another equilibrium or to an unsustainable outcome.[2] Hence, the issue of the sustainability of constant debt per capita is central to the dynamic analysis.[3] Moreover, there is in general more than one steady state equilibrium. Hence there is a second worthy question, beyond the issue of sustainability: towards which equilibrium does the economy converge?

Section 4.1 introduces public debt into the model of chapter 1. The limits of the approach in terms of inter-temporal budget constraint are clearly established in section 4.2. In section 4.3, we analyze the effect of constant deficit policies on capital accumulation and debt dynamics. The difference between

(1993), King and Ferguson (1993), Bertocchi (1994), Uhlig (1998), and Azariadis and Smith (1998).

[2] Renewed interest in sustainability issues has been fostered by the Maastricht Treaty, imposing on European governments the duty to reach a maximum level of debt equivalent to 60% of GDP.

[3] A recent paper by Rankin and Roffia (1999) has a comparable motivation: "There is a need to investigate another aspect of unsustainability: namely, the possibility that, even with a constant stock of debt, fiscal policy may be unsustainable because a steady state equilibrium [...] may not exist. [...] It is necessary to have a good understanding of the technical limits to debt before we can make serious progress in modelling its political limits." As we shall show, the existence of a steady state is not sufficient to guarantee sustainability; stability is also required. Notice also that the analysis of Rankin and Roffia (1999) is carried out in a Cobb–Douglas world, while we would like to analyze this issue with general preferences and production functions, without, e.g., imposing Inada conditions.

debt and bubble dynamics is also clarified. In section 4.4, we analyze the effect of a constant debt policy on capital accumulation and provide a global treatment of the dynamics. Section 4.5 provides applications and extensions.

4.1 DIAMOND'S MODEL WITH DEBT

In this section, we list the changes that should be made in the model of chapter 1 in order to take public debt into account.

4.1.1 The Model

The government has to finance public spending G_t. It can use lump-sum taxes $N_t \tau_t^1$ on the income of the young households, and $N_{t-1} \tau_t^2$ on the income of old people. It can also issue a debt B_t, and it has to repay the debt of the preceding period B_{t-1} plus the accrued interests $r_t B_{t-1}$. The government in this model always honors its debt. We thus have

$$B_t + N_t \tau_t^1 + N_{t-1} \tau_t^2 = (1 + r_t) B_{t-1} + G_t. \tag{4.1}$$

This budget constraints links the three instruments at period t. The government's budget is balanced when

$$N_t \tau_t^1 + N_{t-1} \tau_t^2 = G_t,$$

i.e., total taxes equal spending. The government runs a deficit when $N_t \tau_t^1 + N_{t-1} \tau_t^2 < G_t$; it runs a surplus if the opposite holds.

At the first period $t = 0$, each of the N_{-1} old households is the owner of the same fraction of the installed capital stock K_0 and of the existing debt B_{-1}. We assume that $K_0 > 0$ and $B_{-1} > -K_0$. Their wealth is thus $s_{-1} = (K_0 + B_{-1})/N_{-1}$, and their net income is equal to $R_0 s_{-1} - \tau_0^2$.

The net income of the young individuals is equal to the real wage w_t minus the lump-sum tax τ_t^1 levied by the government. They allocate this income between current consumption c_t and savings s_t. The budget constraint of period t is

$$w_t - \tau_t^1 = c_t + s_t. \tag{4.2}$$

In their second period of life, $t + 1$, they are retired. Their income comes from the return on the savings made at time t minus the taxes imposed on the old generation.[4] Their expected consumption is

$$d_{t+1}^e = R_{t+1}^e s_t - \tau_{t+1}^{2e}. \tag{4.3}$$

---

[4] In Diamond (1965) the government does not impose taxes on the older generation. An extension of Diamond (1965) to a framework with two different taxes is proposed in Ihori (1978).

At time t each *young individual* anticipates a return R_{t+1}^e for his savings and a future tax τ_{t+1}^{2e}. Each young individual maximizes

$$u(c_t) + \beta u(d_{t+1}^e),$$

subject to equations (4.2) and (4.3). Optimal savings are described by using the function of section 3.1.1 defined when the agent receives income in both periods of life:

$$s_t = \tilde{s}(w_t - \tau_t^1, -\tau_{t+1}^{2e}, R_{t+1}^e). \tag{4.4}$$

This savings function is defined provided that the expected life-cycle income is positive:

$$w_t > \tau_t^1 + \frac{\tau_{t+1}^{2e}}{R_{t+1}^e}. \tag{4.5}$$

When his savings s_{t-1} are fixed, each old consumer consumes

$$d_t = R_t s_{t-1} - \tau_t^2.$$

For d_t to be positive, one needs

$$\tau_t^2 < R_t s_{t-1}. \tag{4.6}$$

The behavior of firms remains unchanged. The capital stock $K_t = I_{t-1}$ is installed, their labor demand is defined by $F_L'(K_t, L_t) = w_t$, i.e., $\omega(K_t/L_t) = w_t$, and they distribute their profits to the capital owners: $\pi_t = Y_t - w_t L_t = K_t f'(K_t/L_t)$.

The savings of the young households at time t are used to finance both the public debt and the capital of firms. Since the one-period bonds of the government have the same characteristics (in terms of risk) as the private deposits, debt and capital are substitutes in the portfolios of wealth owners.[5] Investment in physical capital is given by

$$I_t = N_t s_t - B_t.$$

4.1.2 The Temporary Equilibrium

We first define the temporary equilibrium. The temporary equilibrium of period t gives the equilibrium value of the current variables as a function of the past and of the expectations about the future. At period t the existing debt B_{t-1} and capital $K_t = I_{t-1} > 0$ are given. They are linked to the savings of the old through

$$N_{t-1} s_{t-1} = I_{t-1} + B_{t-1}. \tag{4.7}$$

[5] Diamond (1965) calls this case "internal debt." He also studies another case where debt is "external" and domestic wealth owners only detain the stock of capital.

The foresight of the young (τ_{t+1}^{2e} and R_{t+1}^e) is also given. For a given G_t, the government chooses its instruments B_t, τ_t^1, and τ_t^2 in order to satisfy its budget constraint (4.1).

At equilibrium the returns on public debt and private capital are equal: $1 + r_t = R_t$. The labor demand L_t is equal to the labor supply N_t. We deduce that

$$w_t = \omega(k_t) \text{ and } R_t = f'(k_t) \quad \text{with} \quad k_t = \frac{K_t}{N_t}, \tag{4.8}$$

and the government decisions are linked by

$$B_t + N_t \tau_t^1 + N_{t-1} \tau_t^2 = G_t + f'(k_t) B_{t-1}. \tag{4.9}$$

Following (4.6), the taxation of the old should be smaller than their income. The anticipations of the young should verify (4.5) with $w_t = \omega(k_t)$. Furthermore, for private investment to be positive, one needs

$$I_t = N_t s_t - B_t = N_t \tilde{s}(w_t - \tau_t^1, -\tau_{t+1}^{2e}, R_{t+1}^e) - B_t > 0, \tag{4.10}$$

using the savings function (4.4). Equation (4.10) gives a restriction on the government debt, depending on the net wage $w_t - \tau_t^1$ and expectations.

Proposition 4.1 (Existence of a temporary equilibrium with debt)
Given the variables $\{B_{t-1}, s_{t-1}, I_{t-1}\}$ from the previous period for which (4.7) holds, and given government spending G_t and the expected variables R_{t+1}^e and τ_{t+1}^{2e}, there exists a temporary equilibrium with instruments $(B_t, \tau_t^1, \tau_t^2)$ and positive investment if and only if, with $k_t = K_t/N_t = I_{t-1}/N_t$, and prices w_t and R_t given by (4.8), the following conditions hold:

- *the expected life-cycle income of the young household is positive, i.e., equation (4.5) holds;*
- *the consumption of the old household is positive, i.e., equation (4.6) holds;*
- *the three instruments $(B_t, \tau_t^1, \tau_t^2)$ are linked by the budget constraint (4.9);*
- *the debt and tax τ_t^1 allow for positive investment, i.e., equation (4.10) holds.*

4.1.3 The Inter-temporal Equilibrium with Perfect Foresight

An inter-temporal equilibrium with perfect foresight is a sequence of temporary equilibria which verify the assumption of perfect foresight:

$$\forall t \geq 0, \quad \tau_{t+1}^{2e} = \tau_{t+1}^2 \text{ and } R_{t+1}^e = R_{t+1}.$$

It is thus characterized by sequences $(B_t, \tau_t^1, \tau_t^2)$, $(K_t, L_t, Y_t, k_t, I_t)$, (c_t, s_t, d_t), (w_t, R_t), which verify $\forall t \geq 0$:

- $K_t = I_{t-1}$, $L_t = N_t$, $Y_t = F(K_t, N_t)$, $k_t = \frac{K_t}{N_t}$, $w_t = \omega(k_t)$, $R_t = f'(k_t)$;
- $I_t = N_t s_t - B_t > 0$, $s_t = \tilde{s}(w_t - \tau_t^1, -\tau_{t+1}^2, R_{t+1})$, $w_t > \tau_t^1 + \frac{\tau_{t+1}^2}{R_{t+1}}$;

- $B_t + N_t\tau_t^1 + N_{t-1}\tau_{t+1}^2 = G_t + R_t B_{t-1}$;
- $c_t = w_t - \tau_t^1 - s_t, d_t = R_t s_{t-1} - \tau_t^2 > 0.$

Note that, except at $t = 0$ where s_{-1} is given, the condition that $\tau_t^2 < R_t s_{t-1}$ results from the positivity of the life-cycle income (4.5), which implies that the two optimal consumptions are positive.

We now define the variables in intensive form: public spending per capita is $g_t = G_t/N_t$, and debt per capita is $b_t = B_{t-1}/N_t$. Note that the time index associated to b_t is chosen by symmetry with respect to k_t. Both b_t and k_t are pre-determined variables.

The following proposition characterizes the inter-temporal equilibrium in terms of the intensive variables k_t and b_t.

Proposition 4.2 (Characteristics of an inter-temporal equilibrium with debt)
Given the initial conditions $k_0 = K_0/N_0$ and $b_0 = B_{-1}/N_0$, and the path $(g_t)_{t\geq 0}$, an inter-temporal equilibrium with perfect foresight is characterized by the sequences $(k_t, b_t)_{t\geq 0}$ and $(\tau_t^1, \tau_t^2)_{t\geq 0}$, which verify two dynamic equations

$$(1+n)(k_{t+1} + b_{t+1}) = \tilde{s}\big(\omega(k_t) - \tau_t^1, -\tau_{t+1}^2, f'(k_{t+1})\big),$$

$$(1+n)b_{t+1} + \tau_t^1 + \frac{\tau_{t+1}^2}{1+n} = g_t + f'(k_t)b_t,$$

(4.11)

and also verify the constraints $\tau_0^2 < f'(k_0)(1+n)(k_0 + b_0)$ and

$$\forall t \geq 0, \qquad k_{t+1} > 0, \quad \omega(k_t) > \tau_t^1 + \frac{\tau_{t+1}^2}{f'(k_{t+1})}.$$

Proof: It is easy to verify that the equilibrium variables $(B_t), (K_t, L_t, Y_t, k_t, I_t)$, $(c_t, s_t, d_t), (w_t, R_t)$ for all periods t are determined as functions of $(k_t, b_t)_{t\geq 0}$ and $(\tau_t^1, \tau_t^2)_{t\geq 0}$.   ∎

To study this class of equilibria we shall assume more specific policies. In particular, we shall consider constant deficit policies and constant debt policies. However, before the analysis of the dynamics in these two special cases, it is necessary to study the role of debt as a tool for economic policy that depends on the available fiscal instruments. Accordingly, we analyze the restrictions bearing on taxes and debt, with a special focus on the *government inter-temporal budget constraint* and its link to the availability of the different instruments.

4.2 THE INTER-TEMPORAL BUDGET CONSTRAINT OF THE GOVERNMENT

The inter-temporal budget constraint of the government has become a focus of an important literature dealing with the sustainability of government deficit.

In this literature, sustainability should be understood in the sense of solvency: for instance, Ahmed and Rogers (1995) write that "Solvency requires that asymptotically the government cannot leave a debt that has a positive expected present value." To explore the theoretical relevance of the debate we start from the constraint of period t (4.1),

$$B_t + N_t \tau_t^1 + N_{t-1} \tau_t^2 = (1 + r_t) B_{t-1} + G_t,$$

which can be written, after multiplying by ρ_t,

$$\rho_t B_t = \rho_{t-1} B_{t-1} + \rho_t G_t - \rho_t T_t,$$

where $T_t = N_t \tau_t^1 + N_{t-1} \tau_t^2$ is the total of taxes and where the discount factors are defined recursively by

$$\forall t \geq 0, \quad \rho_t = \frac{\rho_{t-1}}{1 + r_t} \quad \text{with} \quad \rho_{-1} = 1.$$

By induction we have

$$\rho_{t_0} B_{t_0} = B_{-1} + \sum_{t=0}^{t_0} \rho_t G_t - \sum_{t=0}^{t_0} \rho_t T_t. \tag{4.12}$$

As noted by Hamilton and Flavin (1986), equation (4.12) causes little controversy, since it is derived from an accounting identity. The interesting question concerns what happen to the left-hand side when t_0 gets large: Where is the actual value of the debt going to?

Assume that the discounted sum of the differences $G_t - T_t$ converges. If the left-hand side of (4.12) goes to zero in the limit,

$$\lim_{t \to \infty} \rho_t B_t = 0, \tag{4.13}$$

then the present value of taxes net of spending should cover the initial debt:

$$\sum_{t=0}^{\infty} \rho_t (T_t - G_t) = B_{-1}. \tag{4.14}$$

Definition 4.1 (Inter-temporal budget constraint of the government)
For a given sequence of discount factors $(\rho_t)_{t \geq 0}$, an initial debt B_{-1}, a sequence of government spending $(G_t)_{t \geq 0}$, and a sequence of lump-sum taxes $(T_t)_{t \geq 0}$, we say that the inter-temporal budget constraint of the government holds if:

- *the discounted value of the difference between spending and taxes is finite;*
- *initial debt is financed by total taxes net of spending, i.e., equation (4.14) holds.*

Equation (4.13) is a necessary and sufficient condition for (4.14) to hold.

In the face of such a constraint, two attitudes are possible. The first one, as in Hamilton and Flavin (1986), consists in testing the statistical implications of equation (4.14) shedding light on whether the government satisfies the inter-temporal budget constraint. If these equations were not supported by the data, one would conclude that the inter-temporal budget constraint need not be satisfied. On the contrary, the second approach to the inter-temporal budget constraint, as in Wilcox (1989), "regards the necessity of the present-value borrowing constraint in a dynamically efficient economy as established on theoretical grounds." The aim of this section is accordingly to investigate whether this second view is correct or not.

In models with representative infinite-lived agents, the condition (4.13) holds when debt is positive. This results from the inter-temporal budget constraint of the representative agent.[6] Indeed,

$$\lim_{t \to \infty} \rho_t (K_t + B_{t-1}) = 0$$

implies the following restriction on the borrowing possibilities of the government:

$$\lim_{t \to +\infty} \sup \, \rho_t B_t \leq 0,$$

and in the case of a positive debt this leads to (4.13).

In overlapping generations models, the inter-temporal budget constraint of the government is not the mirror of the inter-temporal budget constraint of a private agent, since there are no infinite-lived individuals. We shall see that the conclusion on whether the inter-temporal budget constraint of the government should hold depends crucially on the number of available fiscal instruments. When there are two types of taxes (three instruments), there is no restriction on government borrowing. On the contrary, when there is only one type of tax (two instruments), the debt that can decentralize a given trajectory is determined. However, this unique debt trajectory may or may not satisfy the inter-temporal budget constraint of the government, depending on the accumulation regime.

4.2.1 Debt with the Two Types of Lump-sum Taxes

When there are both types of lump-sum taxes, Proposition 3.1 on the decentralization of feasible allocations can be generalized to the case with debt and public spending.

Proposition 4.3 (Decentralization with debt and public spending)
Let $(\check{c}_t, \check{d}_t, \check{k}_{t+1})_{t \geq 0}$ be a feasible trajectory starting at $\check{k}_0 = k_0$ with government spending $(g_t)_{t \geq 0}$, i.e. such that for all $t \geq 0$

$$f(\check{k}_t) = g_t + \check{c}_t + \frac{\check{d}_t}{1+n} + (1+n)\check{k}_{t+1},$$

---

[6] Crettez, Michel, and Wigniolle (1999) provide a careful study of the borrowing restrictions with infinite-lived agents.

which also satisfies for all t ≥ 0

$$u'(\check{c}_t) = \beta f'(\check{k}_{t+1})u'(\check{d}_{t+1}).$$

Then, for any sequence of real numbers $(B_t)_{t \geq -1}$, there exists a sequence of lump-sum taxes $(\tau_t^1, \tau_t^2)_{t \geq 0}$ such that this trajectory $(\check{c}_t, \check{d}_t, \check{k}_{t+1})_{t \geq 0}$, together with $(B_t, \tau_t^1, \tau_t^2)_{t \geq 0}$, is an inter-temporal equilibrium with perfect foresight.

Proof: We define the tax levels which give, for savings equal to $\check{s}_t = (1+n)$ $(b_{t+1} + \check{k}_{t+1})$ and $b_{t+1} = B_t/N_{t+1}$, the consumptions $\check{c}_t$ and $\check{d}_t$:

$$\tau_t^1 = f(\check{k}_t) - \check{k}_t f'(\check{k}_t) - \check{s}_t - \check{c}_t, \tag{4.15}$$

$$\tau_t^2 = f'(\check{k}_t)\check{s}_{t-1} - \check{d}_t. \tag{4.16}$$

The life-cycle income is

$$\omega(\check{k}_t) - \tau_t^1 - \frac{\tau_{t+1}^2}{f'(\check{k}_{t+1})},$$

which, after using (4.15)–(4.16), equals

$$\check{c}_t + \frac{\check{d}_{t+1}}{f'(\check{k}_{t+1})} > 0.$$

This implies that τ_t^1 and τ_{t+1}^2 satisfy the positivity constraint of the life-cycle income. Following the individual arbitrage condition, we have

$$\check{s}_t = \tilde{s}\big(\omega(\check{k}_t) - \tau_t^1, -\tau_{t+1}^2, f'(\check{k}_{t+1})\big),$$

where the function $\tilde{s}(\cdot)$ is defined in equation (3.2). Finally, by substituting $\check{c}_t$ and $\check{d}_t$ in the resource constraint

$$f(\check{k}_t) - g_t - (1+n)\check{k}_{t+1} = \check{c}_t + \frac{\check{d}_t}{1+n}$$

$$= f(\check{k}_t) - \check{k}_t f'(\check{k}_t) - \tau_t^1 - \check{s}_t + \frac{f'(\check{k}_t)\check{s}_{t-1} - \tau_t^2}{1+n}$$

with $\check{s}_t = (1+n)(b_{t+1} + \check{k}_{t+1})$, this conditions becomes

$$f(\check{k}_t) - g_t - (1+n)\check{k}_{t+1} = f(\check{k}_t) - \check{k}_t f'(\check{k}_t) - \tau_t^1 - (1+n)(b_{t+1} + \check{k}_{t+1})$$

$$+ \frac{1}{1+n}\big[f'(\check{k}_t)(1+n)(b_t + \check{k}_t) - \tau_t^2\big],$$

and one obtains the condition (4.11) on the instruments of the government. ∎

With the appropriate choice of taxes (4.15)–(4.16), the condition (4.11) is a consequence of the resource constraint.

This proposition generalizes the decentralization theorem (proposition 3.1) to allow for arbitrary levels of debt. It shows that there is no restriction on public debt as long as the government can tax the two generations freely. This holds because the government has three instruments available in each period,[7] among which any two are sufficient to decentralize a feasible allocation for which the individual life-cycle arbitrage holds. More precisely, one can decentralize any optimal trajectory by fixing arbitrarily the path of any of the three instruments:

1. For a given arbitrary path of debt $(b_t)_{t\geq 0}$, Proposition 4.3 gives the two taxes that should be implemented. With $b_t = 0$ and $g_t = 0$ for all t, we retrieve proposition 3.1.
2. With $(\tau_t^1)_{t\geq 0}$ given arbitrarily and b_0 given by the initial condition, equation (4.15) determines the path of debt $(b_t)_{t\geq 1}$ and equation (4.16) determines the path of taxes $(\tau_t^2)_{t\geq 0}$ that decentralize the optimal allocation.
3. With $(\tau_t^2)_{t\geq 1}$ given arbitrarily and b_0 given by the initial condition, τ_0^2 should be chosen according to equation (4.16) at $t = 0$. $(b_t)_{t\geq 1}$ is now determined by (4.16), and $(\tau_t^1)_{t\geq 0}$ by (4.15).

Note that, in the third scenario, τ_0^2 cannot be given exogenously. Indeed, the only way to obtain the right level of consumption for the first old generation is to use τ_0^2: $\tau_0^2 = f'(k_0)s_{-1} - \check{d}_0$ with k_0 and s_{-1} given.

Public debt appears here as a device to transfer resources between generations. Its effect can be neutralized by an adequate mix of lump-sum taxes. We can obtain the same equilibrium as the one with no debt when the government can tax both generations.

Example: To illustrate an optimal allocation where the constraint (4.13) does not hold, let us take again the case of a log-linear utility function and a Cobb–Douglas production function. For simplicity, we consider an optimal stationary path with an social discount factor γ. From chapter 2 (section 2.4.1), we know that this path is characterized by

$$\check{k} = \left(\frac{\alpha\gamma}{1+n} A \right)^{\frac{1}{1-\alpha}},$$

$$\check{c} = \frac{1 - \alpha\gamma}{1 + \beta/\gamma} A\check{k}^{\alpha},$$

$$\check{d} = \frac{\beta(1+n)}{\gamma} \frac{1 - \alpha\gamma}{1 + \beta/\gamma} A\check{k}^{\alpha}.$$

[7] With an infinite number of periods, this means in fact an infinite number of instruments. Here we analyze the three types of instruments available in each period.

We consider a debt which increases over time according to

$$b_t = \lambda \left(\frac{1}{\gamma}\right)^t, \qquad \text{i.e.} \quad B_t = \lambda \left(\frac{1}{\gamma}\right)^t N_{t+1},$$

where λ is a real positive constant. The initial debt B_0 is distributed to the first old households. Given that

$$\rho_t = R^{-t} = \left(\frac{\gamma}{1+n}\right)^t,$$

the condition (4.13) does not hold; for

$$\lim_{t \to \infty} \rho_t B_t = \lambda.$$

Let us now compute the taxes that will decentralize the optimal allocation, given the above path for debt. The path of taxes is given by (4.15)–(4.16):

$$\tau_t^1 = (1-\alpha)A\check{k}^\alpha - \check{c} - (1+n)(\check{k} + b_{t+1}) = \check{\tau}_t^1 - (1+n)b_{t+1},$$

$$\tau_t^2 = \alpha A\check{k}^{\alpha-1}(1+n)(\check{k} + b_t) - \check{d} = (1+n)^2 b_{t+1} + \alpha A\check{k}^\alpha - \check{d}$$

$$= \check{\tau}_t^2 + (1+n)^2 b_{t+1},$$

using $\alpha A\check{k}^{\alpha-1} = (1+n)/\gamma$ and $b_t/\gamma = b_{t+1}$. Taxes have two components: the transfers without debt, $\check{\tau}_t^1$ and $\check{\tau}_t^2$, i.e., the transfers that would decentralize the given path in the absence of debt ($\lambda = 0$), and a component neutralizing the effect of debt; The transfers without debt,

$$\check{\tau}_t^1 = (1-\alpha)A\check{k}^\alpha - \check{c} - (1+n)\check{k} = \check{\tau}^1 \qquad \forall t,$$

$$\check{\tau}_t^2 = \alpha A\check{k}^\alpha - \check{d} = \check{\tau}^2 \qquad \forall t,$$

are constant through time.

Let us finally compute the aggregate taxes:

$$T_t = \tau_t^1 N_t + \tau_t^2 N_{t-1} = N_t \left(\check{\tau}^1 + \frac{\check{\tau}^2}{1+n}\right)$$

$$= N_t \left(A\check{k}^\alpha - \check{c} - (1+n)\check{k} - \frac{\check{d}}{1+n}\right)$$

$$= 0.$$

Aggregate taxes are zero, implying that the reimbursement of the initial debt λ is postponed forever. The tax on the young decreases continuously over time and tends to $-\infty$. This negative tax amounts to subsidize the young households so that they are able to absorb the increasing debt. Moreover, the tax on the old tends to $+\infty$. For each agent, the government taxes away the wealth it has given to him when young. This debt is a Ponzi debt (see below, section 4.2.3).

4.2.2 Debt with a Restriction of Only One Type of Lump-sum Tax

When there is only one type of taxation available, we can no longer apply proposition 3.1. To decentralize a feasible path, debt is now necessary. We first consider the case with no taxation of the young. Next we consider the case with no taxation of the old and show that, in both cases, there is a restriction on debt at each period. We finally study the consequence of this restriction for the inter-temporal budget constraint.

Taxation of Old Households. When we exclude the taxation of the young households ($\tau_t^1 = 0 \forall t$), the debt that can decentralize a feasible trajectory should satisfy the first-period budget constraint with $\check{s}_t = (1+n)(b_{t+1} + \check{k}_{t+1})$:

$$(1+n)b_{t+1} = \omega(\check{k}_t) - (1+n)\check{k}_{t+1} - \check{c}_t < \omega(\check{k}_t) < f(\check{k}_t),$$

and with the resource constraint of the economy we have

$$(1+n)b_{t+1} = \omega(\check{k}_t) - f(\check{k}_t) + g_t + \frac{\check{d}_t}{1+n} > -f(\check{k}_t).$$

Thus, no taxation of the young implies that the debt in absolute value remains smaller than the national product:

$$\forall t, \qquad |B_t| < \check{Y}_t,$$

since $\check{Y}_t = N_t f(\check{k}_t)$ and $B_t = (1+n)N_t b_{t+1}$.

Taxation of Young Households. When we exclude the taxation on the old households ($\tau_t^2 = 0 \forall t \geq 1$; τ_0^2 should always be chosen to realize $\check{d}_0$), we obtain the following restriction, derived from the second-period budget constraint:

$$(1+n)f'(\check{k}_t)b_t = \check{d}_t - (1+n)f'(\check{k}_t) \cdot k_t.$$

To guarantee a positive $\check{d}_t$, one needs $b_t > -\check{k}_t$. As $f(\check{k}_{t-1}) > (1+n)\check{k}_t$, we obtain

$$b_t > -\check{k}_t > -\frac{f(\check{k}_{t-1})}{1+n}.$$

Moreover, to guarantee a positive capital stock one needs $(1+n)f'(\check{k}_t)b_t < \check{d}_t$. As $\check{d}_t < (1+n)f(\check{k}_t)$, we obtain

$$(1+n)f'(\check{k}_t)b_t < \check{d}_t < (1+n)f(\check{k}_t).$$

We deduce the following two restrictions:

$$B_{t-1} > -\check{Y}_{t-1} \text{ and } \check{R}_t B_{t-1} < \check{Y}_t \qquad \text{for all} \quad t \geq 1.$$

Summary. As a consequence, in the two cases with only one lump-sum tax available, the public debt necessarily verifies the following condition, introduced by Crettez, Michel, and Wigniolle (2000):

$$\forall t \geq 0, \qquad |B_t| < \max\left\{ \check{Y}_t, \frac{\check{Y}_{t+1}}{\check{R}_{t+1}} \right\}. \qquad (4.17)$$

At each date, the public debt in absolute value or the reimbursement of debt cannot exceed the national product. Alternatively, one can see this restriction as a ceiling on the debt–GDP ratio. We have indeed shown the following result:

Proposition 4.4 (Ceiling on the debt–GDP ratio)
There is a ceiling on the debt–GDP ratio,

$$v_t = \max\left[1, \frac{f(\check{k}_{t+1})/f(\check{k}_t)}{f'(\check{k}_{t+1})} \right],$$

such that

$$\frac{|B_t|}{\check{Y}_t} = \frac{|B_t|}{f(\check{k}_t)N_t} < v_t$$

has to hold for a feasible allocation with $(\check{k}_t)_{t\geq 0}$ to be decentralized with debt and one type of lump-sum tax.

If the GDP growth factor $f(\check{k}_{t+1})/f(\check{k}_t)$ is smaller than the gross rate of return on capital, $f'(\check{k}_{t+1})$, the ceiling is equal to one. Otherwise, it is given by the ratio of growth to the rate of return. Let us study the trajectories with a ceiling when $\check{k}_t$ converges to a limit k.

Proposition 4.5 (Efficiency and the inter-temporal budget constraint)
If the feasible sequence $\check{k}_t$ converges towards k with under-accumulation, then any debt with ceiling (4.17) necessarily satisfies the condition (4.13):

$$\lim_{t \to +\infty} \check{p}_t B_t = 0, \qquad where \quad \check{p}_t = \frac{1}{f'(\check{k}_t)}\check{p}_{t-1} \quad and \quad \check{p}_{-1} = 1.$$

If the sequence $\check{k}_t$ converges towards k in over-accumulation, then there exists a debt for which (4.17) holds, but the inter-temporal budget constraint does not hold, since (4.13) is not verified.

Proof: We have

$$\frac{\check{p}_{t+1}\check{Y}_{t+1}}{\check{p}_t\check{Y}_t} = \frac{N_{t+1}f(\check{k}_{t+1})}{\check{R}_{t+1}N_t f(\check{k}_t)} = \frac{1+n}{f'(\check{k}_{t+1})}\frac{f(\check{k}_{t+1})}{f(\check{k}_t)}.$$

We distinguish two cases.

- If $f'(k) = \lim f'(\check{k}_t) > 1 + n$, the above expression converges towards

$$\frac{1 + n}{f'(k)} < 1.$$

Hence, the positive sequence $\check{\rho}_t \check{Y}_t$ converges towards 0. As (4.17) can be written

$$\forall t \geq 0, \qquad |\check{\rho}_t B_t| < \max\{\check{\rho}_t \check{Y}_t, \ \check{\rho}_{t+1} \check{Y}_{t+1}\},$$

we deduce that $\lim_{t \to \infty} \check{\rho}_t B_t = 0$.
- If $f'(k) < 1 + n$, we observe that the sequence $\check{\rho}_t \check{Y}_t$ goes to infinity and that the debt $B_t = \frac{1}{2}\check{Y}_t$ verifies (4.17), but $\check{\rho}_t B_t$ goes to infinity. ∎

Note that when $\check{k}_t$ goes to the golden rule capital stock, a case not considered in proposition 4.5, $\lim \check{\rho}_t \check{B}_t$ can be either nil or strictly positive (see Crettez, Michel, and Wigniolle (2000)).

4.2.3 Ponzi Games

According to the skeptic's dictionary of Carroll (2000), "Following a Ponzi scheme, named after Charles Ponzi who defrauded people in the 1920s using the method, involves getting people to invest in something for a guaranteed rate of return and using the money of later investors to pay off the earlier ones."

We use the following formal definition of Buiter and Kletzer (1994):

Definition 4.2 (Ponzi debt)

A Ponzi debt $(B_t)_{t \geq 0}$ is a sequence of debt that satisfies, for all t,

$$B_t \geq R_t B_{t-1} \quad and \quad B_{-1} > 0.$$

At each date, the new debt covers at least the reimbursement of the debt of the previous period. With such a debt we have for all t

$$\rho_t B_t \geq \rho_{t-1} B_{t-1} \quad and \quad \rho_{-1} B_{-1} > 0.$$

The positive sequence $\rho_t B_t$ is non-decreasing and has a limit which is either a positive real number or $+\infty$. Consequently, the inter-temporal budget constraint of the government does not hold.

It is often explained in the literature that Ponzi debt is excluded in an economy with under-accumulation: "If r is greater than [the growth rate], then government debt will increase faster than the economy, and the Ponzi scheme will eventually be rendered infeasible: The debt will grow so large that

the government will be unable to find buyers for all of it, facing either default or a tax increase." (From *The Handbook of Macroeconomics*, Elmendorf and Mankiw (1999).)

We have seen that, if taxes on both generations are available, any path of debt can be implemented with any given feasible allocation. This implies in particular that Ponzi debt is feasible, whether over-accumulation prevails or not. The example of section 4.2.1 is an example of Ponzi debt with an optimal path (hence with under-accumulation); in this case, generation-specific taxes grow unboundedly, but total taxes are zero (with no public spending).

If there is only one tax available, the usual result of the literature (impossibility of Ponzi debt in an economy displaying under-accumulation) is in line with proposition 4.5. However, we have an additional result: in the case of over-accumulation, the Ponzi debts are subject to the ceiling of proposition 4.4.

4.3 CONSTANT DEFICIT POLICIES

In this section, we consider exogenous constant deficit policies and study the steady states and their stability. The stability property is essential for a meaningful study of the effect of policy changes in the long run.

We assume in this section that the policy of the government is to keep the deficit constant. We also assume that lump-sum taxes and government spending per young are constant. Hence, we consider constant lump-sum taxes $\tau_t^1 = \tau^1$, $\tau_t^2 = \tau^2$ $\forall t$ and constant spending $g_t = g$ $\forall t$. We define the budget deficit per young individual as

$$\delta = g - \tau^1 - \frac{\tau^2}{1+n}.$$

This constant deficit policy implies the following dynamic equation for debt:

$$b_{t+1} = \frac{R_t}{1+n}b_t + \delta,$$

which describes the appropriate level of debt to maintain constant the level δ of the deficit.

We shall study the inter-temporal equilibria with perfect foresight, which are characterized by the following dynamic equations (see proposition 4.2):

$$(1+n)(k_{t+1} + b_{t+1}) = \tilde{s}(\omega(k_t) - \tau^1, -\tau^2, f'(k_{t+1})), \tag{4.18}$$

$$(1+n)b_{t+1} = f'(k_t)b_t + \delta. \tag{4.19}$$

By substitution of b_{t+1}, equation (4.18) becomes

$$(1+n)k_{t+1} = \tilde{s}(\omega(k_t) - \tau^1, -\tau^2, f'(k_{t+1})) - f'(k_t)b_t - \delta. \tag{4.20}$$

A global analysis of this two-dimensional system cannot be carried out in the general case. To give a flavor of the logic of these dynamics, we first consider the associated dynamics obtained by keeping debt constant, $b_{t+1} = b$, in equation (4.18):[8]

$$(1+n)(k_{t+1} + b) = \tilde{s}(\omega(k_t) - \tau^1, -\tau^2, f'(k_{t+1})).$$

Following the same argument as in section 1.5.2 for the model without debt, the dynamics are well defined and monotonic if

$$1 + n - \tilde{s}'_R(\omega(k_t) - \tau_t^1, -\tau_t^2, f'(k_{t+1})) > 0.$$

A steady state k is locally stable if at it we have:

$$\tilde{s}'_{\omega_1}\omega' < 1 + n - \tilde{s}'_R f''.$$

The dynamics obtained by keeping capital constant in equation (4.20) are much simpler:

$$(1+n)b_{t+1} = f'(k)b_t + \delta.$$

They are stable if there is over-accumulation of capital at k, and unstable if there is under-accumulation. As we shall see, these conditions are not sufficient to determine the dynamics in the two-dimensional system, even for local analysis.

We shall proceed by analyzing the different possible steady states and study their local stability. A steady state (k, b) is defined by the following two conditions:

$$(1+n)(k+b) = \tilde{s}(\omega(k) - \tau^1, -\tau^2, f'(k)), \qquad (4.21)$$

$$(1 + n - f'(k))b = \delta. \qquad (4.22)$$

In the sequel we shall use the following assumption of local stability in the associated dynamics:

Assumption A10.
At a steady state (k, b) verifying (4.21)–(4.22), we have

$$\tilde{s}'_{\omega_1}\omega' < 1 + n - \tilde{s}'_R f'',$$

where the arguments of $\tilde{s}$ are $\omega(k) - \tau^1$, $-\tau^2$, and $f'(k)$.

We start by considering balanced budget policies (zero deficit), before analyzing the more complex case with non-zero deficit. The relationship between bubbles and debt is studied in a last section. In all the subsequent analysis we suppose that the golden rule exists (assumption **A5**): $k_{GR} > 0$ is solution to $f'(k_{GR}) = 1 + n$.

---

[8] The global dynamics in the case of constant debt and varying deficit are studied in section 4.4.

4.3.1 Balanced Budget Policies: Local Analysis

When the deficit is nil ($\delta = 0$), equation (4.22) shows that only two possibilities may occur: the capital stock is at the golden rule level, $f'(k) = 1 + n$, and/or the long-term debt is nil, $b = 0$.

The Golden Rule Steady State with Debt.

Proposition 4.6 (The golden rule steady state with debt)
*Assume the existence of the golden rule k_{GR} (assumption **A5**). Given government spending $g < \omega(k_{GR})$ and the tax τ^2 on the old, there exists a unique level of debt b_{GR} such that (k_{GR}, b_{GR}) is a steady state with zero deficit. This level is given by*

$$b_{GR} = \frac{s(\omega(k_{GR}) - g, 1 + n) + \tau^2/(1 + n)}{1 + n} - k_{GR}. \tag{4.23}$$

Proof: Assuming that $\delta = g - \tau^1 - \tau^2/(1 + n) = 0$, (k_{GR}, b_{GR}) is a steady state of the dynamics (4.19)–(4.20) if and only if

$$(1 + n)(k_{GR} + b_{GR}) = \tilde{s}(\omega(k_{GR}) - \tau^1, -\tau^2, 1 + n).$$

Such an equilibrium exists if and only if the life-cycle income is positive:

$$\omega(k_{GR}) - \tau^1 - \frac{\tau^2}{1 + n} = \omega(k_{GR}) - g > 0. \tag{4.24}$$

This inequality $g < \omega(k_{GR})$ imposes an upper bound on government spending. This bound is equal to wage income at the golden rule. When the condition (4.24) holds, there is a unique stationary level of debt b_{GR}, which depends on the distribution (τ^1, τ^2), that allows one to finance g:

$$(1 + n)b_{GR} = \tilde{s}(\omega(k_{GR}) - \tau^1, -\tau^2, 1 + n) - (1 + n)k_{GR}.$$

Using equation (3.3), which links the function $\tilde{s}(\cdot)$ to the standard saving function, we obtain equation (4.23). ∎

Note that given government spending g and the tax on the old τ^2, the tax on the young τ^1 is determined by the condition of zero deficit: $\tau^1 = g - \tau^2/(1 + n)$.

Proposition 4.6 states that, for a given $g < \omega(k_{GR})$ and for any real value of τ^2, there exists a unique value b_{GR}, defined by (4.23), such that (k_{GR}, b_{GR}) is a steady state of the dynamics (4.19)–(4.20). Interestingly, b_{GR} is an increasing function of τ^2. Indeed, a higher τ^2 implies a lower τ^1, allowing in turn more savings in the economy and more debt.

For all these equilibria, the life-cycle income is the same: $\omega(k_{GR}) - g$. Consequently, consumptions and utilities are also the same. They correspond to the golden age (see section 2.1.2) with a fixed government spending. The local stability of this steady state is given by the following proposition.

Proposition 4.7 (Stability of the golden rule steady state with debt)
*Given g and τ^2, assume **A5**, $g < \omega(k_{GR})$, and **A10** at (k_{GR}, b_{GR}) with $\tau^1 = g - \tau^2/(1+n)$. There exists a threshold $\underline{b} < 0$ depending on τ^2 and g such that the steady state (k_{GR}, b_{GR}) with zero deficit is locally stable if $b_{GR} \in (\underline{b}, 0)$. It is a saddle point if b_{GR} lies outside the interval.*

Proof: To study the local dynamics (4.19)–(4.20) we take a first-order Taylor expansion of the system around the steady state (k_{GR}, b_{GR}). This leads to the linear dynamics

$$
\begin{bmatrix} k_{t+1} - k_{GR} \\ b_{t+1} - b_{GR} \end{bmatrix} = \begin{bmatrix} \dfrac{\tilde{s}'_{\omega_1}\omega' - b_{GR}f''}{D_{GR}} & \dfrac{1+n}{D_{GR}} \\ \dfrac{b_{GR}f''}{1+n} & 1 \end{bmatrix} \begin{bmatrix} k_t - k_{GR} \\ b_t - b_{GR} \end{bmatrix},
$$

where

$$
D_{GR} = 1 + n - \tilde{s}'_R(\omega(k_{GR}) - \tau^1, -\tau^2, 1+n)\, f''(k_{GR}).
$$

The assumption **A10** implies $D_{GR} > 0$. The characteristic polynomial is

$$
P(\lambda) = \lambda^2 - \lambda\left(1 + \frac{\tilde{s}'_{\omega_1}\omega' - b_{GR}f''}{D_{GR}}\right) + \frac{\tilde{s}'_{\omega_1}\omega'}{D_{GR}}.
$$

The product of the eigenvalues, $P(0)$, is equal to $\tilde{s}'_{\omega_1}\omega'/D_{GR}$ and belongs to $(0, 1)$ from **A10**. Moreover, we have

$$
P(1) = \frac{b_{GR}f''}{D_{GR}},
$$

$$
P(-1) = 2 + \frac{2\tilde{s}'_{\omega_1}\omega' - b_{GR}f''}{D_{GR}}.
$$

We have $P(-1) > 0$ if and only if $b > \underline{b}$, the threshold $\underline{b}$ being given by

$$
\underline{b} = \frac{2}{f''(k_{GR})}[D_{GR} + s'_w(\omega(k_{GR}) - g, 1+n)\omega'(k_{GR})].
$$

In the case $b_{GR} > 0$, we have $P(1) < 0$. The eigenvalues verify $0 < \lambda_1 < 1 < \lambda_2$, and the steady state is a saddle point. In the case $P(-1) < 0$, the eigenvalues verify $0 > \lambda_1 > -1 > \lambda_2$, and the steady state is a saddle point (with oscillatory dynamics near the steady state). In the case $P(1) > 0$ and $P(-1) > 0$, the modulus of each eigenvalue is smaller than 1, since $P(0) < 1$. ∎

To interpret the assumption **A10** in this case, let us use the results of section 3.1.1. Given that $g = \tau^1 + \tau^2/(1+n)$, we have the following relationship:

$$\tilde{s}(\omega(k_{GR}) - \tau^1, -\tau^2, 1+n) = s(\omega(k_{GR}) - g, 1+n) + \frac{\tau^2}{1+n},$$

$$\tilde{s}'_{\omega_1}(\omega(k_{GR}) - \tau^1, -\tau^2, 1+n) = s'_w(\omega(k_{GR}) - g, 1+n),$$

$$\tilde{s}'_R(\omega(k_{GR}) - \tau^1, -\tau^2, 1+n) = s'_R(\omega(k_{GR}) - g, 1+n)$$
$$- \frac{\tau^2[1 - s'_w(\omega(k_{GR}) - g, 1+n)]}{(1+n)^2}.$$

These imply that **A10** amounts to

$$(1+n - s'_R f'' - s'_w \omega') + \frac{\tau^2(1 - s'_w)f''}{(1+n)^2} > 0.$$

Thus **A10** is equivalent to imposing an upper bound on τ^2.

Proposition 4.7 sets out an important restriction to obtain the stability of the dynamics with debt: $0 > b_{GR} > \underline{b}$. It means in particular that under **A10**, the dynamics around the golden rule steady state cannot be stable if the debt is positive. When the debt is positive, the steady state is a saddle point. This has a particular meaning in the dynamics with bubbles, which is a case without taxes and government spending (this corresponds to a Ponzi game and will be studied in section 4.3.5). In this particular case, the level of debt corresponding to the golden rule is

$$b^0_{GR} = \frac{s(\omega(k_{GR}), 1+n)}{1+n} - k_{GR},$$

and proposition 4.7 can be restated with

$$\underline{b}^0 = \frac{2}{f''(k_{GR})}\left[D^0_{GR} + s'_w(\omega(k_{GR}), 1+n)\omega'(k_{GR})\right].$$

The steady state (k_{GR}, b^0_{GR}) is a saddle point in two cases: $b^0_{GR} > 0$ and $b^0_{GR} < \underline{b}^0$. In the case $0 > b^0_{GR} > \underline{b}^0$, it is stable.

The Steady State with Zero Debt. The other case in which the constant deficit $\delta = \tau^1 + \tau^2/(1+n) - g$ is nil corresponds to a steady state where the debt asymptotically vanishes. At this steady state, the capital intensity verifies

$$(1+n)k = \tilde{s}(\omega(k) - \tau^1, -\tau^2, f'(k)). \tag{4.25}$$

Any steady state of the economy with lump-sum transfers financing public expenditure is also a steady state with zero debt of the economy with debt. The results of chapter 3 can be used to study the existence of steady states:

- If $\tau^2 = 0$, the study of section 3.3.1 applies. A steady state k exists if g is sustainable, i.e., the smallest sustainable initial capital $\underline{k}(g)$ is finite. This condition is equivalent to an upper bound on g, defining the highest sustainable public spending $\bar{g}$.

- If $g = 0$, the study of section 3.1.1 applies, and one obtains conditions on τ^2.
- In the general case there are restrictions on both g and τ^2. By continuity, for $g < \bar{g}$, there is a steady state if τ^2 is small enough.

The local stability of such a steady state is given by the following proposition.

Proposition 4.8 (Stability of the steady state with zero debt)
*Given g and τ^2, and a steady state with zero debt k solution to (4.25) with $\tau^1 = g - \tau^2/(1+n)$, assume **A10** at $(k, 0)$.*

The steady state $(k, 0)$ is locally stable if there is over-accumulation at k ($f'(k) < 1 + n$). It is a saddle point if there is under-accumulation.

Proof: We take a first-order Taylor expansion of the system (4.19)–(4.20) around the steady state $(k, 0)$. This leads to

$$\begin{bmatrix} k_{t+1} - k \\ b_{t+1} \end{bmatrix} = \begin{bmatrix} \frac{s'_w \omega'}{D(k)} & \frac{1}{D(k)} \\ 0 & \frac{f'(k)}{1+n} \end{bmatrix} \begin{bmatrix} k_t - k \\ b_t \end{bmatrix}$$

with

$$D(k) = 1 + n - \tilde{s}'_R f''.$$

The two eigenvalues are thus

$$\lambda_1 = \frac{f'(k)}{1+n}, \qquad \lambda_2 = \frac{s'_w \omega'}{D(k)}.$$

The condition $\lambda_2 < 1$ is given by **A10**, and the proposition follows. ∎

When debt asymptotically vanishes, under assumption **A10**, the stability analysis is exactly the one of the single equation (4.19) with constant capital.

4.3.2 Balanced Budget Policies: Graphical Illustration

To illustrate and extend the analytical and local results derived so far, we first build and study the phase diagram of the two-dimensional dynamics (4.19)–(4.20). We then propose a complete study of the case of logarithmic utility and Cobb–Douglas production. Note that we do not make the assumption **A10** in this global analysis.

At the inter-temporal equilibrium with perfect foresight, the stock of capital of period $t + 1$ and the stock of debt of period $t + 1$ should verify the following system of implicit equations:

$$\Phi(k_{t+1}, b_t, k_t) \equiv k_{t+1} + \frac{f'(k_t)}{1+n} b_t - \frac{\tilde{s}(\omega(k_t) - \tau^1, -\tau^2, f'(k_{t+1}))}{1+n} = 0,$$

$$\Psi(b_{t+1}, b_t, k_t) \equiv b_{t+1} - \frac{f'(k_t)}{1+n} b_t = 0. \tag{4.26}$$

The dynamics of the economy are described by a system of two non-linear first-order difference equations, and interesting insights can be drawn from a phase diagram.

We first characterize the set of points (k_t, b_t) for which there is no change in b_t, i.e., for which $\Psi(b_t, b_t, k_t) = 0$. This set is given by the pairs (k_t, b_t) for which

$$b_t[1 + n - f'(k_t)] = 0$$

holds. This equality defines a cross in the space $\{b, k\}$ that is represented in figure 4.1. The vertical branch is the line $k = k_{\text{GR}}$. The horizontal one is the line $b = 0$. To describe the direction of change in b_t, we remark, using the implicit function $\Psi(b_{t+1}, b_t, k_t) = 0$, that b_{t+1} increases (decreases) with increasing k_t in the case $b_t < 0$ ($b_t > 0$). Hence, for negative b, we have $b_{t+1} < b_t$ at the left of the vertical branch and $b_{t+1} > b_t$ at the right. For positive b, the reverse holds. The corresponding directions of motion are plotted in the figure 4.1.

The set of points (k_t, b_t) for which there is no change in k_t is not easy to characterize. For the function $\Phi(k_t, b_t, k_t)$ to be defined, the life-cycle income at $k_{t+1} = k_t$,

$$\omega(k_t) - \tau^1 - \frac{\tau^2}{f'(k_t)},$$

should be positive. When $\tau^2 \le 0$ (see section 3.2.2 on pensions), the life-cycle income is increasing in k and positive on the set $(\underline{k}, +\infty)$, where $\underline{k}$ is defined

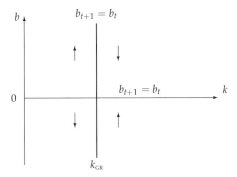

Figure 4.1. The debt motion. The locus where debt is constant is composed of the lines $k = k_{\text{GR}}$ and $b = 0$. The arrows indicate the direction of motion.

by $\omega(\underline{k}) - \tau^1 - \frac{\tau^2}{f'(\underline{k})} = 0.$[9] If $\tau_2 > 0$, the set on which the life-cycle income is positive can be *discontinuous*, which means that the definition set of the phase line under consideration is not an interval. In order to simplify the graphical illustration, we assume that $\tau^2 = 0$. This implies $g = \tau^1$ and allows us to rewrite the above equation (4.26) as

$$(1+n)k_{t+1} + f'(k_t)b_t - s(\omega(k_t) - g, f'(k_{t+1})) = 0. \tag{4.27}$$

Hence, $k_{t+1} = k_t$ if and only if

$$b_t = v(k_t) = \frac{s(\omega(k_t) - g, f'(k_t)) - (1+n)k_t}{f'(k_t)}$$

holds. The limit of the function $v(\cdot)$ when $k \to \underline{k}$ is some negative real number. Using $\lim_{k \to +\infty} s(w, f'(k))/k = 0 \, \forall w > 0$ (as $0 < s(w, R) < w$ and $\lim_{k \to +\infty} w/k = 0$), we find that

$$\lim_{k \to +\infty} v(k) = \frac{-(1+n)k}{f'(k)} = -\infty.$$

Hence, the phase line goes below the horizontal axis when k is near $\underline{k}$ and when k is large. An example of a possible phase line is drawn in figure 4.2 (a Cobb–Douglas example; see below). To describe the direction of change in k_t, we remark, using the implicit function (4.27), that k_{t+1} is decreasing in b_t under the assumption $1 + n - s'_R > 0$. Hence, $k_{t+1} < k_t$ above the curve, and $k_{t+1} > k_t$ below. The corresponding directions of motion are plotted in the figure.

At this stage, we can already deduce the following. Assume that the golden rule is feasible, that is, $\omega(k_{GR}) > g$ (equation (4.24)). On the one hand, if the phase line $k_{t+1} = k_t$ crosses the vertical line $k = k_{GR}$ in the positive orthant,

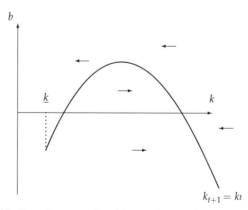

Figure 4.2. A Cobb–Douglas example of the capital motion. The arrows indicate the direction of motion.

[9] Or $\underline{k} = 0$ if the life-cycle income is always positive.

then the steady state golden rule level of debt is positive, and there is at least one other steady state with positive capital and zero debt displaying over-accumulation. This holds because the continuous phase line $k_{t+1} = k_t$ ends below the horizontal axis. On the other hand, if the phase line $k_{t+1} = k_t$ crosses the vertical branch $k = k_{\mathrm{GR}}$ below the horizontal branch $b = 0$, then the steady state golden rule level of debt is negative, and we do not know if there are steady state(s) $(k, 0)$ with zero debt.

We shall provide a exhaustive list of possible cases when the utility function is logarithmic and the production function is Cobb–Douglas. The phase line $k_{t+1} = k_t$ is then defined in the set $(\{g/[A(1 - \alpha)]\}^{1/\alpha}, +\infty)$, and it is given by

$$b_t = v(k_t) = \frac{\frac{\beta}{1+\beta}[A(1 - \alpha)k_t^\alpha - g] - (1 + n)k_t}{A\alpha} k_t^{1-\alpha}$$

The function $v(\cdot)$ is concave for $g = 0$. For $g > 0$, either $v(\cdot)$ is always decreasing or it is increasing on an interval (k_1, k_2) and decreasing outside. k_1 can be either above or below $\underline{k}$. Indeed, we have

$$A\alpha k^\alpha v'(k) = \frac{\beta}{1 + \beta}[A(1 - \alpha)k^\alpha - g(1 - \alpha)] - (1 + n)(2 - \alpha)k,$$

which is a concave function, negative at 0 and for k large enough.

We illustrate the five possible cases. They are presented in figures 4.3 and 4.4.

When $g = 0$, there is a corner steady state at 0, and we have the two cases depicted in figure 4.3. In the left panel, the economy without debt has one positive stable steady state, which is characterized by over-accumulation. As a consequence this steady state is stable for the dynamics with debt. There is also a steady state with the golden rule and a positive debt. This steady state is a saddle point (proposition 4.7). In this case, zero deficit policies can lead to the golden rule, if the initial debt is set at the appropriate level. If the initial debt is

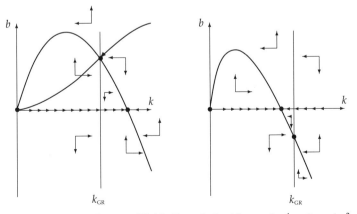

Figure 4.3. The phase diagram (Cobb–Douglas) with $g = 0$, $\tau^1 = 0$, and $\tau^2 = 0$.

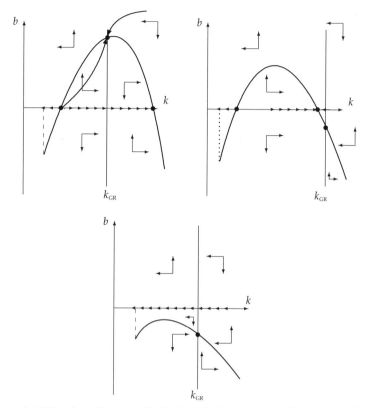

Figure 4.4. The phase diagram (Cobb–Douglas) with $\delta = 0$, $\tau^1 = g$, and $\tau^2 = 0$.

too high, the policy leads the economy to the top left corner, in a region where debt increases unboundedly. If it is too low, debt disappears asymptotically. As in Tirole (1985), if there is only one positive steady state in the economy without debt, the required level exists for any initial capital stock. This case is illustrated in the left panel of Figure 4.3, where the saddle path is represented by the bold line. In the right panel, the economy without debt has a positive stable steady state with under-accumulation. According to proposition 4.8, this steady state is a saddle point, as it is stable in the one-dimensional case and displays under-accumulation. The golden rule steady state has a negative debt. This steady state can be either stable, saddle-point stable, or unstable for the dynamics with debt, depending on the condition established in proposition 4.7 and on whether assumption **A10** holds. Its stability is further studied in the example in section 4.3.5.

When $g > 0$, there are potentially more than one positive steady state in the economy without debt (one-dimensional dynamics). As we have seen in section 3.3.1, for g low enough, we have two steady states, represented in the top panels of figure 4.4. The first one is unstable (and **A10** does not hold in it), and the second stable. The lower steady state is comparable to the lowest sustainable initial capital of section 3.2.2. In the left panel, the higher steady state without debt displays over-accumulation, implying that the golden rule steady state has a positive debt. As in the previous case, zero deficit policies can lead to the golden rule, if the initial debt is set at the appropriate level. This results simply from the saddle-point property of the steady state. Contrary to the previous case, the needed level no longer exists for any initial capital. It exists only for an initial capital larger than the lowest sustainable initial capital. In the right panel, the largest positive steady state of the economy without debt displays under-accumulation, implying that the golden rule steady state displays a negative debt.

In the bottom panel of figure 4.4, public spending is so large that there is no positive steady state equilibrium in the economy without debt. There exists a steady state equilibrium with a golden rule capital stock and a negative debt, which is stable under assumption **A10**. This case reflects the fact that large public spending is sustainable only with a negative debt.

4.3.3 Non-zero Deficit: Local Analysis

In the case where $\delta = g - \tau^1 - \tau^2/(1+n)$ is non-zero, the first steady state condition for the dynamics described by (4.19) and (4.20) is

$$[1 + n - f'(k)]b = \delta \neq 0, \tag{4.28}$$

which implies both $f'(k) \neq 1 + n$ and $b \neq 0$. Hence, the golden rule cannot be a steady state when the deficit is non-zero. However, any other value of k can be the capital stock of a steady state. More precisely, we shall show that there always exist a unique level of deficit $\hat{\delta}(k, \tau^2)$ and debt $\hat{b}(k, \tau^2)$ such that $(k, \hat{b}(k, \tau^2))$ is a steady state. We will start with fixed levels of k and τ^2 and study the corresponding levels of deficit and debt. We next investigate the role played by τ^2 and its effect on the level of debt for a given level of capital. Finally, the local stability properties of this steady state are established. This approach from three different angles does not provide a global analysis of the dynamics, but gives a global view of the set of steady states and their local stability properties.

We first determine the range of deficits compatible with a positive life-cycle income for given capital. The life-cycle income at steady state,

$$\omega(k) - \tau^1 - \frac{\tau^2}{f'(k)} = \delta + \omega(k) - g + \tau^2 \left(\frac{1}{1+n} - \frac{1}{f'(k)} \right),$$

is positive if and only if the deficit is not too small (i.e., the tax on the young is not too large):

$$\delta > \underline{\delta}(k, \tau^2) \equiv g - \omega(k) - \tau^2 \left(\frac{1}{1+n} - \frac{1}{f'(k)} \right).$$

The threshold $\underline{\delta}(k, \tau^2)$ also depends on g, which is fixed. The life-cycle income is equal to $\delta - \underline{\delta}(k, \tau^2)$, and savings are given by

$$\tilde{s}(\omega(k) - \tau^1, -\tau^2, f'(k)) = s(\delta - \underline{\delta}(k, \tau^2), f'(k)) + \frac{\tau^2}{f'(k)}. \qquad (4.29)$$

The second steady state condition: $(1 + n)(k + b) = \tilde{s}$ is equivalent to finding the roots of the function

$$Y = [1 + n - f'(k)][(1 + n)k - \tilde{s} + (1 + n)b].$$

Using equations (4.28) and (4.29), we have

$$Y = [1 + n - f'(k)]\left((1 + n)k - s(\delta - \underline{\delta}(k, \tau^2), f'(k)) - \frac{\tau^2}{f'(k)}\right) + (1 + n)\delta.$$

The following proposition derives a steady state curve $\hat{\delta}(k, \tau^2)$ which gives the level of the deficit corresponding to a steady state k.

Proposition 4.9 (The steady state curve $\hat{\delta}(k, \tau^2)$)
Let $k > 0$ with $f'(k) \neq 1 + n$, and $g \geq 0$ be feasible, i.e. lower than the net production: $f(k) - (1 + n)k > g$. For any tax $\tau^2 \in \mathbb{R}$, there exists a unique value of the deficit $\hat{\delta}(k, \tau^2)$ and of the debt

$$\hat{b}(k, \tau^2) = \frac{\hat{\delta}(k, \tau^2)}{1 + n - f'(k)}$$

for which the pair $(k, \hat{b}(k, \tau^2))$ is a steady state of the dynamics (4.19)–(4.20) with constant deficit.

Proof: For k, g and τ^2 given, Y is an increasing function of δ, defined for $\delta > \underline{\delta}(k, \tau^2)$. Indeed, we have

$$\frac{\partial Y}{\partial \delta} = (1 + n)(1 - s'_w) + f'(k)s'_w > 0$$

with $s'_w = s'_w(\delta - \underline{\delta}(k, \tau^2), f'(k))$ between 0 and 1. Let us study the limits of Y when δ goes to the bounds of the interval $(\underline{\delta}(k, \tau^2), +\infty)$.

- When δ tends to $\underline{\delta}(k, \tau^2)$, $s(\delta - \underline{\delta}(k, \tau^2), f'(k))$ tends to 0, and we have

$$\lim_{\delta \to \underline{\delta}(k,\tau^2)} Y = [1 + n - f'(k)]\left((1 + n)k - \frac{\tau^2}{f'(k)}\right) + (1 + n)\underline{\delta}(k, \tau^2).$$

With

$$\underline{\delta}(k, \tau^2) = g - [f(k) - kf'(k)] - \tau^2\left(\frac{1}{1 + n} - \frac{1}{f'(k)}\right),$$

we obtain

$$\lim_{\delta \to \underline{\delta}(k,\tau^2)} Y = (1 + n)[g + (1 + n)k - f(k)],$$

and this limit is negative if and only if k is feasible in the long run with public spending g, i.e., $f(k) - (1 + n)k > g$.

- When δ tends to ∞, Y is bounded below by

$$(1 + n)[\delta - s(\delta - \underline{\delta}(k, \tau^2), f'(k))] + C(k, \tau^2),$$

where $C(k, \tau^2)$ does not depend on δ. Using the arbitrage condition $u'(\delta - \underline{\delta}(k, \tau^2) - s) = \beta R u'(Rs)$ which defines $s(\delta - \underline{\delta}(k, \tau^2), R)$, we obtain that the limit of $\delta - s(\delta - \underline{\delta}(k, \tau^2), f'(k))$ when δ goes to $+\infty$ is equal to $+\infty$. As a consequence we have

$$\lim_{\delta \to +\infty} Y = +\infty.$$

We thus conclude that the function Y has a root $\hat{\delta}(k, \tau^2)$ belonging to the interval $(\underline{\delta}(k, \tau^2), +\infty)$ if and only if k and g are such that $f(k) - (1 + n)k > g$ holds. As a consequence, since $f'(k) \neq 1 + n$, the pair $(k, \hat{b}(k, \tau^2))$ with $\hat{b}(k, \tau^2) = \hat{\delta}(k, \tau^2)/[1 + n - f'(k)]$ is a steady state for the dynamics described by (4.19) and (4.20). ∎

We now analyze the effect of changing the tax on the old τ^2 on the steady state debt at given capital.

Proposition 4.10 (Effect of τ^2 on the steady state debt)
For a given feasible k, the long-run debt $\hat{b}(k, \tau^2)$ is an increasing function of τ^2 and increases from $-\infty$ to $+\infty$ when τ^2 rises from $-\infty$ to $+\infty$. The deficit $\hat{\delta}(k, \tau^2)$ increases (decreases) with τ^2 if $k > k_{GR}$ ($k < k_{GR}$).

Proof: The derivative of Y with respect to τ^2 can be written, when we take into account the effect of τ^2 on $\underline{\delta}(k, \tau^2)$:

$$\frac{\partial Y}{\partial \tau^2} = [1 + n - f'(k)]\left(-\frac{s'_w}{1 + n} - \frac{1 - s'_w}{f'(k)}\right),$$

and we have from the implicit function theorem that

$$\frac{\partial \hat{\delta}(k, \tau^2)}{\partial \tau^2} = -\frac{\partial Y/\partial \tau^2}{\partial Y/\partial \delta}.$$

Remember that $\partial Y/\partial \delta$ is positive from proposition 4.9.

To study the change in $\hat{\delta}(k, \tau^2)$ and $\hat{b}(k, \tau^2)$ as a function of τ^2, we distinguish two cases.

- When there is under-accumulation of capital, $f'(k) > 1 + n$, $\partial Y/\partial \tau^2$ is positive, and $\hat{\delta}(k, \tau^2)$ is a decreasing function of τ^2. When τ^2 tends to $-\infty$, $\underline{\delta}(k, \tau^2)$ tends to $+\infty$ and $\hat{\delta}(k, \tau^2)$, which is larger than $\underline{\delta}(k, \tau^2)$, also tends to $+\infty$. When τ^2 tends to $+\infty$, we use the fact that $Y = 0$ at $\delta = \hat{\delta}(k, \tau^2)$ to deduce

$$\frac{(1+n)\hat{\delta}(k, \tau^2)}{1+n - f'(k)} = s(\hat{\delta}(k, \tau^2) - \underline{\delta}(k, \tau^2), f'(k)) + \frac{\tau^2}{f'(k)} - (1+n)k$$

$$> \frac{\tau^2}{f'(k)} - (1+n)k,$$

which implies that $\hat{\delta}(k, \tau^2)$ tends to $-\infty$. In this case, $\hat{b}(k, \tau^2) = \hat{\delta}(k, \tau^2)/[1+n - f'(k)]$ is increasing with respect to τ^2, and it increases from $-\infty$ to $+\infty$ when τ^2 rises from $-\infty$ to $+\infty$.

- When there is over-accumulation of capital ($f'(k) < 1+n$), $\hat{\delta}(k, \tau^2)$ is an increasing function of τ^2. When τ^2 tends to $+\infty$, $\underline{\delta}(k, \tau^2)$ tends to $+\infty$, implying that both $\hat{\delta}(k, \tau^2)$ and $\hat{b}(k, \tau^2)$ tend to $+\infty$. From the fact that $Y = 0$ at $\delta = \hat{\delta}(k, \tau^2)$, we deduce

$$\frac{(1+n)\hat{\delta}(k, \tau^2)}{1+n - f'(k)} < \hat{\delta}(k, \tau^2) - \underline{\delta}(k, \tau^2) + \frac{\tau^2}{f'(k)} - (1+n)k$$

$$< \hat{\delta}(k, \tau^2) - g + \omega(k) + \frac{\tau^2}{1+n} - (1+n)k,$$

and

$$\frac{f'(k)\hat{\delta}(k, \tau^2)}{1+n - f'(k)} < -g + \omega(k) + \frac{\tau^2}{1+n} - (1+n)k.$$

Hence, when τ^2 tends to $-\infty$, $\hat{\delta}(k, \tau^2)$ and $\hat{b}(k, \tau^2)$ tend to $-\infty$. ∎

Although τ^2 affects government deficit and debt at given k, it does not affect consumptions or welfare. Indeed, the consumptions are determined by the individual arbitrage condition $u'(c) = \beta f'(k)u'(d)$ and the resource constraint $f(k) = c + d/(1+n) + g + (1+n)k$, which do not depend on τ^2, δ, or b. We find here the same property of the multiplicity of instruments as in the decentralization theorem 4.3.

For a given steady state and for a given deficit and public spending, different financing schemes (τ^1, τ^2, b) are possible. Although the tax mix does not affect the level of the steady state, it is important for its stability type. The local stability properties of the steady state(s) are given by the following proposition.

Proposition 4.11 (Stability of steady states with debt and deficit)
*Given g, τ^2, and k, assume g feasible with k and **A10** at $(k, \hat{b}(k, \tau^2))$ with $\tau^1 = g - \hat{\delta}(k, \tau^2) - \tau^2/(1+n)$. There are two thresholds $\bar{b}$ and $\underline{b}$, $\underline{b} < \bar{b}$:*

$$\bar{b} = \frac{1}{f''}\left(1 - \frac{f'}{1+n}\right)(1 + n - \tilde{s}'_R f'' - \tilde{s}'_{\omega_1}\omega'),$$

$$\underline{b} = \frac{1}{f''}\left(1 + \frac{f'}{1+n}\right)(1 + n - \tilde{s}'_R f'' + \tilde{s}'_{\omega_1}\omega') < 0,$$

such that the steady state $(k, \hat{b}(k, \tau^2))$ *is locally stable if* $\hat{b}(k, \tau^2) \in (\underline{b}, \bar{b})$ *and there is over-accumulation at k. In the case of under-accumulation, there is an additional stability condition:*

$$\frac{f'}{1+n} < \frac{1 + n - \tilde{s}'_R f''}{\tilde{s}'_{\omega_1} \omega'}.$$

The steady state is a saddle point if $\hat{b}(k, \tau^2)$ *lies outside the interval* $(\underline{b}, \bar{b})$. *The argument of* $\tilde{s}$ *are* $\omega(k) - \tau^1, -\tau^2,$ *and* $f'(k)$.

Proof: The dynamic system (4.19)–(4.20) takes the form

$$(1+n)k_{t+1} = \tilde{s}(\omega(k_t) - \tau^1, -\tau^2, f'(k_{t+1})) - f'(k_t)b_t - \delta,$$

$$(1+n)b_{t+1} = f'(k_t)b_t + \delta.$$

We take a first-order Taylor expansion of the system around the steady state $(k, \hat{b}(k, \tau^2))$. This leads to the linear dynamics

$$\begin{bmatrix} k_{t+1} - k \\ b_{t+1} - \hat{b}(k, \tau^2) \end{bmatrix} = \begin{bmatrix} \frac{\tilde{s}'_{\omega_1} \omega' - f''(k)\hat{b}(k,\tau^2)}{\hat{D}} & \frac{-f'(k)}{\hat{D}} \\ \frac{\hat{b}(k,\tau^2)f''(k)}{1+n} & \frac{f'(k)}{1+n} \end{bmatrix} \begin{bmatrix} k_t - k \\ b_t - \hat{b}(k, \tau^2) \end{bmatrix},$$

where

$$\hat{D} = 1 + n - \tilde{s}'_R(\omega(k) - \tau^1, -\tau^2, f'(k))f''(k).$$

Assumption **A10** ensures $\hat{D} > \tilde{s}'_{\omega_1}\omega' > 0$. Replacing $\tilde{s}'_R = s'_R - \frac{\tau^2}{f'(k)^2}(1 - s'_w)$, we obtain

$$\hat{D} = 1 + n - s'_R f''(k) + \frac{\tau^2}{(1+n)^2}(1 - s'_w)f''(k),$$

where $s'_R = s'_R(\hat{\delta}(k, \tau^2) - \underline{\delta}(k, \tau^2), f'(k))$ and $s'_w = s'_w(\hat{\delta}(k, \tau^2) - \underline{\delta}(k, \tau^2), f'(k))$. The characteristic polynomial is

$$P(\lambda) = \lambda^2 - \lambda \left(\frac{f'}{1+n} + \frac{s'_w \omega' - f'' \hat{b}(k, \tau^2)}{\hat{D}} \right) + \frac{f's'_w \omega'}{(1+n)\hat{D}}.$$

The following holds:

$$P(0) = \frac{f's'_w \omega'}{(1+n)\hat{D}} > 0,$$

$$P(1) = \left(1 - \frac{f'}{1+n} \right)\left(1 - \frac{s'_w \omega'}{\hat{D}} \right) + \frac{f''\hat{b}}{\hat{D}},$$

$$P(-1) = \left(1 + \frac{f'}{1+n} \right)\left(1 + \frac{s'_w \omega'}{\hat{D}} \right) - \frac{f''\hat{b}}{\hat{D}}.$$

The condition $P(1) > 0$ is equivalent to $\hat{b} < \bar{b}$ with

$$\bar{b} = \frac{1}{f''} \left(1 - \frac{f'}{1+n} \right) (\hat{D} - s'_w \omega').$$

The condition $P(-1) > 0$ is equivalent to $\hat{b} > \underline{b}$ with

$$\underline{b} = \frac{1}{f''} \left(1 + \frac{f'}{1+n} \right) (\hat{D} + s'_w \omega') < 0.$$

In any case we have $\underline{b} < \bar{b}$. Indeed,

$$|f'' \bar{b}| = \left| 1 - \frac{f'}{1+n} \right| |\hat{D} - s'_w \omega'| < \left(1 + \frac{f'}{1+n} \right) (\hat{D} + s'_w \omega') = f'' \underline{b}.$$

Hence, if $\bar{b} \geq 0$ then $\bar{b} > \underline{b}$. If $\bar{b} < 0$ then $f'' \bar{b} < f'' \underline{b}$, which again implies $\bar{b} > \underline{b}$.

We can characterize the stability type using $P(0)$, $P(1)$, and $P(-1)$. In the case of over-accumulation, **A10** implies $P(0) < 1$. In the case of under-accumulation, $P(0) < 1$ requires another condition, given in the proposition. ∎

From this proposition we learn that stability is possible even when there is under-accumulation, i.e., the dynamics (4.20) with fixed capital are unstable. Stability is ensured by an additional restriction. This restriction holds if k is close to the golden rule level. Note moreover that, with **A10**, $\bar{b}$ is positive when there is under-accumulation and negative otherwise. Hence, in the case of under-accumulation, the upper bound on debt is strictly negative.

With a policy of constant deficit, Proposition 4.11 shows that the local stability conditions are quite restrictive, imposing conditions on the level of debt and on the level of capital (under- vs over-accumulation). When the steady state is stable, there is no special restrictions on the initial debt to ensure convergence (at least locally). When the steady state is a saddle point, there is only one convergence path, which imposes a very strong restriction on the initial debt. Finally, when the steady state is unstable, constant deficit policies should not be implemented. In these last two cases, the economy either converges to another steady state, or follows an unsustainable path.

4.3.4 Non-zero Deficit: Graphical Illustration

We first draw the phase diagram. The set of points (k_t, b_t) for which there is no change in b_t, i.e., $b_{t+1} = b_t$, is given by the pairs (k_t, b_t) for which

$$b_t[1 + n - f'(k_t)] = \delta$$

holds. This function is defined on the set of capital stocks k belonging $(0, +\infty)$, $k \neq k_{GR}$. It is represented in figure 4.5. The function displays a vertical asymptote at $k = k_{GR}$. If $\delta < 0$, which represents a budget surplus, the function is increasing in k_t. In the case of a deficit, it is decreasing. To describe the direction of change in b_t, we remark, using the implicit function $\Psi(b_{t+1}, b_t, k_t) = 0$

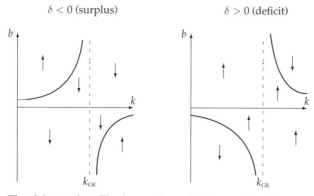

Figure 4.5. The debt motion. The locus where debt is constant is represented. The arrows indicate the direction of motion.

defined in the system (4.26), that b_{t+1} increases (decreases) with increasing k_t in the case $b_t < 0$ ($b_t > 0$). Hence, for negative b, we have $b_{t+1} > b_t$ to the right of the curve and $b_{t+1} < b_t$ to its left. For positive b, we have $b_{t+1} < b_t$ to the right of the curve and $b_{t+1} > b_t$ to its left. The corresponding directions of motion are plotted in the figure.

One conclusion can already be drawn from this partial analysis: it is not possible to run permanently a positive debt with a budget deficit when there is under-accumulation of capital. This conclusion is consistent with the three propositions on local stability.

The second phase line is similar to the one in the analysis with zero deficit. Limiting the analysis to an example, we keep the simplifying assumption $\tau^2 = 0$. The number of steady states and their stability type depend crucially on the policy variable δ. To obtain more satisfactory characterization of the dynamics in the economy with varying debt, proposition 4.9 is very useful. It indeed derives a steady state curve $\hat{\delta}(k, \tau^2)$. We illustrate this in an example. We take the case of a CES production function with low substitution ($\rho = 4$) and a logarithmic utility.[10] The parameters are $\alpha = 1/2, \beta = 0.3, n = 1.097, A = 20$. We assume $g = 0$ and $\tau^2 = 0$, which implies that $\tau^1 = -\delta$. The function $\hat{\delta}(k, 0)$ is plotted in figure 4.6. The values of δ for which there are zero, one, two, three, or four steady states can be clearly identified. We also report on the same figure the function $\hat{\delta}(k, 1)$, i.e., for a non-zero value of τ^2. The figure illustrates proposition 4.10, that the deficit $\hat{\delta}(k, \tau^2)$ increases (decreases) with increasing τ^2 if $k > k_{GR} = 1.57$ ($k < k_{GR}$).

Figure 4.6 shows the ranges of interesting values of δ, for which we can draw phase diagrams. Five phase diagrams are presented in figure 4.7. Looking now at both figures 4.6 and 4.7, we observe the following. When government runs a high deficit per capita, $\delta = 3$, there is no steady state for the economy.

---

[10] Low substitution between productive inputs is useful in that it yields four steady states in the example, which illustrates the great variety of situations and stability types.

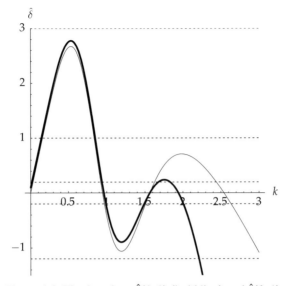

Figure 4.6. The functions $\hat{\delta}(k, 0)$ (bold line) and $\hat{\delta}(k, 1)$.

Lowering the value of δ, we observe first the appearance of two steady states with negative debt (deficit $= 1$), then the appearance of two steady states with positive debt and over-accumulation of capital (deficit $= 0.2$). When δ becomes negative (surplus), the phase line associated with constant debt is completely different and we have three steady states for $\delta = -0.2$. When δ decreases further, the two low steady states disappear and the high steady state with negative debt and over-accumulation remains.

We finally focus on the case $\delta = 0.2$, which displays four steady states. The corresponding phase diagram with the directions of motions is represented in figure 4.8 in a schematic way. Considering only those with a positive debt, the directions of motion suggest that the steady state C is a saddle point. In this case, for a given level of k_0 near the value of k at C, there is only one initial b_0 leading the economy to that steady state. If the initial debt per capita is too high, the economy will move in the northwest direction and the debt will explode. If it is too low, the economy is attracted to the fourth steady state D, which is the only stable steady state. The local stability of the steady states inferred from the arrows is confirmed by the following table, which gives the numerical values of the eigenvalues:

Steady state	k	b	λ_1	λ_2	
A	0.041	−0.019	0.01	11.34	Saddle
B	0.908	−0.041	3.60	4.55	Source
C	1.719	0.588	0.21	2.15	Saddle
D	2.280	0.243	0.09	0.37	Sink

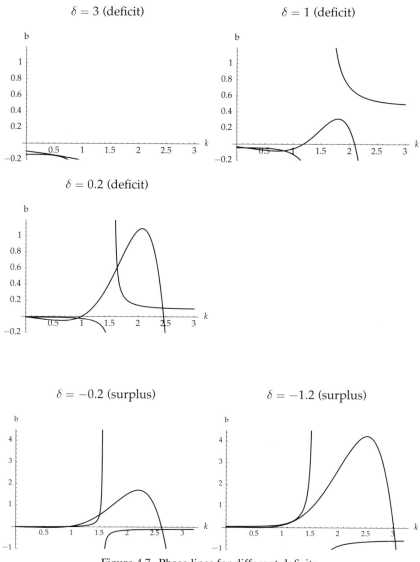

Figure 4.7. Phase lines for different deficits.

4.3.5 Ponzi Debt, Money, and Bubbles

In the model with debt but without taxes and government spending ($\tau^1 = \tau^2 = g = 0$), there is no choice for government other than running a Ponzi debt (see section 4.2.3). The dynamics are given by

$$(1+n)b_{t+1} = f'(k_t)b_t, \tag{4.30}$$

$$(1+n)(b_{t+1} + k_{t+1}) = s(\omega(k_t), f'(k_{t+1})). \tag{4.31}$$

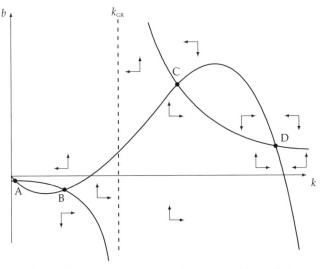

Figure 4.8. The phase diagram. Example with $\delta = 0.2$.

We have the same equations when b is a private asset that does not bring any dividend, i.e., a pure bubble (see Tirole (1985)).[11] A pure bubble is an asset with zero market fundamental (i.e., with no intrinsic value) that does not distribute any dividend. Under perfect foresight, the bubble must bear the same yield as capital. Similarly, b can also describe the case of fiat money, which plays only one role: to absorb a part of savings without providing any other service. The dynamic equations (4.30)–(4.31) are the same in the three cases: debt without government intervention (called Ponzi debt), bubble, and money. There are nevertheless three important differences: First, debt is a pre-determined variable, while a bubble is a forward-looking variable, since there is no related initial condition. Second, a bubble cannot be negative if the corresponding asset can be freely disposed of. On the contrary, a negative debt simply means that the government holds a part of the physical capital of the economy. Third, the model with debt can be analyzed within a truly dynamic approach to equilibrium, i.e., using the notion of temporary equilibrium and inter-temporal equilibrium. The model with bubble should be analyzed within a general equilibrium framework where the Walrasian auctioneer determines the prices of all periods at the same time. Otherwise, the current value of the bubble, which is not predetermined, could well be inconsistent with the forecasted value of the preceding period (expectations are not

---

[11] Note that Tirole (1985) defines $b_t^{(T)} = B_t/N_t$, which changes the lag structure in the equations and the corresponding phase diagram. This implies that his phase line $b_{t+1} = b_t$ is positively sloped, while ours is vertical. This notation is related to the first difference between debt and bubbles mentioned below.

inherited). The difference between the two approaches is further explored in section 5.4.

As in Diamond (1965) and Farmer (1986), we have assumed that public debt is a real variable. This is a natural assumption in an economy without money. Concerning the equilibrium with money, we can also point out some differences from bubbles and debt. If the nominal stock of money is exogenous, the price of money is a non-predetermined variable, and this leads to the same logic as in the model with bubbles.[12] Nevertheless, money is in general issued by some authority which could warrant a positive value of money.

We thus conclude that in analyzing the dynamics described by (4.30)–(4.31), the economic interpretation of the variable b plays a central role in understanding the properties of the model. For example, with debt, we study the sustainability of a given policy. With bubbles we are interested in the existence and the nature of the equilibrium (with asymptotic bubble, for example).

Let us recall the main local stability properties of the steady state equilibria of these dynamics, limiting ourselves to the cases $b \geq 0$, which apply to the three interpretations. There may exist two types of steady states: The golden rule $f'(k_{GR}) = 1 + n$ when the asset b_{GR} is positive, and the steady states with zero value asset ($b = 0$), which correspond to the steady states of the dynamics analyzed in chapter 1.

As we have seen in proposition 4.7, the steady state (k_{GR}, b_{GR}) with

$$b_{GR} = \frac{s(\omega(k_{GR}), 1 + n)}{1 + n} - k_{GR} > 0$$

is a saddle point, which corresponds to the notion of asymptotic bubble in Tirole (1985). Locally, this steady state is the limit of a unique path where, for each value of k_0, there is a unique b_0 which leads to the steady state. Under some assumptions, including that the Diamond steady state equilibrium is unique and characterized by over-accumulation, global uniqueness of this trajectory can be obtained (see Tirole (1985)).

Global Dynamics in an Example of Ponzi Debt. It is possible to study globally the solution to the system (4.30)–(4.31) in an example.

Example: We assume a logarithmic utility function and a Cobb–Douglas production function with total depreciation of capital. The dynamics obey

$$(1 + n)(b_{t+1} + k_{t+1}) = \frac{\beta(1 - \alpha)A}{1 + \beta} k_t^{\alpha},$$

$$(1 + n)b_{t+1} = \alpha A k_t^{\alpha - 1} b_t.$$

---

[12] Alternatively, money can be the support to inter-generational exchange, as in the model of Samuelson (1958) without capital.

Let us define the debt–savings ratio x_t as

$$x_t = \frac{B_t}{N_t s_t} = \frac{(1+n)b_{t+1}}{s_t}.$$

We have

$$x_{t+1} = \frac{\alpha A k_t^{\alpha-1} b_t (1+\beta)}{\beta(1-\alpha) A k_t^{\alpha}} = \frac{\alpha(1+\beta)\, s_{t-1} x_t}{\beta(1-\alpha) k_t (1+n)}$$

and

$$(1+n)k_t = s_{t-1} - (1+n)b_t = s_{t-1}(1-x_t),$$

from which we obtain

$$x_{t+1} = \frac{\alpha(1+\beta)x_t}{\beta(1-\alpha)(1-x_t)}.$$

It is then sufficient to study the dynamics of the ratio x_t, which should always remain lower than one. Indeed, for k to be positive the asset b should always be lower than savings. The dynamics of x_t can then be used to determine the dynamics of k_t and b_t,

$$(1+n)k_{t+1} = (1-x_{t+1})\frac{\beta(1-\alpha)A}{1+\beta} k_t^{\alpha},$$

$$(1+n)b_{t+1} = x_{t+1}\frac{\beta(1-\alpha)A}{1+\beta} k_t^{\alpha},$$

and the corresponding steady states. When the one-dimensional dynamics of x_t are stable, the two-dimensional dynamics of k_t and b_t are stable too. When the one-dimensional dynamics of x_t are unstable, the steady state of the two-dimensional dynamics of k_t and b_t is a saddle point.

The dynamics of x_t has two steady states:

$$x_0^* = 0 \quad \text{and} \quad x_1^* = 1 - \frac{\alpha(1+\beta)}{\beta(1-\alpha)}.$$

x_1^* is positive (negative) if the steady state of the model without asset b of chapter 1, given by

$$k^D = \left(\frac{\beta(1-\alpha)A}{(1+\beta)(1+n)}\right)^{\frac{1}{1-\alpha}},$$

displays over-accumulation (under-accumulation). The possible cases are illustrated in figures 4.9 and 4.10.

- When there is over-accumulation ($k^D > k_{GR}$), the steady state x_1^* is positive, corresponds to the golden rule (k_{GR}, b_{GR}), and is unstable (figure 4.9). With the particular initial condition $x_0 = (1+n)b_0/s_{-1} = x_1^*$ the sequence

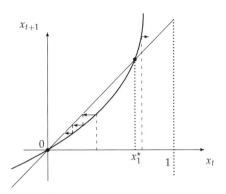

Figure 4.9. Global dynamics in an example: over-accumulation.

(x_t) remains constant and the sequence (k_t, b_t) converges to (k_{GR}, b_{GR}). There is no equilibrium if x_0 is above x_1^*, for then x_t reaches in a finite number of periods a value larger than 1, implying that the asset b can no longer be absorbed by private savings. For any $x_0 < x_1^*$, the dynamics of x_t converges to 0 and the asset value tends to vanish. (k_t, b_t) tends to $(k^D, 0)$. In the two-dimensional dynamics, (k_{GR}, b_{GR}) is a saddle point and $(k^D, 0)$ is stable.

- When there is under-accumulation ($k^D < k_{GR}$), the steady state x_1^* is negative (figure 4.10). In this case, there is no inter-temporal equilibrium with $x_0 > 0$. There is thus no equilibrium with (positive) bubble. However, all the trajectories with a negative initial debt $x_0 < 0$ converge to the golden rule: (k_t, b_t) converges to (k_{GR}, b_{GR}).
- In the limit case $k^D = k_{GR}$, one obtains the same conclusion with $b_{GR} = 0$. In the two-dimensional dynamics with bubbles, there is no inter-temporal equilibrium with perfect foresight. With debt, (k_{GR}, b_{GR}) is stable and $(k^D, 0)$ is a saddle point.

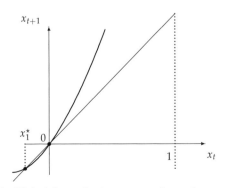

Figure 4.10. Global dynamics in an example: under-accumulation.

This section provides a global analysis of the dynamics with constant debt. We show that the essential information can be gathered in a single planar diagram, thereby allowing us to answer the questions of global stability and sustainability in a comprehensive way by means of a graphical exposition.

In this version of the model, the policy of the government is to keep constant the level of debt per young individual. Hence, $B_{t-1}/N_t = b$ $\forall t$, where b is the target level of debt per capita. We also assume, as in Diamond (1965), that both the lump-sum tax on the old and the level of government spending are zero. The level of taxes required to maintain this level of debt is thus

$$\tau_t^1 = [R_t - (1+n)]b = [f'(k_t) - (1+n)]b \equiv \tau(k_t).$$

4.4.1 Sustainability in the Short Run

We keep the view that sustainability of a given policy is associated with the existence of the corresponding equilibrium.

To study sustainability in the short run we consider the temporary equilibrium. The following variables are given: b, s_{t-1}, $I_{t-1} = N_{t-1}s_{t-1} - N_t b > 0$, R_{t+1}^e. The conditions under which the temporary equilibrium exists are made explicit in the following proposition.

Proposition 4.12 (Existence and uniqueness of the temporary equilibrium)
Given $\{s_{t-1}, I_{t-1}, R_{t+1}^e\}$, *a temporary equilibrium with positive consumptions and investment exists if and only if*

$$s_{t-1} > 0, \tag{4.32}$$

$$\omega(k_t) > \tau(k_t) \equiv b[f'(k_t) - (1+n)], \tag{4.33}$$

$$s(\omega(k_t) - \tau(k_t), R_{t+1}^e) > (1+n)b, \tag{4.34}$$

where $k_t = s_{t-1}/(1+n) - b$. *If it exists, it is unique and can be expressed as a function of* k_t *and* R_{t+1}^e.

Proof: If the equilibrium exists, then $d_t > 0$, $c_t > 0$, and $I_t > 0$. The positivity of consumptions implies the positivity of the incomes of both young and old households. This in turn implies $s_{t-1} > 0$ and $\omega(k_t) > \tau(k_t)$, which are (4.32) and (4.33). The positivity of investment implies that the whole debt should be absorbed, i.e., (4.34).

If (4.32) does not hold, positive consumption of the old is excluded. If (4.33) does not hold, it implies that $\omega(k_t) \leq \tau(k_t)$ and positive consumption of the young is excluded. If (4.34) does not hold, investment is not positive.

The temporary equilibrium is unique, as $\omega(\cdot)$, $f(\cdot)$, $\tau(\cdot)$, and $s(\cdot, R)$ are (single-valued) functions. ■

The three conditions (4.32), (4.33), and (4.34) are closely related to the short-run sustainability of debt policy. The last one can be read as bearing on expectations. The first one is simply $k_t > -b$. The second one relates k_t and b and should be studied carefully.

Let us define the net income of the young households as a function of capital and debt:

$$\tilde{w}(k_t, b) = \omega(k_t) - \tau(k_t) = \omega(k_t) - b[f'(k_t) - (1 + n)].$$

We should study the set $\mathcal{E}_{\tilde{w}}$ of pairs $(k, b) \in \mathbb{R}_{++} \times \mathbb{R}$ which satisfy $\tilde{w}(k, b) > 0$, with

$$\tilde{w}(k, b) = \omega(k) - \varrho(k)b, \quad \text{where} \quad \varrho(k) \equiv f'(k) - (1 + n).$$

We next assume that **A5** holds in order to define a finite positive golden rule capital stock k_{GR}.

- When $k < k_{\mathrm{GR}}$ (under-accumulation of capital), we have $\varrho(k) > 0$ and the condition $\tilde{w}(k, b) > 0$ is equivalent to

$$b < \frac{\omega(k)}{\varrho(k)} \equiv \bar{b}(k).$$

The upper bound on debt, $\bar{b}(k)$, is an increasing function of $k(\omega' > 0$, $\varrho' < 0)$, is positive valued, and has limits

$$\lim_{k \to 0} \bar{b}(k) = \frac{\omega(0)}{\varrho(0+)} \quad \text{and} \quad \lim_{k \to k_{\mathrm{GR}}} \bar{b}(k) = +\infty.$$

The limit $\bar{b}(0+)$ is zero if $\omega(0) = 0$ or $f'(0+) = +\infty$. If $\omega(0) > 0$ and $f'(0+)$ is finite, $\bar{b}(0+)$ is positive.

- When $k > k_{\mathrm{GR}}$ (over-accumulation of capital), we have $\varrho(k) < 0$, and the condition $\tilde{w}(k, b) > 0$ is equivalent to

$$b > \frac{-\omega(k)}{-\varrho(k)} = \frac{-\omega(k)}{1 + n - f'(k)} \equiv \underline{b}(k).$$

The lower bound on debt, $\underline{b}(k)$, is negative, and its limits are

$$\lim_{k \to k_{\mathrm{GR}}} \underline{b}(k) = -\infty \quad \text{and} \quad \lim_{k \to +\infty} \underline{b}(k) = \frac{-\omega(+\infty)}{1 + n - f'(+\infty)}.$$

The derivative of $\underline{b}(k)$ is

$$\frac{f''(k)[(1 + n)k - f(k)]}{[1 + n - f'(k)]^2}$$

Let us define $\tilde{k}$ as the positive root of $f(k) - (1 + n)k$. The existence of the golden rule implies that $\tilde{k}$ is finite (see section 2.1.1). We then have that $f(k) > (1 + n)k$ if and only if $k < \tilde{k}$. The function $\underline{b}(k)$ is increasing in

$(k_{GR}, \tilde{k})$ and decreasing in $(\tilde{k}, +\infty)$. Notice also that

$$\underline{b}(\tilde{k}) = \frac{f(\tilde{k}) - \tilde{k}f'(\tilde{k})}{f'(\tilde{k}) - (1+n)\tilde{k}} = -\tilde{k}.$$

The functions $\bar{b}(k)$ and $\underline{b}(k)$ are represented in figure 4.11. The interpretation is the following. When k is below the golden rule level, running a positive debt requires levying positive taxes, as the interest rate is above the rate of growth (of population). Sustainability thus requires an upper bound $\bar{b}$ on the debt. When k is above the golden rule level, running a negative debt requires levying positive taxes, as the interest rate on government assets is below the rate of growth (of population). Sustainability thus requires a lower bound $\underline{b}$ on the debt.

Finally, the chart should be completed with the condition $k > -b$, which ensures that the old-age consumption is positive. We do not represent the condition of positive investment, which depends on exogenous expectations. Figure 4.11 represents the set where the two conditions (4.32) and (4.33) hold. This set will be denoted by $\mathcal{E}$, and we have

$$\mathcal{E} = \{(k, b) \in \mathbb{R}_{++} \times \mathbb{R}; \ k > -b \text{ and } \tilde{w}(k, b) > 0\}.$$

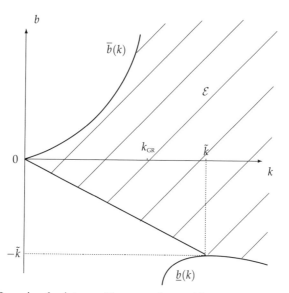

Figure 4.11. Domain of existence. The scope for positive young-age consumption is given by the set of pairs $(k, b) \in \mathbb{R}_{++} \times \mathbb{R}$, which satisfy $\tilde{w}(k, b) > 0$. It is the region between the two curves $\bar{b}(k)$ and $\underline{b}(k)$. The scope for positive old-age consumption is given by the set of pairs (k, b) such that $b > -k$. The set $\mathcal{E}$ is given by the intersection of the two. (To improve the clarity of the picture, the scale of the axes is different.)

4.4.2 Sustainability in the Long Run

We shall study the inter-temporal equilibria with perfect foresight, i.e., when $R^e_{t+1} = f'(k_{t+1})$ and thus

$$k_{t+1} = \frac{1}{1+n} s(\tilde{\omega}(k_t, b), f'(k_{t+1})) - b. \tag{4.35}$$

This dynamical equation links the two periods by equalizing investment in physical capital and bonds with savings.

Given a constant value of b and an initial capital stock $k_0 = K_0/N_{-1}$, an inter-temporal equilibrium with perfect foresight is characterized by a sequence $(k_t)_{t \geq 0}$ with $k_t > 0$ that satisfies for all $t \geq 0$ the condition (4.35). Hence, at the inter-temporal equilibrium with perfect foresight, the stock of capital of period $t + 1$ should verify the following implicit equation:

$$\Delta(k_{t+1}, \tilde{w}(k_t, b), b) \equiv (1+n)(k_{t+1} + b) - s(\tilde{w}(k_t, b), f'(k_{t+1})) = 0. \tag{4.36}$$

This equation defines the dynamics of k_t under perfect foresight. Following the same method as in section 1.5.1, we keep b and $w > 0$ fixed, and investigate whether there exists a solution $k > 0$ to

$$\Delta(k, w, b) \equiv (1+n)(b + k) - s(w, f'(k)) = 0. \tag{4.37}$$

If the net income is $\tilde{w}_t = w$, the savings with perfect foresight $s(w, f'(k_{t+1}))$ should be equal to $(1+n)(b + k_{t+1})$ when the debt per capita b is constant. As the savings $s(w, f'(k_{t+1}))$ are bounded from above by income w, we have

$$\lim_{k \to +\infty} \Delta(k, w, b) = +\infty. \tag{4.38}$$

Before completing the study of the existence of the equilibrium, we introduce an assumption **H3b**. The condition of rational foresight, i.e. the fact that agents coordinates their expectations on a single value of k, supposes that equation (4.37) has a unique solution in k. We thus adapt the assumption **H3** of chapter 1 to the model with constant debt: Given b, for all $w > 0$, equation (4.37) has at most one solution $k > 0$ such that $(k, b) \in \mathcal{E}$.

Assumption H3b.
Given b, for all $w > 0$, for all k such that $(k, b) \in \mathcal{E}$,

$$\Delta(k, w, b) = 0 \quad \Rightarrow \quad \Delta'_k(k, w, b) > 0.$$

A sufficient condition is obviously that $\Delta(k, w, b)$ is always increasing. As we have

$$\Delta'_k(k, w, b) = 1 + n - s'_R(w, f'(k)) f''(k),$$

we obtain the same sufficient condition as in chapter 1 for **H3**. It holds in particular when $s'_R \geq 0$, i.e., the inter-temporal elasticity of substitution is not smaller than one, implying that the substitution effect is not dominated by the income effect.

Assuming **H3b** implies that, for all $k_t > 0$, $k_t > -b$ such that $\tilde{w}(k_t, b) > 0$, there exists at most one solution $k_{t+1} > 0$, $k_{t+1} > -b$ to equation (4.36).

Existence and Monotonicity of Equilibrium Trajectories. The derivative of $\tilde{w}(k, b)$ with respect to k is

$$\frac{\partial \tilde{w}(k, b)}{\partial k} = \omega'(k) - f''(k)b = -f''(k)(k + b),$$

which is positive for $k > -b$. We now have the following proposition:

Proposition 4.13 (Existence and monotonicity of equilibrium trajectories)
*Assume **H3b**, and let $(k_0, b) \in \mathcal{E}$. Then, we have:*

1. *If $\Delta(k_0, \tilde{w}(k_0, b), b) \leq 0$, there exists an inter-temporal equilibrium with perfect foresight with initial capital k_0; the sequence (k_t) is non-decreasing.*
2. *If $\Delta(k_0, \tilde{w}(k_0, b), b) > 0$, then equation (4.36) defines a decreasing sequence (k_t). Either there is a date at which equation (4.36) has no solution, or there is a solution for all t and the inter-temporal equilibrium exists.*

Proof:
1. Consider $t \geq 0$ such that $\Delta(k_t, \tilde{w}(k_t, b), b) \leq 0$. Then there exists $k_{t+1} \geq k_t$ such that $\Delta(k_{t+1}, \tilde{w}(k_t, b), b) = 0$, for the continuous function $\Delta(k, \cdot)$ of k, is negative or nil at k_t and positive for k large enough (equation (4.38)). As we have $k_{t+1} \geq k_t > -b$, we have $\tilde{w}(k_{t+1}, b) \geq \tilde{w}(k_t, b)$. As $\Delta(\cdot)$ is decreasing with respect to $\tilde{w}$, we deduce that

$$\Delta(k_{t+1}, \tilde{w}(k_{t+1}, b), b) \leq 0.$$

The first result is proven by induction for all $t \geq 0$; the sequence (k_t) exists and is non-decreasing. Moreover, it is strictly increasing if it is not constant (case $\Delta(k_0, \tilde{w}(k_0, b), b) < 0$).
2. Assume now that $\Delta(k_t, \tilde{w}(k_t, b), b) > 0$ at $t \geq 0$ with $(b, k_t) \in \mathcal{E}$, and assume that there exists k_{t+1} such that (4.36) holds. Let us use the simplified notation $\tilde{\Delta}_t(k) = \Delta(k, \tilde{w}(k_t, b), b)$. If k_{t+1} were greater than k_t, we would have, following **H3b**,

$$\frac{\partial \tilde{\Delta}_t}{\partial k}(k_{t+1}) > 0 \quad \text{and} \quad \tilde{\Delta}_t(k_{t+1}) = 0.$$

As Δ is increasing in k at k_{t+1}, there exists ϵ such that $k_{t+1} - \epsilon > k_t$ and $\tilde{\Delta}_t(k_{t+1} - \epsilon) < 0$. Then $\tilde{\Delta}(k)$ crosses the horizontal axis between k_t and $k_{t+1} - \epsilon$. We would then have two solutions, which is excluded.

We deduce that k_{t+1} should necessarily be smaller than k_t: as long at it is defined, the sequence k_{t+1} is decreasing and satisfies $\tilde{w}(k_{t+1}, b) < w(k_t, b)$ and, if $\tilde{w}(k_{t+1}, b) > 0$, $\Delta(k_{t+1}, \tilde{w}(k_{t+1}, b), b) > 0$. ∎

We have thus established the existence of the inter-temporal equilibrium in the case $\Delta(k_0, \tilde{w}(k_0, b), b) \leq 0$ and the monotonicity of the dynamics in that case. However, the inter-temporal equilibrium may not exist for certain initial conditions such that $\Delta(k_0, \tilde{w}(k_0, b), b) > 0$. In that case, at a given date, either the net income becomes negative, or savings are not sufficient to finance the debt. The debt b is therefore not sustainable.

From the monotonicity result we deduce that an inter-temporal equilibrium – if it exists – necessarily converges. Such a limit is a steady state. We now study the set of steady states in detail.

The Steady State Curve $\hat{b}(k)$. Capital $\bar{k} > 0$ is a steady state of the dynamics described by (4.36) if $\Delta(\bar{k}, \tilde{w}(\bar{k}, b), b) = 0$. We analyze the set of the steady states

$$\psi(k, b) = \Delta(k, \tilde{w}(k, b), b) = (1+n)(b+k) - s(\tilde{w}(k, b), f'(k)) = 0$$

in the set $\mathcal{E}$, and we shall show that $\psi = 0$ defines a function $\hat{b}(k)$ for k feasible in the long run: $0 < k < \tilde{k}$, with $\tilde{k}$ such that $f(\tilde{k}) = (1+n)\tilde{k}$. We have the following proposition:

Proposition 4.14 (The steady state curve)
The equation

$$\Delta(k, \tilde{w}(k, b), b) = 0$$

has a unique solution $\hat{b}(k)$ for all positive capital feasible in the long run ($0 < k < \tilde{k}$) such that $(k, \hat{b}(k)) \in \mathcal{E}$. The function $\hat{b}(k)$ is continuously differentiable, and its limits are $\hat{b}(\tilde{k}-) = -\tilde{k}$ and $\hat{b}(0+) \geq 0$. We have $\hat{b}(0+) > 0$ if and only if $\bar{b}(0+) > 0$.

We call $b = \hat{b}(k)$ the steady state curve, linking together the steady state value of capital to the level of debt.

Proof: We first study the existence and uniqueness of $\hat{b}$ and compute its limits. The partial derivatives of $\psi(k, b)$ with respect to b is

$$\psi'_b = \Delta'_{\tilde{w}}\tilde{w}'_b + \Delta'_b = s'_w[f'(k) - (1+n)] + 1 + n$$
$$= s'_w f'(k) + (1+n)(1 - s'_w) > 0,$$

as $0 < s'_w < 1$.

1. When $k < k_{GR}$ (under-accumulation of capital), $\tilde{w}(k, b) > 0 \Leftrightarrow b < \bar{b}(k)$. As $\psi(b, k) < (1 + n)(b + k)$, we have

$$\lim_{b \to -\infty} \psi(b, k) = -\infty.$$

Moreover, by definition of $\bar{b}(k)$ we have $\lim_{b \to \bar{b}(k)} \tilde{w}(k, b) = 0$, which implies

$$\lim_{b \to \bar{b}(k)} \psi(b, k) = (1 + n)[\bar{b}(k) + k] > 0,$$

as $\bar{b}(k) = \omega(k)/\varrho(k)$ is positive. As a consequence, for all $k > 0$ the function $\psi(k, b)$ is increasing in b, from $-\infty$ to a positive value. There thus exists $\hat{b}(k) < \bar{b}(k)$ unique such that $\psi(k, \hat{b}(k)) = 0$, where $\hat{b}(k)$ is the value of the debt such that k is a steady state. The limits of the function $\hat{b}(k)$ are as follows:
- When $\bar{b}(0) = 0$ ($\omega(0) = 0$ or $f'(0+) = +\infty$), we deduce from $\hat{b}(k) < \bar{b}(k)$ that

$$\limsup_{k \to 0} \hat{b}(k) \leq 0.$$

We also have

$$\liminf_{k \to 0} \hat{b}(k) = \liminf_{k \to 0} s(\tilde{w}(k, \hat{b}(k)), f'(k)) \geq 0.$$

As $\liminf \leq \limsup$, the two limits are equal at 0 and

$$\lim_{k \to 0} \hat{b}(k) = 0.$$

- When $\bar{b}(0) > 0$ ($\omega(0) > 0$ and $f'(0+) < +\infty$), the limit $\check{b}$ of $\hat{b}(k)$ when k tends to zero, if it exists, satisfies $\psi(0, \check{b}) = 0$, where

$$\psi(0, \check{b}) = (1 + n)\check{b} - s(\omega(0) - \varrho(0)\check{b}, f'(0)).$$

The limit when $k \to 0$ of $\psi(k, \check{b})$ is defined for $\check{b} < \bar{b}(0)$. We deduce from $\psi'_b(0, \check{b}) > 0$ and $\psi(0, 0) = -s(\omega(0), f'(0)) < 0$ that $\check{b} > 0$ is the unique solution to $\psi(0, \check{b}) = 0$ and that it verifies $0 < \check{b} < \bar{b}(0)$. Moreover, for any sequence (k_t) converging to 0, all the limit points b of $\hat{b}(k_t)$ verify $\psi(0, b) = 0$ and thus coincides with $\check{b}$. This implies that the limit of $\hat{b}(k)$ when k goes to 0 exists and is equal to $\check{b}$.

Concerning the limit when k tends to k_{GR}, $\tilde{w}(k, b)$ tends to $\omega(k_{GR})$, and the limit of $\hat{b}(k)$ is b_{GR} (the same argument as above can be applied).
2. When $k > k_{GR}$ (over-accumulation of capital), $\tilde{w}(k, b) > 0 \Leftrightarrow b > \underline{b}(k)$. As

$$\psi(b, k) > (1 + n)(b + k) - \tilde{w}(b, k)$$
$$> (1 + n)(b + k) - \omega(k) + (f'(k) - (1 + n))b$$
$$> (1 + n)k - \omega(k) + f'(k)b,$$

we have

$$\lim_{b \to +\infty} \psi(b, k) = +\infty.$$

Moreover, we have $\lim_{b \to \underline{b}(k)} \tilde{w}(k, b) = 0$, which implies

$$\lim_{b \to \underline{b}(k)} \psi(b, k) = (1 + n)[\underline{b}(k) + k] = \frac{1 + n}{\varrho(k)}[\omega(k) - \varrho(k)k]$$

$$= \frac{1 + n}{-\varrho(k)}[(1 + n)k - f(k)].$$

This limit is negative if and only if $k < \tilde{k}$. As a consequence, since the function $\psi(k, b)$, is increasing in b, there exists, for $k < \tilde{k}$, a unique $\hat{b}(k) > \underline{b}(k)$ such that $\psi(k, \hat{b}(k)) = 0$. The limits of the function $\hat{b}(k)$ are

$$\lim_{k \to k_{GR}} \hat{b}(k) = b_{GR} = \frac{s(\omega(k_{GR}), 1 + n)}{1 + n} - k_{GR},$$

and

$$\lim_{k \to \tilde{k}} \hat{b}(k) = \underline{b}(\tilde{k}) = -\tilde{k}.$$

For $k > \tilde{k}$, we have $\forall b > \underline{b}(k)$, $\psi(k, b) > 0$.

Finally, the continuity and differentiability of $\hat{b}$ result from the implicit function theorem. ∎

Two examples of possible $\hat{b}(k)$ are represented in figures 4.12 and 4.13.

Example: With a logarithmic utility function, we have

$$\psi(b, k) = (1 + n)(b + k) - \frac{\beta}{1 + \beta}[\omega(k_t) - bf'(k_t) + b(1 + n)],$$

and

$$\hat{b}(k) = \frac{\beta\omega(k) - (1 + \beta)(1 + n)k}{1 + n + \beta f'(k)}.$$

4.4.3 Characteristics of Inter-temporal Equilibria

It is now possible to characterize the inter-temporal equilibria, their existence, and the nature of their dynamics by using the function $\hat{b}(k)$.

Proposition 4.15 (Characteristics of inter-temporal equilibria)
We assume **H3b** *and let* $(b, k_0) \in \mathcal{E}$*. Then, when* $k_0 < \tilde{k}$*, there are three possibilities for b:*

A. *If $b < \hat{b}(k_0)$, the inter-temporal equilibrium with initial state k_0 exists and is unique, and the sequence $(k_t)_{t\geq0}$ is increasing and converges to a steady state $\bar{k}$; $\bar{k}$ is the smallest steady state greater than k_0.*

B. *If $b = \hat{b}(k_0)$, k_0 is a steady state equilibrium: the inter-temporal equilibrium exists, and the sequence $(k_t)_{t\geq0}$ is constant and equal to (k_0).*

C. *if $b > \hat{b}(k_0)$, we have three possible situations:*
- *If there exists a steady state equilibrium $0 < \bar{k} < k_0$, then the inter-temporal equilibrium exists, and the sequence $(k_t)_{t\geq0}$ is decreasing and converges to the largest steady state which is smaller than k_0.*
- *If there is no inter-temporal equilibrium starting from k_0, then there is no steady state smaller than k_0.*
- *If there is an inter-temporal equilibrium starting from k_0, but there is no steady state smaller than k_0, then the sequence $(k_t)_{t\geq0}$ converges to 0 (poverty trap).*

When $k_0 \geq \tilde{k}$,

D. *The condition $\tilde{w}(k_0, b) > 0$ implies that $\psi(k_0, b)$ is positive and we have the same properties as in case C ($b > \hat{b}(k_0)$).*

Proof: A: If $b < \hat{b}(k_0)$, then $\psi(k_0, b) < \psi(k_0, \hat{b}(k_0)) = 0$. We are in case 1 of proposition 4.13 (with strict inequality). Then the inter-temporal equilibrium

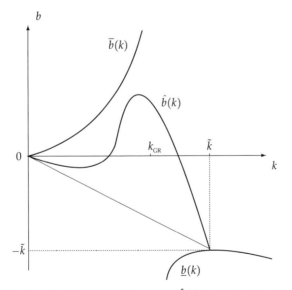

Figure 4.12. The steady state curve. The curve $\hat{b}(k)$ is plotted for the case where $\hat{b}(0+) = 0$ and $\tilde{k}$ is finite. This case arises, e.g., with a logarithmic utility function and a CES production function with low substitutability.

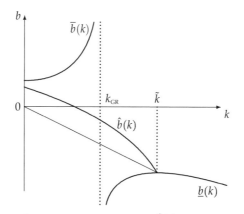

Figure 4.13. The steady state curve. The curve $\hat{b}(k)$ is plotted for the case where $\hat{b}(0+) > 0$. This case arises, e.g., with a logarithmic utility function and a CES production function with high substitutability.

exists, it is unique according to **H3b**, and the sequence (k_t) is increasing. Let us show that it is bounded. We have

$$(1+n)(k_{t+1}+b) < \tilde{w}(k_t, b) = \omega(k_t) - \varrho(k_t)b,$$

and

$$\frac{k_{t+1}}{k_t} < \frac{1}{1+n}\left(\frac{\omega(k_t)}{k_t} - \frac{\varrho(k_t)b}{k_t}\right) - \frac{b}{k_t}.$$

The limit of the right-hand side is nil when k_t tends to $+\infty$, as $\varrho(+\infty) = f'(+\infty) - (1+n)$ is finite, and the limit of $\omega(k)/k$ when k tends to $+\infty$ is equal to 0 (see appendix A.1.3). Thus we have that, for k_t large enough, $k_{t+1} < k_t$, which is excluded. The increasing sequence (k_t) is bounded.

We deduce that the sequence (k_t) converges to the limit $\bar{k}$, which is a steady state equilibrium. As monotonic dynamics never goes from one side of a steady state to the other (see appendix A.3.1), $\bar{k}$ is the smallest steady state larger than k_0.

B: In the case where $b = \hat{b}(k_0)$, the conclusion results directly from the definition of $\hat{b}(\cdot)$.

C: If $b > \hat{b}(k_0)$, then $\psi(k_0, b) > \psi(k_0, \hat{b}(k_0)) = 0$. We are in case 2 of proposition 4.13. As long as it exists, the equilibrium sequence (k_t) is decreasing.

- If there exists a steady state equilibrium $0 \leq \bar{k}_0 < k_0$, we apply the same method as in the proof of case A.
- The second claim is logically equivalent to the first one.
- If the inter-temporal equilibrium exists, the corresponding (decreasing) monotonic sequence $(k_t)_{t \geq 0}$ necessarily has a limit. Since there is no steady state, this limit is zero.

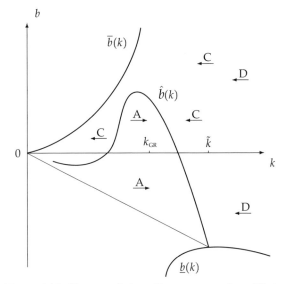

Figure 4.14. Characteristics of inter-temporal equilibria.

D: If $k_0 \geq \tilde{k}$ and $(k_0, b) \in \mathcal{E}$, we have $\psi(k_0, b) > 0$. Then we are in case 2 of proposition 4.13, and the analysis developed for C can be applied. ∎

This proposition is related to two results derived earlier. First, the poverty trap case mentioned in the proposition is in fact a corner steady state of the economy with debt (see sections 1.6.1 and 1.6.3). Second, considering a stable stationary equilibrium, the inter-temporal government budget constraint holds if and only if under-accumulation prevails at the equilibrium. Obviously, if over-accumulation prevails, the growth rate of debt, which equals the growth rate of population, is larger than the interest rate, and the inter-temporal government budget constraint does not hold. In that case, though, the inter-temporal equilibrium exists and debt is sustainable. This illustrates the results in section 4.2.2.

As shown in figure 4.14, we have now a simple geometrical tool to analyze the dynamics of capital. Locally stable (unstable) steady states are located on the downward (upward) sloping branches of the function $\hat{b}(\cdot)$.

4.4.4 Policy Implications

The main policy issues are as follows: On the one hand, not every level of debt is compatible with the existence of equilibrium. On the other hand, any level of capital between 0 and the upper limit $\tilde{k}$ given by $f(\tilde{k}) = (1 + n)\tilde{k}$ can be implemented as an equilibrium. In particular, one can reach the golden rule with either $b \geq 0$ and $b < 0$. Debt can also be used to avoid a poverty trap. We detail these issues in turn.

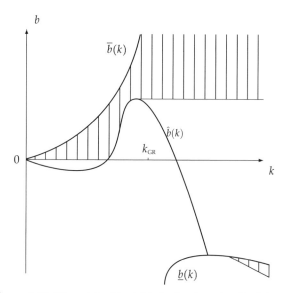

Figure 4.15. Unsustainable debts in the domain of existence.

Sustainability. Sustainability means that an inter-temporal equilibrium with constant debt exists. As shown in figure 4.15, three different unsustainable situations can occur.

In the first situation the economy starts above the maximum of the steady state curve. Debt is too large, implying that the over-taxed young households do not save enough to maintain a constant private capital stock, as the burden of debt is excessive. As productive capital falls, wage incomes become at some point insufficient to cover the tax payments, and the temporary equilibrium with this level of debt no longer exists.

In the second situation, the economy starts to the left of the steady state curve. Debt is too large with respect to the initial capital stock, and the conclusion is the same as in the previous case.

The third case arises when the debt is negative and the initial stock of capital is large. In this situation the interest rate is lower than the growth rate of the population, and households have to pay taxes to finance the government investment program. The stock of capital (and hence wage income) decreases, and at some point households are no longer able to sustain this situation. Note in the figure the range to the right of the $\hat{b}(k)$ curve where over-accumulation implies that the growth rate of debt is larger than the interest rate. In this range the inter-temporal government budget constraint does not hold, but the inter-temporal equilibrium exists and debt is sustainable.

Poverty Traps. We have seen in proposition 4.15 that 0 can be a limit of the equilibrium trajectory (poverty trap). This cases arises only if debt is positive

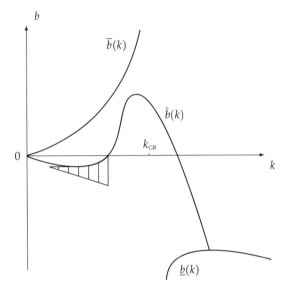

Figure 4.16. Escapes from a poverty trap.

or nil. Indeed, when the government holds private assets ($b < 0$), we have

$$(1+n)k_{t+1} = s_t - b > -b > 0,$$

and capital is bounded below by the constant quantity held by the government.

Moreover, negative public debt can be used to escape from a poverty trap under certain circumstances. As illustrated in figure 4.16, negative debt allows one to escape from a poverty trap when (i) the corner steady state is locally stable in the economy without debt, (ii) the initial capital stock lies in the range of stability of the corner steady state, and (iii) the curve $\hat{b}(k)$ is increasing at k_0, which guarantees that some level of debt $b^\star$ exists such that $b^\star < \hat{b}(k_0)$. In this case, running a negative debt would put the economy on a path that converges to a high steady state level of capital. This policy amounts to "nationalizing" part of the capital stock detained by the first old generation, thereby allowing the government to distribute the dividends of this capital to the young generation by means of a negative tax. This inter-generational transfer enables a high level of investment, which allows the capital stock to grow.

Notice also that the size of the negative debt that is necessary to escape from the poverty trap depends on the distance between the actual stock of capital and the lowest (unstable) steady state. Near this steady state very little negative debt is sufficient. The further one is from the steady state, the higher the necessary level of negative debt will be. At some point it is impossible to escape from the trap, as the required level of debt would violate the positivity constraint on private investment.

Golden Rule. As the curve $\hat{b}(k)$ is always defined at k_{GR}, there always exists a level of debt such that the golden rule capital stock is a steady state. However, nothing says that this steady state equilibrium is locally or globally stable. Our analysis allows us to obtain conditions where this is the case. When the golden rule equilibrium is locally stable, i.e., when $\hat{b}'(k_{GR}) < 0$, the constant debt policy with $b = \hat{b}(k_{GR})$ leads to the golden rule if k_0 is not too low.

One main point of the analysis of Diamond (1965) was to show that debt causes a rise (a fall) in the utility level of an individual living in long-run equilibrium if the competitive equilibrium without debt is inefficient (efficient). This result applies to a stable long-run equilibrium, which requires in our framework $\hat{b}'(k) < 0$. In this case, a rise in debt reduces the stock of capital, which increases the steady state utility in the case $k > k_{GR}$.

Proposition 4.16 (Debt and welfare)
For a given b and a stable steady state k, public debt has a positive (negative) effect on welfare if there is over-accumulation (under-accumulation) at k.

Proof: This can be shown by differentiating

$$U(c, d) = u(\omega(k) - (1 + n)(k + b) - \tau(k)) + \beta u(f'(k)(1 + n)(b + k))$$
$$= u(\omega(k) - (1 + n)k - bf'(k)) + \beta u(f'(k)(1 + n)(b + k))$$

with respect to k and b. This leads to

$$\frac{dU}{db} = u'(c) \left([\omega' - (1 + n) - bf''] \frac{dk}{db} - f' \right)$$
$$+ \beta u'(d) \left([f''(k + b) + f'] \frac{dk}{db} + f' \right) (1 + n).$$

Simplifying with the arbitrage condition $u'(c) = \beta f' u'(d)$, we get that dU/db is of the sign of

$$\left([\omega' - (1 + n) - bf''] \frac{dk}{db} - f' \right) + \left[\left(\frac{f''}{f'}(k + b) + 1 \right) \frac{dk}{db} + 1 \right] (1 + n)$$
$$= (1 + n - f') \left(1 + \frac{f''}{f'}(k + b) \frac{dk}{db} \right),$$

since $\omega' = -kf''$. This expression is of the same sign as $1 + n > f'$ if $dk/db < 0$ (stability). ∎

A noteworthy situation arises when the golden rule steady state equilibrium is unstable, which is characterized by $\hat{b}'(k_{GR}) > 0$. In this case, although a level of debt always exists such that the golden rule capital stock is a steady state, a policy of constant debt is unable to lead to the golden rule (unless the initial capital stock is already at the golden rule level). From proposition 4.15, if the debt is set such that $b = \hat{b}(k_{GR})$ and the initial capital stock is larger that k_{GR}, we have $b < \hat{b}(k_0)$, so that the inter-temporal equilibrium exists and is unique, and the sequence (k_t) is increasing. Moreover, it converges to a steady state higher than the golden rule level, and thus is characterized by over-accumulation of capital. If the initial capital stock is smaller that k_{GR}, then $b > \hat{b}(k_0)$, and, as long as it exists, the equilibrium sequence (k_t) is decreasing. Either it converges to a steady state characterized by under-accumulation, or it converges to zero, or the equilibrium ceases to be defined after a finite number of periods.

Example: The framework developed above can be used to obtain the conditions under which the golden rule equilibrium with constant debt is stable or unstable. Let us take a Cobb–Douglas production function $f(k) = Ak^\alpha$ and a logarithmic utility function $U(c, d) = \ln c + \beta \ln d$. Then the steady state curve is given by

$$\hat{b}(k) = \frac{(1 - \alpha)\beta A k^\alpha - k(1 + n)(1 + \beta)}{1 + n + Ak^{\alpha-1}\alpha\beta}.$$

Differentiating with respect to k, we obtain that $b'(k)$ is of the sign of

$$[(1 - \alpha)\beta R - (1 + n)(1 + \beta)](1 + n + \beta R) + (1 - \alpha)^2\beta^2 R^2/\alpha$$
$$- (1 + n)(1 + \beta)(1 - \alpha)\beta R,$$

where $R(k) = A\alpha k^{\alpha-1}$. Computing this expression at the golden rule, i.e., for $R = 1 + n$, we obtain that $\hat{b}'(k_{GR})$ is of the sign of

$$\frac{\beta^2}{\alpha}[(1 - \alpha)^2 - \alpha] - 2\beta - 1,$$

which is negative for $1 - \alpha \leq \sqrt{\alpha}$ (i.e., $\alpha > 0.38$). When the opposite inequality holds (say $\alpha = 1/3$), there is a weak restriction on β ($\beta < 6.5$ for $\alpha = 1/3$). Hence, if the weight attached to future consumption is not too large and the share of capital in production is reasonable, Diamond's golden rule equilibrium with constant debt is stable. Notice that the condition does not depend on n.

4.5 APPLICATIONS AND EXTENSIONS

We present here two extensions of the previous analysis. In the first one, we study an example where the policy amounts to keeping constant the debt–GDP ratio. In the second one, we look at a numerical example where constant deficit policies are responsible for everlasting fluctuations.

4.5.1 Constant Debt–Output Ratio

In the above sections, we have analyzed constant deficit and debt policies. It is fair to recognize that real world policies are often expressed in per output terms. With a logarithmic utility and Cobb–Douglas production, proportional policy rules are easy to analyze. Let us assume a logarithmic utility and zero taxes on the old households, which implies a savings function

$$s_t = \frac{\beta}{1+\beta}(1-\tau_t)w_t,$$

where $\tau_t \in (0,1)$ is a proportional tax rate on wage income. The budget of the government is

$$B_t = R_t B_{t-1} - \tau_t w_t N_t. \tag{4.39}$$

Assume a constant debt–output ratio

$$\frac{B_t}{Y_t} = b.$$

The taxes that maintain the budget balanced are

$$\tau_t w_t = b\frac{R_t}{1+n}y_{t-1} - by_t, \qquad \text{with} \quad y_t = \frac{Y_t}{N_t}.$$

With a Cobb–Douglas production function $y_t = Ak_t^\alpha$, these taxes are equal to

$$\tau_t w_t = bA\left(\frac{R_t}{1+n}k_{t-1}^\alpha - k_t^\alpha\right).$$

The dynamics are then given by

$$(1+n)k_{t+1} = \frac{\beta}{1+\beta}(1-\tau_t)w_t - by_t,$$

$$(1+n)k_{t+1} = \frac{\beta Ak_t^\alpha}{1+\beta}\left((1-\alpha) - b\frac{\alpha Ak_t^{-1}}{1+n}k_{t-1}^\alpha + b\right) - bAk_t^\alpha. \tag{4.40}$$

Dividing by Ak_t^α and rearranging, we find

$$\frac{(1+n)k_{t+1}}{Ak_t^\alpha} = \frac{\beta(1-\alpha)-b}{1+\beta} - \frac{\beta b\alpha}{1+\beta}\frac{Ak_{t-1}^\alpha}{(1+n)k_t}. \tag{4.41}$$

Hence the dynamics follow a difference equation of order 2. With $B_0 = bY_0 = bF(K_0, N_0)$, initial conditions B_{-1} and K_0 allow us to compute

$$\tau_0 = \frac{R_0 B_{-1} - bY_0}{N_0 w_0}$$

from equation (4.39), and

$$(1+n)k_1 = \frac{\beta}{1+\beta}(1-\tau_0)w_0 - by_0$$

from equation (4.40). Hence, both k_0 and k_1 are determined by the initial conditions.

It is useful to rewrite the expression (4.41) as giving the dynamics of the investment rate

$$z_{t+1} = \frac{(1+n)k_{t+1}}{Ak_t^\alpha}.$$

We then obtain a first-order difference equation

$$z_{t+1} = \frac{\beta(1-\alpha) - \flat}{1+\beta} - \frac{\beta\flat\alpha}{1+\beta}\frac{1}{z_t} \tag{4.42}$$

that can be studied first. Once the dynamics in z are known, those of k can be easily deduced. Hence, with a constant debt–output ratio, the dynamics of dimension 2 can be solved recursively.

The steady state investment rates are the solution to

$$P(z) = z^2 - \frac{\beta(1-\alpha) - \flat}{1+\beta}z + \frac{\beta\flat\alpha}{1+\beta} = 0.$$

Three cases have to be considered, depending on whether $\flat < 0$, $\flat = 0$, or $\flat > 0$:

- In the case of negative debt, if $\flat < 0$, the dynamics (4.42) are defined in $\mathbb{R}_{++}$. They are oscillatory and converge to a unique globally stable steady state z^* which is the positive root of $P(z)$. These dynamics have been studied in section 1.8.9. For the steady state z^* to be an equilibrium, it should be smaller than 1. This requires $P(1) > 0$, i.e. $\flat > -1$. Moreover, for the dynamics to stay in $(0, 1)$, there is a restriction on the initial condition z_1 such that $z_2 < 1$.
- In the case of zero debt, z is constant and equal to $\beta(1-\alpha)/(1+\beta)$. Equation (4.41) is the equation (1.21) of chapter 1.
- In the case of positive debt, if $\flat > 0$, the dynamics (4.42) are defined in $\mathbb{R}$ as long as $z \neq 0$. They are monotonic. The condition $z_{t+1} > 0$ requires a not too large debt–GDP ratio:

$$\flat < \beta(1-\alpha).$$

For the dynamics to stay in $(0, 1)$, it is necessary to have at least one steady state in the interval. A first condition is the existence of a steady state, i.e., the discriminant of $P(z)$ is non-negative:

$$\left(\frac{\beta(1-\alpha) - \flat}{1+\beta}\right)^2 \geq 4\frac{\beta\alpha\flat}{1+\beta}.$$

With $0 < \flat < \beta(1-\alpha)$, this leads to

$$\beta(1-\alpha) \geq 2\sqrt{(1+\beta)\beta\flat\alpha} + \flat, \tag{4.43}$$

which imposes an upper bound on the debt $\bar{\flat}$, viz., $\flat \leq \bar{\flat} < \beta(1-\alpha)$. The roots of $P(z) = 0$ are positive, since the coefficient of z in $P(z)$ is negative. To pursue the analysis, we draw the function ϕ corresponding to the dynamics

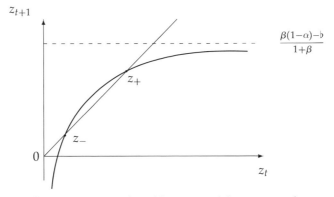

Figure 4.17. Dynamics with constant debt–output ratio.

(4.42): $z_{t+1} = \phi(z_t)$. This function is increasing and concave and is plotted in figure 4.17 (assuming $\flat < \bar{\flat}$). We see that the dynamics converge to z_+. From the figure, there are two additional conditions for the existence of equilibrium: $z_+ < 1$ (steady state investment rate smaller than one) and $z_1 \geq z_-$ (to converge to z_+). The conditions for $z_+ < 1$ are $P(1) > 0$ and $P(0) < 1$, implying that both roots are below 1. $P(1) > 0 \Leftrightarrow \flat > -1$ and is thus verified for positive debt. $P(0) < 1$ requires another condition on $\flat$: $\flat < (1 + \beta)/(\alpha\beta)$. This condition always holds for $\flat < \bar{\flat}$, since the opposite of the inequality (4.43) is verified for $\flat \geq (1 + \beta)/(\alpha\beta)$.

To conclude, the policy of fixing a constant debt–GDP ratio is compatible with the existence of a steady state equilibrium for a ratio belonging to $(-1, \bar{\flat})$. Given the initial state z_1, the existence of an inter-temporal equilibrium starting from z_1 requires an additional restriction.

4.5.2 Deficits and Cycles

In proposition 4.11, we have studied the stability of steady states when the government follows a policy of fixing the deficit. The local stability of some steady states may well be characterized by complex roots. In this case, oscillations in output and debt will occur. This point was already studied by Farmer (1986) in the case of zero deficit (he thus consider near-golden-rule dynamics). We develop here an example of a constant, non-zero deficit. We numerically compute some trajectories in the presence of complex roots. The numerical exercise allows us to describe the trajectory when the steady state is locally unstable; this is interesting because the trajectory does not necessarily explode but may follow a regular pattern.

We take a logarithmic utility function with $\beta = 0.3$ and a CES production function with $\rho = 4$, $\alpha = 0.5$, and $A = 10$ (a low level of total factor productivity

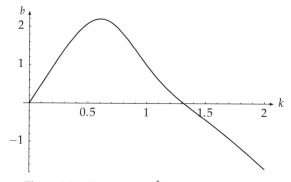

Figure 4.18. The function $\hat{\delta}(k, 0)$ in the example.

turns out to be necessary to obtain Farmer's results). The other parameters
are $g = 0$, $\tau^2 = 0$, and $n = 1.097$. A first set of useful information can be drawn
from figure 4.18, which represents the steady state curve $\hat{\delta}(k, 0)$ of proposition
4.9 for the chosen parameters. We observe that for a deficit δ between 2.2
and 0 two steady states exist. For δ negative there is one steady state, and for
δ above 2.2 there is no steady state. We will now look at the dynamics for
different values of δ (Farmer considers the dynamics for different values of a
technological parameter).

We represent in figure 4.19 the phase diagram for $\delta = 0.06$. The low steady
state does not appear in the picture, as it displays low capital ($k < 0.7$). The
steady state we consider is thus at the intersection of the two phase lines
with $b = -0.39$ and $k = 1.29$. We have also plotted a trajectory starting from
$b_0 = -0.7$, $k_0 = 1.29$. This trajectory converges to the steady state following
oscillations. The computed eigenvalues are stable and complex; they equal
$0.391 \pm 0.908i$ with a modulus of 0.989.

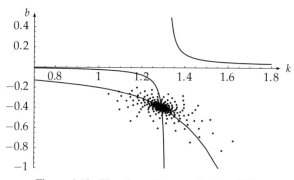

Figure 4.19. The phase diagram for $\delta = 0.06$.

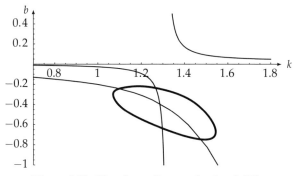

Figure 4.20. The phase diagram for $\delta = 0.076$.

If one increases the deficit slightly, the system loses its stability. The critical point is $\delta = 0.07172$, where the modulus of both eigenvalues is 1.[13] For $\delta = 0.076$ the steady state is locally unstable. The eigenvalues have now a modulus of 1.004. Any trajectory starting close to the steady state diverges from the steady state but does not explode. It converges to a closed curve, shown in figure 4.20. Also, any trajectory starting slightly outside the closed curve converges to it.

The picture changes completely if the deficit is increased further. Figure 4.21 is shown for $\delta = 0.095$. The closed curve transforms into what the literature calls a *strange attractor*.[14] Again, if the initial conditions lie inside the attractor, the trajectory will converge to it and the economy will be characterized by everlasting fluctuations.

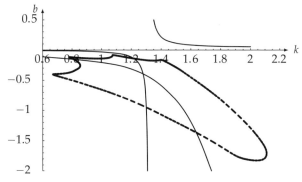

Figure 4.21. The phase diagram for $\delta = 0.095$.

---

[13] This critical point is called in the literature a Hopf bifurcation for maps, or a Naimark–Sacker bifurcation. See Hale and Koçak (1991) and Wiggins (1990).
[14] Pintus, Sands, and de Vilder (2000) study these transformations in detail.

When δ increases further, the equilibrium will no longer exists, as the trajectory would at some point entail a negative stock of capital.

The endogenous cycles computed above arise only if the government pursues a particular policy, viz., maintaining the deficit constant. Notice that the range of values of δ for which never-ending fluctuations arise is rather small. One might also wonder whether such cycles can be reproduced in models with individuals living more than two periods.[15]

4.6 CONCLUSION

In this chapter we have analyzed economic policies when the government budget is not balanced period after period, i.e. when there is a public debt. In particular, we have been interested in studying the restrictions on debt policy and the effect of policies on capital accumulation.

A first central result is that there is no restriction on government borrowing when the government can freely tax the two generations. While fiscal instruments are limited by the fact that the life-cycle income of the agents must be kept positive, there is no specific constraint on debt policy. Furthermore, two instruments are enough to decentralize any feasible allocation respecting the household arbitrage condition. If two lump-sum taxes are available, the given allocation can be decentralized for any arbitrary path of public debt. For instance, the debt may well follow an explosive path if the government subsidizes the young households so that they are able to absorb the debt, and taxes this wealth away when they are old. This shows that there is no theoretical reason to require that the government satisfy its inter-temporal budget constraint in overlapping generations models. But some restrictions apply when only young (or only old) people are taxed, even when there is over-accumulation of capital.

We have then analyzed the dynamics of debt and capital under two different policies: constant (zero or non-zero) deficit per capita and constant debt per capita. In the first case, the analysis is essentially local, although a global view of the steady states can be obtained. In the second case, we propose a global analysis of the dynamics, which allows us to study the sustainability of constant debt policies. Considering now the whole set of results of this analysis, we retain two main elements and a general conclusion.

First, a level of debt such that the golden rule capital stock is a steady state always exists provided that public spending is reasonable. However, a constant debt policy may be unable to lead the economy to the golden rule. In the case where the debt of the golden rule is positive, a constant zero deficit policy leads to a saddle path. It can thus implement the golden rule only for a specific level of the initial debt.

---

[15] Aiyagari (1989) argues that cycles tend to disappear when life spans get large in overlapping generations models, provided that the future is discounted positively by households. He proves the result for an exchange economy and cycles of fixed periods.

Second, if the initial capital stock is low and/or government spending is very high, implying that the economy is threatened by a poverty trap, negative debt can be useful to escape from the trap. With a constant deficit policy, this escape from the trap requires a sufficiently negative initial debt. With a constant debt policy, it means we must not be too far from the lowest positive steady state.

In addition, two policies are clearly not sustainable: to maintain a constant deficit with a too high initial debt, and to maintain a constant debt with a too low initial capital.

The general conclusion to the stability analysis is that none of the policies considered is stable per se. According to the values of the parameters, one can obtain local or global stability, saddle points, or unstable steady states. This implies that a debt policy should be carefully thought through as a function of the characteristics and current state of the economy.

Finally, we propose in this chapter a clear presentation of the differences between debt and bubbles. The three important differences are: First, debt is a pre-determined variable, while a bubble is a forward-looking variable with no initial condition. Second, a bubble cannot be negative if the corresponding asset can be freely disposed of. On the contrary, a negative debt simply means that the government holds a part of the physical capital of the economy. Third, the model with debt can be analyzed within a truly dynamic approach to equilibrium. The model with bubbles should be analyzed within a general equilibrium framework where the Walrasian auctioneer determines the prices of all periods at the same time, a condition for the existence of an equilibrium with *rational bubbles*.

FIVE

Further Issues

This chapter offers a treatment of four important issues: altruism, education, inter-generational externalities, and general equilibrium in macroeconomics.[1] The first three topics involve inter-generational linkages in one way or another; this is why they require the use of the overlapping generations model. Altruism implies bequests; education needs funding by older generations; inter-generational externalities model the inheritance of standard-of-living aspirations. The last topic studies the link between the overlapping generations model and the Arrow–Debreu approach to general equilibrium.

Altruism is an important topic in that it gives a motive to parents for leaving bequests to their children. In the real world, inter-generational resource transfers consist mainly of pensions (chapter 3), public debt (chapter 4), and private bequests. Section 5.1 explains how dynastic altruism provides a motive for bequest and studies the problem of the altruistic household. It then draws the consequences of altruism for pension and debt policy.

Parents' influence on children is not limited to resource transfers; two other important influences are human capital spillovers (section 5.2) and taste spillovers (section 5.3). These two spillovers are in general responsible for two externalities: A positive one linked to the transmission of human capital from one generation to the other, and a negative one related to the inheritance of standard-of-living aspirations from the parents. The first one has given rise to many articles dealing with education as an engine of growth. They stress the idea that individual-specific human capital is increasing in the human capital of the previous generation and this can be responsible for sustained growth. The second spillover stems for the fact that in a growing economy, successive generations are raised in increasingly richer households and hence develop successively higher standard-of-living aspirations.

---

[1] We do not intend to provide an in-depth analysis of these different fields, but only to show the reader how the previous chapters can be extended and applied to wider issues.

The question of the fourth section – the link between our approach and Arrow–Debreu general equilibria – is important. Indeed, we have developed a framework based on the notions of temporary equilibrium and inter-temporal equilibrium; another strand of the literature that studies the overlapping generations model (without capital) uses the atemporal general equilibrium approach with complete markets (extending the Arrow–Debreu framework to infinite horizon). The comparison provided in section 5.4 will help to put into perspective the approach chosen for this book and to highlight its use for policy issues.

5.1 DYNASTIC ALTRUISM: A BEQUEST MOTIVE

Bequests and inter vivos gifts are responsible for large inter-generational transfers. They account, together with private savings, for an important part of individual wealth. Bequests can either be unintentional (accidental) or intentional (voluntary). In the first case, as in Abel (1985), one assumes lifetime uncertainty; a precautionary demand for savings arises to avoid low levels of consumption in the event of a long life. When death occurs, the household is holding some wealth, which is passed on to the children as an accidental bequest. This eventuality arises because of lack of complete markets for annuity securities. In the second case, which is the one we consider in this section, dynastic altruism (i.e., from parents to children) provides a motive for leaving bequests to the descendants. Altruism within the family can be seen as an application of social interaction theory (Becker (1974)).

5.1.1 Modeling Voluntary Bequests

We extend the model of the preceding chapters (two-period-lived households supplying labor when young and being retired when old) to allow for private transfers from each household to its $1 + n$ children. Taking the budget constraint of chapter 4 (see equations (4.2) and (4.3)), we introduce the variables x_t and x_{t+1}. x_t is the quantity of goods received by a young household from its parents at time t. x_{t+1} is the amount of good given by an old household to each of its children. The constraints are

$$w_t + x_t - \tau_t^1 = c_t + s_t, \tag{5.1}$$

$$d_{t+1} + (1+n)x_{t+1} = R_{t+1}\, s_t - \tau_{t+1}^2. \tag{5.2}$$

Let us recall that w_t denotes wages, τ_t^1 and τ_{t+1}^2 are the lump-sum taxes bearing on young and old households respectively, c_t and d_{t+1} stand for consumption when young and old respectively, s_t stands for savings, and R_{t+1} is the interest factor. Note that x_t and x_{t+1} represent inter vivos gifts, but the literature calls them bequests. As all households of the same generation are identical, they all receive the same gift. There is an important additional constraint for the household born in t:

$$x_{t+1} \geq 0. \tag{5.3}$$

This non-negativity constraint on bequests forbids the parents to take away resources from their children.

The Objective Function. The utility from consuming when young and old is the same as in the preceding chapters:

$$U_t = U(c_t, d_{t+1}) = u(c_t) + \beta u(d_{t+1}).$$

Moreover, following Barro (1974), an altruistic household enjoys the well-being of its children. Denoting by V_{t+1} the well-being of each of the $1 + n$ children, we assume that the well-being (or the total utility) of an household born in t is given by

$$V_t = U_t + \gamma V_{t+1}. \tag{5.4}$$

The parameter $\gamma > 0$ is called the *degree of altruism*. It is alternatively possible to define

$$V_t = U_t + \tilde{\gamma}(1 + n)V_{t+1},$$

where $\tilde{\gamma}$ applies to the sum of the utilities of the (identical) $1 + n$ children. We obtain (5.4) by defining $\gamma = \tilde{\gamma}(1 + n)$.[2]

The relationship (5.4) links the total utility of a household to that of its children. It introduces a dependency between this utility and the utilities of all descendants. Indeed, although each generation cares only about its children, these children care about their own children, i.e., $V_{t+1} = U_{t+1} + \gamma V_{t+2}$, etc. Every household will thus act taking into account this series of links, and the altruistic household born at t will act taking into account its infinite dynasty. By induction, the total utility can be written as follows, for all $T > t$:

$$V_t = \sum_{\theta=t}^{T-1} \gamma^{\theta-t} U_\theta + \gamma^{T-t} V_T,$$

and, if the total utilities satisfy the limit condition

$$\lim_{T\to\infty} \gamma^{T-t} V_T = 0, \tag{5.5}$$

we have

$$V_t = \sum_{\theta=t}^{\infty} \gamma^{\theta-t} U_\theta,$$

---

[2] A refinement of this approach is to consider that the degree of altruism depends on the number of children, i.e., $\gamma = \gamma(n)$; see Barro and Becker (1989) and an application in Doepke (1999).

i.e., the total utility of a young household born in t is equal to the discounted sum (with a factor γ) of the life-cycle utilities of its descendants.

Expectations. After having written the objective function of an altruistic household, one should determine what are its decision variables and its expectations. A household of any generation $\theta \geq t$ chooses c_θ, s_θ, $d_{\theta+1}$, and $x_{\theta+1}$, taking as given the prices w_θ and $R_{\theta+1}$, the taxes τ_θ^1 and $\tau_{\theta+1}^2$, and the bequest from its parents x_θ. It maximizes his total utility V_θ subject to the constraints (5.1), (5.2), and (5.3) at $t = \theta$. With this information a young household in t which foresees all future prices and taxes can compute the optimal decisions of all its descendants. These future choices depend on its own choice x_{t+1}.

The assumption of perfect foresight bears here on all future taxes and prices. At time t the information set $\mathcal{P}_t$ contains prices $(w_{\theta+1}, R_{\theta+1})$ and taxes $(\tau_{\theta+1}^1, \tau_{\theta+1}^2)$ for all future periods $\theta \geq t$. This assumption is obviously restrictive but necessary for the coherence of the anticipations made by all cohorts, in the sense that $\mathcal{P}_t$ is the union of $\mathcal{P}_{t+1}$ with $(w_{t+1}, R_{t+1}, \tau_{t+1}^1, \tau_{t+1}^2)$.

Under the assumption of perfect foresight, the maximum of total utility is given by the following recursive relation:

$$V_t^\star\left(x_t + w_t - \tau_t^1, \mathcal{P}_t\right)$$
$$= \max_{c_t, s_t, d_{t+1}, x_{t+1}} \left\{u(c_t) + \beta u(d_{t+1}) + \gamma V_{t+1}^\star\left(x_{t+1} + w_{t+1} - \tau_{t+1}^1, \mathcal{P}_{t+1}\right)\right\}. \quad (5.6)$$

The maximum is taken subject to the constraints (5.1), (5.2), and (5.3). For any $t \geq 0$, $V_t^\star(x_t + w_t - \tau_t^1, \mathcal{P}_t)$ is the maximum of utility of a young household born in t when its first-period income is $x_t + w_t - \tau_t^1$, and its information set is $\mathcal{P}_t$. It is the utility it gets when it maximizes the sum of his life-cycle utility plus the utility (weighted by γ) that its children can reach with the bequest x_{t+1}, given that every member of the dynasty anticipate the same prices and taxes.

Compared to the infinite sum approach, the definition of the altruistic household problem based on (5.6) links together the total utilities of all generations. An important feature of this definition is to consider explicitly the decisions of the household born in t only.

The Dynastic Optimal Problem. Equation (5.6) is the Bellman equation of an infinite horizon problem. It links the value functions $V_t^\star$ and $V_{t+1}^\star$. Note that these value functions do depend on time through the paths of prices and taxes. The dynamics of bequests is obtained by eliminating s_t with (5.1)–(5.2):

$$x_{t+1} = \frac{1}{1+n}\left[R_{t+1}\left(x_t + w_t - \tau_t^1 - c_t\right) - \tau_{t+1}^2 - d_{t+1}\right]. \quad (5.7)$$

This dynamic equation also depends on time through prices and taxes. The objective whose maximum is $V_0^\star(x_0 + w_0 - \tau_0^1, \mathcal{P}_0)$ can be written in infinite horizon as the maximum of

$$\sum_{t=0}^{\infty} \gamma^t \left[u(c_t) + \beta u(d_{t+1}) \right], \tag{5.8}$$

subject to the constraints (5.7) and

$$c_t > 0, \qquad d_{t+1} > 0, \quad \text{and} \quad x_{t+1} \geq 0. \tag{5.9}$$

x_0 and the *parameters* w_0, τ_0^1, and $\mathcal{P}_0$ are given. We can now prove the existence of the optimal solution using the method developed in appendix A.4.1 and characterize its properties.[3]

Proposition 5.1 (Optimal solution of the altruistic household)
Given $x_0 \geq 0$ and the current and anticipated prices and taxes (w_0, τ_0^1, and $\mathcal{P}_0$), we consider the following assumptions:

   (i) *the personal lifetime incomes $\Omega_t = w_t - \tau_t^1 - \tau_{t+1}^2 / R_{t+1}$ are all positive;*
   (ii) *the dynastic objective (5.8) is bounded for all feasible paths of consumptions and bequests;*
   (iii) *there exists a path of consumptions and zero bequests such that the objective (5.8) is finite.*

Then, there exists a unique solution to the dynastic optimal problem. All the value functions V_t^* for all $t \geq 0$ are defined, continuous, increasing, concave, and differentiable. They verify the Bellman equation (5.6).

Proof: We apply the dynamic optimization method of appendix A.4.1 where the dynamics of the stock variable is given by (5.7) and where the control variables (c_t, d_{t+1}) belong to the set of feasible decisions:

$$Q_t(x) = \{(c, d) \in \mathbb{R}^2; \ c > 0, \ d > 0, \ \text{and } R_{t+1}c + d \leq R_{t+1}x_t + R_{t+1}\Omega_t\}.$$

$\Omega_t = w_t - \tau_t^1 - \tau_{t+1}^2 / R_{t+1}$ is the personal life-cycle income to which bequests should be added to obtain the total life-cycle income. It gives us a lower bound on the effective life-cycle income. The dynastic problem of maximizing (5.8) subject to (5.7)–(5.9) is a time-varying problem to which all the results of appendix A.4.1 apply. We first check the assumptions **B0**, **B1**, **B2**, and **B3** of the appendix.

- Assumption (i) implies that the dynamics are defined on $I = \mathbb{R}_+$ (assumption **B0**): for all $x \in I = \mathbb{R}_+$, $Q_t(x)$ is not empty, since the personal life-cycle income Ω_t is positive for all $t \geq 0$. Then, for all $(c_t, d_{t+1}) \in Q_t(x_t)$, the quantity $x_{t+1} = [R_{t+1}(x_t + \Omega_t - c_t) - d_{t+1}]/(1 + n)$ is positive or nil, i.e., $x_{t+1} \in I$.

---

[3] Although this appendix is written without time-dependent dynamics, all the definitions and results remains valid under time-dependent dynamics (Michel (1990a)).

- Assumption (ii) means that feasible payoffs are bounded from above (assumption **B1**) and is verified when the following holds:

$$\sum_{t=0}^{\infty} \gamma^t \bar{U}_t(\bar{x}_t) < +\infty,$$

where the life-cycle utility with maximum bequest is

$$\bar{U}_t(\bar{x}_t) = \sup\{u(c) + \beta u(d); \ (c, d) \in Q_t(\bar{x}_t)\},$$

and where the sequence of maximum bequests $(\bar{x}_t)$ is defined by $\bar{x}_{t+1} = R_{t+1}(\bar{x}_t + \Omega_t)/(1+n)$, $\bar{x}_0 = x_0$ given.
- Assumption (iii) implies that there exists at least one feasible trajectory such that the payoff is finite (assumption **B2**) and holds if there exists a sequence $(c_t, d_{t+1})_{t \geq 0}$ such that

$$c_t > 0, \qquad d_{t+1} > 0, \qquad c_t + \frac{d_{t+1}}{R_{t+1}} \leq \Omega_t, \quad \text{and} \quad \sum_{t=0}^{\infty} \gamma^t U(c_t, d_{t+1}) > -\infty.$$

- Finally, the convexity of the optimization problem (assumption **B3**) holds because $\forall t \geq 0$, the set $\mathcal{A}_t$ with elements $(a, x, y) \in \mathbb{R} \times I \times I$ defined by

$$\exists (c, d) \in Q_t(x) \quad \text{such that} \quad U(c, d) \geq a \text{ and } y = \frac{R_{t+1}(x + \Omega_t - c) - d}{1 + n}$$

is convex.

Under these assumptions there exists an optimal solution $(c_t^\star, d_{t+1}^\star, x_{t+1}^\star)_{t \geq 0}$ to the dynastic problem, given x_0 and all the parameters. The value functions $V_t^\star$ are then defined, continuous, increasing, and concave with respect to x_t, for all $x_t > 0$. Moreover, $V_t^\star$ is differentiable, and we have

$$V_t^{\star\prime}\left(x_t^\star + w_t - \tau_t^1, \mathcal{P}_t\right) = \frac{\partial V_t^\star\left(x_t^\star + w_t - \tau_t^1, \mathcal{P}_t\right)}{\partial x_t} = u'(c_t^\star). \qquad (5.10)$$

Indeed, for $x_t^\star$ positive we apply proposition A.16 with the functions $c_t(x) = x - x_t^\star + c_t^\star$, $d_{t+1} = d_{t+1}^\star$, which gives the same value of $x_{t+1}^\star$ from $x_t = x$ (see assumption **B4**).

Finally, the same properties hold for $V_t^\star$ at $x = 0$ when $x_t^\star = 0$, because the optimization problem is defined to the left of $x = 0$. It is indeed possible to consider negative values of x such that $c_t(x) = x + c_t^\star$ remains positive. One might then define $V_t^\star(x + w_t - \tau_t^1, \mathcal{P}_t)$ for negative x's such that the life-cycle income $x + \Omega_t$ is positive. This merely amounts to modifying, in the optimization problem, the value of the parameter $w_t' = w_t - \epsilon$ with $\epsilon > 0$ such that $\Omega_t - \epsilon > 0$. ∎

To characterize the optimal solution for the altruistic household, we may also apply the necessary and sufficient conditions of appendix A.4.2:

Proposition 5.2 (Characteristics of the solution for the altruistic household)
Under assumptions (i), (ii), and (iii) of proposition 5.1, the solution to the dynastic optimal problem is characterized by the following necessary and sufficient conditions:

$$\forall t \geq 0, \qquad u'(c_t^*) = R_{t+1}\beta u'(d_{t+1}^*), \tag{5.11}$$

$$\forall t \geq 0, \qquad \gamma u'(c_{t+1}^*) - (1+n)\beta u'(d_{t+1}^*) \leq 0 \quad (= 0 \text{ if } x_{t+1}^* > 0), \tag{5.12}$$

$$\lim_{t \to \infty} \gamma^t u'(c_t^*)x_t^* = 0. \tag{5.13}$$

Proof: Proposition A.17 of appendix A.4.2 applies to time-varying problems (see Michel (1990a)). The Lagrangian of period t, $\mathcal{L}_t$, is equal to the sum of the life-cycle utility $u(c_t) + \beta u(d_{t+1})$ with the increase in the shadow value of x_t over the period, $\gamma p_{t+1}x_{t+1} - p_t x_t$:

$$\mathcal{L}_t = u(c_t) + \beta u(d_{t+1}) + \frac{\gamma}{1+n} p_{t+1}[R_{t+1}(x_t + \Omega_t - c_t) - d_{t+1}] - p_t x_t.$$

This Lagrangian attains its maximum at $(c_t^*, d_{t+1}^*, x_t^*)$ on the set of the (c_t, d_{t+1}, x_t) such that $x_t \geq 0$, $c_t > 0$, $d_{t+1} > 0$, and $R_{t+1}c_t + d_{t+1} \leq R_{t+1}(x_t + \Omega_t)$. We assign a multiplier λ_t to this latter constraint, and we obtain

$$u'(c_t^*) = \frac{\gamma}{1+n} p_{t+1}R_{t+1} + \lambda_t R_{t+1}, \tag{5.14}$$

$$\beta u'(d_{t+1}^*) = \frac{\gamma}{1+n} p_{t+1} + \lambda_t, \tag{5.15}$$

$$-p_t + \frac{\gamma}{1+n} p_{t+1}R_{t+1} + \lambda_t R_{t+1} \leq 0 \quad (= 0 \text{ if } x_t^* > 0). \tag{5.16}$$

Moreover, λ_t is equal to zero when the latter constraint is not binding, i.e., when $x_{t+1}^* > 0$.

Equation (5.11) can be deduced directly from (5.14) and (5.15). The condition $p_t \geq u'(c_t^*)$ (from (5.14) and (5.16)) applies also to $t+1$: $p_{t+1} \geq u'(c_{t+1}^*)$, and we have from (5.15)

$$\frac{\gamma}{1+n} p_{t+1} = \beta u'(d_{t+1}^*) - \lambda_t \leq \beta u'(d_{t+1}^*),$$

which implies

$$\gamma u'(c_{t+1}^*) \leq \gamma p_{t+1} \leq (1+n)\beta u'(d_{t+1}^*).$$

Moreover, if $x_{t+1}^* > 0$, the above conditions hold with equality:

$$p_{t+1} = u'(c_{t+1}^*) \quad \text{and} \quad \frac{\gamma}{1+n} p_{t+1} = \beta u'(d_{t+1}^*).$$

Thus, (5.12) holds.

The transversality condition

$$\lim_{t \to +\infty} \gamma^t p_t x_t^\star = 0$$

is necessary and sufficient (because the trajectory $x_t = 0$ is feasible and gives a finite value of the objective function; see the discussion after proposition A.17). As we have $\forall t \geq 0$, $p_t x_t^\star = u'(c_t^\star) x_t^\star$, we obtain (5.13).

Conversely, if the conditions (5.11), (5.12), and (5.13) hold, it is sufficient to chose a sequence of shadow prices such that

$$u'(c_{t+1}^\star) \leq p_{t+1} \leq \frac{\beta}{\gamma}(1 + n)u'(d_{t+1}^\star),$$

and to define

$$\lambda_t = \beta u'(d_{t+1}^\star) - \frac{\gamma}{1 + n} p_{t+1}$$

to obtain the conditions (5.14), (5.15), and (5.16). ∎

Equation (5.11) simply reflects the arbitrage condition of the households over their life-cycle. The transversality condition (5.13) which corresponds to the marginal form of equation (5.5) ensures that the households are able to evaluate the utility of their children, and thus to compute their total utility.

The First Old Generation. Up to now, the initial level of bequest x_0 was treated as an initial condition. Although this is often assumed in the literature for convenience, one should recognize that x_0 is in fact chosen by the first old generation, the *initial father*. This generation lives together with the young households born in $t = 0$ for which the above study has been performed. The N_{-1} first old households detain the installed capital stock K_0 and thus receive an income $R_0 s_{-1}$, where $s_{-1} = K_0/N_{-1}$. These agents, which are altruistic, choose their consumption d_0 and the bequest x_0 to maximize their utility:

$$\beta u(d_0) + \gamma V_0^\star(x_0 + w_0 - \tau_0^1, \mathcal{P}_0),$$

subject to the constraints

$$R_0 s_{-1} - \tau_0^2 = d_0 + (1 + n)x_0 \quad \text{and} \quad x_0 \geq 0.$$

By assumption, they have computed the total utility of their children as a function of their bequest x_0. Following the concavity and differentiability of $V_0^\star$, their optimal choice is characterized by

$$-(1 + n)\beta u'(d_0^\star) + \gamma V_0^{\star\prime}(x_0^\star + w_0 - \tau_0^1, \mathcal{P}_0) \leq 0 \quad (= 0 \text{ if } x_0^\star > 0).$$

Using the relationship (5.10), we obtain

$$-(1 + n)\beta u'(d_0^\star) + \gamma u'(c_0^\star) \leq 0 \quad (= 0 \text{ if } x_0^\star > 0). \tag{5.17}$$

The optimal level of the bequest x_0^* is thus determined by (5.17) given the initial condition s_{-1}. Equation (5.17) is the same as equation (5.12) at $t = -1$ and describes the arbitrage made by the first old individuals between consuming themselves or enhancing the consumption of their children through bequests.

The same analysis can be applied to the old living in any period $t + 1$. These households maximize their utility

$$\beta u(d_{t+1}) + \gamma V_{t+1}^*(x_{t+1} + w_{t+1} - \tau_{t+1}^1, \mathcal{P}_{t+1}),$$

subject to the constraints

$$R_{t+1} s_t^* - \tau_{t+1}^2 = d_{t+1} + (1+n)x_{t+1} \quad \text{and} \quad x_{t+1} \geq 0.$$

Their optimal choice is characterized by equation (5.12).

5.1.2 Marginal Analysis of Bequests

We now study how optimal consumptions and bequests are modified when there are marginal exogenous changes in the interest factor and in the income of the parents and/or the children. To study these issues formally, we consider the optimal decisions (c_t, d_{t+1}, x_{t+1}) when bequests are positive. These decisions are the solution to the following system of equations (from equations (5.7), (5.10), (5.11), and (5.12)):

$$u'(c_t) = R_{t+1}\beta u'(d_{t+1}), \tag{5.18}$$

$$(1+n)\beta u'(d_{t+1}) = \gamma u'(c_{t+1}) = \gamma V_{t+1}^{*\prime}(x_{t+1} + w_{t+1} - \tau_{t+1}^1, \mathcal{P}_{t+1}), \tag{5.19}$$

$$c_t + \frac{d_{t+1}}{R_{t+1}} + \frac{1+n}{R_{t+1}}x_{t+1} = \Omega_t + x_t, \tag{5.20}$$

given x_t, Ω_t, R_{t+1}.

Rise in Parents' Income. Let us first consider the effect of a rise in parents' income Ω_t. When the interest factor R_{t+1} and all other future prices and taxes are held fixed, the first two equations (5.18)–(5.19) show that c_t, d_{t+1}, and x_{t+1} should move in the same direction (remember that the value function is concave in its argument). In the face of a rise in parental income Ω_t, the additional resources are shared between the three components of expenditures c_t, d_{t+1}, and x_{t+1}. Hence, we have

$$0 < \frac{\partial x_{t+1}}{\partial \Omega_t} < 1.$$

The same holds in the face of an exogenous rise in the bequest x_t.

Rise in the Interest Factor. A rise in the interest factor makes it optimal for the parents to substitute consumption across time both in *personal* terms (the ratio $u'(c_t)/u'(d_{t+1})$ increases) and in *dynastic* terms (the ratio $u'(c_t)/u'(c_{t+1})$ increases, since the ratio $u'(c_{t+1})/u'(d_{t+1})$ is unchanged).

To identify the sign of the effect on the optimal bequest, notice first that equation (5.19) is not directly affected by the rise in the interest rate R_{t+1}. This implies that d_{t+1} and x_{t+1} move in the same direction. We next rewrite the equation (5.18) as

$$\frac{u'(c_t)}{u'(d_{t+1})} = R_{t+1}\beta.$$

In the face of a rise in R_{t+1}, two cases may arise: either c_t increases, requiring an increase in d_{t+1} and hence in x_{t+1}, or c_t decreases, savings s_t increase, and $R_{t+1}s_t$ increases, implying that both d_{t+1} and x_{t+1} increase. Hence, we have in both cases

$$\frac{\partial x_{t+1}}{\partial R_{t+1}} > 0.$$

Parents thus leave a larger bequest and consume more in their old age when the interest factor increases.

Rise in Children's Income. To study how a gain in children's income $w_{t+1} - \tau_{t+1}^1$ affects the allocations c_t, d_{t+1}, and x_{t+1}, we add the actual value of the children's personal income, $(w_{t+1} - \tau_{t+1}^1)(1+n)/R_{t+1}$, to both sides of equation (5.20), which gives

$$c_t + \frac{d_{t+1}}{R_{t+1}} + \frac{1+n}{R_{t+1}}\omega_{t+1} = \Omega_t + x_t + \left(w_{t+1} - \tau_{t+1}^1\right)\frac{1+n}{R_{t+1}},$$

where $\omega_{t+1} = x_{t+1} + w_{t+1} - \tau_{t+1}$. The two arbitrage equations (5.18)–(5.19) imply that c_t, d_{t+1}, and ω_{t+1} should move in the same direction when the left-hand side $\Omega_t + x_t + (w_{t+1} - \tau_{t+1}^1)(1+n)/R_{t+1}$ changes. Thus, we have

$$0 < \frac{\partial \omega_{t+1}}{\partial\left(w_{t+1} - \tau_{t+1}^1\right)} < 1,$$

and thus

$$-1 < \frac{\partial x_{t+1}}{\partial\left(w_{t+1} - \tau_{t+1}^1\right)} < 0.$$

It is thus optimal to increase the three quantities $c_t, d_{t+1}, \omega_{t+1}$, which requires a drop in bequests x_{t+1}. This illustrates the fact that, as long as bequests are operative (i.e., $x_t > 0 \; \forall t$), the altruistic model predicts that the whole amount of resources of the dynasty is shared across its members.

The marginal effects we have studied are at the basis of many empirical studies on the effectiveness of parental altruism. (See, for instance, the contradictory results of Wilhelm (1996) and Laitner and Juster (1996). A more recent study is in Laitner and Ohlsson (2001).) In particular, they test the prediction that if one increases the present-value income of the children by one unit and decreases that of the parents by one unit, the optimal bequest should compensate this change in the distribution of income and be reduced by one unit. The intuition behind this prediction of the model is the following (from Altonji, Hayashi, and Kotlikoff (1992)): "If parents and children are altruistically linked, their consumption will be based on a collective budget constraint, and the distribution of consumption between parents and children will be independent of the distribution of their incomes." This prediction is closely related to the neutrality of lump-sum transfers when generations are altruistically linked. It is the subject of the next subsection.

5.1.3 Altruism and the Neutrality of Economic Policy

In the model with infinite-lived agents, the lump-sum taxation policy and public debt policy are neutral. This means that the choice of the households depends only on the discounted value of the flow of taxes, not on their distribution across time.

We have seen in the previous section that the behavior of an altruistic household is characterized by the resolution of an infinite horizon problem. It is thus natural to study under which conditions there is neutrality of economic policy in an inter-temporal equilibrium with perfect foresight and dynastic altruism. In this context, neutrality would imply that any change in the inter-generational transfers made by the government through taxes and debt are compensated by changes in private inter-generational transfers (bequests).

We start by defining the inter-temporal equilibrium with perfect foresight and altruism. Next we study the equivalence between this equilibrium and the planner's optimal solution. When they are equivalent, the allocation does not depend on policies, and neutrality holds.

The Inter-temporal Equilibrium with Altruism. Firms act as in chapter 1: In period t, the stock of capital K_t is installed and results from the investment decision of the preceding period: $K_t = I_{t-1}$. Labor demand equalizes the marginal product of labor with the wage w_t: $\omega(K_t/L_t) = F'_L(K_t, L_t) = w_t$. Profits are distributed to the owners of the capital stock: $\pi_t = f'(K_t/L_t)K_t = R_t K_t$. Thus, we have

$$\omega(K_t/L_t) = w_t \quad \text{and} \quad f'(K_t/L_t) = R_t. \tag{5.21}$$

With national debt, savings are used to finance both productive capital and government debt:

$$N_t s_t = I_t + B_t = K_{t+1} + N_{t+1}b_{t+1}. \tag{5.22}$$

With public spending and lump-sum taxes, the dynamics of debt can be written, as in chapter 4,

$$(1+n)b_{t+1} = R_t b_t + \delta_t = R_t b_t + g_t - \tau_t^1 - \frac{\tau_t^2}{1+n}. \tag{5.23}$$

The households' behavior analyzed in the preceding subsection is defined for given taxes and prices from $t = 0$ to $t = +\infty$, i.e., for $(w_t, R_t, \tau_t^1, \tau_t^2)_{t \geq 0}$ given. There are restrictions on these taxes and prices for the indirect utility functions of the households of each generation to be defined. These indirect utility functions are the value functions $V_t^\star$ of an infinite horizon problem, and the assumptions made in proposition 5.1 should be fulfilled. Under these assumptions, given the initial condition $s_{-1} = (1+n)(k_0 + b_0)$, the sequence $(d_t^\star, x_t^\star, c_t^\star, s_t^\star)_{t \geq 0}$ is characterized by the budget constraints $\forall t \geq 0$:

$$x_t^\star + w_t - \tau_t^1 = c_t + s_t^\star \quad \text{and} \quad R_t s_{t-1}^\star - \tau_t^2 = d_t^\star + (1+n)x_t^\star \quad \text{and} \quad x_t^\star \geq 0, \tag{5.24}$$

by the two marginal conditions $\forall t \geq 0$:

$$u'(c_t^\star) = R_{t+1}\beta u'(d_{t+1}^\star), \tag{5.25}$$

and

$$\gamma u'(c_t^\star) - (1+n)\beta u'(d_t^\star) \leq 0 \quad (= 0 \text{ if } x^\star > 0), \tag{5.26}$$

and by the transversality condition

$$\lim_{t \to \infty} \gamma^t u'(c_t^\star)x_t^\star = 0. \tag{5.27}$$

When the conditions (5.21)–(5.27) hold simultaneously with $s_t = s_t^\star$, and the labor market and the product market clear in all periods, i.e.,

$$L_t = N_t \quad \text{and} \quad F(K_t, L_t) = N_t c_t^\star + N_{t-1}d_t^\star + N_t g_t + K_{t+1},$$

there is an inter-temporal equilibrium with perfect foresight in the economy with altruistic households.

Note that, in the economy with altruistic households, the assumption of perfect foresight is much more stringent than in the models of the preceding chapters. Indeed, each agent has to anticipate all future prices and taxes. If the equilibrium is not unique, which cannot be insured by a simple general condition, there is the need to coordinate the expectations. One can then simply suppose that all prices and taxes are announced at $t = 0$, as is the case in the general equilibrium model of section 5.4.[4]

---

[4] This problem appears even more severely in the model with two-sided altruism, with $t = -\infty, \ldots, +\infty$. See Kimball (1987).

We can recast the conditions of the inter-temporal equilibrium by replacing the prices by their expression (5.21) as a function of $k_t = K_t/N_t$. We then obtain the following proposition.

Proposition 5.3 (Inter-temporal equilibrium with altruism)
Consider an economy with altruistic households, lump-sum taxes, public debt, and public spending. Given the initial conditions $k_0 > 0$; b_0, $s_{-1} = (1+n)(k_0 + b_0) > 0$, and the sequences of policies $(\tau_t^1, \tau_t^2)_{t \geq 0}$ and $(g_t)_{t \geq 0}$, the inter-temporal equilibrium with perfect foresight is characterized by a sequence $(c_t^\star, d_t^\star, x_t^\star, k_{t+1}, b_{t+1})_{t \geq 0}$, such that:

1. *With the prices $w_t = \omega(k_t)$ and $R_t = f'(k_t)$ the total utilities $V_t^\star$ of all generations are defined.*
2. *The following conditions hold:*

$$u'(c_t^\star) = f'(k_{t+1})\beta u'(d_{t+1}^\star),\tag{5.28}$$

$$\gamma u'(c_t^\star) - (1+n)\beta u'(d_t^\star) \leq 0 \quad (= 0 \text{ if } x_t^\star > 0),\tag{5.29}$$

$$f(k_t) = c_t^\star + \frac{d_t^\star}{1+n} + g_t + (1+n)k_{t+1},\tag{5.30}$$

$$(1+n)b_{t+1} = f'(k_t)b_t + g_t - \tau_t^1 - \frac{\tau_t^2}{1+n},\tag{5.31}$$

$$(1+n)x_t^\star = f'(k_t)(1+n)(k_t + b_t) - \tau_t^2 - d_t^\star \geq 0,\tag{5.32}$$

$$\lim_{t \to \infty} \gamma^t u'(c_t^\star)x_t^\star = 0.\tag{5.33}$$

Proof: All the conditions of the proposition hold at equilibrium. Let us show that they are sufficient. Defining $s_t^\star = (1+n)(k_{t+1} + b_{t+1})$, we obtain the second-period budget constraint leading equation (5.32) by one period. Eliminating g_t with the equations (5.30) and (5.31), we obtain

$$s_t^\star = (1+n)(k_{t+1} + b_{t+1}) = f(k_t) - c_t^\star - \frac{d_t^\star}{1+n} + f'(k_t)b_t - \tau_t^1 - \frac{\tau_t^2}{1+n}.$$

Using (5.32) to eliminate b_t, we obtain

$$s_t^\star = f(k_t) - k_t f'(k_t) - c_t^\star - \tau_t^1 + x_t^\star,$$

which gives with $w_t = \omega(k_t) = f(k_t) - k_t f'(k_t)$ the first-period budget constraint. Hence all the conditions characterizing the behavior of households, firms, and government are fulfilled. ∎

Neutrality of Economic Policy. To study the neutrality of economic policy we establish the conditions under which the inter-temporal equilibrium with perfect foresight is equivalent to the planner's optimal solution. By doing so, we ensure that the market allocation is the optimal allocation and is not affected by lump-sum transfers and/or debt.

Proposition 5.4 (Neutrality of policy)
If $(c_t^*, d_t^*, x_t^*, k_{t+1}, b_{t+1})_{t \geq 0}$ is an inter-temporal equilibrium with perfect foresight for which bequests are positive at all dates,

$$\forall t \geq 0, \qquad x_t^* > 0,$$

and the following transversality condition holds:

$$\lim_{t \to \infty} \gamma^t u'(c_t^*) k_t f'(k_t) = 0, \tag{5.34}$$

then the sequence $(c_t^*, d_t^*, k_{t+1})_{t \geq 0}$ is the optimal allocation chosen by the planner with a discount factor γ.

Proof: The necessary and sufficient conditions of proposition 2.12 hold with the implicit price $q_t = f'(k_t) u'(c_t^*)$. With positive bequests at all dates we have that the condition (5.29) holds with equality, which implies

$$(1+n)\beta u'(d_t^*) f'(k_t) = \gamma u'(c_t^*) f'(k_t) = \gamma q_t. \tag{5.35}$$

Equation (2.23) thus holds, which implies through equation (5.30) that (2.21) holds. By assumption, the transversality condition (2.20) holds. Finally, the dynamics of q_t given by (2.22) is obtained using (5.28) and (5.35). ∎

Hence, any inter-temporal equilibrium with positive bequests for which the transversality condition (5.34) holds does not depend on the policy choices (transfers and/or debt) as long as these choices remain compatible with the existence of this equilibrium. Public debt and lump-sum pensions do not matter in this framework. Any modification to these variables is offset by a change in private transfers. This neutrality property is similar to the one we find in models with infinite-lived agents. It as been much debated in the literature and has led to many empirical studies. Two classical surveys including both theoretical and applied aspects are those of Bernheim (1987) and Seater (1993).[5]

The overlapping generations model with altruism can be thought of as a micro foundation for the infinite horizon representative agent model. There are however three important differences from the model with infinite-lived agents.

First, all bequests must be positive.[6] The old generation cannot take resources from the future. For the equivalence result to hold, this should be true at all dates. There is no such restriction in the model with infinite-lived agents.

---

[5] A more recent discussion of the empirical methodology is provided by Cardia (1997).
[6] Or, at least in the limit case, bequests can be zero with equation (5.29) holding with equality.

Second, there is the condition that all dynastic indirect utility functions are defined, requiring that each generation take its life-cycle decisions knowing the effect of the bequest it leaves on the welfare of the next generation. An agent with infinite life computes at the initial period all its future decisions as a function of future prices and taxes.

The third difference comes from the transversality condition. For the altruistic agents, the discounted value of bequests tends to zero. For the infinite-lived agent, the discounted value of wealth tends to zero. The wealth of a representative infinite-lived agents includes all the assets of the economy. On the contrary, the bequest of one altruistic agent who lives two periods[7] only includes the wealth transmitted to the next generation. In the special case where the debt is non-negative ($b_t \geq 0 \; \forall t$) and the second-period tax is non-negative ($\tau_t^2 \geq 0 \; \forall t$), we have

$$(1+n)x_t^\star \leq (1+n)f'(k_t)k_t - \tau_t^2 - d_t^\star < (1+n)f'(k_t)k_t,$$

and the transversality condition of the planner,

$$\lim_{t\to\infty} \gamma^t q_t k_t = \lim_{t\to\infty} \gamma^t u'(c_t^\star)f'(k_t)k_t,$$

implies that of the altruistic agent,

$$\lim_{t\to\infty} \gamma^t u'(c_t^\star)x_t^\star.$$

But the converse is not necessarily true.

5.1.4 When are Bequests Positive?

From the preceding analysis, it results that private intergenerational transfers are able, under the conditions detailed in proposition 5.4, to neutralize public intergenerational transfers (debt, pensions), and Ricardian equivalence holds (Barro (1974)). In that case, overlapping generations models have similar properties to models with infinite-lived agents. On the other hand, if the optimal bequests are zero at all dates, the model with altruistic agents leads to the same decisions as in the overlapping generations model without altruism.

Proposition 5.4 requires positive bequests. An interesting question is to study the conditions under which it will indeed be optimal for the old households of all generations to leave bequests to their children. Weil (1987) and Abel (1987) have shown under particular assumptions that bequests are operative in the long run if the intensity of altruism γ is strong enough;[8] we illustrate this result in the example below.

---

[7] In the model with altruistic agents who live one period only, there is no individual saving and the whole wealth of the economy is transmitted through bequests.

[8] Their result is extended by Thibault (2000).

Another important issue is related to the role of public debt, which increases the wealth of old households to the detriment of the young households when taxes are mainly levied on the young generation. In Gevers and Michel (1998), bequests can be positive in the economy with debt although they are zero in the same economy without debt. In this section, we investigate the effect of public debt on the positivity of bequests in an example.

Example: Taking again the example of section 2.4.1, we know that with a logarithmic utility and a Cobb–Douglas production function, the optimal allocation is given by

$$c_t = \frac{1 - \alpha\gamma}{1 + \beta/\gamma} A k_t^\alpha,$$

$$d_t = \frac{\beta(1 + n)}{\gamma} \frac{1 - \alpha\gamma}{1 + \beta/\gamma} A k_t^\alpha,$$

$$k_{t+1} = \frac{\alpha\gamma}{1 + n} A k_t^\alpha$$

in the absence of government intervention ($g_t = 0$, $b_t = 0$, $\tau_t^1 = \tau_t^2 = 0$). The private transfer that implements the optimal allocation is

$$(1 + n)x_t = (1 + n)k_t f'(k_t) - d_t$$

$$= (1 + n)\alpha A k_t^\alpha - d_t = (1 + n)\left(\alpha - \frac{\beta(1 - \alpha\gamma)}{\gamma + \beta}\right) A k_t^\alpha.$$

This transfer is positive if and only if the altruism factor is large enough, i.e.,

$$\gamma > \frac{\beta(1 - \alpha)}{\alpha(1 + \beta)}.$$

In this case the inter-temporal equilibrium with altruistic households coincides with the optimal planner's solution, as all the conditions of proposition 5.4 are met. On the contrary, when the altruism factor is low,

$$\gamma < \frac{\beta(1 - \alpha)}{\alpha(1 + \beta)},$$

the positivity constraint on bequests binds, and equilibrium prices and quantities with altruistic households are the same as in the inter-temporal equilibrium with selfish households (chapter 1). Indeed, when bequests are nil, each household consumes its life-cycle income. Nevertheless, the total utilities enjoyed by households are different.

Consider now a constant public debt b, detained by the first old households and financed by a lump-sum tax on the young households:

$$\tau_t^1 = [f'(k_t) - (1 + n)]b \quad \text{and} \quad \tau_t^2 = 0.$$

The private transfer that allows one to implement the optimal allocation is now

$$(1+n)x_t = (1+n)(k_t + b) f'(k_t) - d_t$$

$$= (1+n)\alpha A k_t^{\alpha-1} \left[b + \left(1 - \frac{\beta(1-\alpha\gamma)}{\alpha(\gamma+\beta)} \right) k_t \right].$$

This relationship allows us to derive a condition on debt such that bequests are positive at time t:

$$x_t > 0 \quad \Leftrightarrow \quad b > \left(\frac{\beta(1-\alpha\gamma)}{\alpha(\gamma+\beta)} - 1 \right) k_t.$$

Given the optimal k_t, there always exists a level of debt leading to positive private transfers, $x_t > 0$ for all t.

At the steady state where the modified golden rule holds, we have

$$\gamma \alpha A k_\gamma^{\alpha-1} = 1 + n,$$

and the condition $x > 0$ in the long run becomes

$$b > \left(\frac{\beta(1-\alpha\gamma)}{\alpha(\gamma+\beta)} - 1 \right) \left(\frac{\gamma\alpha A}{1+n} \right)^{\frac{1}{1-\alpha}}.$$

When the degree of altruism is too low to generate positive bequests in the economy without debt, i.e., $\gamma < \beta(1-\alpha)/\alpha(1+\beta)$, the right-hand side is positive; with a sufficiently high level of public debt, bequests become positive, and the equilibrium with altruistic households coincides with the optimal planner's allocation. The explanation is the following. In the absence of policy, the old households would like to make negative transfers to their children, but they cannot. When the government makes such transfers through public debt, and even more, then the private transfers that partly compensate the public transfers are positive. This example illustrates the difference between the model with altruistic households and the one with infinite-lived consumers. The infinite-lived consumer can make transfers in either direction, and debt is always neutral.

In the above example, we have derived simple conditions under which bequests are positive and the competitive inter-temporal equilibrium coincides with the planner's allocation. In more general models such analytical conditions are only valid for steady state equilibria. Non-steady-state cases can be tackled using numerical methods. In particular, the positivity constraint on bequests may bind temporarily along the dynamic adjustment. If it binds at least once, the equivalence result does not hold and policies are no longer neutral. We illustrate this in the following numerical example.

A Numerical Example. Let the economy start from a steady state situation with

$$u(c) = \ln c, \qquad f(k) = \frac{2Ak}{1+k},$$

and the numerical values of section A.5.3, i.e. $\beta = 0.3, n = 1.025^{30} - 1, A = 20, g = 6$. The government finances its spending with $\tau^1 = 3.762, b = 0.03, \tau^2 = 5$. Households are altruistic with $\gamma = \beta = 0.3$. The steady state displays positive bequests and is given by

$$c = 7.18, \qquad d = 15.056, \qquad k = 1.392, \qquad x = 0.377.$$

Assume now that agents forecast at time $t = 1$ that government spending will temporarily rise to $g = 6.6$ at $t = 3$. We consider the optimal allocation and two different financing scenarios.

In table 5.1, we first present the optimal path of capital. Capital should rise before the shock in order to share the burden of the shock with the first generation and to increase production possibilities for $t = 3$. At $t = 3$ government spending rises and investment falls, implying that capital at $t = 4$ is reduced. The optimal capital then returns to its steady state value.

In the first scenario, the whole burden of additional spending is supported by the young generation at $t = 3$ through an increase in τ^1. In this case, bequests remain positive over all the dynamic adjustment, and the allocation is the optimal one. Bequests even rise at the time of the shock to compensate the over-taxed young generation.

In the second scenario, the old households living in $t = 3$ are taxed more. τ^2 is adjusted to finance additional spending. These agents are no longer willing to leave a positive bequest to their offspring. They would even like to implement a negative bequest, but it is impossible. As a consequence, $x_t = 0$ at $t = 3$. The allocation thus differs from the optimal one, but in the long run altruism is operative and capital converges to the modified golden rule.

We finally consider whether the government can finance its additional spending by issuing new debt, without changing taxes. We shall see that

Table 5.1. *Neutrality of Policy*

Time	Optimal	Scenario 1		Scenario 2	
t	k_t	x_t	k_t	x_t	k_t
1	1.3922	0.3798	1.3922	0.3808	1.3922
2	1.3950	0.3927	1.3950	0.4010	1.3963
3	1.4199	0.5226	1.4199	0.0000	1.4339
4	1.3720	0.4669	1.3720	0.3918	1.3886
5	1.3852	0.4080	1.3852	0.3817	1.3909
$+\infty$	1.3922	0.3765	1.3922	0.3765	1.3922

Table 5.2. *Dynamics with Ponzi Debt*

t	x_t	k_t	b_t	$\gamma^t u'(c_t)x_t$
1	0.3798	1.3922	0.0300	0.0159
2	0.3927	1.3950	0.0300	0.0049
3	0.5226	1.4199	0.0297	0.0020
4	2.4788	1.3720	0.3130	0.0028
5	7.1673	1.3852	0.9914	0.0024
$+\infty$	$+\infty$	1.3922	$+\infty$	0.0023

this strategy is incompatible with the existence of equilibrium because the transversality condition on the households bequests would be violated. Since the debt $b_t = B_{t-1}/N_t$ increases at $t = 4$ and taxes remain constant, the additional interest payments are financed by issuing more debt. Since $f'(k_t)$ is larger than $1 + n$, debt follows an exploding path after $t = 3$. The implicit intergenerational transfer performed by the increasing public debt is compensated, period after period, by rising bequests. The parents who detain the public debt give to their children the resources to make them able to buy this debt. With constant tax policies, equation (5.31) leads to

$$b_{t+1} = \frac{f'(k_t)}{1+n}b_t + \delta \qquad \text{for} \quad t \geq 4$$

with $\delta = g - \tau^1 - \tau^2/(1+n)$. In the long run government debt grows at rate $f'(k_y)/(1 + n) = 1/\gamma$. Using equation (5.32), x_t grows at the same rate and tends to infinity. The term $\gamma^t x_t$ does not converge to zero, and the transversality condition is violated.

To illustrate the problem we have computed in table 5.2 a path using the first-order conditions. The table shows the exploding path of debt and bequests after time 4 and gives the value of the term $\gamma^t u'(c_t)x_t$. This term decreases from $t = 1$ to $t = 3$ and would have gone to zero if there were no shock at $t = 3$.

We conclude from this example that the neutrality property of debt does not allow one to run Ponzi debts. The transversality condition of the altruistic household should hold for the inter-temporal equilibrium to exist.

5.2 HUMAN CAPITAL AND EDUCATION

In a growing economy, each generation normally has more resources at its command on reaching adulthood. These additional resources result on the one hand from the increase in productivity linked to the accumulation of physical capital by the previous generation. On the other hand, they result from the accumulation of human capital as children inherit knowledge and skills from their parents and enhance their bequeathed abilities by training and education. The theory of human capital initiated by Becker (1964) studies how the allocation of education time or resources affects the future productivity of the workers through their skill level. In this context, education is an important factor of economic growth, and the inter-generational knowledge spillovers are essential to economic development. This view is consistent with the large fraction of growth attributed to improvements in the quality of labor services (see Denison (1974), Goldin (1994), and Nehru, Swanson, and Dubey (1995)).

The importance of human capital for growth was stressed by Uzawa (1965), Lucas (1988), and Azariadis and Drazen (1990). In particular, they show that the crucial element for explaining permanent endogenous development is the presence of a positive externality that makes individual-specific human capital increasing in aggregate human capital and/or in the human capital of the previous generation.

5.2.1 Modeling Education

There are two main sources of human capital accumulation: learning-by-doing and education. In this section, we are exclusively interested in education, as education and its financing are crucially related to inter-generational matters.

Education usually takes place at the beginning of the life cycle. The overlapping generations model allows us to capture this explicitly. The simplest way to model it is to assume three-period-lived households. The first period is devoted to education, the second to active life, and the last to retirement. It is convenient to assume that there is neither work nor explicit consumption in the first period (the consumption of the children is included in the consumption of the parents).

Education allows people to accumulate human capital through three different channels. These channels are affected by decisions taken during the first period of life. First there is a decision on individual education spending in terms of goods. The financing of this spending can be achieved either through parental funding or through the market. In this latter case, children borrow to finance education spending. Second, there is a decision on the length of education; to capture this aspect one should assume a tradeoff between education and leisure (and/or earnings) during the first period of life. Third, public spending on education can be financed by levying taxes on the preceding generations.

Human capital also depends on external effects. On the one hand, the young individual inherits part of the human capital of the parents. This reflects cultural transmission within the family. On the other hand, the capital accumulation of an agent also hinges on other agents' stock (through for instance the quality of their teachers), or on the aggregate level of the stock, therefore allowing for cross-individual spillover.

It is generally assumed that human capital is homogeneous, and is measured by the quantity of labor in efficiency units. In this case, the human capital of period t is by definition the sum of the workers' human capital.[9]

---

[9] For a more elaborate way to aggregate human capital, see Benabou (1996).

Finally, a model with education is an appropriate place to introduce heterogeneous agents, assuming that individuals can have different family backgrounds and hence different levels of human capital. This type of heterogeneity is often used in the literature (e.g., Benabou (1996), Glomm and Ravikumar (1992), and de la Croix and Monfort (2000)) to study the interplay between inequality and growth and the role of education finance. To model heterogeneity in a simple way, we assume that each generation consists of a continuum of households. Children within a generation are differentiated by the stock of human capital of their parents. As in the literature on the subject, we assume a constant population: $n = 0$.[10]

At time 0, each household i of the initial adult generation is endowed with human capital $h_{i,0} > 0$.[11] Human capital of adults is distributed according to a probability distribution function $\Gamma_0(\cdot)$.

The initial distribution is given, and the subsequent distributions will evolve over time at equilibrium. The average human capital is

$$\bar{h}_t = \int h_t \, d\Gamma_t(h_t).$$

Normalizing the total population to 1, $\bar{h}_t$ is also the supply of efficient labor.

In the sequel, we shall use the following distribution:

Definition 5.1 (Log distribution)
The log distribution of human capital is the distribution of the logarithm of human capital, associated to Γ_t:

$$\ell_t = \ln h_t, \qquad \Lambda_t(\ell_t) = \Gamma_t(\exp \ell_t).$$

Then, the average human capital is given by

$$\bar{h}_t = \int \exp \ell_t \, d\Lambda_t(\ell_t). \tag{5.36}$$

The production of goods at time t with physical capital K_t and human capital input H_t is given by $\Upsilon_t = F(K_t, H_t)$. Defining the capital–efficient-labor ratio

$$\kappa_t = \frac{K_t}{H_t},$$

the production function in intensive form is $f(\kappa_t) = F(\kappa_t, 1)$. The wage per

---

[10] To model population growth, we can assume a continuum of families of the same size, assume that each family has N_t members born at t, and that N_t grows at a rate n over time. This introduces an additional level of aggregation, the family. Such an approach can be interesting for modeling the dynamics of population when families have different numbers of children, as illustrated in de la Croix and Doepke (2001).

[11] To avoid trivial poverty traps for certain households, we exclude the case of zero initial human capital.

efficiency unit is given by

$$w_t = F'_H(K_t, H_t) = \omega(\kappa_t).$$

Thus, the wage income of an individual with human capital h_t is $w_t h_t$.

An important aspect of human capital accumulation is its inter-generational transmission. Several authors have measured the inter-generational correlation of income. Dearden, Machin, and Reed (1997) for Britain, and Solon (1992) for the United States, conclude that the father–son correlation in income is at least 0.4, which is large given that the intergenerational transmission of human capital is affected by many external factors such as ability shocks, etc. This portrays a society where social mobility is relativity small. In the models we shall present, this aspect is reflected in that the human capital of a household born in $t + 1$ depends on the human capital of his parent.

In the first sections, we study the frameworks where education is costly in terms of goods, and analyze how growth and inequality are affected by the type of education funding. Another opportunity cost of education can be thought of in terms of loss of working time. This is especially true at the margin: longer study can entail a shorter working life. This tradeoff is modeled by Azariadis and Drazen (1990). This leads to a more complicated model in that labor supply is now made endogenous.[12] We shall propose a simple version of Azariadis and Drazen (1990) in the last section.

5.2.2 Parental Funding: Private vs Public Education

In this section, we include capital accumulation in a modified version of the model of Glomm and Ravikumar (1992) (without child leisure but with physical capital). We then compare the equilibrium arising when parents directly finance their children's education with the equilibrium where parents vote for taxes that finance education. We are mostly interested in comparing the growth rates in the two regimes as well as the evolution of inequalities. Inequalities are measured by the variance of the distribution of human capital across households, which amounts to measuring the variance of labor income.

The only difference between two households lies in their human capital stock and hence in their income. The utility function of one household is logarithmic:

$$\ln c_t + \beta \ln d_{t+1} + \gamma \ln e_t.$$

It depends on consumption when adult (c_t), on consumption when old (d_{t+1}), and on the total amount spent on children's education (e_t). This last element reflects the ad hoc altruism factor, which is referred in the literature as *joy*

---

[12] As when one introduces endogenous labor supply in the standard overlapping generations model (Reichlin (1986), Nourry (2001), and Cazzavillan and Pintus (2001)), such an approach leads to two-dimensional dynamics with one forward-looking variable.

of giving (or "warm glove"), because parents have a taste for giving (see e.g., Andreoni (1989)). More precisely, the utility obtained from leaving a bequest or making a gift depends only on the size of the bequest or the gift. The parameter $\gamma > 0$ is the ad hoc altruism factor.[13]

The production function for human capital is

$$h_{t+1} = \psi e_t^\theta h_t^{1-\theta}, \qquad 0 < \theta < 1, \quad \psi > 0. \tag{5.37}$$

ψ is a productivity parameter. The stock of human capital is assumed to depend on education spending e_t. Moreover, it also depends on parents' human capital. This introduces the intergenerational externality mentioned above. The Cobb–Douglas formulation is chosen for simplicity.[14]

Two versions of the model are considered. In the private funding case, the parents decide directly over e_t, the amount of resource they give to their own children. In the public funding case, all children receive the same amount, which is collected by levying a proportional tax τ_t on wage income. We consider the two cases in turn.

Private Funding. When young, the representative household benefits from education spending and builds his human capital stock; his consumption is included in his parents' consumption. The adults supply inelastically h_t units of human capital and earn $w_t h_t$. This income is allocated to consumption, education spending e_t, and savings s_t for future consumption. When old, households spend all their saving and accrued interest on consumption. We implicitly assume that children are not allowed to borrow on capital markets to complete the amount given by the parents. As a consequence, parental education funding rests only on family resources. The problem of the household is thus to maximize utility subject to

$$w_t h_t = c_t + s_t + e_t,$$

$$d_{t+1} = R_{t+1} s_t.$$

The first-order conditions for this problem are

$$s_t = \frac{\beta}{1 + \beta + \gamma} w_t h_t, \tag{5.38}$$

$$e_t = \frac{\gamma}{1 + \beta + \gamma} w_t h_t. \tag{5.39}$$

---

[13] Abel and Warshawsky (1988) have derived an estimation of the joy-of-giving parameter consistent with a given degree of rational altruism. They use a calibrated model where households live for 60 periods and 30 periods elapse between the births of successive generations.

[14] More generally, other functions with constant returns to scale can be considered. With such functions, there are aggregate constant returns with respect to reproducible factors, which are conditions for sustained endogenous growth.

Replacing e_t by its optimal value from (5.39) in the production function of human capital (5.37), we obtain the following relation:

$$h_{t+1} = \mathcal{G}w_t^\theta h_t \qquad (5.40)$$

with

$$\mathcal{G} = \psi \left(\frac{\gamma}{1+\beta+\gamma}\right)^\theta.$$

Equation (5.40) shows that the growth factor of the human capital depends on a constant $\mathcal{G}$ and on the wage per efficiency unit, w_t. We can already see here that the human capital of every individual will grow at the same rate. We also directly obtain the growth rate of average human capital $\bar{h}_t$ as

$$\frac{\bar{h}_{t+1}}{\bar{h}_t} = \mathcal{G}w_t^\theta. \qquad (5.41)$$

Equation (5.40) is linear in the logarithm of human capital, $\ell_t = \ln h_t$:

$$\ell_{t+1} = \ell_t + \ln\left(\mathcal{G}w_t^\theta\right)$$

With the log distribution of human capital,

$$\Lambda_t(\ell) = \Gamma_t(\exp \ell),$$

the dynamics of this distribution (see appendix A.6.1) is given by

$$\Lambda_{t+1}(\ell) = \Lambda_t\left(\ell - \ln\left(\mathcal{G}w_t^\theta\right)\right). \qquad (5.42)$$

As in the preceding chapters, the equilibrium on the labor market,

$$H_t = \bar{h}_t,$$

and the distribution of profits to the owners of capital imply that the prices should be equal to marginal productivities:

$$w_t = \omega(\kappa_t) = f(\kappa_t) - \kappa_t f'(\kappa_t) \quad \text{and} \quad R_t = f'(\kappa_t),$$

where $\kappa_t = K_t/\bar{h}_t$.

The capital of the next period is built from the savings of the adults:

$$K_{t+1} = \int s_t \, d\Gamma_t(h) \equiv \bar{s}_t,$$

which implies, using the savings function (5.38),

$$K_{t+1} = \kappa_{t+1}\bar{h}_{t+1} = \frac{\beta}{1+\beta+\gamma}w_t\bar{h}_t. \qquad (5.43)$$

An inter-temporal equilibrium can now be defined as follows:

Definition 5.2 (Inter-temporal equilibrium – private funding of education)
Given the initial distribution of wealth s_{-1} over old households, the initial cap-
ital stock $K_0 = \bar{s}_{-1}$ and the initial log distribution Λ_0 of human capital, an
inter-temporal equilibrium with private funding is a sequence of prices $\{w_t, R_t\}$,
aggregate variables $\{K_{t+1}, \bar{h}_{t+1}, \kappa_{t+1}\}$, and distributions of human capital, sav-
ings, and education spending such that:

- *prices $\{w_t, R_t\}$ verify $w_t = \omega(\kappa_t)$, $R_t = f'(\kappa_t)$ with $\kappa_t = K_t/\bar{h}_t$;*
- *the capital market clears, i.e., equation (5.43) holds;*
- *the log distribution of human capital Λ_t follows (5.42), and $\bar{h}_t$ is given by*
  (5.36);
- *the distribution of savings and education spending result from the distribution*
  of human capital through the individual decisions (5.38) and (5.39).

The distribution of the individual consumptions also results from the distribution of human capital.

Dynamics of Aggregate Variables. To further characterize the equilibrium, one
might substitute for $\bar{h}_{t+1}$ in (5.43) its value from (5.41). Using the equilibrium
value of w_t, we obtain the following dynamic equation in κ:

$$\kappa_{t+1} = \frac{\beta}{(1 + \beta + \gamma)\mathcal{G}} \omega(\kappa_t)^{1-\theta}.$$

Under the assumption **H2**, the dynamics in κ are monotonic and bounded,
thus converging to a steady state κ_∞. The wage per unit of human capital, w_t,
converges to $w_\infty = \omega(\kappa_\infty)$, and the growth rate of human capital converges to

$$\lim_{t \to \infty} \frac{\bar{h}_{t+1}}{\bar{h}_t} = \mathcal{G}w_\infty^\theta.$$

In the particular case of a Cobb–Douglas production function, the steady
state κ_∞ is unique and does not depend on κ_0. Then, the initial human capital
distribution does not affect the long-run growth rate.[15] More generally, the
steady state κ_∞ only depends on $\kappa_0 = K_0/\bar{h}_0$.

Dynamics of Distributions. As far as inequalities are concerned, the mean
μ_t and the variance σ_t^2 of the log distribution of human capital follow (see
appendix A.6.1)

$$\mu_{t+1} = \mu_t + \ln \mathcal{G} + \theta \ln w_t,$$

$$\sigma_{t+1}^2 = \sigma_t^2 = \sigma_0^2.$$

We deduce that the distribution of the logarithm of human capital keeps the
same standard error over time. There is however no limiting distribution,

---

[15] On the effect of of the initial distribution of human capital see also Galor and Zeira (1993).

because households have an ever growing income when $\mathcal{G}w_\infty^\theta > 1$. In this context it makes sense to explore the possibility of a limiting distribution for the transformed variable

$$\hat{h}_t = \frac{h_t}{\bar{h}_t}.$$

The individual transition function is given by $\hat{h}_{t+1} = \hat{h}_t$, which implies that the transformed distribution remains constant over time and the limiting distribution is the distribution of $\hat{h}_0$.

More can be said when the initial distribution is a log-normal distribution as in Glomm and Ravikumar (1992), i.e., the log distribution Λ_0 is normal. In this case, the distribution Λ_t remains normal for all t. Moreover, the link between then mean μ_t of Λ_t and average human capital $\bar{h}_t$ is given by (see appendix A.6.2)

$$\ln \bar{h}_t = \mu_t + \frac{\sigma_t^2}{2} = \mu_t + \frac{\sigma_0^2}{2}.$$

To conclude, we have seen that when the resources devoted to the education of a given child only rely on the child's family income, there are no convergence forces at work; inequalities as measured by the variance of the logarithm of income remain constant over time.

Let us now turn our attention to the public way of financing education.

Public Funding. Under the public system, a government levies taxes on a nationwide basis and uses revenues to finance education spending. All children receive the same amount, which is collected by levying a proportional tax τ_t on wage income:

$$e_t = \bar{e}_t = \tau_t w_t \bar{h}_t. \tag{5.44}$$

Households first vote for a tax rate, then choose how much to save. We solve their problem backward. The savings that maximize utility for a given level of taxes and net income $(1 - \tau_t)w_t h_t$ are given by

$$s_t = \frac{\beta}{1 + \beta}(1 - \tau_t)w_t h_t. \tag{5.45}$$

The preferred tax rate of the adult household is obtained by maximizing the indirect utility function

$$\ln(w_t h_t - s_t - \bar{e}_t) + \beta(\ln R_{t+1} s_t) + \gamma \ln \bar{e}_t,$$

knowing how much he will save (5.45), and how much he will receive for education (5.44). After substitution this amounts to maximizing

$$(1 + \beta)\ln(1 - \tau_t) + \gamma \ln \tau_t,$$

which yields

$$\tau_t = \tau = \frac{\gamma}{1 + \beta + \gamma}. \tag{5.46}$$

The chosen tax rate is constant over time and the same for all individuals. It can be checked that with this tax rate, the savings function is the same as in the model with private funding and thus equation (5.43) holds.

The tax rate is determined by means of majority voting. As the resulting tax rate does not depend on the type of household, this can alternatively be seen as unanimity voting. For simplicity we assume that only those who are affected by the tax, i.e., the households that work, will vote. The tax rate (5.46) will emerge from this voting process.

Each household thus benefits from the following amount of public education:

$$\bar{e}_t = \frac{\gamma}{1 + \beta + \gamma} w_t \bar{h}_t. \tag{5.47}$$

Substituting this expression in equation (5.37), individual human capital will accumulate according to

$$h_{t+1} = \mathcal{G} w_t^\theta \, \bar{h}_t^\theta \, h_t^{1-\theta}, \tag{5.48}$$

or, in logarithms,

$$\ell_{t+1} = (1 - \theta)\ell_t + \ln\left(\mathcal{G} w_t^\theta \, \bar{h}_t^\theta\right).$$

Hence, the evolution of the log distribution functions is defined by

$$\Lambda_{t+1}(\ell) = \Lambda_t \left(\frac{\ell - \ln\left(\mathcal{G} w_t^\theta \bar{h}_t^\theta\right)}{1 - \theta} \right), \tag{5.49}$$

which is less simple than in the previous case, as the average of the h_t intervenes in the expression.

An inter-temporal equilibrium can now be defined as follows:

Definition 5.3 (Inter-temporal equilibrium – public funding of education)
Given the initial wealth distribution s_{-1}, the initial capital stock $K_0 = \bar{s}_{-1}$, and the initial log distribution of human capital Λ_0, an inter-temporal equilibrium with public funding is a sequence of prices $\{w_t, R_t\}$, aggregate variables $\{K_{t+1}, \bar{h}_{t+1}, \kappa_{t+1}, \tau_t, \bar{e}_t\}$, and distributions of human capital and savings such that

- *prices $\{w_t, R_t\}$ verify $w_t = \omega(\kappa_t)$, $R_t = f'(\kappa_t)$ with $\kappa_t = K_t/\bar{h}_t$;*
- *the capital market clears, i.e., equation (5.43) holds;*
- *taxes are determined by (5.46), and education spending by (5.47);*
- *the log distribution of human capital follows (5.49), and $\bar{h}_t$ is given by (5.36);*
- *the distribution of savings results from the distribution of human capital through the individual decision (5.45).*

Some simple results can however be derived from (5.48).[16] The mean μ_t and variance σ_t^2 of the log distribution of human capital follow

$$\mu_{t+1} = (1-\theta)\mu_t + \ln\left(\mathcal{G}w_t^\theta \bar{h}_t^\theta\right), \tag{5.50}$$

$$\sigma_{t+1}^2 = (1-\theta)^2 \sigma_t^2. \tag{5.51}$$

Thus, the variance goes to zero, and inequalities tend to disappear. One might derive additional results in two special cases: when the support of the initial distribution is a closed and bounded interval, and when the initial distribution is log-normal.

Compact Support. When the support of the initial distribution is a compact interval, we look at the distribution of the transformed variable $\hat{h}_t = h_t/\bar{h}_t$, and obtain the following result.

Proposition 5.5 (Reduction of inequalities with public funding)
Consider an inter-temporal equilibrium with public funding. Assume that the initial distribution of human capital Γ_0 has a compact support $[a_0, b_0]$, $0 < a_0 < b_0$. Then the support of the distribution of the relative human capital $\hat{h}_t$ collapses to the single point $\{1\}$.

Proof: By induction, using equation (5.48), the support of Γ_t is a compact interval $[a_t, b_t]$, and we have

$$\frac{b_{t+1}}{a_{t+1}} = \left(\frac{b_t}{a_t}\right)^{1-\theta}.$$

This is obtained by applying (5.48) to a_t and b_t, then taking their ratio. As a consequence, the ratio b_t/a_t converges to 1. The support of the distribution of $\hat{h}_t$, $[a_t/\bar{h}_t, b_t/\bar{h}_t]$, is included in

$$\left[\frac{a_t}{b_t}, \frac{b_t}{a_t}\right],$$

since $a_t \le \bar{h}_t \le b_t$. This interval collapses to a single point. ∎

From the previous proposition, the limit of the support of the distribution of the $\hat{h}_t$ collapses to a single point. To study the dynamics of aggregate variables, we consider the ratio

$$\frac{h_{t+1}}{\bar{h}_t} = \mathcal{G}w_t^\theta \hat{h}_t^{1-\theta}.$$

---

[16] A complete characterization of the dynamics of the distributions of human capital in the general case would require the use of techniques developed, a.o., by Futia (1982) and Hopenhayn and Prescott (1992). Moreover there is a special difficulty linked to the fact that human capital may grow unboundedly.

This ratio belongs to the interval

$$\mathcal{G}w_t^\theta \left[\left(\frac{a_t}{b_t}\right)^{1-\theta}, \left(\frac{b_t}{a_t}\right)^{1-\theta} \right].$$

The aggregate growth rate $\bar{h}_{t+1}/\bar{h}_t$ belongs to the same interval. More precisely,

$$\frac{\bar{h}_{t+1}}{\bar{h}_t} = \bar{\lambda}_t \mathcal{G}w_t^\theta,$$

where $\bar{\lambda}_t$ is the mean of $\hat{h}_t^{1-\theta}$. The dynamics of κ_t given in (5.43) verify

$$\kappa_{t+1} = \frac{\beta}{(1+\beta+\gamma)\mathcal{G}} \frac{1}{\bar{\lambda}_t} \omega(\kappa_t)^{1-\theta}.$$

Since $\bar{\lambda}_t$ belongs to an interval which collapses to $\{1\}$, κ_t has a limit κ_∞ and w_t goes to w_∞. Hence,

$$\lim_{t \to +\infty} \frac{\bar{h}_{t+1}}{\bar{h}_t} = \mathcal{G}w_\infty^\theta.$$

In the case where the steady state κ_∞ is unique, it is the same as in the model with private funding, and the long-term growth rates are identical in the two funding systems.

We conclude that the public funding system has the virtue of reducing the inequalities (there is no other sources of convergence in the model). This is because it redistributes resources through taxation, allowing the less educated families to catch up. Moreover, in this version of the model, public schooling does not introduce any distortion or external effect, and the long-run growth rate under the public system converges to that of the private system in the case of a unique steady state.

Log-Normal Distribution. The above result has been derived in the case of a compact support of the initial distribution. If the support of the initial distribution is an infinite interval, we can still characterize the dynamics of inequalities if the initial distribution $\Gamma_0(h)$ is log-normal (or the log distribution Λ_0 is normal). In this case, the distribution will remain log-normal over time. However, the variance of the underlying normal distribution will decrease (equation (5.51)). To describe the evolution of $\bar{h}_t$ we use equations (5.50)–(5.51) and $\ln \bar{h}_t = \mu_t + \sigma_t^2/2$, which implies after some manipulations that

$$\ln \bar{h}_{t+1} = \ln \mathcal{G} + \theta \ln w_t + \ln \bar{h}_t - \frac{(1-\theta)\theta}{2}\sigma_t^2. \tag{5.52}$$

Comparing with equation (5.41), there are two differences from the private system. First, the w_t are different (but converge to the same w_∞ when the steady state is unique). Second, there is an additional term in the public system which involves the variance of the distribution. This last term reduces the growth rate of the average the human capital in the public system but tends to disappear in the long run.

The intuition for the variance effect is as follows. Given the way human capital accumulates (5.37), it would be more efficient to devote more resources to the more skilled households, since the productivity of education spending depends on the family background. Hence, the public system entails a loss of efficiency, which is more important if the variance is high.

To compare the two systems with respect to capital and wages, we assume a Cobb–Douglas production function: $f(\kappa_t) = A\kappa_t^\alpha$. Taking logarithms, we replace $\ln \bar{h}_{t+1}$ in equation (5.43) by its value from (5.52) and find that

$$\ln \kappa_{t+1} = \ln \left(\frac{\beta}{(1+\beta+\gamma)\mathcal{G}} [(1-\alpha)A]^{1-\theta} \right) + \alpha(1-\theta)\ln \kappa_t + \frac{\theta(1-\theta)}{2}\sigma_t^2.$$

Starting from the same initial condition in both systems, this implies that κ_t (and thus w_t) is higher in the public system than in the private one. This higher wage increases the growth rate underlying (5.41) and may or may not compensate the negative effect of the variance.

To further investigate the growth differential between the two systems, we define the variables $\Delta \ln x_t = \ln x_t(\text{public}) - \ln x_t(\text{private})$, and we denote the variance of the log distribution in the public system by ς. To compare both systems we should solve

$$\Delta \ln \kappa_{t+1} = \alpha(1-\theta)\Delta \ln \kappa_t + \frac{\theta(1-\theta)}{2}\varsigma_t^2,$$

$$\Delta \ln \frac{\bar{h}_{t+1}}{\bar{h}_t} = \theta\alpha \Delta \ln \kappa_t - \frac{\theta(1-\theta)}{2}\varsigma_t^2,$$

$$\varsigma_{t+1}^2 = (1-\theta)^2 \varsigma_t^2$$

with $\Delta\kappa_0 = 0$ and $\varsigma_0^2 = 4$ given. The parameters that affects this system are θ, α, and the initial condition ς_0^2. We set $\alpha = 0.3$. In table 5.3, we present the evolution of the difference between the two systems for two values of θ. In both cases, the capital stock is higher in the public system, as predicted. Moreover, when θ is large, the family background does not matter much in education; the variance decreases quickly, implying that its negative effect on growth in the public system does not last long. Hence in the first case, the public system grows slower in the beginning – the variance effect dominates – and faster after 4 periods. When θ is small, the variance decreases slowly, and the public system always grows at a slower pace than the private one.

Table 5.3. *Difference between Public and Private Systems*

t	$\theta = 0.5$			$\theta = 0.25$		
	$\Delta \ln \kappa_t$	ς_t^2	$\Delta \ln \frac{\bar{h}_{t+1}}{\bar{h}_t}$	$\Delta \ln \kappa_t$	ς_t^2	$\Delta \ln \frac{\bar{h}_{t+1}}{\bar{h}_t}$
0	0.0000	4.0000		0.0000	4.0000	
1	0.5000	1.0000	−0.5000	0.3750	2.2500	−0.3750
2	0.2000	0.2500	−0.0500	0.2953	1.2656	−0.1828
3	0.0613	0.0625	−0.0013	0.1851	0.7119	−0.0965
4	0.0170	0.0156	0.0014	0.1084	0.4005	−0.0529
5	0.0045	0.0039	0.0006	0.0619	0.2253	−0.0294
6	0.0012	0.0010	0.0002	0.0351	0.1267	−0.0165

Extensions. The above framework can be extended in several directions. A first possibility, à la Becker and Lewis (1973), consists in introducing an additional determinant of human capital accumulation: the effort made by the parents to educate their children. Denote this effort by l_t. Equation (5.37) should be modified to incorporate this factor. For example,

$$h_{t+1} = \psi \, l_t \, e_t^\theta \, h_t^{1-\theta}.$$

Of course this effort has a cost either in terms of disutility[17] or in terms of opportunity cost. If it is the time spent rearing the children, it then reduces the time spent at work and modifies the first-period budget constraint:

$$w_t h_t (1 - l_t) = c_t + s_t + e_t.$$

In this case, the growth differential between the two financing systems is altered. Indeed, the time spent with the children is not taxed. Hence, in the presence of taxes, the parents will choose to work less and to remain with their children longer, which will in turn increase the pace of human capital accumulation. Economic growth will tend to be higher in the public regime than in the private one (see Wigniolle (1994)).

Another determinant of human capital accumulation is the effort made by the children, denoted λ_t. In this case, followed by Glomm and Ravikumar (1992), equation (5.37) becomes

$$h_{t+1} = \psi \, \lambda_{t-1} \, e_t^\theta \, h_t^{1-\theta},$$

and one should add a term in $\ln(1 - \lambda_{t-1})$ to the utility function:

$$\ln c_t + \beta \ln d_{t+1} + \gamma \ln e_t + \chi \ln(1 - \lambda_{t-1}).$$

This leads to an individual optimization problem with three decisions, $(\lambda_{t-1}, s_t, e_t)$. Compared to the previous approach, we now find the inverse result: The

---

[17] If l_t is an effort, it should enter the utility function of the parents negatively.

public system introduces a distortion in the choice of effort made by the children that will hamper growth. Indeed, in the private regime, the children take into account that more effort when young – and hence more resources when adult – will allow them to increase the quality of education for their children, e_t. In the public regime, they view their individual contribution to the quality of public education through taxes as negligible. This is a typical case of fiscal externality. Economic growth will thus tend to be higher in the private regime.

A further extension is to assume that the individual capital accumulation also hinges on an aggregate human capital index or on some other individuals' stock or average, therefore allowing for cross-individual spillover. For example,

$$h_{t+1} = \psi e_t^\theta h_t^{\chi(1-\theta)} \bar{h}_t^{(1-\chi)(1-\theta)},$$

or

$$h_{t+1} = \psi e_t^\theta (h_t + \zeta \bar{h}_t)^{1-\theta}.$$

This effect introduces convergence forces into the model. In the second formulation, the importance of the spillover in the human capital accumulation process is parametrized by $\zeta < 1$, which captures the fact that the transmission of knowledge from one individual to the other is affected by distance and other factors. Such a framework can be used to study regional spillovers as in de la Croix and Monfort (2000), or to build international growth models where cross-border spillovers are affected by integration.[18]

Finally, there may be a link between public education, which requires a transfer from the parents to the children, and pay-as-you-go pensions, inducing a transfer in the other direction. Indeed, when parents retire, the labor income of their children, which has been built thanks to taxes they paid, is taxed in turn to finance their own social security benefits. Kaganovich and Zilcha (1999) study the interaction of these two potential outlays of public revenues. Their conclusions depends greatly on the values of the parameters and in particular on the ad hoc altruism factor.

5.2.3 Market Funding

Under the market funding system,[19] households finance their education by borrowing on the capital market and do not rely on public resources. We therefore assume that individuals have perfect access to capital market and can use their human capital as collateral to finance their education spending. One

---

[18] This idea is developed by Rivera-Batiz and Romer (1991a) and (1991b) in a model with research and development. See also Michel and Vidal (2000).

[19] This version of the model is an adaptation of Michel (1993).

important difference from the preceding system is that education spending no longer rests on gift motives but on the return to human capital.

One may thus adopt the standard utility function of chapter 1. The life cycle of each household is the same as in the previous section except concerning education spending: When young at $t-1$, the representative household builds his human capital stock; it borrows e_{t-1} from the capital market. The adults supply inelastically h_t units of human capital and earn $w_t h_t$, where w_t is the wage per unit of human capital and h_t is the level of human capital of the household. This income is allocated to purchasing consumption goods, reimbursing the debt $R_t e_{t-1}$, and saving s_t for future consumption. When old, households spend all their saving and accrued interest on consumption. The two budget constraints are thus

$$w_t h_t = c_t + s_t + R_t e_{t-1},$$

$$d_{t+1} = R_{t+1} s_t.$$

Human capital accumulates as in equation (5.37):

$$h_t = \psi e_{t-1}^{\theta} h_{t-1}^{1-\theta}. \tag{5.53}$$

Agents chose education spending and savings, subject to the budget constraints.[20]

The optimal choice of savings obeys the same rule as in section 1.3.3, where the first period income is now

$$\Omega_t = w_t h_t - R_t e_{t-1}.$$

We accordingly obtain a saving function

$$s_t = s(\Omega_t, R_{t+1}), \tag{5.54}$$

which is the same for all individuals, since they all have the same preferences. The first-order condition for e_{t-1} leads to

$$e_{t-1} = \left(\psi \theta \frac{w_t}{R_t}\right)^{\frac{1}{1-\theta}} h_{t-1}. \tag{5.55}$$

Hence, education spending increases the wage rate. The interest factor has a negative effect on education spending, as it is part of the cost of education.

Equations (5.55) and (5.53) allow to study the dynamics of the distribution of human capital. Substituting e_{t-1} from (5.55) in (5.53), we obtain

$$h_t = \psi \left(\psi \theta \frac{w_t}{R_t}\right)^{\frac{\theta}{1-\theta}} h_{t-1} \quad \text{and} \quad \Omega_t = (1-\theta) w_t h_t.$$

---

[20] Since there is no disutility of education in the utility function, the problem can be solved in two steps: e_{t-1} can be obtained by maximizing the life-cycle income $w_t \psi e_{t-1}^{\theta} h_{t-1}^{1-\theta} - R_t e_{t-1}$. Given this choice, savings maximize utility.

The evolution of the log distribution follows for $t \geq 1$:

$$\Lambda_t(\ell) = \Lambda_{t-1}\left\{\ell - \ln\left[\psi\left(\psi\theta\frac{w_t}{R_t}\right)^{\frac{\theta}{1-\theta}}\right]\right\}. \tag{5.56}$$

The set of initial data includes the distributions of initial wealth s_{-1} and of the debt of the first adults e_{-1}, the log distribution Λ_0, and the initial stock of capital, which verifies $K_0 + \bar{e}_{-1} = \bar{s}_{-1}$. The first adults choose $s_0 = s(\Omega_0, R_1)$ with $\Omega_0 = w_0 h_0 - R_0 e_{-1}$. The first old consume $d_0 = R_0 s_{-1}$.

Firms use the same production function as in the preceding section. The stock of capital per unit of human capital is $\kappa_t = K_t/H_t$, and prices are equal to marginal productivities: $w_t = \omega(\kappa_t)$ and $R_t = f'(\kappa_t)$.

The equilibrium on the financial market should take into account spending on education. This is the most specific feature of this model: physical and human capital compete to be funded. Savings are thus allocated to investment in physical capital and in human capital:

$$K_{t+1} + \bar{e}_t = \bar{s}_t,$$

where $\bar{e}_t$ and $\bar{s}_t$ are the means of e_t and s_t in the population normalized to 1. This gives, with $H_t = \bar{h}_t$,

$$\kappa_{t+1}\bar{h}_{t+1} + \bar{e}_t = \bar{s}_t. \tag{5.57}$$

An inter-temporal equilibrium can now be defined as follows:

Definition 5.4 (Inter-temporal equilibrium – market funding of education)
Given the set of initial data, an inter-temporal equilibrium with market funding is a sequence of prices $\{w_t, R_t\}$, aggregate variables $\{K_{t+1}, \bar{h}_{t+1}, \kappa_{t+1}\tau_{t+1}, \bar{s}_t, \bar{e}_t\}$, and distributions of human capital, savings, and education spending such that:

- *prices $\{w_t, R_t\}$ verify $w_t = \omega(\kappa_t)$ and $R_t = f'(\kappa_t)$ with $\kappa_t = K_t/\bar{h}_t$;*
- *the capital market clears, i.e., equation (5.57) holds;*
- *the log distribution of human capital follows (5.56), and $\bar{h}_t$ is given by (5.36);*
- *the distribution of savings and education spending result from the distribution of human capital through the individual decisions (5.54) and (5.55) with $\Omega_t = (1 - \theta)w_t h_t$ for $t \geq 1$, and $\Omega_0 = w_0 h_0 - R_0 e_{-1}$. The variables $\bar{s}_t$ and $\bar{e}_t$ are the means of these distributions.*

The dynamics of the moments of the log distribution of human capital follow

$$\mu_{t+1} = \mu_t + \ln\left[\psi\left(\psi\theta\frac{w_{t+1}}{R_{t+1}}\right)^{\frac{\theta}{1-\theta}}\right],$$

$$\sigma_{t+1}^2 = \sigma_t^2.$$

We thus have the same properties as in the model with parental funding: the distribution of $\ln h_t$ keeps the same standard error over time, since the constant term is common to all households. Hence, the market funding system does not reduce inequalities, as measured by this standard error. The key to this result is that, although households have different human capital, they will invest at the same *rate*:

$$\frac{e_{t-1}}{h_{t-1}} = \left(\psi\theta\frac{w_t}{R_t}\right)^{\frac{1}{1-\theta}}.$$

To study the aggregate dynamics we use the deflated variable $\hat{e}_{t-1}$, which verifies

$$\hat{e}_{t-1}\frac{e_{t-1}}{h_{t-1}} = \left(\psi\theta\frac{\omega(\kappa_t)}{f'(\kappa_t)}\right)^{\frac{1}{1-\theta}} \equiv \mathcal{E}(\kappa_t),$$

giving a static relationship between $\hat{e}_{t-1}$ and κ_t. This implies

$$h_{t+1} = \psi\mathcal{E}(\kappa_{t+1})^\theta h_t,$$
$$\bar{h}_{t+1} = \psi\mathcal{E}(\kappa_{t+1})^\theta \bar{h}_t.$$

The total stock of capital can be expressed as

$$K_{t+1} = \kappa_{t+1}\bar{h}_{t+1} = \kappa_{t+1}\psi\mathcal{E}(\kappa_{t+1})^\theta \bar{h}_t.$$

Assuming that preferences are homothetic, savings are proportional to income (see section 1.8.4). The propensity to save, $\zeta(R_{t+1})$, only depends on the interest factor. Aggregate savings are given by

$$\bar{s}_t = \zeta(f'(\kappa_{t+1}))(1-\theta)\omega(\kappa_t)\bar{h}_t.$$

Using $\bar{e}_t = \mathcal{E}(\kappa_{t+1})\bar{h}_t$, the equilibrium (5.57) is given by

$$\kappa_{t+1}\mathcal{E}(\kappa_{t+1})^\theta + \mathcal{E}(\kappa_{t+1}) = \zeta(f'(\kappa_{t+1}))(1-\theta)\omega(\kappa_t). \qquad (5.58)$$

The dynamics of κ_t are autonomous: they are defined by equation (5.58) which is a deterministic non-linear difference equation of the first order. The solution to this equation determines the dynamics of the distribution (5.56), and of the growth factor $\psi\mathcal{E}(\kappa_{t+1})^\theta$ of human capital.

Example: With a logarithmic utility function and a Cobb–Douglas production function, we have

$$\omega(\kappa_t) = A(1-\alpha)\kappa_t^\alpha,$$

$$\mathcal{E}(\kappa_{t+1}) = \left(\psi\theta\frac{1-\alpha}{\alpha}\kappa_{t+1}\right)^{\frac{1}{1-\theta}} \equiv B\kappa_{t+1}^{\frac{1}{1-\theta}},$$

$$\zeta(f'(\kappa_{t+1})) = \frac{\beta}{1+\beta}.$$

The capital market equilibrium (5.58) can be simplified and leads to

$$(B^\theta + B)\kappa_{t+1}^{\frac{1}{1-\theta}} = \frac{\beta}{1+\beta}(1-\theta)(1-\alpha)A\kappa_t^\alpha,$$

or

$$\kappa_{t+1} = M\kappa_t^{\alpha(1-\theta)},$$

where M is a positive constant. These dynamics converge to a steady state, which is globally stable.

Extensions. Since Auerbach and Kotlikoff's (1987) seminal book, several examples of computable overlapping generations model with exogenous growth can be found in the literature. These models extend the initial model by incorporating several features such as trade openness, multi-sectoral production, generational accounting, and life uncertainty. Few of them endogenize the formation of human capital and the rate of productivity growth. Docquier and Michel (1999) provide a simulation exercise on the basis of a simple model with three periods of life and market funding. Fougère and Mérette (1999) use a similar growth specification, but allow for education investment in each period of life and do not take into account the huge government intervention in education financing. One of the biggest problems arising with numerical endogenous growth models is the choice of a human capital technology specification and the calibration of its parameters. Though there is a large consensus on the production function of consumption and investment goods, there is no real evidence on the choice of the production function of human capital. In general the simulation results are too sensitive to the various calibrations of the production function of human capital, and the growth effect of policy changes are unrealistically strong. This issue in tackled in Hendricks (1999) and Bouzahzah, de la Croix, and Docquier (2001).

Concerning individual decisions on human capital, it has been argued that education is a typical long-run investment project whose risky nature is widely accepted and incorporated in the literature on human capital (see e.g., Schultz (1961)). Different innate abilities to take advantage of education, length of life, the effects of family background are some of the identified sources of uncertainty characterizing the returns to educational investment, and hence future labor earnings. This can be modeled by adding a random term ε_t to the human capital accumulation, for example,

$$h_{t+1} = \psi e_t^\theta h_t^{1-\theta} \varepsilon_t.$$

In this context, Rillaers (2000) studies how unemployment benefits may affect investment in education on behalf of risk averse individuals.

Another interesting extension is to introduce government education spending and study the interplay between public and private spending. Michel (1993) and de la Croix (2001) assume that public spending is financed through a lump-sum tax bearing on the adult generation and that it affects the production of human capital in the following way:

$$h_{t+1} = \psi e_t^\theta \phi(g_t),$$

or, for an endogenous growth version,

$$h_{t+1} = \psi e_t^\theta g_t^\lambda h_t^{1-\theta-\lambda}.$$

In this last version, the ratio of public spending on education to human capital, $\hat{g}$, is crucial to determining the dynamic properties. When $\hat{g}$ (and hence taxes) increases, the households will lower their private spending on education, since their disposable income has been reduced. The total effect on growth includes two components:[21] the favorable one is the efficiency gain in the accumulation of human capital, and the negative one is linked to the reduction in savings caused by taxation. There is a growth-maximizing level of public spending. After this point, increasing public spending reduces growth, as the tax effect dominates the efficiency effect on the accumulation of human capital.

5.2.4 The Tradeoff between Studying and Working

If accumulating human capital needs time, each individual has to allocate his time endowment between working and producing human capital. This problem was first studied by Ben-Porath (1967) in a partial equilibrium setup. Beginning his life cycle, an individual has to choose how long he will accumulate human capital before entering the labor market. By studying early in his life, he maximizes the time during which this investment will be productive. Azariadis and Drazen (1990) have formulated this problem in an overlapping generations model where households live two periods. In the first period of life, they devote their time to both activities, producing human capital and working. In the second period, they benefit from the human capital accumulated when young and work.

We present here a simplified version of Azariadis and Drazen (1990) inspired by d'Autume and Michel (1994). Again, each generation consists of a continuum of households, with unit mass. Each individual lives for two periods, say adulthood and old age. Each adult inherits a fraction δ of the parents' human capital. A share of time λ_t is spent to build up human capital, and $1 - \lambda_t$ to work. The first-period income is allocated between consumption and savings:

$$(1 - \lambda_t)w_t \delta h_t = c_t + s_t, \tag{5.59}$$

---

[21] Compare Barro (1990), in which public spending affects the production function of goods directly.

where w_t is the wage per unit of human capital and h_t the human capital of the old generation at time t. When old, the human capital depends on the time spent on education when adult:

$$h_{t+1} = \psi(\lambda_t)\delta h_t. \tag{5.60}$$

The function ψ is assumed increasing and concave and satisfies

$$\lim_{\lambda \to 0} \psi'(\lambda) = +\infty.$$

This ensures that it is always optimal to spend a strictly positive time span to built human capital.

When old, the household consumes both labor earnings and capital income:

$$d_{t+1} = R_{t+1}s_t + w_{t+1}h_{t+1}. \tag{5.61}$$

From equations (5.59), (5.60), and (5.61), the life-cycle income is proportional to the inherited human capital δh_t:

$$\Omega_t = \delta h_t \left((1 - \lambda_t)w_t + \frac{w_{t+1}}{R_{t+1}}\psi(\lambda_t) \right).$$

As λ_t does not enter the utility function, we can solve the problem in two separate steps, and the optimal length of schooling will not depend on the shape of the utility function. The optimal length of schooling maximizes the life-cycle income, which yields

$$\psi'(\lambda_t) = w_t \frac{R_{t+1}}{w_{t+1}}. \tag{5.62}$$

This equation represents the tradeoff between studying and working. The benefit of a marginal increase in the schooling periods is more income in the second period: $\psi'(\lambda_t)w_{t+1}/R_{t+1}$. The cost is less income today, w_t. This relationship implies that the length of schooling depends positively on the discounted future wage (the benefit from education) and negatively on the current wage (the opportunity cost). We also see that the time devoted to schooling does not depend on the inherited human capital, and will thus be the same for everyone.[22]

Equation (5.62) implies thus that all households of a given period t choose the same fraction λ_t. λ_t depends only on prices: $\lambda_t = \psi^{-1}(w_t R_{t+1}/w_{t+1})$. There is therefore no reduction in inequalities:

$$h_{t+1} = \delta\psi(\lambda_t)h_t,$$

and

$$\bar{h}_{t+1} = \delta\psi(\lambda_t)\bar{h}_t.$$

---

[22] At equilibrium λ_t is necessarily smaller than one. It would otherwise imply negative aggregate savings and capital.

The initial log distribution of human capital Λ_0 is given. The evolution of the log distribution follows

$$\Lambda_{t+1}(\ell) = \Lambda_t\left(\ell - \ln\left[\delta\psi(\lambda_t)\right]\right). \tag{5.63}$$

As in the private and market funding cases, the distribution of $\hat{h}_t = h_t/\bar{h}_t$ remains constant over time.

We use equation (5.62) to compute life-cycle income:

$$\Omega_t = (1 - \lambda_t)w_t\delta h_t + \frac{w_{t+1}}{R_{t+1}}\psi(\lambda_t)\delta h_t = \left(1 - \lambda_t + \frac{\psi(\lambda_t)}{\psi'(\lambda_t)}\right)w_t\delta h_t.$$

As it is proportional to h_t, one could write the model with a homothetic utility function. In this case, using the results of section 3.1.1 (in particular equation (3.3)), one gets

$$s_t = \tilde{s}((1 - \lambda_t)\delta h_t w_t, \delta w_{t+1}\psi(\lambda_t)h_t, R_{t+1});$$

with homothetic utility this would be linear in h_t. Assuming for simplicity that the life-cycle utility is log-linear, we have

$$U_t = \ln c_t + \beta \ln d_{t+1}.$$

The consumption choice is obtained by maximizing the life-cycle utility under the constraint

$$c_t + \frac{d_t}{R_{t+1}} = \Omega_t.$$

We obtain

$$c_t = \frac{1}{1 + \beta}\Omega_t, \tag{5.64}$$

and

$$s_t = (1 - \lambda_t)w_t\delta h_t - c_t. \tag{5.65}$$

From equations (5.64) and (5.65), savings are given by

$$s_t = \frac{1}{1 + \beta}\left(\beta(1 - \lambda_t) - \frac{\psi(\lambda_t)}{\psi'(\lambda_t)}\right)w_t\delta h_t. \tag{5.66}$$

We assume a Cobb–Douglas technology for firms, which leads to $w_t = (1 - \alpha)A\kappa_t^\alpha$ and $R_t = \alpha A\kappa_t^{\alpha-1}$, with $\kappa_t = K_t/H_t$.

The supply of labor from the old individuals is $\bar{h}_t$. The supply from the young ones is $(1 - \lambda_t)\delta\bar{h}_t$. The equilibrium on the labor market requires

$$H_t = [1 + (1 - \lambda_t)\delta]\bar{h}_t.$$

Equation (5.66) defines a linear relation between savings and human capital for each household; we aggregate them and obtain the equilibrium on the capital market:

$$K_{t+1} = \bar{s}_t = \frac{1}{1+\beta}\left(\beta(1-\lambda_t) - \frac{\psi(\lambda_t)}{\psi'(\lambda_t)}\right)w_t\delta\bar{h}_t. \tag{5.67}$$

Given an initial stock of capital K_0 and an initial log distribution of human capital over the first old generation $\Lambda_0(\cdot)$, an inter-temporal equilibrium is, in this example, a sequence of prices $\{w_t, R_t\}$ verifying $w_t = (1-\alpha)A\kappa_t^\alpha$, and $R_t = \alpha A\kappa_t^{\alpha-1}$, aggregate variables $\{K_{t+1}, \bar{h}_{t+1}, \kappa_{t+1}\}$ and distributions of human capital Λ_t which determines the distribution of other individual variables $\{s_t, \lambda_t\}$. These sequences are such that each household chooses savings s_t and schooling according to (5.62) and (5.66). The human capital accumulates according to equation (5.60), and its distribution follows (5.63). The clearing condition (5.67) on the capital market holds.

We describe the dynamics of the economy in terms of κ and λ. Aggregate human capital is given by

$$H_{t+1} = [1 + (1-\lambda_{t+1})\delta]\bar{h}_{t+1} = [1 + (1-\lambda_{t+1})\delta]\delta\psi(\lambda_t)\bar{h}_t,$$

which, after replacing the equilibrium wage by its value, allows us to rewrite equation (5.67) as

$$\kappa_{t+1}[1 + (1-\lambda_{t+1})\delta]\psi(\lambda_t) = \frac{1}{1+\beta}\left(\beta(1-\lambda_t) - \frac{\psi(\lambda_t)}{\psi'(\lambda_t)}\right)A(1-\alpha)\kappa_t^\alpha. \tag{5.68}$$

Here the labor supply is endogenous. As λ_t verifies

$$\psi'(\lambda_t) = w_t\frac{R_{t+1}}{w_{t+1}} = \frac{\alpha A\kappa_t^\alpha}{\kappa_{t+1}}, \tag{5.69}$$

the dynamics have two dimensions; substituting λ_t and λ_{t+1} from (5.69) in (5.68) leads to a second-order difference equation in κ. Since there is only one initial condition, κ_0, there is one pre-determined variable and one forward-looking variable. However, thanks to the assumptions we have made on utility and production functions, the dynamic system can be solved recursively and the dynamics can be studied in a simple way. Indeed, replacing κ_{t+1} from (5.69) in (5.68) leads to

$$1 - \lambda_{t+1} = \frac{1-\alpha}{\delta\alpha(1+\beta)}\beta(1-\lambda_t)\frac{\psi'(\lambda_t)}{\psi(\lambda_t)} - \frac{1}{\delta} - \frac{1-\alpha}{\delta\alpha(1+\beta)}, \tag{5.70}$$

which can be rewritten as

$$x_{t+1} = B_1 x_t\frac{\psi'(1-x_t)}{\psi(1-x_t)} - B_2 \equiv \phi(x_t),$$

with $x_t = 1 - \lambda_t$ and $B_1, B_2 > 0$.

When x_t increases from 0 to 1, $\phi(x_t)$ goes from $-B_2$ to $+\infty$ and there exists a steady state between 0 and 1 (see figure 5.1). This steady state is unique,

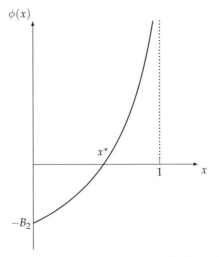

Figure 5.1. The forward-looking dynamics in Azariadis and Drazen (1990).

because $\phi(x)$ is monotonical increasing in x:

$$\phi'(x) = B_1 \left[\frac{\psi'(1-x)}{\psi(1-x)} - \frac{x\psi''(1-x)}{\psi(1-x)} + x \left(\frac{\psi'(1-x)}{\psi(1-x)} \right)^2 \right] > 0.$$

Moreover, the steady state $x^\star$ is unstable, because $\phi'(x^\star)$ is larger than one:

$$\phi'(x^\star) > B_1 \frac{\psi'(1-x^\star)}{\psi(1-x^\star)} = 1 + \frac{B_2}{x^\star} > 1.$$

This implies that the forward-looking variable λ_t has to jump to its steady state value $\lambda^\star = 1 - x^\star$ at the initial date. Otherwise, the trajectory implied by the unstable monotonic dynamics would lead λ_t outside the interval $(0, 1)$. The perfect foresight dynamics are thus characterized by $\lambda_t = \lambda^\star$ for all t. The dynamics of the capital/labor ratio will then follow, from (5.69),

$$\kappa_{t+1} = w_t \frac{R_{t+1}}{w_{t+1}} = \frac{\alpha A \kappa_t^\alpha}{\psi'(\lambda^\star)}.$$

The dynamics of κ converge to a steady state $\kappa^\star$ which is globally stable. The dynamics of the human capital stocks follow

$$h_{t+1} = \delta \psi(\lambda^\star) h_t,$$

and its log distribution follows

$$\Lambda_{t+1}(\ell) = \Lambda_t(\ell - \ln[\delta \psi(\lambda^\star)]).$$

Hence, the growth rate is constant and depends on the parameters α, β, δ and on the function $\psi(\cdot)$.

Extension: Threshold Externalities and Poverty Traps. In their model with ho-mogeneous households, Azariadis and Drazen (1990) assume a positive ex-ternality from the total human capital of the society on the function ψ. With heterogeneous households, we can assume that the average human capital affects learning positively:

$$h_{t+1} = \xi(\lambda_t, \bar{h}_t)h_t.$$

In this case, the equality between the individual specific λ's is preserved. λ_t, the same for all households, verifies

$$\xi'_\lambda(\lambda_t, \bar{h}_t) = w_t \frac{R_{t+1}}{w_{t+1}}.$$

To keep things simple, assume $\xi(\lambda_t, \bar{h}_t) = \psi(\lambda_t)\eta(\bar{h}_t)$ with $\eta(\cdot)$ increasing and bounded. Then the $\psi(\cdot)$ and $\psi'(\cdot)$ of the previous model are multiplied by $\eta(\cdot)$, and their ratio is unchanged. Equation (5.70) remains valid, and we obtain the same constant value $\lambda_t = \lambda^*$ as a perfect foresight equilibrium. However, the dynamics of human capital are altered. We have

$$h_{t+1} = \delta\psi(\lambda^*)\eta(\bar{h}_t)h_t,$$

and

$$\bar{h}_{t+1} = \delta\psi(\lambda^*)\eta(\bar{h}_t)\bar{h}_t.$$

If there exists a threshold $\tilde{h}$ such that $\delta\psi(\lambda^*)\eta(\tilde{h}) = 1$, the economy will be caught in a poverty trap if $\bar{h}_0 < \tilde{h}$, since the sequence $(\bar{h}_t)_{t\geq 0}$ is decreasing and converges to 0 (see figure 5.2). On the contrary, if $\bar{h}_0 > \tilde{h}$, the sequence $(\bar{h}_t)_{t\geq 0}$ is increasing and tends toward infinity. The growth factor in the long run equals $\delta\psi(\lambda^*)\eta(+\infty)$, which is finite. Knowing the dynamics of $\bar{h}_t$, we can

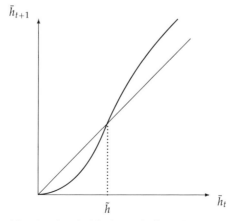

Figure 5.2. The threshold of Azariadis and Drazen (1990).

deduce those for κ:

$$\kappa_{t+1} = \frac{\alpha}{\psi'(\lambda^\star)\eta(\bar{h}_t)} A\kappa_t^\alpha.$$

Since $\eta(\bar{h}_t)$ converges towards a limit – $\eta(0)$, $\eta(\tilde{h})$, or $\eta(+\infty)$ depending on whether $\bar{h}_0$ is smaller than, equal to, or larger than $\tilde{h}$ – the sequence $(\kappa_t)_{t \geq 0}$ converges to the corresponding limit.

5.3 INTER-GENERATIONAL EXTERNALITIES

Parents' influence on children is not limited to resource transfers (section 5.1) or human capital spillovers (section 5.2). Becker (1992) notices that "The habits acquired as a child or young adult generally continue to influence behavior even when the environment changes radically. For instance, Indian adults who migrate to the United States often eat the same type of cuisine they had in India, and continue to wear the same type of clothing.[...] Childhood-acquired habits then continue, even though these would not have developed if the environment when growing up had been the same as the environment faced as an adult.[...]" A comprehensive survey of evidence of vertical transmission (i.e., from parents to children), including the fear of insects but also career aspirations, is provided in Boyd and Richerson (1985). These vertical transmission mechanisms are modeled in different strands of literature. All of them lead to the conclusion that intergenerational taste externalities are particularly important for thinking about long-term evolution processes like growth.

The involuntary transmission of tastes from one generation to the next has, as far as we know, rarely been formalized in economics.[23] Besides its inter-generational aspect, the idea of bequeathed tastes reflects the effect of past decisions on the perception of current outcomes. In the context of consumption, this clearly refers to the models of habit formation initiated by Duesenberry (1949) and developed afterwards by many others. The empirical studies in this literature have always been developed in the framework of infinite-lived agents. They often find strong support in favor of time non-separable preferences (for a recent study see de la Croix and Urbain (1998)). Moreover, there is convincing experimental support for supposing a habituation mechanism by which the most salient events are progressively absorbed into the new baseline against which further events are judged (see Brickman, Coates, and Janoff-Belman (1978)). Finally, as studied by de la Croix (1998), one empirical implication of the habit formation models is that reported satisfaction levels do not necessarily increase over time in line with economic development. This is consistent with the empirical evidence

---

[23] Two exceptions are Jones (1984) and Bisin and Verdier (2000). Jones (1984) analyses traditions of behavior within a workplace. He analyzes a model in which "it is through conformism between neighboring generations that we generate traditions passed down from one generation to the next."

provided by Easterlin (1995). The fact that "an Indian will, on average, be twice as well off as his grandfather" (Lucas (1988)) does not mean that his satisfaction level has increased, as standard-of-living norms will have risen too.

As this view is relatively non-standard, we need to expand more on the foundations of the idea of inherited tastes in neighboring disciplines.

The inter-generational spillover can take the form of what social scientists call social capital. Following Coleman (1990), physical capital is wholly tangible, being embodied in equipment; human capital is embodied in the individuals through skills and knowledge; social capital is embodied in the relations among persons. The family relationships are important vectors of social capital allowing for inter-generational spillovers. Chapter 22 of Coleman (1990) analyzes how different family structures generate social capital and how the decline in the role of the family in recent decades can be important for the social capital of the next generations. In Coleman (1990), social capital can be seen as a vector of growth; he does not investigate situations in which some sort of social capital can hamper the growth process.

The most comprehensive analysis of inter-generational spillovers can be found in the work of Cavalli-Sforza and Feldman (1981) and Boyd and Richerson (1985). After having assessed the importance of social learning within the family, Boyd and Richerson (1985) build different models in which the distribution of beliefs, attitudes, and values in a population is transmitted and modified. In Cavalli-Sforza and Feldman (1981), the vertical transmission of culture is measured using the Stanford survey of beliefs and values. Vertical transmission appears clearly important concerning dietary habits, religious habits, sports participation, and political interest. The authors next study the interaction between the inheritance of culture and the environment. Their socio-biological approach is not that far from the economic approach, in which the role of the natural selection is played by market forces.

5.3.1 Inter-generational Taste Externalities in the Competitive Economy

Let us consider how an inter-generational taste externality modifies some of the results of chapters 1 and 2. For simplicity, we assume here constant population ($n = 0$).

The Utility Function. Inter-generational taste externalities can be modeled in the following way. The utility v of consumption in the first period of life is modified and depends on a stock variable a_t, which is interpreted as family social capital.[24]

---

[24] One can also introduce in the utility function the services from another stock variable in order to model cultural goods. Family capital and cultural goods differ from ordinary durable goods because there is no second-hand market for them (see Champarnaud and Michel (2000)). Another stock variable in the utility function that can be responsible for externalities is environmental quality, as in Jouvet, Michel, and Vidal (2000).

We thus have $v(c_t, a_t)$, and we may distinguish two cases depending on the sign of the inter-generational spillover.

When $v'_a > 0$, the consumption of the parents has a positive influence on the utility of their children. This is the case for instance when the children learn an "art of living" with their parents; this stock of cultural knowledge presents some durability and still exerts a positive influence when the children become adults. The effect of a on the consumption behavior of the new adult depends on v''_{ca}. If $v''_{ca} < 0$, the marginal utility, i.e., the *desire to consume*, is reduced by the stock of cultural knowledge; when for instance the households have learned how to draw a maximum satisfaction from what they consume, and we say that they are *repleted*. If $v''_{ca} > 0$, the desire for consumption is increasing in the parents' consumption and we say that there is *addiction*.

When $v'_a < 0$, which is the case studied in this section, parents' consumption has a negative influence on children's utility. As in the psychological models of the "goal-achievement gap," the instantaneous satisfaction depends on the gap between the actual consumption and the aspirations, i.e., the consumption of the previous generation. If $v''_{ca} < 0$, the aspiration effect generates distaste. If $v''_{ca} > 0$ the aspirations serve as a benchmark consumption level determining a goal to reach for the new generation. They induce a desire for catching up, pushing the new generation to consume more than what their parents did. The utility function used in de la Croix (1996) and (2001) and in de la Croix and Michel (2001) and (1999) displays this catching-up effect. They use the following utility of a representative individual:

$$v(c_t, a_t) + u(d_{t+1}).$$

Aspirations a_t are linked to the consumption of the parents when adults:

$$a_t = c_{t-1}. \tag{5.71}$$

We assume that the depreciation rate of aspirations (i.e. forgetting) is high, so that they no longer affect the evaluation of consumption when old. This simplifying assumption proxies the idea that aspirations are less important for older persons.[25]

Moreover, we should assume

$$v'_c > 0, \quad v'_a < 0, \quad v''_{cc} < 0, \quad v''_{aa} < 0, \quad \text{and} \quad v''_{ca} > 0.$$

The assumption $v_{ca} > 0$ amounts to postulating that a rise in aspirations increases the marginal utility of (i.e., the desire for) consumption. We also assume

---

[25] This is supported by the empirical observation that reported satisfaction increases from the age of 30 onwards. On the basis of their empirical study on job satisfaction, Clark, Oswald, and Warr (1996) conclude that "the rise in job satisfaction at these ages could come from *reduced aspirations*, due to a recognition that there are few alternative jobs available once a worker's career is established [...]. Alternatively, aspirations themselves could remain the same, but older workers might put less weight on such comparisons [...]."

that v is strictly concave:

$$v''_{cc}v''_{aa} - (v''_{ca})^2 > 0.$$

The Competitive Equilibrium. The model is a simple extension of the one in chapter 1. Each generation lives three periods. The young generation has no decision to take and only inherits life standard aspirations a_t from its parents. The adult generation sells one unit of labor inelastically at some real wage w_t, consumes the quantity c_t, and saves s_t for next period consumption by holding capital. The old generation spends all its savings from the previous period and consumes d_{t+1}. The maximization program of the individual is to choose $\{c_t, d_{t+1}\}$ in order to

$$\max v(c_t, a_t) + u(d_{t+1})$$

subject to $c_t = w_t - s_t$, $d_{t+1} = R_{t+1}s_t$, prices, and a_t given. This problem is the same as in chapter 1 except that marginal utility is conditional on a parameter a_t. The first-order condition

$$v'_c(c_t, a_t) = R_{t+1}u'(d_{t+1}) \qquad (5.72)$$

allows us to define a saving function of the form

$$s_t = s(w_t, R_{t+1}, a_t). \qquad (5.73)$$

Its partial derivative with respect to a_t is

$$s'_a = \frac{v''_{ca}}{v''_{cc} + R^2_{t+1}u''} < 0.$$

The effect of rising aspirations is to reduce savings, because it increases the desire for consumption when young.

As in the model of chapter 1, The competitive behavior of firms and the equalization between realized and distributed profits lead to the equalization of marginal productivities to marginal costs: $R_t = f'(k_t)$ and $w_t = f(k_t) - k_t f'(k_t) = \omega(k_t)$, where $k_t = K_t/L_t$. At equilibrium $L_t = N$.

The equilibrium condition in the capital market implies

$$k_{t+1} = s_t.$$

Using (5.73) and $a_{t+1} = c_t = w_t - s_t$, the competitive equilibrium is characterized by a sequence $(k_t, a_t)_{t \geq 0}$, which satisfies

$$k_{t+1} = s(\omega(k_t), f'(k_{t+1}), a_t),$$
$$a_{t+1} = \omega(k_t) - s(\omega(k_t), f'(k_{t+1}), a_t). \qquad (5.74)$$

We thus conclude that the dynamics is of dimension two. Both variables are predetermined, as there are two initial conditions, the initial capital stock k_0 and the initial aspiration level $a_0 = c_{-1}$. We now study an example of competitive dynamics with Cobb–Douglas production and logarithmic utility.

Example: The inter-temporal utility of the typical adult has a specific functional form:

$$\ln(c_t - \theta a_t) + \beta \ln(d_{t+1}).$$

$\theta \in \,]0, 1[$ measures the intensity of the effect of the inter-generational spillover. Assuming an interior solution, the decision problem of the household has a unique solution characterized by the following saving function:

$$s_t = \frac{\beta}{1 + \beta}(w_t - \theta a_t).$$

Savings do not depend on the interest rate, and aspirations affect savings negatively. When aspirations are low, the adult generation has a sober lifestyle and savings are high. When aspirations are high compared to wage income, adults spend much on consumption to maintain a life standard similar to that of their parents, and their propensity to save is low.

Production is through a Cobb–Douglas constant-returns-to-scale technology: $f(k_t) = Ak_t^\alpha$. The competitive behavior of firms leads to $R_t = \alpha \, k_t^{\alpha-1}$, and $w_t = (1 - \alpha)k_t^\alpha$. The dynamics (5.74) are

$$k_{t+1} = \frac{\beta}{1 + \beta}\left[(1 - \alpha)Ak_t^\alpha - \theta a_t\right],$$

$$a_{t+1} = \frac{1}{1 + \beta}(1 - \alpha)Ak_t^\alpha + \frac{\beta}{1 + \beta}\theta a_t.$$

There is a unique non-trivial steady state (k, a):

$$k = \left(\frac{\beta(1 - \alpha)(1 - \theta)A}{(1 + \beta(1 - \theta))}\right)^{\frac{1}{1-\alpha}},$$

$$a = \frac{k}{\beta(1 - \theta)}.$$

It can be checked that $\partial k / \partial \theta < 0$, implying that the stationary capital stock per head is lower in the economy with bequeathed tastes than in the standard Diamond economy. This is essentially due to the fact that aspirations affect savings negatively.[26]

---

[26] This result holds even if aspirations are not completely forgotten after one period, provided that their effect is stronger on the adults than on the old.

We linearize the dynamic system around the steady state (k, a). This leads to

$$\begin{bmatrix} a_{t+1} - a \\ k_{t+1} - k \end{bmatrix} = \begin{bmatrix} \dfrac{\beta\theta}{1+\beta} & \dfrac{\alpha(1+\beta(1-\theta))}{\beta(1+\beta)(1-\theta)} \\ \dfrac{-\beta\theta}{1+\beta} & \dfrac{\alpha(1+\beta(1-\theta))}{(1+\beta)(1-\theta)} \end{bmatrix} \begin{bmatrix} a_t - a \\ k_t - k \end{bmatrix}.$$

The determinant D of the Jacobian matrix of the linearization of the dynamic system is

$$D = \frac{\alpha\theta[1 + \beta(1 - \theta)]}{(1 + \beta)(1 - \theta)}.$$

Its trace T is

$$T = \frac{\alpha[1 + \beta(1 - \theta)] + \beta\theta(1 - \theta)}{(1 + \beta)(1 - \theta)}.$$

Let $\hat\theta$ be the root smaller than one of $D = 1$:

$$\hat\theta = \frac{(1 + \beta)(1 + \alpha) - \sqrt{(1 + \beta)^2(1 + \alpha)^2 - 4\alpha\beta(1 + \beta)}}{2\alpha\beta}.$$

Non-hyperbolicity may arise only if there is at least one eigenvalue equal to 1 (case a), or if there is at least one eigenvalue equal to -1 (case b), or if the two eigenvalues are complex conjugates with modulus 1 (case c). A necessary condition for case a is that $D = T + 1$. This would happen if $\beta = -(1 + \alpha)/[1 + \theta + \alpha(1 - \theta)] < 0$, which is excluded given the domain of these parameters. A necessary condition for case b is that $-D = T + 1$. This would happen if $\beta = [1 + \alpha - \theta(1 - \alpha)]/[(1 + \alpha)(\theta^2 - 1)] < 0$, which is also excluded given the domain of the parameters. Case c arises if $D = 1$ and $T \in [-2, 2]$, which is true only if $\theta = \hat\theta$ (notice that cases in which $\theta = \hat\theta$, $D = 1$, and $T > 2$ arise only when some parameters take their values outside their domains). As the determinant D (which equals the product of the eigenvalues) is increasing in θ, the steady state is stable (unstable) when $\theta < \hat\theta$ ($\theta > \hat\theta$).

This result establishes that for all possible values of the parameters in their admissible domain, there is only one value $\hat\theta$ of θ in which the fixed point is a non-hyperbolic equilibrium, i.e., in which at least one of the eigenvalues of the Jacobian matrix of the linearized system has unit modulus. In that case, the linear approximation cannot be used to determine stability. In all other cases, the proposition establishes that if θ is smaller (greater) than $\hat\theta$, the fixed point is stable (unstable). If the effect of aspirations on utility is strong enough, the steady state is unstable.

In addition to the result on stability, it is possible to define a domain for θ inside which the dynamics of the system is characterized by oscillations. Indeed, dynamics around (k, a) are oscillatory if $\theta \in]\underline\theta, \hat\theta[\cup]\hat\theta, \bar\theta[$, where $\underline\theta$ and $\bar\theta$ are the real roots of the discriminant of the characteristic polynomial of the Jacobian matrix. When $\theta \in (\underline{\theta}, \bar{\theta})$, the corresponding eigenvalues are complex numbers, leading to (local) oscillations around (k, a). For instance, with $\alpha = 0.3$ and $\beta = 0.3$, we have $\hat{\theta} = 0.7856$, $\underline{\theta} = 0.1030$, and $\bar{\theta} = 0.9189$.

The spillover from one generation to the next has two components: (a) savings finance the capital stock required to produce and to pay the wages of the next generation; this process, which transforms income/savings of the old into income for the young, displays decreasing returns; (b) past consumption levels of the parents generate life standard aspirations for the young generation, leading them to spend more on consumption; this process is linear. At one point, due to the decreasing returns in the production process, the inter-generation spillover in terms of higher wages is not sufficient to cover the spillover in terms of higher aspirations. This leads to a drop in savings to maintain the life standard and induces a recession. When the subsequent impoverishment is strong enough, aspirations have reverted to lower levels, allowing a rise in savings and the start of an expansion period. Depending on the relative strength of the two effects, this process converges or not to the steady state.

5.3.2 The Optimal Allocation

This framework developed above introduces an externality that is not taken into account by non-altruistic parents. This externality should be taken into account by a benevolent planner. We thus consider a central planner who chooses the allocation of output in order to maximize the present discounted value of current and future generations. Assuming that the central planner's discount factor is γ, the social welfare function takes the following form (as in chapter 2, equation (2.8)):

$$\sum_{t=0}^{\infty} \gamma^{t+1} \left(v(c_t, a_t) + \frac{1}{\gamma} u(d_t) \right).$$

The resource constraint of the economy has the usual form:

$$f(k_t) = c_t + d_t + k_{t+1},$$

and $a_{t+1} = c_t$ holds. The control variables are $(c_t, d_t)_{t \geq 0}$, and the state variables are $(k_t, a_t)_{t \geq 0}$. The initial conditions are a_0 and k_0. We substitute $a_t = c_{t-1}$ and $d_t = f(k_t) - k_{t+1} - c_t$ in the objective. The first-order conditions for a maximum are

$$v_c'(c_t, a_t) + \gamma v_a'(c_{t+1}, a_{t+1}) = \frac{1}{\gamma} u'(d_t),$$

$$\frac{1}{\gamma} u'(d_t) = u'(d_{t+1}) f'(k_{t+1}).$$

The first equation is a condition for the optimal allocation of consumption between the adult and the old generation, which are alive at the same time. The marginal utility of consumption of adults, corrected to internalize the taste externality, is equalized to the marginal utility of consumption of the old. Note that, due to the presence of the taste externality and contrary to the model of chapter 1, this planner's first-order condition does not respect the first-order condition the individual chooses for himself in a market economy (equation (5.72)). The second equation is the usual condition describing the optimal intertemporal allocation.

The marginal conditions characterizing the dynamics of the optimal economy are described by the following system of four first-order non-linear difference equations:

$$\gamma v_a'(c_{t+1}, c_t) = \frac{1}{\gamma} u'(d_t) - v_c'(c_t, a_t),$$

$$u'(d_{t+1}) f'(k_{t+1}) = \frac{1}{\gamma} u'(d_t), \qquad (5.75)$$

$$a_{t+1} = c_t,$$

$$k_{t+1} = f(k_t) - d_t - c_t,$$

in which a_t and k_t are predetermined, and c_{t+1} and d_{t+1} are anticipated variables

Study of the Steady State. A steady state $\{a, k, c, d\}$ of this optimal economy is defined by $a = c, c + d = f(k) - k$, and

$$f'(k) = \frac{1}{\gamma}, \qquad (5.76)$$

$$v_c'(c, a) = \frac{1}{\gamma} u'(d) - \gamma v_a'(c, a), \qquad (5.77)$$

Equation (5.76) is the modified golden rule. Hence, the introduction of bequeathed tastes does not modify the optimal steady state stock of capital, which remains at the modified golden rule level k_γ. Equation (5.77) shows that the marginal utility of adults should be larger in the economy with inherited tastes than in the Diamond (1965) economy; this implies that they consume less.

There is a particular difficulty coming from equation (5.77), in that the existence and uniqueness of steady state consumption is not obvious. To find a sufficient condition for the existence of a steady state, we substitute $a = c$ and $d = f(k) - k - c$ in (5.77), and we obtain

$$0 = \gamma v_a'(c, c) + v_c'(c, c) - \frac{1}{\gamma} u'(f(k_\gamma) - c - k_\gamma) \equiv \phi(c).$$

Steady state consumption levels should satisfy $\phi(c) = 0$. To derive a condition under which there is at least one c such that $\phi(c) = 0$, we look at the value of

$\phi(\cdot)$ at extreme values for c. We have

$$\lim_{d \to 0} u'(d) = +\infty \quad \Rightarrow \quad \lim_{c \to f(k_\gamma) - k_\gamma} \phi(c) = -\infty.$$

Since $\phi(c)$ is continuous on the interval $(0, f(k_\gamma) - k_\gamma)$, there exists at least one c such that $\phi(c) = 0$ if

$$\lim_{c \to 0} [\gamma v'_a(c, c) + v'_c(c, c)] = \lim_{c \to 0} \phi(c) > 0.$$

This equation states that the negative effect of habits does not offset the gain in welfare linked to a rise in consumption, when $c = 0$. In particular, the existence of the steady state is guaranteed as long as the world is not Veblenian: Veblen believed that the welfare of a typical person primarily depends on his relative income position. In that case, the value of a social capital causing envy exactly offsets the value of own consumption. A rise in all incomes in a community by the same percentage would not improve anyone's welfare in Veblen's world (see Becker (1974), Veblen (1934)).

Let us consider the uniqueness of the steady state. A sufficient condition for uniqueness is

$$\phi'(c) = v''_{cc} + (1 + \gamma)v''_{ca} + \gamma v''_{aa} + \gamma^{-1} u'' < 0.$$

This is always guaranteed, for instance, if

$$v''_{cc} + (1 + \gamma)v''_{ca} + \gamma v''_{aa} \leq 0. \tag{5.78}$$

Notice that given the concavity of $u(c, a)$, the condition (5.78) is always satisfied for $\gamma = 1$. In the other cases, (5.78) imposes a restriction on v''_{ca} conditionally on γ, v''_{cc}, and v''_{aa}:

$$v''_{ca} \leq \frac{|v''_{cc}| + \gamma |v''_{aa}|}{1 + \gamma}.$$

This condition is satisfied for every γ as long as $v''_{ca} \leq |v''_{cc}|$ and $v''_{ca} \leq |v''_{aa}|$. If not, there is a restriction on γ.

Local Dynamics. Assuming that the steady state exists and is unique, we investigate whether the optimal solution defined by (5.75) converges to the steady state. Since there are two anticipated variables in the system, two (and only two) eigenvalues of its linearization should have a modulus larger than one. de la Croix and Michel (1999) show that under the condition (5.78), the stationary state is a saddle point. Moreover, the sign of the following function Δ allows one to characterize the local dynamics:

$$\Delta \equiv \left[v''_{cc} + \gamma v''_{aa} + v''_{ca} \left(1 + \gamma + \frac{\gamma^2 u'}{u''} f'' \right) \right]^2 + 4\gamma v''_{ca} u' f''.$$

If $\Delta > 0$, the four eigenvalues are real and the local dynamics are monotonic. If $\Delta < 0$, the eigenvalues are complex and the local dynamics display damped oscillations.

The condition $\Delta > 0$ is always satisfied if e.g., $v''_{ca} = 0$, which corresponds to the case in which inherited tastes do not affect the marginal utility of consumption when adult (the standard monotonicity result for optimal growth). More surprisingly, the condition $\Delta > 0$ is satisfied if u'' or f'' is close enough to zero, i.e., if $u(\cdot)$ and $f(\cdot)$ are not too concave. Indeed, a small u'' implies a large value of the squared term, and a small f'' implies a small value of the second – negative – term. Notice also that, even when $\gamma = 1$ (i.e., the planner does not discount the future at all), the condition $\Delta > 0$ is not necessarily satisfied. This implies that the optimal dynamics around the golden rule can be characterized by damped oscillations.

5.3.3 Extensions

When households are altruistic, the parents will take into account the effect of their own consumption on the bequeathed habits. Quoting Becker (1992) again, "they would try to direct the evolution of children's preferences toward raising the utility of children. For example, parents may refrain from smoking even when that gives them much pleasure because their smoking raises the likelihood that the children will smoke. Or they may take children to church, even when not religious, because they believe exposure to religion is good for children. Indeed, many parents stop going after their children leave home." Hence, the optimal behavior of the parents is to promote self-restraint. Applying equation (5.4), the utility of an altruistic household adult in t is

$$\mathcal{V}_t = v(c_t, a_t) + u(d_{t+1}) + \beta \mathcal{V}_{t+1}.$$

In de la Croix and Michel (2001), we have first analyzed in details the dynamics in two regimes, one with and the other without bequest. The regime with (positive) bequest is similar to the analysis of the central planner. The regime without bequest is new. In that case, the parents internalize the intergenerational spillover and direct the evolution of children's aspirations towards raising their utility by restraining their own consumption standard, all other things being equal. We have shown that, in that case, altruism always enhances the accumulation of capital. In the case of over-accumulation, altruism can thus amplify the inefficiency related to the over-accumulation of capital.

Concerning the stability of the equilibrium, inherited standard-of-living aspirations can be responsible for damped oscillations in the regime with positive bequests and for damped or exploding oscillations in the regime with no bequest. Altruism reduces the scope for instability in this last regime. Furthermore, in an example nesting the Barro (1974)–Weil (1987) model, we have shown that bequests can be positive even if this is never the case in the Barro–Weil economy. This is because parents wish to provide their children with more resources to fulfill their inherited aspirations.

Another extension consists in analyzing the dynamics of growth when two externalities are present: inherited human capital and inherited aspirations.

As stressed in section 5.2, the crucial element for explaining sustained growth is the presence of a *positive* externality that makes individual-specific human capital increasing in the human capital of the previous generation. However, as emphasized by Easterlin (1971), income growth from one generation to another is a two-edged sword. His argument is that "in a steadily growing economy, successive generations are raised in increasingly affluent households and hence develop successively higher living aspirations." This "intergenerational taste effect" is the negative externality studied above that makes the future generations more and more demanding along the growth process. Extending the model of section 5.2.3, de la Croix (1998) studies the equilibrium where the maximization program of the individual is

$$\max_{c_t, s_t, d_{t+1}, e_{t-1}} v(c_t, a_t) + u(d_{t+1}),$$

subject to

$$c_t + s_t = w_t h_t - R_t e_{t-1},$$

$$d_{t+1} = R_{t+1} s_t,$$

$$h_t = \phi(h_{t-1}, e_{t-1}).$$

The state variables a_t and h_{t-1} responsible for the inter-generational externalities are given. The principal finding of is that the interaction of these two externalities leads to more complex dynamics. This arises because higher human capital of parents has two competing effects: It increases the incentive to invest in education via the transmission of human capital on the one hand. On the other hand, a high level of parents' human capital, implying that their consumption is high, lowers children's propensity to save via the aspiration effect. The dynamics that result depend on the relative strengths of these two effects. In particular, there can be poverty traps: an economy with slightly lower initial education or slightly higher aspirations than a critical surface will stagnate, whilst one on the other side of the critical surface will grow.

The preceding model is used by Croissant and Jean-Pierre (2001) to study the impact of international aid (transfers) on developing countries. Aid increases current consumption and future aspirations, reduces savings, and thus lowers the resources available to finance education spending. This negative habit effect might counteract the direct positive effect on the resources of the economy.

5.3.4 Conclusion

The standard approach to economics is to assume that agents maximize an objective function with preferences that depend at any point in time on the control variables chosen at that time (consumption, leisure). These preferences are, by definition, independent of past choices and others' choices. This simplification is quite useful in addressing many economic issues, but it is fair to recognize that a large number of choices depend very much on past actions and inter-individual relationships. Accordingly, the standard micro-economic approach to preferences has been extended to incorporate past experiences and social forces into tastes in order to analyze issues like addiction, peer pressure, and catching up. Our aim is to use these *extended preferences* to model the making of standard-of-living aspirations in an inter-generational context and their effect on macro-economic variables; we then analyze to what extent these mechanisms provide plausible explanations of why growth is not a steady process and how fluctuations in output and employment are propagated. We show in particular that this assumption introduces a mechanism that can be responsible for oscillations.

We conclude that the microeconomic approach to extended preferences can be fruitful in analyzing macroeconomic issues like cycles and growth. Including past consumption expenditure in the utility function is helpful in modeling the desire to maintain or enhance an inherited standard of living. Many further extensions are possible. In pursuing this line of research, one should however keep in mind that when one puts things like status into the utility function, one is in danger of losing the discipline standard economic modeling provides (Postlewaite (1999)). A careful analysis of both the theoretical and the empirical foundations of the modeling choices is thus required to build parsimonious macro-economic models with endogenous tastes.

5.4 MACRO-ECONOMICS AND GENERAL EQUILIBRIUM

In his book, Farmer (1993) argues for the future of macro-economics as a branch of general equilibrium theory. His main theme is that macro-economics is best viewed as the study of equilibrium environments in which the welfare theorems break down. This approach allows him to discuss the role of policy in a context in which it may serve some purpose.

This book is clearly in line with that statement. However, the above claim may cover different approaches to general equilibrium. The assumptions about the completeness of markets, the existence of goods given in nominal terms, the time span considered, and the initial conditions are all interrelated in an intricate way. We intend to provide here some clarifications of these issues.

There are two main streams in the formulation of the overlapping generations model. The first one is the one followed in this book. In this stream, initiated by Allais (1947) and Diamond (1965), the inter-temporal equilibrium is a sequence of temporary equilibria with perfect foresight on the return on savings. The good produced in this period is the numeraire of the temporary equilibrium of this period. The only way to transfer resources to the future is to buy capital goods: Productive capital is the only support to savings.

The second one directly flows from the Walrasian general equilibrium approach in Arrow and Débreu (1954) and Debreu (1959) and assumes the existence of markets for all goods. Extending their approach to a model with an infinite number of periods, one assumes that there is a full set of futures markets open before the economy starts to operate and that all exchanges for future goods can be contracted. In this complete market approach, inter-generational exchange needs no support; any good can be sold or purchased between all agents which supply and demand this good.[27] In this general formulation, one may assume that time goes from $-\infty$ to $+\infty$. In the usual approach, time goes from 0 to $+\infty$ and all markets open at date 0. There is also an initial stock of capital K_0, and one then needs to specify the owners of this stock.

Our main conclusion will be that the model developed along the lines of Diamond (1965) belongs to the general equilibrium family with an infinite number of agents and goods. More precisely, it is the equilibrium in the the Arrow–Debreu economy from 0 to $+\infty$ where the initial stock of capital K_0 belongs to the first old generation.[28] For the economy from $-\infty$ to $+\infty$, there is no initial condition, and even for a given level of capital at date 0, the Arrow–Debreu equilibrium is not determined. Imposing the meaningful assumption of Diamond that physical capital is the only support for savings, the equilibrium becomes determined.

We start by studying the structure of the economy with the Arrow–Debreu full set of markets. We then define the sequence equilibrium from $-\infty$ to $+\infty$ and the Arrow–Debreu market equilibria from 0 to $+\infty$. We then compare the different approaches and end with an example.

5.4.1 Modeling Arrow–Debreu Market Equilibria

There are two types of agents, consumers and firms, and there is an infinite sequence of periods going from $-\infty$ to $+\infty$. In this approach there is no initial condition. An alternative approach consists in introducing a condition at $t = 0$, which will be considered later.

In each period t, there are two goods, a physical good with price P_t, which can be consumed or accumulated as capital, and labor with price W_t. Agents behave competitively. At each date t, N_t consumers are born and live for two periods.

As in the Arrow–Debreu approach, all agents are defined by their endowment and preferences. Firms are defined by their production set. There is no explicit property of firms as the firms do not make pure profit at equilibrium (constant return to scale). There is an infinity of agents and markets.[29]

---

[27] In the overlapping generations model where households have a finite lifetime, we should assume that each agent has a representative which can intervene on his behalf on all markets.

[28] The distribution of this initial capital among the members of the first old generation does not matter; the important assumption bears on the inter-generational distribution of initial capital.

[29] For an extension of the Arrow–Debreu approach to an infinity of goods, see Bewley (1972).

A consumer born at date t is endowed with one unit of labor in period t. His income consists in the nominal wage W_t that he receives at t. He purchases c_t units of the good produced in period t at a price P_t, and d_{t+1} units of the good produced in period $t+1$ at a price P_{t+1}. Each young individual maximizes (compare with (1.5))

$$u(c_t) + \beta u(d_{t+1})$$
$$\text{s.t.} \quad W_t \geq P_t c_t + P_{t+1} d_{t+1},$$
$$c_t \geq 0, \quad d_{t+1} \geq 0.$$

The decision of the household thus depends on the prices W_t, P_t, and P_{t+1}. In principle, each household can buy any good produced in the economy (from $-\infty$ to $+\infty$). However, only goods produced at t and $t+1$ enter in the utility function of the agent born in t.

The representative firm produces one good Y_t with two inputs: L_t units of labor and $K_t = I_{t-1}$ units of goods produced in period $t-1$, bought at the price P_{t-1}: $Y_t = F(K_t, L_t)$. The function F is the standard neo-classical production function. The firm maximizes its profit:

$$P_t Y_t - P_{t-1} K_t - W_t L_t$$
$$\text{s.t.} \quad Y_t \leq F(K_t, L_t),$$
$$K_t \geq 0, \quad L_t \geq 0.$$

Hence, this firm intervenes in three markets: the physical good produced in $t-1$ (capital input), the labor of time t, and the physical good of time t (output). Its production set is[30]

$$\{(-L_t, -I_{t-1}, Y_t); Y_t \leq F(I_{t-1}, L_t), I_{t-1} \geq 0, L_t \geq 0\}.$$

Let (P_t, W_t) be an infinite sequence of positive prices, t going from $-\infty$ to $+\infty$. Under the hypothesis **H1** on the utility function, the consumers' maximization problem leads to the following standard first-order conditions:

$$u'(c_t) = \lambda_t P_t,$$
$$\beta u'(d_{t+1}) = \lambda_t P_{t+1},$$
$$W_t = P_t c_t + P_{t+1} d_{t+1},$$

where λ_t is the Lagrange multiplier of the budget constraint. The arbitrage condition is thus

$$u'(c_t) = \frac{P_t}{P_{t+1}} \beta u'(d_{t+1}),$$

---

[30] Considering that investment and installed capital are different goods, we can equivalently consider two types of firms with the following production sets: the investment firm, whose production set is $\{(-I_{t-1}, K_t); K_t \leq I_{t-1}, K_t \geq 0\}$, and the producing firm with $\{(-L_t, -K_t, Y_t); Y_t \leq F(K_t, L_t), K_t \geq 0, L_t \geq 0\}$.

to be compared with equation (1.7) of chapter 1. The system of first-order condition characterizes demand functions that are well defined in each period. These functions,

$$c_t = c(W_t, P_t, P_{t+1}), \tag{5.79}$$

$$d_{t+1} = d(W_t, P_t, P_{t+1}), \tag{5.80}$$

are homogeneous of degree 0 with respect to the prices. They are related to the savings function of chapter 1 through

$$c(W_t, P_t, P_{t+1}) = \frac{W_t}{P_t} - s\left(\frac{W_t}{P_t}, \frac{P_t}{P_{t+1}}\right),$$

and

$$d(W_t, P_t, P_{t+1}) = \frac{P_t}{P_{t+1}} s\left(\frac{W_t}{P_t}, \frac{P_t}{P_{t+1}}\right).$$

Under the hypothesis **H2** the firm produces a positive quantity of good if and only if the marginal productivities are equal to the factor prices:

$$P_t F'_L(K_t, L_t) = W_t, \tag{5.81}$$

$$P_t F'_K(K_t, L_t) = P_{t-1}, \tag{5.82}$$

which imply zero profit by Euler's theorem.

5.4.2 Arrow–Debreu Market Equilibria from $-\infty$ to $+\infty$

Definition 5.5 (Arrow–Debreu equilibrium)
An Arrow–Debreu equilibrium with positive production is a sequence of positive prices (P_t, W_t) and of non-negative quantities (c_t, d_t, K_t, L_t), t going from $-\infty$ to $+\infty$, such that for all t the following equations are satisfied:

$$L_t = N_t, \tag{5.83}$$

$$F(K_t, L_t) = N_t c_t + N_{t-1} d_t + K_{t+1}, \tag{5.84}$$

together with the individual equilibrium conditions (5.79), (5.80), (5.81), (5.82).

Equation (5.83) is the equilibrium condition on the labor market, and equation (5.84) is the equilibrium condition on the market of the physical good. These two conditions applied to each period are necessary to define the equilibrium. Indeed, Walras's law cannot be used in this economy with an infinite number of goods.

Proposition 5.6 (Characterization of an Arrow–Debreu equilibrium)
An Arrow–Debreu equilibrium is characterized by a sequence of positive capital stocks (K_t) which satisfy the following equation:

$$F(K_t, N_t) = N_t \tilde{c}(K_t, K_{t+1}) + N_{t-1} \tilde{d}(K_{t-1}, K_t) + K_{t+1}, \qquad (5.85)$$

where

$$\tilde{c}(K_t, K_{t+1}) = c(F_L'(K_t, N_t), 1, F_K'(K_{t+1}, N_{t+1})^{-1}),$$
$$\tilde{d}(K_{t-1}, K_t) = c(F_L'(K_{t-1}, N_{t-1}), 1, F_K'(K_t, N_t)^{-1}).$$

Proof: Equation (5.85) is obtained from (5.83) and (5.84) by using the homogeneity of the demand functions (5.79) and (5.80) and the values of the relative prices given by (5.81) and (5.82). Conversely, if a sequence (K_t) satisfies (5.85) for all t, then $L_t = N_t$, $c_t = \tilde{c}(\cdot)$, and $d_t = \tilde{d}(\cdot)$, and the relative prices satisfying (5.81) and (5.82) determine a unique equilibrium. Only the normalization of prices is not fixed. ∎

Equation (5.85) is a second-order difference equation in K_t, and the value of K_t in one date is generally not sufficient to determine the equilibrium. We illustrate this in an example (section 5.4.5). The comparison with the intertemporal equilibrium approach of section 1.4 will help to interpret the result.

Before this comparison let us clarify in what sense definition 5.5 corresponds to an Arrow–Debreu equilibrium. As in the Arrow–Debreu system, the agents are defined by the preferences and their endowment, and firms are defined by their production set. All prices are such that markets clear at all time. Although there are infinite numbers of agents and markets, there are only a finite number of agents announcing positive demand or supply on each market. To complete the picture, one might suppose that all agents are represented with their supply and demand before the economy starts to operate and production takes place.

5.4.3 Sequence Equilibrium from $-\infty$ to $+\infty$

In section 1.5, we have defined an inter-temporal equilibrium with perfect foresight as a sequence of temporary equilibria where physical capital is the support of savings:

$$K_{t+1} = N_t s_t, \qquad (5.86)$$

with

$$s_t = s(F_L'(K_t, N_t), F_K'(K_{t+1}, N_{t+1})). \qquad (5.87)$$

This equilibrium is a sequence equilibrium, as it specifies restrictions on the availability of markets at a sequence of dates (Radner (1972)). We define a sequence equilibrium as follows:

Definition 5.6 (Sequence market equilibrium)
A sequence equilibrium is a path (c_t, d_t, s_t, K_t) with t going from $-\infty$ to $+\infty$ such that equations (5.86)–(5.87) hold for all t and the consumptions are defined by

$$c_t = F_L'(K_t, N_t) - s_t \quad and \quad d_t = F_K'(K_t, N_t)s_{t-1}.$$

There is a clear difference between this sequence equilibrium and the Arrow–Debreu general equilibrium. The first type is characterized by a first-order difference equation:

$$K_{t+1} = N_t s(F_L'(K_t, N_t), F_K'(K_{t+1}, N_{t+1})), \tag{5.88}$$

and the second type is characterized by a second-order difference equation (5.85). However, we can show that

Proposition 5.7 (Sequence equilibrium as a general equilibrium)
The sequence equilibrium (solution to (5.88)) is an Arrow–Debreu equilibrium (solution to (5.85)) in the economy from $-\infty$ to $+\infty$.

Proof: By definition of the sequence equilibrium, the consumptions levels are given by

$$c_t = F_L'(K_t, N_t) - s(F_L'(K_t, N_t), F_K'(K_{t+1}, N_{t+1}))$$
$$= \tilde{c}(K_t, K_{t+1}),$$
$$d_t = F_K'(K_t, N_t)s_{t-1}$$
$$= \tilde{d}(K_{t-1}, K_t).$$

We deduce from equation (5.88) that

$$N_t c_t = N_t F_L'(K_t, N_t) - K_{t+1},$$
$$N_{t-1} d_t = F_K'(K_t, N_t)K_t.$$

Hence, we have

$$N_t c_t + N_{t-1} d_t + K_{t+1} = K_t F_K'(K_t, N_t) + N_t F_L'(K_t, N_t) = F(K_t, N_t),$$

by the Euler theorem. With the expressions of $c_t = \tilde{c}(\cdot)$ and $d_t = \tilde{d}(\cdot)$ we obtain equation (5.85) which characterized an Arrow–Debreu equilibrium. ∎

Any equilibrium where physical capital is the sole support for savings is an Arrow–Debreu equilibrium: it is indeed a particular case of a general equilibrium which satisfies the additional condition

$$N_{t-1}\, \tilde{d}(K_{t-1}, K_t) = K_t F'_K(K_t, N_t),$$

i.e., the equality between the consumption of the old agents and the income of capital. This is also equivalent to the equality between the savings of the young agents and the investment in the capital stock:

$$K_{t+1} = N_t s_t = N_t \frac{W_t}{P_t} - N_t \tilde{c}(K_t, K_{t+1}).$$

The sequence equilibrium, which is similar to the model of chapter 1 but with t going from $-\infty$ to $+\infty$, can thus be seen as a special case of an Arrow–Debreu market general equilibrium in which the unique possible support for savings is the stock of physical capital. Without any restriction on the support of savings, there is a wider set of general equilibria, as if there were other supports to savings. This will be further analyzed in an example (section 5.4.5).

5.4.4 Arrow–Debreu Equilibria from 0 to $+\infty$

We have so far assumed that time goes from $-\infty$ to $+\infty$, so that we do not need any initial condition. When time goes from 0 to $+\infty$, it is necessary to specify the endowment of the agents in period 0. In the Diamond model, the definition of the temporary equilibrium implies that the real capital stock existing in period 0 belongs to the agents which are old in $t = 0$. In the Arrow–Debreu approach, we are not obliged to make this assumption.

The firm in period 0 uses labor as the sole input and produces

$$Y_0 = F_0(L) = F(K_0, L).$$

Its production set is

$$\{(-L, Y);\ L \geq 0,\ 0 \leq Y \leq F(K_0, L)\}.$$

Maximizing its profit $P_0 Y - W_0 L$, one obtains a profit level

$$\pi_0 = P_0 F(K_0, L_0) - W_0 L_0 = P_0 F'_K(K_0, L_0) K_0$$

with the demand for labor L_0 defined by

$$P_0 F'_L(K_0, L_0) = W_0.$$

At equilibrium, $L_0 = N_0$. In the Arrow–Debreu logic, the profits are distributed to the agents, who detain given shares of this firm.

If one assumes that the first old agents detain the total amount of shares and that these shares are equally distributed among them, each old agent receives π_0 / N_{-1}. Maximizing their utility, they consume their whole income:

$$P_0 d_0 = \frac{\pi_0}{N_{-1}} = P_0 F'_K(K_0, N_0) \frac{K_0}{N_{-1}}.$$

Proposition 5.8 (Arrow–Debreu equilibrium with private ownership)
An Arrow–Debreu equilibrium from 0 to $+\infty$ with initial capital K_0 equally detained by the first old agents coincides with the inter-temporal equilibrium defined in chapter 1: equation (5.88) holds for all t.

Proof: At time 0 we have $N_{-1} d_0 = F_K'(K_0, N_0) K_0$, and the equilibrium condition (5.85) at time 0 is

$$F(K_0, N_0) = N_0 \tilde{c}(K_0, K_1) + N_{-1} d_0 + K_1,$$

from which we deduce that

$$N_0 \tilde{c}(K_0, K_1) = F(K_0, N_0) - K_0 F_K'(K_0, N_0) - K_1$$
$$= N_0 F_L'(K_0, N_0) - K_1.$$

Thus,

$$K_1 = N_0[F_L'(K_0, N_0) - \tilde{c}(K_0, K_1)]$$
$$= N_0 s(F_L'(K_0, N_0), F_K'(K_1, N_1)).$$

The condition (5.88) is thus verified at time 0. Using the resource constraint of young agent in $t = 0$, we have

$$P_1 d_1 = W_0 - P_0 c_0$$

$$d_1 = \frac{P_0}{P_1} \left(\frac{W_0}{P_0} - c_0 \right)$$

$$= F_K'(K_1, N_1)[F_L'(K_0, N_0) - \tilde{c}(K_0, K_1)] = F_K'(K_1, N_1) \frac{K_1}{N_0},$$

which implies that the following holds:

$$N_0 d_1 = F_K'(K_1, N_1) K_1.$$

The same reasoning as above, using equation (5.85) at time 1, implies

$$K_2 = N_1 s(F_L'(K_1, N_1), F_K'(K_2, N_2)).$$

By induction, the condition (5.88) holds for all t and the Arrow–Debreu market equilibrium coincides with the inter-temporal equilibrium of chapter 1. ∎

Instead of giving all the shares to the old agents, one might have different property allocation schemes and thus different economies. For example, the young agents at time 0 might well be born with some shares. By doing so, we modify the demands of the agents, and their consumptions will depend on their share of profits. We thus have different Arrow–Debreu economies indexed by the property allocation scheme. In each of these economies, the equilibrium is determined. Choosing the assumption of Diamond that all shares belong to the first old, we select one of these economies. Stated otherwise, the Diamond economy is the Arrow–Debreu economy where initial old agents consume the entire remuneration of capital, i.e. with the particular value of d_0 given by

$$d_0 = \left(\frac{K_0}{N_{-1}} \right) F'_K(K_0, N_0). \tag{5.89}$$

A Note on the Monetary Approach. Equation (5.89) can be used to discuss the difference between the Allais (1947)–Diamond (1965) approach and the general equilibrium approach with nominal goods or explicit money.

In the Allais–Diamond approach, there is an important restriction which leads to determinacy[31] of the equilibrium: There is no good given in "nominal" value (all goods are real). This is reflected by the determination of d_0.

With explicit money as unique medium of exchange, the general equilibrium approach is a priori restricted to incomplete markets. One agent can demand a consumption good in a pure exchange economy only if he/she holds some money allowing him/her to buy this good (see for example Balasko and Shell (1981)).[32] Money might co-exist with another support for savings, like capital as in Benhabib and Laroque (1988), provided that it has the same rate of return. If the nominal stock of money is exogenous, the price of money is a non-predetermined variable. This leads to the same logic as in the model with bubbles (see section 4.3.5), and indeterminacy of equilibrium might prevail. Considering equation (5.89), it is not enough to fix a nominal value of endowment D_0 for the equilibrium to be determined. In the general equilibrium approach, any price normalization like the choice of P_0 is possible for a given general equilibrium which is characterized only by relative prices. The choice of P_0 modifies the real endowment $d_0 = D_0/P_0$ and thus the general equilibrium. This is the reason why the general equilibrium is not determined when old agents hold a fixed amount of a nominal asset like money. Kehoe and Levine (1985) provide a general treatment of this issue.

---

[31] Determinacy means local uniqueness.

[32] Samuelson (1958) studies exchange economies in which there are two types of equilibria, with or without wealth transmission between different generations. In the simple model with one good per period and two-period-lived agents, the equilibrium without intergenerational exchange is the autarkic equilibrium at which all agents consume their endowment; this equilibrium is unique. The equilibria with inter-generational exchange generally use money, which is the unique non-perishable good, and which has no intrinsic utility, but has a positive value resulting from the belief of the agents (the social contrivance of Samuelson (1958)). This belief in money may be implicit (Gale (1973), Geanakoplos (1987)). In Grandmont (1985), there is money, consumption, and labor. Money has the same role as in the pure exchange economy: it is the unique durable good, having the role of supporting savings. Moreover, in the "monetary" general equilibrium approach, the value of money is positive, implying that there is a restriction that agents cannot transfers wealth to the past. The restriction may or may not be binding, depending on whether agents are willing to make such transfers.

5.4.5 Example

We consider the simple case in which the number of consumers born at date t is constant: $N_t = N$. Their utility is logarithmic, $U(c, d) = \ln(c) + \beta \ln(d)$, and the production function is Cobb–Douglas, $F(K, L) = K^\alpha L^{1-\alpha}$. The consumers' demand functions are

$$c_t = \frac{1}{1 + \beta} \frac{W_t}{P_t},$$

$$d_{t+1} = \frac{\beta}{1 + \beta} \frac{W_t}{P_{t+1}}.$$

The firm's optimality conditions are

$$(1 - \alpha) \left(\frac{K_t}{L_t} \right)^\alpha = \frac{W_t}{P_t},$$

$$\alpha \left(\frac{L_t}{K_t} \right)^{1-\alpha} = \frac{P_{t-1}}{P_t}.$$

Setting $k_t = K_t/N$, the equation (5.85) has the following form:

$$k_t^\alpha = \frac{1}{1 + \beta}(1 - \alpha)k_t^\alpha + \frac{\beta}{1 + \beta}(1 - \alpha)k_{t-1}^\alpha \alpha k_t^{\alpha-1} + k_{t+1}. \qquad (5.90)$$

Let us define the investment rate as

$$x_t = \frac{k_{t+1}}{k_t^\alpha}.$$

With this definition, equation (5.90) is equivalent to the two-equation system

$$k_{t+1} = x_t k_t^\alpha,$$

$$x_t = \alpha + (1 - \alpha)\frac{\beta}{1 + \beta} - \frac{\beta}{1 + \beta}\frac{\alpha(1 - \alpha)}{x_{t-1}}. \qquad (5.91)$$

Any sequence (x_t) satisfying (5.91) is monotonic, and there are two constant solutions to

$$x^S = \alpha \quad \text{and} \quad x^D = (1 - \alpha)\frac{\beta}{1 + \beta}.$$

As we shall see, $x_t = x^D$ corresponds to the dynamics of the Diamond equilibrium, and $x_t = x^S$ defines dynamics leading to the golden rule.

To analyze the dynamics in the two cases $x^S < x^D$ and $x^S > x^D$, we denote by $\underline{x}$ the lower of the two and by $\bar{x}$ the larger.[33] We represent them in figure 5.3

---

[33] Here, the sequence of x_t is similar to the dynamics in the exchange economy studied by Gale (1973).

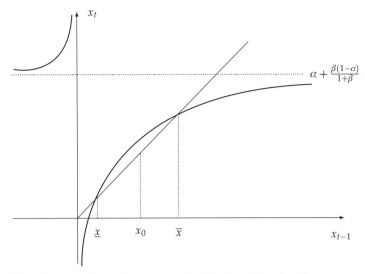

Figure 5.3. The general equilibrium dynamics. The transition function crosses the 45°
line at two points; there are thus two steady states. $\underline{x}$ is the lower and $\bar{x}$ the higher.
Any position x_{t_0} below $\underline{x}$ leads to a negative value for x_t for some $t > t_0$. A sequence
with a position $x'_{t_0} > \bar{x}$ has taken a negative value for some $t < t_0$. But for values of x
belonging to the interval $(\underline{x}, \bar{x})$, there exists a sequence x_t, t going from $-\infty$ to $+\infty$,
which belongs to this interval and satisfies $x_{t_0} = x$.

in the case $\underline{x} \neq \bar{x}$. Any position x_{t_0} smaller than $\underline{x}$ leads to a negative value for
x_t for some $t > t_0$. The sequence with a position $x'_{t_0} > \bar{x}$ has taken a negative
value for some $t < t_0$. But for values of x belonging to the interval $(\underline{x}, \bar{x})$, there
exists a sequence x_t, t going from $-\infty$ to $+\infty$, which belongs to this interval,
and satisfies $x_{t_0} = x$. When x is interior to the interval, $\underline{x} < x_{t_0} < \bar{x}$ then all
these sequences satisfy

$$\lim_{t \to -\infty} x_t = \underline{x} \quad \text{and} \quad \lim_{t \to +\infty} x_t = \bar{x}.$$

Only in the particular case $\underline{x} = \bar{x}$, i.e., $\alpha = (1 - \alpha)\frac{\beta}{1+\beta}$, is the sequence of positive valued x_t which is the solution to (5.91) unique, viz. the constant sequence
$x_t = \underline{x} = \bar{x}$.

In the general case, $\alpha \neq (1 - \alpha)\frac{\beta}{1+\beta}$, any arbitrary value of x_0 belonging
to $(\underline{x}, \bar{x})$ determines a positive sequence x_t that is a solution to (5.91), and
any arbitrary positive value of k_0 determines, with x_t, a unique sequence
satisfying

$$k_{t+1} = x_t k_t^{\alpha}.$$

All these sequences of positive capital stocks satisfy the equilibrium condition
(5.90).

Hence, given any $k_0 > 0$ and any $x_0 \in (\underline{x}, \bar{x})$ there exists a unique Arrow–Debreu general equilibrium (x_t, k_t) taking these values at $t = 0$.

When time goes from 0 to $+\infty$, the initial value of the capital stock is given. There remains one dimension of indeterminacy for the solution. The Arrow–Debreu equilibrium is then determined by the property scheme of the firm in period 0.

Let us now study the Diamond equilibrium as a special case of the Arrow–Debreu general equilibrium approach. Equation (5.88) in intensive terms is

$$k_{t+1} = \frac{\beta}{1 + \beta}(1 - \alpha)k_t^\alpha. \tag{5.92}$$

As $x_t = k_{t+1}k_t^{-\alpha}$, we see that this Arrow–Debreu equilibrium is obtained with the constant sequence:

$$x_t = x^D = \frac{\beta}{1 + \beta}(1 - \alpha).$$

The dynamics of k_t converge to

$$k^D = \left(\frac{\beta}{1 + \beta}(1 - \alpha)\right)^{\frac{1}{1-\alpha}}.$$

For the other constant solution $x_t = x^S = \alpha$, the dynamics of k_t satisfy[34] $k_{t+1} = \alpha k_t^\alpha$ and k_t converges to the golden rule capital stock,

$$k^S = k_{\mathrm{GR}} = \alpha^{1/(1-\alpha)},$$

when t goes to $+\infty$.

Considering a general solution $(x_t, k_t)_{t \geq 0}$, we now consider whether it possible to find simple assets which allow us to make explicit the supports of savings. To do so we shall need the notions, developed in section 2.1, of golden rule and over-accumulation. We distinguish two cases depending on the relative size of k^S and k^D.

The Over-accumulation Case: $k^D > k^S$ (i.e. $x^D > x^S$). In the Diamond model, there is over-accumulation of capital when the steady state to which the economy converges, k^D, is larger than the golden rule capital stock k^S. This occurs when the following holds:

$$\alpha < \frac{\beta}{1 + \beta}(1 - \alpha).$$

---

[34] For these dynamics, savings are equal to profit: $K_{t+1} = F'(K_t, N)K_t$.

Consider a sequence $(k_t, x_t)_{t \geq 0}$ satisfying $k_{t+1} = x_t k_t^\alpha$ and equation (5.91); we assume that the sequence x_t satisfies

$$x^S = \alpha \leq x_t < \frac{\beta}{1+\beta}(1-\alpha) = x^D.$$

According to their demand functions, old agents consume

$$d_t = \frac{\beta}{1+\beta}\frac{W_{t_1}}{P_t} = \frac{\beta}{1+\beta}(1-\alpha)k_{t-1}^\alpha \alpha k_t^{\alpha-1} = \frac{\beta}{1+\beta}(1-\alpha)\alpha\frac{k_t^\alpha}{x_{t-1}}.$$

When x_{t-1} is smaller than $x^D = \frac{\beta}{1+\beta}(1-\alpha)$, then d_t is larger than αk_t^α. The consumption of the old agents exceeds the income from capital. This implies that old agents hold other assets than the capital stock asset. Such assets have no real counterpart; they pay no dividend: they are bubbles. As shown in chapter 4, rational bubbles exist when the Diamond economy is in over-accumulation. The bubble is an asset sold by the old agents to the young agents; for the agents to hold both assets (capital and the bubble) at equilibrium, the increase in its price should be equal to the interest rate. In the example, its level b_t per young agent satisfies

$$(1+r_t)(b_t + k_t) = d_t,$$

and

$$b_t = \frac{\beta}{1+\beta}(1-\alpha)k_{t-1}^\alpha = \left(\frac{x^D}{x_{t-1}} - 1\right)k_t.$$

In the case of over-accumulation, the set of solutions includes, in addition to the Diamond equilibrium, all the sequences of temporary equilibria with rational bubbles.

The Under-accumulation Case: $k^D < k^S$ (i.e. $x^D < x^S$). In the Diamond model, there is under-accumulation of capital when the steady state to which the economy converges, k^D, is smaller than the golden rule capital stock k^S. This occurs when

$$\alpha > \frac{\beta}{1+\beta}(1-\alpha).$$

We assume that the sequence x_t satisfies

$$x^S = \alpha \geq x_t > \frac{\beta}{1+\beta}(1-\alpha) = x^D.$$

Using the same method as above, it can be shown that the consumption of the old is smaller than the corresponding capital income. This case is more difficult to interpret: Solutions are Diamond equilibria with "negative bubbles."

5.4.6 Conclusion

Time plays a different role in the Diamond equilibrium and in the Arrow–Debreu equilibrium. The Diamond economy is a sequence economy (Radner (1972)), i.e., a general equilibrium model in discrete time including specific provision for the availability of markets at a sequence of dates. As stressed by Starr (1987), "This model is in contrast with the Arrow–Debreu model with a full set of futures markets. There, all exchanges for current and future goods [...] are transacted on a market at a single point in time. In the Arrow–Debreu model, there is no need for markets to reopen in the future; economic activity in the future consists simply of the execution of the contracted plans. The Arrow–Debreu model with a full set of futures markets appears unsatisfactory in that it denies commonplace observation: Futures markets for goods are not generally available [...]. The sequence economy model is an alternative that allows formalization and explanation of these observations."

We have shown that the Diamond equilibrium studied in this book coincides with the Arrow–Debreu equilibrium where the unique possible support for savings is the stock of capital. It has the great advantage of being determined under reasonable assumptions. This advantage should not be minimized. Indeed, the interpretation of indeterminacy in the overlapping generations general equilibrium is rather curious: "The equilibrium prices have to be known or foreseen from the beginning of time, even though a finite number of the (infinitely many) agents are alive at the beginning of time. This would not be totally absurd if the equilibrium were unique, so that all agents, once they began to make economic decisions, could calculate and foresee the same sequence of equilibrium prices. With indeterminacy of equilibrium, the agents who are active at the beginning of time must (jointly) pick an equilibrium, and then make sure that all succeeding generations are informed and convinced about the details of the one that they have chosen." (Radner (1991).) In the overlapping generations model, it would be as if expectations were inherited.

Technical Appendices

In these appendices, we have gathered a review of some techniques that are used in the main text. They cover the properties of production functions (section A.1), a simple presentation of useful tools in infinitesimal calculus (section A.2), and some results in dynamical analysis (section A.3). They also provide an exposition of optimization methods, including the value function (section A.4.1) and the Lagrangian approach with the associated transversality conditions (section A.4.2); the description of our numerical examples and a numerical method for deterministic non-linear forward-looking models (section A.5); and some results on the dynamics of distributions with a summary of the characteristics of normal and log-normal distributions (section A.6).

A.1 PRODUCTION FUNCTIONS

A.1.1 Homogeneity

Definition A.1 (Homogeneity)
A function $F(K, L) : \mathbb{R}_{++} \times \mathbb{R}_{++} \to \mathbb{R}_{++}$ is said to be homogeneous of degree
x if

$$F(\lambda K, \lambda L) = \lambda^x F(K, L) \qquad \forall \lambda > 0.$$

Hence, the function $F(K, L)$ is homogeneous of degree one if

$$F(\lambda K, \lambda L) = \lambda F(K, L) \qquad \forall \lambda > 0. \tag{A.1}$$

We assume that $F(\cdot, \cdot)$ is twice continuously differentiable. The first derivatives of a homogeneous function $F(\cdot, \cdot)$ of degree one are themselves homogeneous of degree zero. Indeed, taking the derivatives of both sides of equation (A.1) with respect to K leads to

$$\lambda F'_K(\lambda K, \lambda L) = \lambda F'_K(K, L).$$

Simplifying by λ leads to

$$F'_K(\lambda K, \lambda L) = F'_K(K, L),$$

showing that F'_K is homogeneous of degree zero.

Similarly, the second order derivatives of a homogeneous function of degree one F are homogeneous of degree -1:

$$\lambda F''_{KK}(\lambda K, \lambda L) = F''_{KK}(K, L).$$

Using the fact that, $\forall K, L > 0$,

$$F(K, L) = L F\left(\frac{K}{L}, 1\right),$$

the average productivities can be expressed as functions of K/L alone:

$$\frac{F(K, L)}{K} = \frac{F(K/L, 1)}{K/L} \quad \text{and} \quad \frac{F(K, L)}{L} = F\left(\frac{K}{L}, 1\right).$$

The marginal productivities can also be expressed as functions of K/L alone:

- By the homogeneity of degree zero of $F'_K(K, L)$,

$$F'_K(K, L) = F'_K\left(\frac{K}{L}, 1\right).$$

- By differentiation of $F(K, L) = L F(K/L, 1)$, we obtain

$$F'_L(K, L) = F\left(\frac{K}{L}, 1\right) - \frac{K}{L} F'_K\left(\frac{K}{L}, 1\right). \tag{A.2}$$

A property of homogeneous functions of degree one is Euler's theorem:

Proposition A.1 (Euler's theorem)
If the function $F(K, L) : \mathbb{R}_{++} \times \mathbb{R}_{++} \to \mathbb{R}_{++}$ is homogeneous of degree 1, we have

$$F(K, L) = F'_K(K, L)K + F'_L(K, L)L \qquad \forall K, L > 0 \tag{A.3}$$

This result is directly obtained by multiplying both sides of equation (A.2) by L.

We may differentiate (A.3) with respect to K to derive the properties of the second derivative F''_{KK}:

$$F''_{KL}(K, L) = -\frac{K}{L} F''_{KK}(K, L).$$

Similarly, we differentiate (A.3) with respect to L:

$$F''_{KL}(K, L) = -\frac{L}{K} F''_{LL}(K, L).$$

Hence, $F''_{LL}(K, L)$ has always the same sign as $F''_{KK}(K, L)$, and $F''_{KL}(K, L)$ has the opposite sign. Moreover, we have

$$F''_{LL}(K, L) F''_{KK}(K, L) - F''_{KL}(K, L)^2 = 0.$$

A.1.2 Limits of $f(k)$ and $f'(k)$

In this subsection, we study the implications of **H2** on the production function. We have

$$F(K, L) = Lf(k), \qquad k = \frac{K}{L}, \qquad f(k) = F(k, 1).$$

Assume now **H2**: For all $k > 0$, one has $f(k) > 0$, $f'(k) > 0$, and $f''(k) < 0$.

We first notice that any monotonic function defined in $]0, +\infty[$ admits limits at the end points of the interval (i.e. when $k \to 0$ and $k \to +\infty$). These limits are finite or infinite.

- The limit of $f(k)$ when $k \to 0$, $k > 0$ is finite and non-negative, because $f(k)$ is increasing and bounded from below by 0:

$$f(0+) = \lim_{k \to 0, k > 0} f(k) \in \mathbb{R}_+.$$

  With $f(0) = f(0+)$, f is continuous on $\mathbb{R}_+$.
- The limit of $f(k)$ when $k \to +\infty$ is positive, finite or infinite:

$$f(+\infty) = \lim_{k \to +\infty} f(k) \in \mathbb{R}_{++} \cup \{+\infty\}.$$

- The limit of the marginal productivity of capital, $f'(k)$, when $k \to 0$, $k > 0$, is positive, finite or infinite, since $f'(k)$ is decreasing and positive:

$$f'(0+) = \lim_{k \to 0, k > 0} f'(k) \in \mathbb{R}_{++} \cup \{+\infty\}.$$

- The limit of $f'(k)$ when $k \to +\infty$ is finite and non-negative, because $f'(k)$ is decreasing and bounded from below by 0:

$$f'(+\infty) = \lim_{k \to +\infty} f'(k) \in \mathbb{R}_+.$$

Example: The CES production function is given by

$$f(k) = A[\alpha k^{-\rho} + (1 - \alpha)]^{-1/\rho}, \qquad \rho > -1, \quad \rho \neq 0,$$

$$f'(k) = \alpha A[\alpha + (1 - \alpha)k^\rho]^{-\frac{1+\rho}{\rho}}.$$

For $\rho = 0$, we have (see below, the Cobb–Douglas as a limit case)

$$f(k) = Ak^\alpha, \qquad f'(k) = \alpha Ak^{\alpha-1}$$

The limits of the function are

$$\lim_{k \to 0, k > 0} f(k) = \begin{cases} A(1-\alpha)^{-1/\rho} & \text{for} \quad -1 < \rho < 0, \\ 0 & \text{for} \quad \rho \geq 0, \end{cases}$$

$$\lim_{k \to +\infty} f(k) = \begin{cases} +\infty & \text{for} \quad -1 < \rho \leq 0, \\ A(1-\alpha)^{-1/\rho} & \text{for} \quad \rho > 0. \end{cases}$$

The production $f(0)$ is not equal to 0 with a CES function if $\rho < 0$, i.e., if production factors are high substitutes. In that case, it is possible to produce without capital. The function $f(k)$ is bounded from above when $\rho > 0$, i.e., when factors are complements in the production process.

The limits of the derivatives are

$$\lim_{k \to 0, k > 0} f'(k) = \begin{cases} +\infty & \text{for} \quad -1 < \rho \leq 0, \\ A\alpha^{-1/\rho} & \text{for} \quad \rho > 0, \end{cases}$$

$$\lim_{k \to +\infty} f'(k) = \begin{cases} A\alpha^{-1/\rho} & \text{for} \quad -1 < \rho < 0, \\ 0 & \text{for} \quad \rho \geq 0. \end{cases}$$

The marginal productivity of capital does not necessarily tend to zero when $k \to +\infty$. Indeed, when factors are high substitutes, the marginal productivity tends to a positive constant.

A.1.3 The Marginal Productivity of Labor

The marginal productivity of labor is given by

$$\omega(k) = f(k) - kf'(k) = F'_L(K, L) > 0.$$

Let us analyze the properties of $\omega(k)$. We first notice that $\omega(k)$ is increasing:

$$\omega'(k) = -kf''(k) > 0.$$

Let us show that it is positive valued. The function $f(\cdot)$ is continuous on $[0, k]$ and differentiable on $]0, k[$. Following the mean value theorem for derivatives (see section A.2.1), $\exists \theta, 0 < \theta < 1$, such that

$$f(k) - f(0) = kf'(\theta k).$$

Since $f'(k)$ is decreasing, $f'(\theta k) > f'(k)$, and we deduce that

$$\omega(k) = f(k) - kf'(k) > f(0) \geq 0.$$

Hence, $\omega(k) > 0 \ \forall k > 0$.
    Moreover, $f(k) > \omega(k) > f(0)$ implies

$$\omega(0) = \lim_{k \to 0, k > 0} \omega(k) = f(0),$$

and we have also

$$\lim_{k \to 0} kf'(k) = 0.$$

A.1.4 The Limit of $\omega(k)/k$

The assumption **H2** implies that

$$\lim_{k \to +\infty} \frac{\omega(k)}{k} = 0.$$

To demonstrate this property, we first notice that $\omega(k)/k$ measures the gap between the average and the marginal productivity of capital:

$$\frac{\omega(k)}{k} = \frac{f(k)}{k} - f'(k).$$

The ratio $f(k)/k$ is decreasing (derivative $= -\omega(k)/k^2 < 0$) and positive; it admits thus a limit $l_1 \geq 0$ when $k \to +\infty$. $f'(k)$ is decreasing and positive; it admits thus a limit $l_2 \geq 0$ when $k \to +\infty$. We apply the mean value theorem for derivatives (section A.2.1) to k and $2k$:

$$f(2k) - f(k) = (2k - k)f'(k(1 + \theta)) \qquad \text{with} \quad 0 < \theta < 1.$$

This yields

$$\frac{2f(2k)}{2k} - \frac{f(k)}{k} = f'(k(1 + \theta)).$$

Taking the limit when $k \to +\infty$, we obtain $2l_1 - l_1 = l_2, l_1 = l_2$, and

$$\lim_{k \to +\infty} \frac{\omega(k)}{k} = l_1 - l_2 = 0.$$

The limit on the other side of its definition interval,

$$\lim_{k \to 0} \frac{\omega(k)}{k},$$

may not exist if both $f(k)/k$ and $f'(k)$ go to $+\infty$ when k goes to zero. In the Cobb–Douglas case, we have

$$\frac{\omega(k)}{k} = A(1 - \alpha)k^{-\alpha}.$$

Hence, $\omega(k)/k$ goes to $+\infty$ when k goes to zero. With the CES production function, we have for the high substitution case that $\omega(0) > 0$, and hence $\omega(k)/k$ goes to $+\infty$ when k goes to zero. In the low substitution case, we have

$$\omega(k) = A(1 - \alpha)(\alpha k^{-\rho} + 1 - \alpha)^{-\frac{1}{\rho} - 1},$$

$$\frac{\omega(k)}{k} = A(1 - \alpha)\left(\alpha k^{\frac{-\rho^2}{1+\rho}} + (1 - \alpha)k^{\frac{\rho}{1+\rho}}\right)^{-\frac{1+\rho}{\rho}},$$

and $\omega(k)/k$ goes to zero when k goes to zero. Two examples are presented in figure A.1.

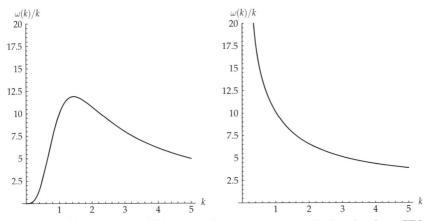

Figure A.1. The function $\omega(k)/k$. The left panel represents the function for a CES production function with low substitution ($\rho > 0$). The limit of the function at 0 is 0. The right panel represents the function for a CES production function with high substitution ($\rho < 0$). The limit of the function at 0 is infinite.

A.1.5 The Cobb–Douglas Function as a Limit Case

We show that the Cobb–Douglas production function can be obtained as a limit case of the CES production function when $\rho \to 0$. As the production function is homogeneous of degree one, the proof can be done on the intensive form. Taking logarithms, we compute the limit when $\rho \to 0$ of

$$-\frac{1}{\rho} \ln[\alpha k^{-\rho} + (1 - \alpha)] + \ln A.$$

This expression can be rearranged into

$$-\frac{1}{\rho} \ln[1 + \alpha(k^{-\rho} - 1)] + \ln A.$$

Recognizing that $\ln(1 + x) \sim x$ when $x \to 0$, we obtain

$$-\frac{1}{\rho} \ln[1 + \alpha(k^{-\rho} - 1)] \sim -\frac{1}{\rho}\alpha(k^{-\rho} - 1).$$

Since $y - 1 \sim \ln y$ when $y \to 1$, we obtain

$$-\frac{1}{\rho}\alpha(k^{-\rho} - 1) \sim -\frac{1}{\rho}\alpha \ln(k^{-\rho}).$$

Hence,

$$\lim_{\rho \to 0} -\frac{1}{\rho} \ln[\alpha k^{-\rho} + (1 - \alpha)] + \ln A = \alpha \ln k + \ln A.$$

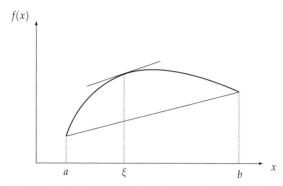

Figure A.2. The mean value theorem for derivatives.

A.2.1 The Mean Value Theorem for Derivatives

The mean value theorem for derivatives that we use is various proofs is the following:

Proposition A.2 (Mean value theorem for derivatives)
If $f(x)$ is a real valued function that is continuous in $[a, b]$ and differentiable in $]a, b[$, then there exists a point $\xi \in]a, b[$ such that $[f(b) - f(a)]/(b - a) = f'(\xi)$.

In geometrical terms, there is always a point $\{\xi, f(\xi)\}$ with $a < \xi < b$ at which the tangent to the function is parallel to the line passing through $\{a, f(a)\}$ and $\{b, f(b)\}$ (figure A.2).

A.2.2 The Implicit Function Theorem

Consider the equation $f(x, y) = 0$. The implicit function theorem gives us the conditions under which the above equation can be solved for y as a function of x: $y = \phi(x)$.

Proposition A.3 (Implicit function theorem)
Let $f(x, y)$ be continuously differentiable near to (x_0, y_0) at which $f(x_0, y_0) = 0$ and $f'_y(x_0, y_0) \neq 0$. Then, near (x_0, y_0) it is possible to solve the implicit equation $f(x, y) = 0$ uniquely for y in the form $y = \phi(x)$ (i.e., there exists $\epsilon_1 > 0$ and $\epsilon_2 > 0$ such that for any x satisfying $|x - x_0| < \epsilon_1$ there exists a unique y such that $|y - y_0| < \epsilon_2$ and $f(x, y) = 0$), and we have

$$\phi'(x_0) = -\frac{f'_x(x_0, y_0)}{f'_y(x_0, y_0)}.$$

A.2.3 Limits, lim sup, and lim inf

Because we are working in a discrete time environment, sequences are fundamental objects manipulated in this book.

Definition A.2 (Sequence)
A sequence in a set S is a function whose domain is the set of positive integers and whose values are in S.

The definition of a sequence as being a function will allow us to describe sequences in the same terms as one would use to describe functions: monotonic, bounded, increasing, etc.

Definition A.3 (Sub-sequence)
A sub-sequence of $(x_0, x_1, x_2, \ldots)$ is an infinite sequence $(x_{t_1}, x_{t_2}, x_{t_3}, \ldots)$ with $t_1 < t_2 < t_3 < \cdots$.

Let $(x_t)_{t \geq 0}$ be a sequence in $\mathbb{R}$. This sequence can either admit a limit or not. In the special case where (x_t) is a monotonic sequence, we can apply the fundamental theorem of sequences:

Proposition A.4 (Fundamental theorem of sequences)
Every increasing or decreasing sequence in $\mathbb{R}$ tends to a limit which is finite or infinite.

Consider any sequence (x_t) in $\mathbb{R}$. If the limit of (x_t) does not exist, we can define a monotonic sequence $(\bar{x}_t)$ which will admit a limit. For any $t > 0$ we consider

$$\bar{x}_t = \sup_{s \geq 0} x_{t+s} \quad \in \quad \mathbb{R} \cup \{+\infty\}.$$

Here sup is the supremum of the terms of the sub-sequence starting at t.[1]

Clearly the sequence $(\bar{x}_t)$ is monotonic and non-increasing in $\mathbb{R} \cup \{+\infty\}$:

$$\bar{x}_{t+1} \leq \bar{x}_t,$$

and

$$\bar{x}_t = \sup\{x_t, \bar{x}_{t+1}\}.$$

We next introduce the following definition:

---

[1] Notice that a sequence can well be bounded above without having a maximum element. The sup is thus not necessarily reached. Any subset in $\mathbb{R}$ admits a sup in $\mathbb{R} \cup \{+\infty\}$.

Definition A.4 (Limit superior)

The limit superior of x_t, $\limsup_{t\to+\infty} x_t$, is the limit of the sequence $(\bar{x}_t)$:

$$\limsup_{t\to+\infty} x_t = \lim_{t\to+\infty} \sup_{s\geq 0} x_{t+s} = \lim_{t\to+\infty} \bar{x}_t.$$

Since the sequence $(\bar{x}_t)$ is monotonic, its limit always exists, finite or infinite. It is the largest limit of the sub-sequences of (x_t), which converges in $\mathbb{R} \cup \{+\infty\}$. Hence, some subsequences converge to the lim sup and no subsequence converges to a larger number.

Similarly we define

$$\underline{x}_t = \inf_{s\geq 0} x_{t+s} \in \mathbb{R} \cup \{-\infty\}.$$

Clearly the sequence $(\underline{x}_t)$ is monotonic and non-decreasing in $\mathbb{R} \cup \{-\infty\}$. We next define

$$\liminf_{t\to+\infty} x_t = \lim_{t\to+\infty} \inf_{s\geq 0} x_{t+s} = \lim_{t\to+\infty} \underline{x}_t$$

Thus, $\liminf_{t\to+\infty} x_t$ is the smallest limit of the sub-sequences of (x_t) which converge. Some subsequence converges to it, and no subsequence converges to a number smaller than it. Since the sequence $(\underline{x}_t)$ is monotonic, this limit always exists.

When the sequence (x_t) is bounded in $\mathbb{R}$ (i.e., $\exists a, b \in \mathbb{R}$ such that $a < x_t < b$ $\forall t$), then the lim inf and lim sup are finite.

Notice also that $\lim x_t$ exists if and only if $\limsup x_t$ and $\liminf x_t$ are equal. This is for instance the case in the example $\sin(t+1)/(t+1)$, represented in figure A.3: we have $\limsup_{t\to+\infty} = \liminf_{t\to+\infty} = 0$, and the sequence

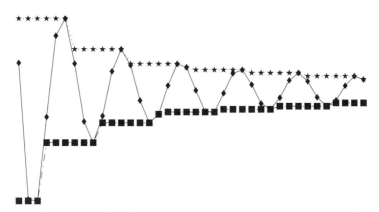

Figure A.3. lim sup and lim inf are monotonic. The sequence $x_t = \sin(t+1)/(t+1)$ is defined in an interval of time and represented by the diamonds. $\bar{x}_t$ is represented by the stars. $\underline{x}_t$ is represented by the squares. $\bar{x}_t$ and $\underline{x}_t$ are monotonic sequences.

converges. A simple example of non-convergence is $x_t = (-1)^t$, where $\lim \sup_{t \to +\infty} = 1$ and $\lim \inf_{t \to +\infty} = -1$.

A.2.4 Limit Points of Multi-dimensional Sequences

Let $(x_t)_{t \geq 0}$ be a sequence in $\mathbb{R}^n$. The point $\bar{x} \in \mathbb{R}^n$ is a limit point (sometimes called cluster point or accumulation point) of x if there exists a sub-sequence x_s of x converging to $\bar{x}$. Stated otherwise:

Definition A.5 (Limit point)
A point $\bar{x}$ is a limit point of the sequence $(x_t)_{t \geq 0}$ if every neighborhood of $\bar{x}$ contains an infinite number of elements of the sequence $(x_t)_{t \geq 0}$.

The theorem used in the main text is the following:

Proposition A.5 (Bounded sequences)
Any sequence in $\mathbb{R}^n$ which is bounded admits at least one limit point $\bar{x} \in \mathbb{R}^n$.

For a one-dimensional sequence (x_t), lim sup x, if it is finite, is the largest limit point of (x_t). Similarly, lim inf x, if finite, is the smallest. The limit of (x_t) exists if and only if all the limit points coincide.

Example: take the sequence $(1, 2, 3, 4, 1, 2, 3, 4, 1, 2, 3, 4, \ldots)$. Then lim sup $= 4$, lim inf $= 1$, and 1, 2, 3, and 4 are limit points.

A.3 DYNAMICAL ANALYSIS

A.3.1 Monotonic Dynamics

Let $l(x)$ be a function defined on some interval $\mathcal{J}$ of $\mathbb{R}$ with values in $\mathcal{J}$. The time path given an initial state $x_0 \in \mathcal{J}$, and the equation

$$x_{t+1} = l(x_t)$$

is uniquely defined. A steady state $x \in \mathcal{J}$ is a solution to $x = l(x)$.

Proposition A.6 (Monotonic dynamics)
If $l(x)$ is continuous and non-decreasing on $\mathcal{J}$, the time path satisfying $x_{t+1} = l(x_t)$ given x_0 is a monotonic sequence. This sequence either converges to a steady state $\bar{x} \in \mathcal{J}$ or goes to a boundary of the interval $\mathcal{J}$. It never goes from one side of a steady state to the other.

Proof: Assume for example $x_t \geq x_{t-1}$. Then we have $l(x_t) \geq l(x_{t-1})$, since l is non-decreasing and $x_{t+1} = l(x_t) \geq x_t = l(x_{t-1})$. Thus, if $l(x_0) \geq x_0$ then $x_1 \geq x_0$ and the inequality $x_{t+1} \geq x_t$ holds for all $t \geq 0$: the sequence x_t is non-decreasing.

Similarly, if $l(x_0) \leq x_0$ the sequence x_t is non-increasing.

A monotonic sequence in $\mathcal{J}$ admits a limit which is finite or infinite. When this limit is a point $\bar{x} \in \mathcal{J}$, then we have, since l is continuous,

$$l(\bar{x}) = \lim_{t \to +\infty} l(x_t) = \lim_{t \to +\infty} x_{t+1} = \bar{x},$$

and $\bar{x}$ is a steady state.

If the limit does not belong to $\mathcal{J}$, it is an end point of the interval (which may be infinite).

Finally, consider any steady state $\bar{x} \in \mathcal{J}$, and assume for example $x_0 \le \bar{x}$. Then $x_1 = l(x_0) \le l(\bar{x}) = \bar{x}$, and by induction for all t, $x_t \le \bar{x}$. Similarly if $x_0 \ge \bar{x}$ then $x_t \ge \bar{x}$ for all t. ∎

A.3.2 Local Stability (Dimension One)

Let $l(x)$ be a function defined on some interval $\mathcal{J}$ of $\mathbb{R}$ with values in $\mathcal{J}$. The time path, given an initial state $x_0 \in \mathcal{J}$ and the equation $x_{t+1} = l(x_t)$, is uniquely defined.

A steady state solution $\bar{x}$ to $\bar{x} = l(\bar{x})$ which is interior to $\mathcal{J}$ is locally stable if for any initial value x_0 near enough to $\bar{x}$, the dynamics starting from x_0 converge to $\bar{x}$.[2] Formally, there exists $\varepsilon > 0$ such that $(\bar{x} - \varepsilon, \bar{x} + \varepsilon) \subset \mathcal{J}$ and for any $x_0 \in (\bar{x} - \varepsilon, \bar{x} + \varepsilon)$ the corresponding dynamics satisfy

$$\lim_{t \to +\infty} x_t = \bar{x}.$$

At a corner steady state like 0, when l is defined on $\mathbb{R}_+$, the corner local stability of 0 is defined similarly but for $x_0 \in (0, \varepsilon)$.

Definition A.6 (Hyperbolicity)
Assume l is continuously differentiable in $\mathcal{J}$. Let $\bar{x}$ be a steady state $\in \mathcal{J}$. If $|l'(\bar{x})| = 1$, then $\bar{x}$ is non-hyperbolic. If $|l'(\bar{x})| \ne 1$, $\bar{x}$ is hyperbolic.

If $\bar{x}$ is non-hyperbolic, its stability type cannot be determined on the basis of its first derivative (the stability type is determined by the terms of the second order).

Proposition A.7 (First-order stability condition)
Let $\bar{x}$ be a hyperbolic steady state $\in \mathcal{J}$. Then

- *if $|l'(\bar{x})| < 1$ then $\bar{x}$ is locally stable;*
- *if $|l'(\bar{x})| > 1$ then $\bar{x}$ is unstable, i.e., it is not locally stable.*

---

[2] This notion of stability is the most commonly used in economics. In dynamical theory, one adds to the condition of convergence the requirement that, when starting near the limit, the sequence not go too far away from it. Formally, $\forall \varepsilon > 0$, $\exists y > 0$ such that $\forall x_0 \in (\bar{x} - y, \bar{x} + y)$, all the terms $x_t \in (\bar{x} - \varepsilon, \bar{x} + \varepsilon)$, $\forall t \ge 0$. This additional condition holds under the assumption of proposition A.7.

Proof: Assume $|l'(\bar{x})| < 1$. Consider b such that $|l'(\bar{x})| < b < 1$. By continuity of $l'(x)$, we have $|l'(x)| < b$ on some interval $(\bar{x} - \varepsilon, \bar{x} + \varepsilon)$ with $\varepsilon > 0$. For any x in this interval, we have, using the mean value theorem for derivatives (section A.2.1),

$$l(x) - l(\bar{x}) = (x - \bar{x})l'(\bar{x} + \theta(x - \bar{x})) \quad \text{with} \quad 0 < \theta < 1,$$

and since $\bar{x} + \theta(x - \bar{x})$ belongs to $(\bar{x} - \varepsilon, \bar{x} + \varepsilon)$,

$$|l(x) - l(\bar{x})| < b|x - \bar{x}|.$$

Thus, for any $x_0 \in (\bar{x} - \varepsilon, \bar{x} + \varepsilon)$, the sequence $x_{t+1} = l(x_t)$ starting at x_0 verifies

$$|x_{t+1} - \bar{x}| = |l(x_t) - l(\bar{x})| < b|x_t - \bar{x}|,$$

and by induction, $x_t \in (\bar{x} - \varepsilon, \bar{x} + \varepsilon)$ for all t and

$$|x_t - \bar{x}| < b^t|x_0 - \bar{x}|,$$

the sequence x_t converges to $\bar{x}$ for all $x_0 \in (\bar{x} - \varepsilon, \bar{x} + \varepsilon)$, and $\bar{x}$ is locally stable. This also implies that the whole sequence remains in the neighborhood of $\bar{x}$. The same proof applies to a corner steady state with $x_0 \in (0, \varepsilon)$.

Assume $|l'(\bar{x})| > 1$, and consider b such that $|l'(\bar{x})| > b > 1$. The same argument as before implies that, for any x in the interval $(\bar{x} - \varepsilon, \bar{x} + \varepsilon)$,

$$|l(x) - l(\bar{x})| > b|x - \bar{x}|,$$

and for a sequence $x_{t+1} = l(x_t)$,

$$|x_t - \bar{x}| > b^t|x_0 - \bar{x}|, \tag{A.4}$$

but only for the terms x_t which belong to $(\bar{x} - \varepsilon, \bar{x} + \varepsilon)$. Since for the sequence x_t verifying (A.4) and $x_0 \neq \bar{x}$ the distance $|x_t - \bar{x}|$ increases geometrically, this distance becomes larger than ε after a finite number of dates. The convergence to $\bar{x}$ implies $|x_t - \bar{x}| < \varepsilon$ after some date t_0, for all $t \geq t_0$, and the preceding result applied to the starting position x_{t_0} excludes this possibility. Hence, for any $x_0 \neq \bar{x}$ the sequence $x_{t+1} = l(x_t)$ does not converge to $\bar{x}$. ∎

The different basic stability types are illustrated in figure A.4.

A.3.3 Linear Dynamics in the Plane

Let us consider the linear dynamics in $\mathbb{R}^2$:

$$\begin{aligned} x_{t+1} &= ax_t + by_t, \\ y_{t+1} &= cx_t + dy_t, \end{aligned} \tag{A.5}$$

or, using matrix notation,

$$\begin{pmatrix} x_{t+1} \\ y_{t+1} \end{pmatrix} = A \begin{pmatrix} x_t \\ y_t \end{pmatrix}, \qquad A = \begin{pmatrix} a & b \\ c & d \end{pmatrix}.$$

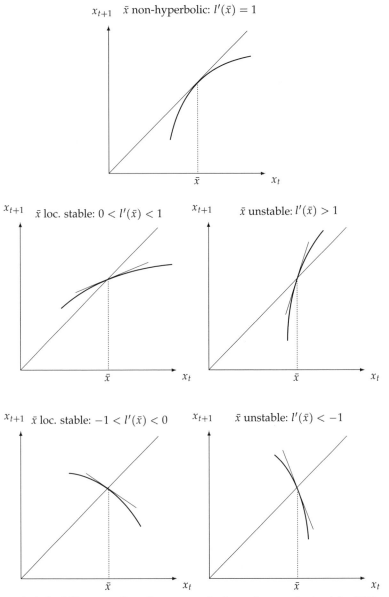

Figure A.4. Stability types. Locally monotonic dynamics are obtained for $l'(\bar{x}) < 0$, and oscillatory dynamics for $l'(\bar{x}) > 0$. $l'(\bar{x}) = 1$ is the non-hyperbolic case.

Let

$$V = \begin{pmatrix} v \\ w \end{pmatrix}$$

be an eigenvector associated to an eigenvalue λ:

$$V \neq 0 \quad \text{and} \quad AV = \lambda V.$$

This means that v and w are not both zero and verify $(a - \lambda)v + bw = 0$ and $cv + (d - \lambda)w = 0$. There exists such an eigenvector if and only if the determinant of the matrix of the coefficients is equal to 0, i.e.,

$$P(\lambda) = \begin{vmatrix} a - \lambda & b \\ c & d - \lambda \end{vmatrix} = 0.$$

$P(\lambda) = (a - \lambda)(d - \lambda) - bc = \lambda^2 - (a + d)\lambda + ad - bc$ is the characteristic polynomial. Its roots are the eigenvalues. We distinguish two cases, according as the eigenvalues are real or complex.

Distinct Real Eigenvalues. Assume that $P(\lambda)$ admits two real roots $\lambda_1 \neq \lambda_2$. This is the case when the discriminant $(a + d)^2 - 4(ad - bc)$ is positive.

Proposition A.8 (Linear dynamics in the plane)
Let V_i be an eigenvector associated to the eigenvalue λ_i, $i = 1, 2$. Any solution to the system (A.5) can be written as

$$\begin{pmatrix} x_t \\ y_t \end{pmatrix} = p\lambda_1^t V_1 + q\lambda_2^t V_2, \tag{A.6}$$

and p and q are uniquely determined by the initial values x_0 and y_0.[3]

$$pV_1 + qV_2 = \begin{pmatrix} x_0 \\ y_0 \end{pmatrix}. \tag{A.7}$$

This property results simply from the definitions and from the fact that the set of solutions is a two-dimensional vector space. For $i = 1, 2$, $\lambda_i^t V_i$ is a solution to (A.5), since

$$A(\lambda_i^t V_i) = \lambda_i^t AV_i = (\lambda_i^{t+1} V_i),$$

and these solutions are linearly independent, since $\lambda_1 \neq \lambda_2$.
   Excluding the cases in which $|\lambda_1| = 1$ or $|\lambda_2| = 1$,[4] we have the following results:

---

[3] In the absence of initial values, all possible solutions are obtained by varying p and q.
[4] In the linear case, it is possible to study the case $|\lambda_1| = 1$ and/or $|\lambda_2| = 1$, but these results do not extend to the non-linear case.

- If $|\lambda_1| \leq |\lambda_2| < 1$, then

$$\text{for all } \begin{pmatrix} x_0 \\ y_0 \end{pmatrix}, \qquad \lim \begin{pmatrix} x_t \\ y_t \end{pmatrix} = \begin{pmatrix} 0 \\ 0 \end{pmatrix},$$

  and the steady state $(0, 0)$ is stable in $\mathbb{R}^2$. Any value for (x_0, y_0) will lead the dynamics to the steady state. The steady state $(0, 0)$ is said to be a *sink*.
- If $1 < |\lambda_1| \leq |\lambda_2|$, all trajectories starting from

$$\begin{pmatrix} x_0 \\ y_0 \end{pmatrix} \neq \begin{pmatrix} 0 \\ 0 \end{pmatrix}$$

  explode. The steady state $(0, 0)$ is unstable. It is said to be a *source*.
- If $|\lambda_1| < 1 < |\lambda_2|$, there exists a unique direction along which the dynamics converge to $(0, 0)$: only for $q = 0$ does the sequence

$$\begin{pmatrix} x_t \\ y_t \end{pmatrix} = p\lambda_1^t V_1$$

  converge to $(0, 0)$. There is a one-dimensional set of initial conditions

$$\begin{pmatrix} x_0 \\ y_0 \end{pmatrix} \in \{pV_1; \; p \in \mathbb{R}\},$$

  which leads to convergence. This implies that for a given x_0, there is only one value of y_0 such that the trajectory converges to the steady state, and this value is given by $y_0 = x_0 w_1/v_1$. Any other initial condition $(q \neq 0)$ leads the dynamics to explode. The steady state $(0, 0)$ is said to be a *saddle point*.[5]

The long-term dynamics is defined by the largest root in absolute value. Indeed, if $|\lambda_1| > |\lambda_2|$,

$$\begin{pmatrix} x_t \\ y_t \end{pmatrix} = \lambda_1^t \left[pV_1 + q \left(\frac{\lambda_2}{\lambda_1} \right)^t V_2 \right],$$

which is equivalent to $\lambda_1^t pV_1$ for large t, when $p \neq 0$.

Thus, we have the following property: Assume $|\lambda_1| > |\lambda_2|$ and $p \neq 0$. Then

- if $\lambda_1 > 0$, the long-run dynamics are monotonic;
- if $\lambda_1 < 0$, the long-run dynamics are oscillating.

Multiple Real Eigenvalues. In the case where $P(\lambda)$ has equal roots $\lambda_1 = \lambda_2 = \lambda$, which arises when $(a + d)^2 - 4(ad - bc) = 0$, the mathematical problem is more complicated but the results are the same. Two sub-cases can be distinguished: (a) The two eigenvectors V_1 and V_2 are still linearly independent, and

---

[5] Some authors use the term "stable in the saddle-point sense." See, e.g., Levhari and Liviatan (1972).

the results are the same as above. (b) Otherwise, we have

$$\begin{pmatrix} x_t \\ y_t \end{pmatrix} = \lambda^t (pV + qt\,W).$$

Consequently,

- If $|\lambda| < 1$, all trajectories converge to $(0, 0)$, which is globally stable in $\mathbb{R}^2$.
- If $|\lambda| > 1$, all trajectories starting from

$$\begin{pmatrix} x_0 \\ y_0 \end{pmatrix} \neq \begin{pmatrix} 0 \\ 0 \end{pmatrix}$$

explode, and $(0, 0)$ is unstable. It is a source.

Complex Eigenvalues. $P(\lambda)$ admits two complex roots: $\lambda_1 = \alpha + i\beta$ and $\lambda_2 = \alpha - i\beta$. Indeed, any complex eigenvalues of a real square matrix must occur in conjugate pairs. This is the case when $(a + d)^2 - 4(ad - bc) < 0$. The same mathematical analysis can be made in the set of complex solutions. When the initial conditions (x_0, y_0) are real, then the solution given by (A.6)–(A.7) is real. There are then two possibilities:

- If $\alpha^2 + \beta^2 = |\lambda_1|^2 = |\lambda_2|^2 < 1$, all trajectories converge to $(0, 0)$, which is globally stable in $\mathbb{R}^2$.
- If $\alpha^2 + \beta^2 > 1$, all trajectories starting from

$$\begin{pmatrix} x_0 \\ y_0 \end{pmatrix} \neq \begin{pmatrix} 0 \\ 0 \end{pmatrix}$$

explode, and $(0, 0)$ is unstable.

A.3.4 Local Stability of Non-linear Dynamics (Dimension 2)

Let $f(x, y)$ and $g(x, y)$ be differentiable functions defined on some open subset $\mathcal{J}$ of $\mathbb{R}^2$. We assume that for all $(x, y) \in \mathcal{J}$, $(f(x, y), g(x, y)) \in \mathcal{J}$. The time path, given an initial state $(x_0, y_0) \in \mathcal{J}$, and the system of equations

$$x_{t+1} = f(x_t, y_t),$$
$$y_{t+1} = g(x_t, y_t)$$

are uniquely defined. A steady state $(\bar{x}, \bar{y})$ solution to $\bar{x} = f(\bar{x}, \bar{y})$ and $\bar{y} = g(\bar{x}, \bar{y})$ which is interior to $\mathcal{J}$ is locally stable if for any initial value (x_0, y_0) near enough to $(\bar{x}, \bar{y})$, the dynamics starting from (x_0, y_0) converge to $(\bar{x}, \bar{y})$. Formally, there exists $\varepsilon > 0$ such that for any (x_0, y_0) such that

$$|x_0 - \bar{x}| + |y_0 - \bar{y}| < \varepsilon,$$

the corresponding dynamics satisfy

$$\lim_{t \to +\infty} x_t = \bar{x} \quad \text{and} \quad \lim_{t \to +\infty} y_t = \bar{y}.$$

Let us take a first-order Taylor expansion of $f(\cdot)$ around a steady state:

$$f(x, y) - f(\bar{x}, \bar{y}) \simeq f'_x(\bar{x}, \bar{y})(x - \bar{x}) + f'_y(\bar{x}, \bar{y})(y - \bar{y}),$$

and similarly for $g(\cdot)$. Consider the linear dynamics

$$\begin{pmatrix} x_{t+1} - \bar{x} \\ y_{t+1} - \bar{y} \end{pmatrix} = \bar{A} \begin{pmatrix} x_t - \bar{x} \\ y_t - \bar{y} \end{pmatrix}, \tag{A.8}$$

where $\bar{A}$ is a 2×2 matrix of the derivatives of $f(\cdot)$ and $g(\cdot)$ taken at the point $(\bar{x}, \bar{y})'$, called the *Jacobian matrix*:

$$\bar{A} = \begin{pmatrix} f'_x(\bar{x}, \bar{y}) & f'_y(\bar{x}, \bar{y}) \\ g'_x(\bar{x}, \bar{y}) & g'_y(\bar{x}, \bar{y}) \end{pmatrix}.$$

The linear system (A.8) can now be analyzed with the tools of section A.3.3.

Definition A.7 (Hyperbolicity in the plane)
Assume $f(\cdot)$ and $g(\cdot)$ continuously differentiable in $\mathcal{J}$. Let $(\bar{x}, \bar{y})$ be a steady state $\in \mathcal{J}$. If the moduli of the eigenvalues of the Jacobian are different from 1 ($|\lambda_1| \neq 1$ and $|\lambda_2| \neq 1$), then $\bar{x}$ is hyperbolic. If either $|\lambda_1| = 1$ or $|\lambda_2| = 1$, $\bar{x}$ is non-hyperbolic.

If the steady state is non-hyperbolic, its stability type cannot be determined on the basis of its eigenvalues (the stability type is determined by the terms of second order.)

Excluding non-hyperbolic steady states, three cases are possible:

- If $|\lambda_1| \leq |\lambda_2| < 1$, the steady state is locally stable. Any initial condition will lead the dynamics to the steady state. The steady state $(\bar{x}, \bar{y})$ is said to be a *sink*.
- If $1 < |\lambda_1| \leq |\lambda_2|$, the steady state is unstable: for any initial condition different from the steady state, the trajectories are locally exploding. The steady state is said to be a *source*.
- If $|\lambda_1| < 1 < |\lambda_2|$, the steady state is a saddle point. For a given initial condition on one variable, there is only one initial value of the other variable such that the trajectory converges to the steady state. Any other value for this variable would lead the trajectory to locally explode.

When the eigenvalues are real and their moduli lie on the same side of 1, the steady state is also called a (stable or unstable) *node*.

From a practical point of view, it is often easier to use the trace and the determinant of the Jacobian matrix. Indeed, the eigenvalues λ_1 and λ_2 are the roots of the characteristic polynomial

$$P(\lambda) = \lambda^2 - T\lambda + D,$$

where $T = f'_x + g'_y$ is the trace of the Jacobian matrix $\bar{A}$, and $D = f'_x g'_y - f'_y g'_x$

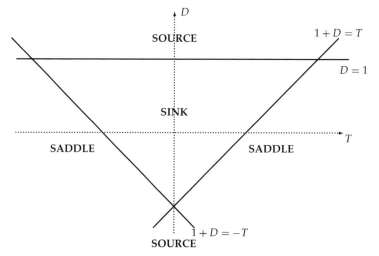

Figure A.5. Analysis of local stability. When $|1 + D| < |T|$, the steady state is a saddle. When $|1 + D| > |T|$ and $|D| < 1$, the steady state is a sink. When $|1 + D| > |T|$ and $|D| > 1$, the steady state is a source.

is its determinant. We can then distinguish the following cases, illustrated in Figure A.5:

- $P(1)P(-1) = (1 + D)^2 - T^2 < 0 \iff |1 + D| < |T|$. There is one and only one real root belonging to $(-1, 1)$. The steady state is a saddle.
- $P(1)P(-1) = (1 + D)^2 - T^2 > 0 \iff |1 + D| > |T|$.
  - $|D| < 1$. Either the roots are complex and $|\lambda_1|^2 = |\lambda_2|^2 = D < 1$, or the roots are real and both belong to $]-1, 1[$. The steady state is locally stable (a sink).
  - $|D| > 1$. Either the roots are complex and $|\lambda_1|^2 = |\lambda_2|^2 = D > 1$, or the roots are real and do not belong to $[-1, 1]$. The steady state is unstable (a source).

A.3.5 Bifurcations of Monotonic Dynamics

The study of bifurcations comes naturally into play when we are interested in studying the effect of changes in a parameter a on a dynamic system. In this section, we study the bifurcations arising in dynamic systems of order one when the dynamics are locally monotonic near a point $(\bar{x}, \bar{a})$.

Let us parametrize the difference equation of section A.3.1:

$$x_{t+1} = l(x_t, a)$$

Consider a parameter value $\bar{a}$, and suppose that there is a steady state $\bar{x}$ such that $l(\bar{x}, \bar{a}) = \bar{x}$ and $l'_x(\bar{x}, \bar{a}) > 0$.

If $\bar{x}$ is hyperbolic ($l'_x(\bar{x}, \bar{a}) \neq 1$), one can apply the implicit function theorem to the function $g(x, a) = l(x, a) - x$ in a neighborhood of $(\bar{x}, \bar{a})$. This allows one to define x as a function of a and to study the effect of changing the value of the parameter a on the dynamics. It is thus possible to obtain a function $x = \phi(a)$. We also conclude that near $\bar{a}$ there exists a steady state $x = l(x, a)$ in a neighborhood of $\bar{x}$ which has the same stability properties as $\bar{x}$.

If $\bar{x}$ is non-hyperbolic ($l'_x(\bar{x}, \bar{a}) = 1$), one cannot apply the implicit function theorem to infer the existence of a function $x = f(a)$. We should then distinguish two cases, depending on the value of $l'_a(\bar{x}, \bar{a})$.

When $l'_a(\bar{x}, \bar{a}) \neq 0$, one can apply the implicit function theorem to the function $g(x, a) = l(x, a) - x = 0$ in a neighborhood of $(\bar{x}, \bar{a})$ to show that there exists a function $a = h(x)$ for x near $\bar{x}$ with $g(\bar{x}, h(\bar{x})) = 0$ and $\bar{a} = h(\bar{x})$. Differentiating $g(x, h(x)) = 0$ and evaluating at $x = \bar{x}$ yields

$$g'_x(\bar{x}, h(\bar{x})) + g'_a(\bar{x}, h(\bar{x})) \, h'(\bar{x}) = 0.$$

Since $g'_x(\bar{x}, \bar{a}) = 0$ and $g'_a(\bar{x}, \bar{a}) = l'_a(\bar{x}, \bar{a}) \neq 0$, we have

$$h'(\bar{x}) = 0.$$

We thus have three possible cases: either the function $h(x)$ attains a maximum at $h(\bar{x})$, or it attains a minimum, or there is an inflection point at $\bar{x}$. We should thus study the second-order derivatives of the function $h(\cdot)$. Twice differentiating $g(x, h(x)) = 0$ and evaluating at $x = \bar{x}$ yields

$$g''_{xx}(\bar{x}, h(\bar{x})) + g''_{xa}(\bar{x}, h(\bar{x}))h'(\bar{x}) + g''_{ax}(\bar{x}, h(\bar{x}))h'(\bar{x})$$
$$+ g''_{aa}(\bar{x}, h(\bar{x}))(h'(\bar{x}))^2 + g'_a(\bar{x}, h(\bar{x}))h''(\bar{x}) = 0.$$

Since $h'(\bar{x}) = 0$, we have

$$g''_{xx}(\bar{x}, h(\bar{x})) + g'_a(\bar{x}, h(\bar{x}))h''(\bar{x}) = 0$$

and thus

$$h''(\bar{x}) = -\frac{g''_{xx}(\bar{x}, h(\bar{x}))}{g'_a(\bar{x}, h(\bar{x}))} = -\frac{l''_{xx}(\bar{x}, h(\bar{x}))}{l'_a(\bar{x}, h(\bar{x}))}.$$

The function $a = h(x)$ thus admits a local maximum (minimum) if $h''(\bar{x}) < 0$ (> 0). There is an inflection point if $h''(\bar{x}) = 0$ and $h'''(\bar{x}) \neq 0$. The three cases are represented in figure A.6. We now have the necessary material to define the following.

Definition A.8 (Tangent bifurcation)
Let $\bar{a}$ be a value of the parameter a, and $\bar{x}$ be a non-hyperbolic steady state of the dynamics $x_{t+1} = l(x_t, \bar{a})$. If the equation $x = l(x, a)$ has in the neighborhood of $(\bar{x}, \bar{a})$ a unique differentiable solution $a = h(x)$ which has a local maximum or a local minimum at $\bar{x}$, we say that the dynamics $x_{t+1} = l(x_t, a)$ undergo a tangent bifurcation at $(\bar{a}, \bar{x})$.

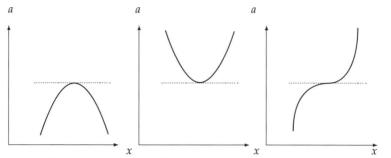

Figure A.6. The function $a = h(x)$. The function admits a local maximum (minimum) at $\bar{x}$ if $h'' < 0\ (> 0)$. There is an inflection point if $h'' = 0$ and $h''' \neq 0$.

A sufficient condition for such a bifurcation to occur is given by the following proposition:

Proposition A.9 (Sufficient condition for a tangent bifurcation)
Sufficient conditions for $\bar{a}$ to be a tangent bifurcation of the dynamics $x_{t+1} = l(x_t, a)$ are

$$l'_x(\bar{x}, \bar{a}) = 1,$$
$$l'_a(\bar{x}, \bar{a}) \neq 0,$$
$$l''_{xx}(\bar{x}, \bar{a}) \neq 0.$$

Note that the condition $h'' \neq 0$ is not necessarily required to have a tangent bifurcation. In the case $h'' = 0$, one should study the higher order derivatives of $h(\cdot)$.

Finally, we can state the main property of the tangent bifurcation:

Proposition A.10 (Properties of a tangent bifurcation)
Assume that the conditions of proposition A.9 hold. The system $x_{t+1} = l(x_t, a)$ has two hyperbolic steady states on one side of $\bar{a}$, exactly one steady state at $\bar{a}$, and none on the other side. Whenever two equilibria exist, one is stable and the other is unstable.

Proof: Consider the case where the function $a = h(x)$ admits a local maximum $\bar{a}$ at $x = \bar{x}$. This implies the existence of two steady states for $a < \bar{a}$ and the non-existence of steady states for $a > \bar{a}$. The opposite conclusion is obtained when $a = h(x)$ has a local minimum.

For one steady state x near $\bar{x}$ and $a = h(x)$, we consider the eigenvalue $l'_x(x, h(x))$. Computing its derivative with respect to x and evaluating it near

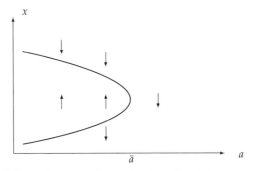

Figure A.7. Local dynamics near a tangent bifurcation. There are two steady states on one side of $\bar{a}$, exactly one steady state at $\bar{a}$, and none on the other side. Whenever two equilibria exist, one is stable and the other is stable.

the bifurcation point, one gets

$$\frac{\mathrm{d}l'_x(x, h(x))}{\mathrm{d}x} = l''_{xx}(\bar{x}, \bar{a}) \neq 0.$$

As l'_x is continuous, the eigenvalue is monotonic with respect to x and the stability conclusions follow. ∎

When $l'_a(\bar{x}, \bar{a}) = 0$, other types of bifurcations arise. One distinguished generally the transcritical bifurcation with $l''_{xx} \neq 0$ and $l''_{xa} \neq 0$ and the pitchfork bifurcation with $l''_{xx} = 0, l'''_{xxx} \neq 0$ (see Wiggins (1990)). They are however rather uncommon in economic models.

   A convenient tool to represent the effect of the parameter under consideration on the dynamics is to draw a bifurcation diagram. The bifurcation diagram for a tangent bifurcation is presented in figure A.7. The lines represent the steady states as a function of the parameter a. The arrows indicate the dynamics and the stability type. What actually happens is the merging and disappearance of two hyperbolic equilibria at the bifurcation point.[6]

Example: One simple example of a tangent bifurcation is the following. Consider the function $l(x, a) = a - x^2$. The point $\bar{a} = -1/4$ is a tangent bifurcation point, as we have

$$\bar{x} = l(\bar{x}, -1/4) = -1/2,$$

$$l'_x(\bar{x}, -1/4) = -2\bar{x} = 1,$$

$$l''_{xx}(\bar{x}, -1/4) = -2 < 0,$$

$$l'_a(\bar{x}, -1/4) = 1 \neq 0.$$

---

[6] In a two-dimensional system, the tangent bifurcation is often called a "saddle–node" bifurcation because the two equilibria are respectively a saddle and a node (i.e., the eigenvalues are real and their moduli are on the same side of 1).

A.4 DYNAMIC OPTIMIZATION

A.4.1 The Value Function

We consider a state variable x_t which belongs to an interval I of $\mathbb{R}$; its motion through time is governed by the following equation:

$$x_{t+1} = \phi(x_t, C_t) = \phi(x_t, c_t^1, c_t^2, \ldots, c_t^n). \tag{A.9}$$

The vector of control variables $C_t = (c_t^1, c_t^2, \ldots, c_t^n)$ of time t has an influence on the evolution of the stock. We assume that the initial stock $\bar{x}_0$ is given by

$$x_0 = \bar{x}_0, \tag{A.10}$$

and that the set of feasible decisions in t, denoted $Q(x_t)$, depends on the level of the stock x_t:

$$C_t \in Q(x_t). \tag{A.11}$$

In general, the set of feasible decisions is delimited by constraints depending on x_t.

A sequence $(x_t, C_t), t = 0, 1, \ldots$, which satisfies (A.9), (A.10), and (A.11) is called a *feasible trajectory* starting from $\bar{x}_0$.

Example: We illustrate the dynamic optimization under constraint with a simple example of optimal growth with constant population. $x_t = k_t$ is the stock of capital, $I = \mathbb{R}_{++}$ is an interval of $\mathbb{R}$, c_t and d_t are the consumption levels, $y_t = f(k_t)$ is the production function, and the equation of motion for the stock of capital is

$$k_{t+1} = f(k_t) - c_t - d_t = \phi(k_t, c_t, d_t).$$

The set of feasible consumption levels is delimited by the positivity constraints and by the resource constraint:

$$Q(k_t) = \{(c_t, d_t) \in \mathbb{R}^2; \ c_t > 0, \ d_t > 0, \ c_t + d_t < f(k_t)\}.$$

Another approach allows for zero consumption. In that case, we define

$$\tilde{Q}(k_t) = \{(c_t, d_t) \in \mathbb{R}^2; \ c_t \geq 0, \ d_t \geq 0, \ c_t + d_t \leq f(k_t)\}.$$

We consider a payoff function, depending on the stock variable and on the decisions at each date:

$$g(x_t, C_t) = g(x_t, c_t^1, c_t^2, \ldots, c_t^n).$$

Given a positive discount factor δ, the objective is to maximize the discounted flow of payoffs

$$\max \sum_{t=0}^{\infty} \delta^t g(x_t, C_t)$$

on the set of *feasible* trajectories starting from $\bar{x}_0$, i.e. those which verify (A.9), (A.10), and (A.11).

Example: In the optimal growth problem the payoff function is the utility function; the objective is to maximize the discounted sum of utilities:

$$\max \sum_{t=0}^{\infty} \delta^t U(c_t, d_t).$$

U is a function defined on the set $\mathbb{R}^2_{++}$ (or on $\mathbb{R}^2_+$ when zero consumptions are admissible).

We next define the value function of state x as the upper bound of the discounted sum of the payoffs that are feasible starting from $\bar{x}_0$. We consider the following assumptions:

Assumption B0.
For all element x of I, $Q(x)$ is non-empty, and for all vectors C in the subset $Q(x)$ of $\mathbb{R}^n$, $\phi(x, C)$ is defined and belongs to I, i.e., the dynamics are defined on I.

Example: With a production function $f(k) : \mathbb{R}_{++} \to \mathbb{R}_{++}$, the dynamics are defined on $\mathbb{R}_{++}$, because for all $k \in \mathbb{R}_{++}$ and for all pairs $(c, d) \in Q(k)$, $\phi(k, c, d)$ is defined and belongs to $\mathbb{R}_{++}$. Similarly, $\mathbb{R}_{++}$ is replaced by $\mathbb{R}_+$ when zero consumptions are admissible.

Assumption B1.
For C given, the functions $\phi(x, C)$ and $g(x, C)$ are non-decreasing with respect to x. The upper bound of $\phi(x, C)$ with respect to C in $Q(x)$ belongs to I:

$$\bar{\phi}(x) = \sup_{C \in Q(x)} \phi(x, C) \in I.$$

The upper bound of $g(x, C)$ with respect to C in $Q(x)$ is finite:

$$\bar{g}(x) = \sup_{C \in Q(x)} g(x, C) \in \mathbb{R}.$$

For any initial condition $\bar{x}_0$, there exists a constant b_0 and a scalar $\delta_0 > \delta$ such that the sequence $\bar{x}_t$ defined by

$$\bar{x}_{t+1} = \bar{\phi}(\bar{x}_t) \qquad \forall t \geq 0$$

satisfies

$$\delta_0^t \bar{g}(\bar{x}_t) \leq b_0 \qquad \forall t \geq 0.$$

Assumption **B1** ensures that the highest possible payoff with the highest possible state remains bounded.

Example: In the optimal growth problem with $\phi(k, c, d) = f(k) - c - d$ and

$$Q(k) = \{(c, d) \in \mathbb{R}^2; \ c > 0, \ d > 0, \text{ and } c + d < f(k)\},$$

we have

$$\bar{\phi}(k) = f(k), \qquad \bar{g}(k) = \sup\{U(c, d); \ (c, d) \in Q(k)\}.$$

- With $f(k) = Ak^\alpha$, the sequence $\bar{k}_t$ is bounded and the assumption **B1** holds for any $\delta < 1$, since there exists δ_0 such that $1 > \delta_0 > \delta$.
- In the linear case, $f(k) = Ak$, the sequence $\bar{k}_t$ that is the solution of $\bar{k}_{t+1} = f(\bar{k})$ is given by $\bar{k}_t = A^t \bar{k}_0$; considering $U(c, d) = c^a + d^a$, we have $\bar{g}(k) = 2(f(k)/2)^a$, and

$$\delta_0^t \bar{g}(k_t) = \delta_0^t 2 \left(\frac{A^t \bar{k}_0}{2} \right)^a$$

is bounded for all $t \geq 0$ if and only if $\delta_0 A^a \leq 1$; this holds for some $\delta_0 > \delta$ if and only if $\delta A^a < 1$.

As is illustrated in the above example, the assumption **B1** imposes a bound on the growth of feasible payoffs, in order to keep the discounted sum bounded. We now have the following proposition on the convergence[7] of the infinite sum:

Proposition A.11 (Convergence of the infinite sum)
Under the assumptions **B0** *and* **B1**, *every discounted sum of feasible payoffs is defined and has values in* $\mathbb{R} \cup \{-\infty\}$:

$$\sum_{t=0}^{\infty} \delta^t g(x_t, C_t) = \lim_{T \to +\infty} \sum_{t=0}^{T} \delta^t g(x_t, C_t) \in \mathbb{R} \cup \{-\infty\}.$$

Proof: If $x_t \leq \bar{x}_t$ at time t, which holds in particular at $t = 0$ because $x_0 = \bar{x}_0$, we have by induction that this inequality holds for any t:

$$x_{t+1} = \phi(x_t, C_t) \leq \bar{\phi}(x_t) \leq \bar{\phi}(\bar{x}_t) = \bar{x}_{t+1}.$$

We also have

$$g(x_t, C_t) \leq \bar{g}(x_t) \leq \bar{g}(\bar{x}_t).$$

As a consequence, the sequence

$$S_T = \sum_{t=0}^{T} \delta^t [g(x_t, C_t) - \bar{g}(\bar{x}_t)]$$

---

[7] In $\mathbb{R} \cup \{-\infty\}$.

is non-increasing, since each term of the sum is negative or nil ($S_T - S_{T-1} = \delta^T[g(x_T, C_T) - \bar{g}(\bar{x}_T)] \leq 0$). The sequence S_T has thus a limit in $\mathbb{R} \cup \{-\infty\}$. We may also, without restriction, assume that $\bar{g}(\bar{x}_t) \geq 0$ (it is sufficient that we replace $\bar{g}(\bar{x}_t)$ by $\max\{0, \bar{g}(\bar{x}_t)\}$). Following the assumption **B1**, we have

$$\bar{S}_T = \sum_{t=0}^{T} \delta^t \bar{g}(\bar{x}_t) \leq \sum_{t=0}^{T} \frac{\delta^t}{\delta_0^t} b_0 = \frac{1}{1 - \delta/\delta_0} b_0,$$

as $\sum_{t=0}^{\infty} (\delta/\delta_0)^t = 1/(1 - \delta/\delta_0)$. The increasing sequence $\bar{S}_T$ has thus a finite limit. We deduce that the sequence of finite sums of discounted payoffs $\sum_{t=0}^{T} g(x_t, C_t)$ has a limit in $\mathbb{R} \cup \{-\infty\}$. ∎

It is then enough that there exists at least one feasible trajectory such that this limit is finite, to be allowed to define the value function.[8]

Assumption B2.
For all $\bar{x}_0 \in I$, there exists a feasible path $(x_t, C_t)_{t \geq 0}$, starting at $\bar{x}_0$, such that the sequence

$$\sum_{t=0}^{T} \delta^t g(x_t, C_t)$$

is bounded below when $T \to +\infty$.

Proposition A.12 (The value function)
*Under the assumptions **B0**, **B1**, and **B2**, the function*

$$\mathcal{V}(\bar{x}_0) = \sup \left\{ \sum_{t=0}^{\infty} \delta^t g(x_t, C_t); \ (x_t, C_t) \text{ feasible from } \bar{x}_0 \right\}$$

is defined on I and satisfies $\forall x \in I$

$$\mathcal{V}(x) = \sup\{g(x, C) + \delta \mathcal{V}(\phi(x, C)); \ C \in Q(x)\}. \tag{A.12}$$

Proof: Following the assumption **B1**, the infinite sums belongs to $\mathbb{R} \cup \{-\infty\}$. They are moreover bounded above by a constant:

$$\sum_{t=0}^{\infty} \delta^t g(x_t, C_t) \leq \sum_{t=0}^{\infty} \delta^t \bar{g}(\bar{x}_t) \leq \frac{b_0}{1 - \delta/\delta_0}.$$

Following **B2**, there exists at least one sequence (x_t, C_t) for which the sum is finite. Then the upper bound $\mathcal{V}(\bar{x}_0)$ is finite.

---

[8] To make the assumption for all feasible trajectories is more restrictive and would not apply to a logarithmic or CIES utility function with $\sigma < 1$.

Take $x_0 \in I$. For any C_0 chosen in $Q(x_0)$, the following state is $y = \phi(x_0, C_0)$. For any feasible trajectory (x_t, C_t) starting at x_0 such that $x_1 = y$, we have

$$\sum_{t=0}^{\infty} \delta^t g(x_t, C_t) = g(x_0, C_0) + \delta \sum_{t=0}^{\infty} \delta^t g(x_{t+1}, C_{t+1}).$$

We first take the upper bound at given C_0 on the set of feasible trajectories for which $x_1 = \phi(x_0, C_0)$:

$$g(x_0, C_0) + \sup \sum_{t=1}^{\infty} \delta^t g(x_t, C_t) = g(x_0, C_0) + \delta V(\phi(x_0, C_0)).$$

We next take the upper bound on $C_0 \in Q(x_0)$, and we obtain the Bellman equation (A.12). ∎

The following proposition shows that the optimal path is the solution to the Bellman equation (A.12) at each date.

Proposition A.13 (Characteristics of optimal trajectories)
Under the assumptions **B0, B1,** *and* **B2,** *a feasible path* $(x_t^\star, C_t^\star)$ *starting from* $x_0^\star = \bar{x}_0$ *is optimal if and only if we have for all t*

$$V(x_t^\star) = g(x_t^\star, C_t^\star) + \delta V(x_{t+1}^\star). \tag{A.13}$$

Proof: Necessary condition: If a path is optimal from $x_0^\star = \bar{x}_0$, then, for all t, the path $(x_{t+i}^\star, C_{t+1}^\star)_{i\geq 0}$ is optimal from $x_t^\star$: if that were not the case, it would be possible to increase the objective by a change in the path after time t.[9] We have thus, for all t,

$$V(x_t^\star) = \sum_{i=0}^{\infty} \delta^i g(x_{t+i}^\star, C_{t+i}^\star),$$

from which we deduce equation (A.13).
  Sufficient condition: Applying equation (A.13), we obtain by induction

$$V(\bar{x}_0) = \sum_{t=0}^{T} \delta^t g(x_t^\star, C_t^\star) + \delta^{T+1} V(x_{T+1}^\star). \tag{A.14}$$

Using the bounds $\bar{x}_{t+1} = \bar{\phi}(\bar{x}_t)$ and $\bar{g}(\bar{x}_t)$ defined from $\bar{x}_0$ with the assumption **B1**, we obtain

$$V(x_t^\star) = \sup \left\{ \sum_{i=1}^{\infty} \delta g(x_{t+i}, C_{t+i}); \text{ feasible trajectories starting from } x_t^\star \right\}$$

[9] This is the principle of Bellman (1957). In a planning problem in which there is no reaction of private agents, time consistency is not an issue.

$$\leq \sum_{i=0}^{\infty} \delta^i \bar{g}(\bar{x}_{t+i})$$

$$\leq \sum_{i=0}^{\infty} \delta^i \frac{b_0}{\delta_0^{t+i}} = \frac{1}{\delta_0^t} \frac{b_0}{1 - \frac{\delta}{\delta_0}},$$

and thus

$$\delta^t \mathcal{V}(x_t^\star) \leq \left(\frac{\delta}{\delta_0} \right)^t \frac{b_0}{1 - \frac{\delta}{\delta_0}},$$

from which we deduce that

$$\limsup_{t \to +\infty} \delta^t \mathcal{V}(x_t^\star) \leq 0. \tag{A.15}$$

Taking the limit of (A.14) when $T \to +\infty$, we have

$$\mathcal{V}(\bar{x}_0) \leq \sum_{t=0}^{+\infty} \delta^t g(x_t^\star, C_t^\star),$$

as $\limsup_{T \to +\infty} \delta^{T+1} \mathcal{V}(x_{T+1}^\star) \leq 0$. As $\mathcal{V}(\bar{x}_0)$ is the upper bound of the values of the objective for all feasible trajectories starting from $\bar{x}_0$, there is strict equality, and the trajectory $(x_t^\star, C_t^\star)$, which realizes the upper bound is optimal. ∎

Under the assumptions **B0**, **B1**, and **B2**, in order to prove that there exists an optimal path and to study its properties, it is sufficient to show that $\forall x$

$$\max_C g(x, C) + \delta \mathcal{V}(\phi(x, C))$$

attains its bound on $Q(x)$ at $C^\star(x) \in Q(x)$. Then, the trajectory defined by induction from $\bar{x}_0$ by

$$C_t^\star = C^\star(x_t^\star) \quad \text{and} \quad x_{t+1}^\star = \phi(x_t^\star, C_t^\star)$$

satisfies equation (A.13), as

$$g(x_t^\star, C_t^\star) + \delta \mathcal{V}(x_{t+1}^\star) = \sup_{C \in Q(x_t^\star)} \{g(x_t^\star, C) + \delta \mathcal{V}(\phi(x_t^\star, C))\} = \mathcal{V}(x_t^\star).$$

Remark that for the optimal solution to exist, it is not sufficient to have that the value function is defined. More precisely, the Bellman equation (A.12) and the necessary condition (A.13) are verified by the value function if this function is defined (with values in $\mathbb{R}$). But the sufficient property of proposition A.13 that ensures the existence of a solution is obtained with the limit property (A.15). This property results from the boundedness condition $\delta_0^t \bar{g}(\bar{x}_t) \leq b_0 \, \forall t$ in **B1**. However, to study the properties of the value function, we only need the existence of this function, not this boundedness condition.

An essential property used to show that the value function attains its bound on $Q(x)$, is the continuity of this function. This continuity property is a consequence of the concavity of the value function of a convex problem.

Assumption B3.
The set $\mathcal{A}$ of the feasible triplets of payoff, current stock, and resulting stock is convex. Formally, $\mathcal{A}$ is the set of elements (a, x, y) of $\mathbb{R} \times I \times I$ for which there exists $C \in Q(x)$ such that $a \leq g(x, C)$ and $y = \phi(x, C)$.

The inequality bearing on a weakens the assumption of convexity; it allows one to realize all gains which are inferior to a given feasible gain.

Example: If the functions $f(k)$ and $U(c, d)$ are concave and increasing, the optimization problem is convex.

Proposition A.14 (Continuity of the value function)
*Under the assumptions **B0**, **B1**, **B2**, and **B3**, the value function is concave on I and is continuous on the interior of I.*

Proof: Let x_0^1 and x_0^2 be two points of I, and let $\lambda \in [0, 1]$. By definition of the value function, there exist feasible trajectories (x_t^i, C_t^i) starting from x_0^i for $i = 1, 2$ such that

$$\sum_{t=0}^{\infty} \delta^t g(x_t^i, C_t^i) > V(x_0^i) - \epsilon \tag{A.16}$$

for $\epsilon > 0$. We apply the hypothesis of the convexity of the set $\mathcal{A}$ of the triplets of feasible payoff, current stock, and resulting stock. The elements (a_t^i, x_t^i, y_t^i) defined by $a_t^i = g(x_t^i, C_t^i)$ and $y_t^i = \phi(x_t^i, C_t^i)$, $i = 1, 2$, belongs to $\mathcal{A}$, and hence their convex combination

$$(a_t^\lambda, x_t^\lambda, y_t^\lambda) = \lambda(a_t^1, x_t^1, y_t^1) + (1 - \lambda)(a_t^2, x_t^2, y_t^2)$$

also belongs to $\mathcal{A}$. As a consequence, there exists $C_t^\lambda \in Q(x_t^\lambda)$ such that $y_t^\lambda = \phi(x_t^\lambda, C_t^\lambda)$ and

$$a_t^\lambda \leq g(x_t^\lambda, C_t^\lambda).$$

We also have, $\forall t$, $x_{t+1}^\lambda = \lambda x_{t+1}^1 + (1 - \lambda)x_{t+1}^2 = \lambda y_t^1 + (1 - \lambda)y_t^2 = y_t^\lambda = \varphi(x_t^\lambda, C_t^\lambda)$. Hence, the sequence $(x_t^\lambda, C_t^\lambda)_{t \geq 0}$ is feasible from x_0^λ, which implies

$$V(x_0^\lambda) \geq \sum_{t=0}^{\infty} \delta^t g(x_t^\lambda, C_t^\lambda) \geq \sum_{t=0}^{\infty} \delta^t a_t^\lambda.$$

Moreover, we have $a_t^\lambda = \lambda a_t^1 + (1 - \lambda)a_t^2 = \lambda g(x_t^1, C_t^1) + (1 - \lambda)g(x_t^2, C_t^2)$, implying

$$V(x_0^\lambda) \geq \lambda \sum_{t=0}^{\infty} \delta^t g(x_t^1, C_t^2) + (1 - \lambda) \sum_{t=0}^{\infty} \delta^t g(x_t^2, C_t^2),$$

and, following (A.16),

$$V(x_0^\lambda) \geq \lambda V(x_0^1) + (1 - \lambda) V(x_0^2) - \epsilon.$$

The inequality being satisfied for all $\epsilon > 0$, we deduce that the function V is concave on I. Moreover, a function which is concave on an interval is necessarily continuous on the interior of this interval. ∎

We further obtain the monotonicity of the value function under an additional assumption on the set $Q(x)$ (see assumption 4.6 of Stokey and Lucas (1989)).

Proposition A.15 (Monotonicity of the value function)
*Assume that **B0**, **B1**, and **B2** hold, and suppose that*

$$\forall x \in I, \quad \forall x' \in I, \qquad x \leq x' \Rightarrow Q(x) \subseteq Q(x').$$

Then the value function V is non-decreasing on the set I.

Proof: Let $x_0 \leq x_0'$ and take $\epsilon > 0$. There exists a feasible trajectory $(x_t, C_t)_{t \geq 0}$ starting from x_0 such that

$$\sum_{t=0}^{\infty} \delta^t g(x_t, C_t) \geq V(x_0) - \epsilon.$$

We define a trajectory $(x_t', C_t)_{t \geq 0}$ starting from x_0' by induction: if $x_t' \geq x_t$ (which in particular holds at $t = 0$), then $x_{t+1}' = \phi(x_t', C_t)$ is defined as $C_t \in Q(x) \Rightarrow C_t \in Q(x_t')$, and we have (as g and ϕ are monotonic with respect to x) $g(x_t', C_t) \geq g(x_t, C_t)$ and

$$x_{t+1}' = \phi(x_t', C_t) \geq \phi(x_t, C_t) = x_{t+1}.$$

As the trajectory $(x_t', C_t)_{t \geq 0}$ is feasible from x_0', we have

$$V(x_0') \geq \sum_{t=0}^{\infty} \delta^t g(x_t', C_t) \geq \sum_{t=0}^{\infty} \delta^t g(x_t, C_t) \geq V(x_0) - \epsilon.$$

As we have $V(x_0') \geq V(x_0) - \epsilon$ for all $\epsilon > 0$, $V(x_0') \geq V(x_0)$ is necessary. ∎

Example: In the optimal growth problem, the set $Q(k) = \{(c, d) \in \mathbb{R}^2; c > 0, d > 0, \text{ and } c + d < f(k)\}$ satisfies the assumptions of Proposition A.15.

The differentiability of the value function is useful for studying stationary optimal paths. To study the differentiability of V with respect to $\bar{x}$, we assume the following: near given state and controls $(\bar{x}, \bar{C})$, for a small change in the state, it is possible to change the controls in order to leave the next period state unchanged.

Assumption B4.
The function g is differentiable at $(\bar{x}, \bar{C})$, and there exists an ad hoc differentiable function $\tilde{C}(x)$ defined on a neighborhood V of $\bar{x}$ such that $\tilde{C}(\bar{x}) = \bar{C}$ and $\forall x \in V$, $\tilde{C}(x) \in Q(x)$ and $\phi(x, \tilde{C}(x)) = \phi(\bar{x}, \bar{C})$.

Example: In the optimal growth problem, given $\bar{k}$, $\bar{c}$, and $\bar{d}$ positive, and given the next period capital stock $\bar{k}_+ = f(\bar{k}) - \bar{c} - \bar{d} > 0$, **B4** says that, with a current capital stock, different from but near to $\bar{k}$, there exist consumptions $\tilde{c}(k)$ and $\tilde{d}(k)$ such that the capital stock of the next period remains unchanged. For example, keeping d constant, we have $\tilde{d}(k) = \bar{d}$ and $\tilde{c}(k) = f(k) - \bar{d} - \bar{k}_+$.

Proposition A.16 (Differentiability of the value function)
Assume that **B0**, **B1**, **B2**, *and* **B3** *hold and that* **B4** *holds at* $(\bar{x}, \bar{C})$ *such that*

$$V(\bar{x}) = g(\bar{x}, \bar{C}) + \delta V(\phi(\bar{x}, \bar{C})). \tag{A.17}$$

Then, V is differentiable at $\bar{x}$, and its derivative is

$$V'(\bar{x}) = \frac{\partial g}{\partial x}(\bar{x}, \bar{C}) + \sum_{i=1}^{n} \frac{\partial g}{\partial c^i}(\bar{x}, \bar{C}) \frac{\partial \tilde{c}^i}{\partial x}(\bar{x}).$$

Proof: For all $x \in V$ we have

$$V(x) \geq g(x, \tilde{C}(x)) + \delta V(\phi(x, \tilde{C}(x))) = g(x, \tilde{C}(x)) + \delta V(\phi(\bar{x}, \bar{C})).$$

Using equation (A.17) and $\bar{C} = \tilde{C}(\bar{x})$, we deduce

$$V(x) - V(\bar{x}) \geq g(x, \tilde{C}(x)) - g(\bar{x}, \tilde{C}(\bar{x})).$$

A concave function which is bounded below in a neighborhood of $\bar{x}$ by a differentiable function of $\bar{x}$ is itself differentiable at $\bar{x}$, and the two derivatives are equal (see figure A.8). We thus have

$$V'(\bar{x}) = \frac{d}{dx} g(x, \tilde{C}(x)) \Big|_{x=\bar{x}}$$

$$= \frac{\partial g}{\partial x}(\bar{x}, \bar{C}) + \sum_{i=1}^{n} \frac{\partial g}{\partial \tilde{c}^i}(\bar{x}, \bar{C}) \frac{\partial \tilde{c}^i}{\partial x}(\bar{x}). \qquad \blacksquare$$

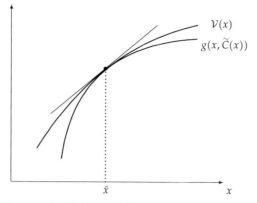

Figure A.8. Differentiability of the value function.

Example: In the optimal growth problem, we have

$$V'(k) = \frac{dU(\tilde{c}(k), \bar{d})}{dk} = U_c'(\bar{c}, \bar{d})\, f'(\bar{k}).$$

A.4.2 Necessary and Sufficient Conditions for Optimality

We now study the same problem as in appendix A.4.1 in a different way, viz., we maximize

$$\sum_{t=0}^{\infty} \delta^t g(x_t, C_t),$$

such that

$$x_{t+1} = \phi(x_t, C_t) \quad \text{and} \quad C_t \in Q(x_t)$$

with a given initial condition $x_0 = \bar{x}_0$.

We define the Lagrangian corresponding to the shadow prices $q_t, t = 0, 1, 2, \ldots$:

Definition A.9 (Lagrangian of period t)
The Lagrangian $L_t(x_t, C_t)$ of period t is obtained as the sum of the payoff $g(x_t, C_t)$ with the increase in the value of the stock:

$$L_t(x_t, C_t) = g(x_t, C_t) + \delta q_{t+1}\phi(x_t, C_t) - q_t x_t.$$

Notice that x_t is evaluated at the price q_t, and x_{t+1} is evaluated at the discounted price δq_{t+1}.

A feasible trajectory $(x_t^\star, C_t^\star)$ is supported by a sequence of shadow prices (q_t) if, for every integer $t \geq 0$, the Lagrangian $L_t(x_t, C_t)$ attains its maximum at $(x_t^\star, C_t^\star)$ on the set of vectors (x_t, C_t) which verify $x_t \in I$ and $C_t \in Q(x_t)$. We then have

$$\mathcal{L}_t(x_t^\star, C_t^\star) = \max_{x_t \in I, C_t \in Q(x_t)} \mathcal{L}_t(x_t, C_t)$$

for all $t \geq 0$.

Proposition A.17 (Necessary and sufficient conditions for optimality)
Let us consider a feasible trajectory $(x_t^\star, C_t^\star)$ starting from $\bar{x}_0$ and for which $x_t^\star$ is interior to I for all $t \geq 0$. Under the assumptions **B0**, **B1**, **B2**, *and* **B3**, *the trajectory $(x_t^\star, C_t^\star)$ is optimal if and only if there exists a sequence of shadow prices (q_t) such that*

- *the trajectory $(x_t^\star, C_t^\star)$ is supported by the sequence of shadow prices (q_t);*
- *for any other feasible trajectory (x_t, C_t) starting from $\bar{x}_0$, such that*

$$\sum_{t=0}^{\infty} \delta^t g(x_t, C_t)$$

is finite, we have

$$\lim_{t \to +\infty} \delta^t q_t (x_t - x_t^\star) \geq 0. \qquad (A.18)$$

The necessary condition is derived with multi-dimensional stocks by Michel (1990a). The sufficient condition is standard (see, e.g., Arrow and Kurz (1970)) and does not require **B1** and **B2**.

The condition (A.18) is the transversality condition. It means that the discounted value of the optimal stock (evaluated at the shadow price) is exhausted in the long run and that the value of any other feasible stock should be greater than or equal to that of the optimal stock. The necessary condition only applies to the feasible trajectories with finite payoffs.[10]

Two particular cases are of special importance.

- *In the usual economic case where $x_t \geq 0$ (stock of capital) and $q_t \geq 0$ (non-negative shadow value of the capital stock), a sufficient condition for (A.18) is*

$$\lim_{t \to +\infty} \delta^t q_t x_t^\star = 0,$$

i.e., the limit of the discounted value of the optimal stock is zero. Indeed, this implies, when $q_t x_t \geq 0$,

$$\lim_{t \to +\infty} \delta^t q_t (x_t - x_t^\star) \geq - \lim_{t \to +\infty} \delta^t q_t x_t^\star = 0.$$

---

[10] Because of **B1**, finite payoffs are equivalent to $\sum_{t=0}^{\infty} \delta^t g(x_t, C_t) > -\infty$ (non-infinite loss).

This condition is also necessary when there exists a feasible trajectory (x_t, C_t) with $x_t = 0 \ \forall t \geq T$ and for which there are finite payoffs, i.e.,

$$\sum_{t=0}^{\infty} \delta^t g(x_t, C_t) > -\infty.$$

Indeed, for this feasible trajectory we have

$$-\lim_{t \to +\infty} \delta^t q_t x_t^* \geq 0.$$

Then, a $q_t \geq 0$ and $x_t^* \geq 0$ implies $\lim_{t \to +\infty} \delta^t q_t x_t^* = 0$.

Example: In the optimal growth problem, the stock of capital can always be reduced by increasing consumption, which implies $q_t \geq 0$. The transversality condition

$$\lim_{t \to +\infty} \delta^t q_t k_t = 0$$

is sufficient. It is also necessary when the trajectory with zero capital is feasible and leads to finite payoffs: $f(0) > 0$ or, for the problem allowing for zero consumptions, $U(0, 0)$ finite.

- *When the stock of any feasible trajectory is bounded and when there exist two feasible trajectories starting from x_0, (x_t^1, C_t^1) and (x_t^2, C_t^2) with finite payoffs such that*

$$\lim_{t \to +\infty} x_t^1 - x_t^* > 0 \quad and \quad \lim_{t \to +\infty} x_t^2 - x_t^* < 0,$$

the transversality condition is equivalent to

$$\lim_{t \to +\infty} \delta^t q_t = 0,$$

and the limit of the discounted shadow price is zero. The significance of this special case is the following: if there exists one feasible trajectory above the optimal one and another one below in the long run, then the optimal stock is worthless and its discounted shadow price is zero.[11]

In the assumptions used so far, there is no condition of differentiability. Indeed, it is the assumption of convexity of the optimization problem that allows us to obtain a necessary and sufficient optimality condition. If, moreover, the functions ϕ and g are differentiable and if (x_t^*, C_t^*) is interior to the set on which we maximize $\mathcal{L}$, we obtain the following first-order conditions:

$$\frac{\partial \mathcal{L}_t(x_t^*, C_t^*)}{\partial x_t} = 0 \quad and \quad \frac{\partial \mathcal{L}_t(x_t^*, C_t^*)}{\partial c_t^i} = 0, \quad i = 1, 2, \ldots, n.$$

---

[11] An economic example linked to optimal growth can be found in the satiation case of Ryder and Heal (1973) and de la Croix (1998).

Example: In the optimal growth problem, the Lagrangian of period t is

$$\mathcal{L}_t = U(c_t, d_t) + \delta q_{t+1}(f(k_t) - c_t - d_t) - q_t k_t,$$

and the first-order optimality conditions are

$$q_t = \delta q_{t+1} f'(k_t^\star),$$

and

$$\frac{\partial U(c_t^\star, d_t^\star)}{\partial c_t} = \delta q_{t+1} = \frac{\partial U(c_t^\star, d_t^\star)}{\partial d_t}.$$

A.5 CALIBRATION AND SIMULATION

The majority of calibrated overlapping generations models consider agents living more than two periods in order to be able to address policy issues in a not too distant future. Some authors, however, carefully calibrate two-period models (see for example Ambler (2000)).

In this section, we first calibrate two overlapping generations economies that should be understood as numerical examples. Calibration means that we choose the parameter values in order to reproduce a list of data characteristics. Other characteristics can then be used to investigate to what extent the model generates accurate predictions with respect to them. In a last sub-section, we explain how to compute numerically the solution to a non-linear dynamic model with perfect foresight.

A.5.1 The Cobb–Douglas Model

We first take a simple logarithmic utility function $U(c, d) = \ln c + \beta \ln d$ and a Cobb–Douglas production function $f(k) = Ak^\alpha$. This amounts to assuming that the inter-temporal elasticity of substitution in consumption is equal to one and that factors of production are substitutes with an elasticity of one. We also assume that capital depreciates fully after one period, which is not unrealistic in our setup.[12] The parameter A is simply a scale parameter when the production function is Cobb–Douglas and the utility is homogeneous. We set it to 20 to get steady state capital around 1. We choose the parameter n in order to match a long-run growth rate of total output of 2.5% per year. This corresponds to the long-run growth of U.S. GDP over the twentieth century. For a period of 30 years, $1 + n$ equals 2.097. There remains two parameters to calibrate, α and β. We chose these parameters following the standard choice in the RBC literature (see the different contributions in Cooley (1995)), which leads to a share of labor in added value of $\alpha = 1/3$ and a quarterly psychological

---

[12] Even if one assumes a rather low annual depreciation rate of 5%, 79% of the stock of capital is depreciated after 30 years.

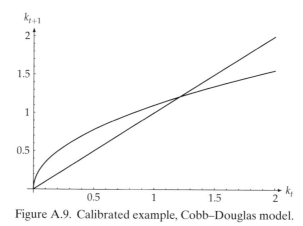

Figure A.9. Calibrated example, Cobb–Douglas model.

discount factor[13] of 0.99. The parameter β is thus set equal to $0.99^{120} = 0.3$. The transition function $k_{t+1} = g(k_t)$ corresponding to our parameter choice is plotted in figure A.9.

The extent to which these parameters are reasonable can be assessed by looking at other steady state characteristics. We shall look at the implied saving rate, interest rate, and speed of convergence.

The positive steady state is equal to $k = 1.21$. At this steady state, the savings rate (savings over production),

$$\frac{N_t s_t}{Y_t} = \frac{1+n}{A} k^{1-\alpha},$$

is 15.38%. This is broadly consistent with the evidence reported in Maddison (1992).[14] The interest rate on an annual basis,

$$\sqrt[30]{A \alpha k^{\alpha-1}} - 1,$$

is equal to 5.18%, and the annual capital/output ratio is 2.2, both of which are in conformity with actual data. One can also compute the convergence speed around the steady state. It is given by

$$\frac{k_{t+1} - k_t}{k - k_t} \simeq 1 - g'(k).$$

This speed on an annual basis is given by $1 - \sqrt[30]{g'(k)}$ and is equal to 3.6%. This is too quick compared to the majority of empirical studies, which estimate it around 2% per year. Hence, the transition function is "too horizontal" near the steady state to reproduce a realistic speed of convergence.

---

[13] This last parameter is usually calibrated to match the long-run interest rate in models with infinite-lived agents.

[14] Maddison (1992) provides historical estimates of long-run savings rates for 11 countries.

A.5.2 The Model with a CES Production Function

Forty years ago, Arrow, Chenery, Minhas, and Solow (1961) taught us that economic analysis based on a unit elasticity of substitution between labor and capital often leads to unduly restrictive conclusions. For example, estimates for developed countries consistently find that the elasticity of substitution is not different from unity, but much lower values have been found for LDCs.[15] This may reflect more limited technological options in emerging economies, i.e., entrepreneurs choosing from the set of technologies in current or local use rather than on the broader set of all potential technologies.

Let us consider an economy with a CES production function $f(k) = A(\alpha k^{-\rho} + 1 - \alpha)^{-1/\rho}$ with $\rho = 1$, and a logarithmic utility $U(c, d) = \ln c + \beta \ln d$. The assumption $\rho = 1$ implies that the elasticity of substitution between capital and labor is $1/2$. In this case,

$$f(k) = \frac{Ak}{\alpha + (1 - \alpha)k}.$$

The parameters $A = 20$, $n = 2.097$, $\beta = 0.3$ are set as in the previous calibration exercise (Cobb–Douglas). α is set to obtain a labor share in production of $2/3$. This yields $\alpha = 0.49$. We round it to $\alpha = 1/2$. The corresponding transition function $k_{t+1} = g(k_t)$ is plotted in figure A.10.

There are two positive steady states, $k = 0.54$ and $k = 1.86$. At the stable steady state, the savings rate is 15%, the interest rate on an annual basis is 5.42%, and the annual capital/output ratio is 2.15. They are all in conformity with actual data. One can also compute the convergence speed around the steady state. This speed on an annual basis is equal to 1.19%. As the transition function is steeper around the stable steady state than in the previous example,

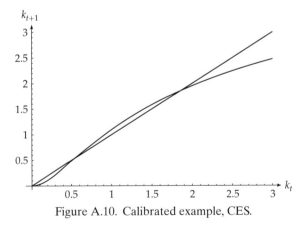

Figure A.10. Calibrated example, CES.

---

[15] For example, Sosin and Fairchild (1984) find an average elasticity of $1/2$ using a sample of 221 Latin American firms in the 1970s.

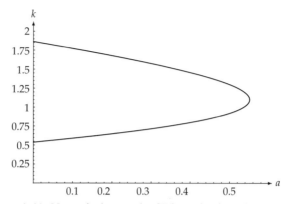

Figure A.11. Numerical example, CES production with pensions.

this example generates a high speed of convergence. Note also that both steady states are in the under-accumulation regime.

A.5.3 Introduction of Policies in the Model with CES Production

In the previous example, we considered public pensions financed by lump-sum taxes on the young agents. Keeping the same parameters as in the previous sub-section, figure A.11 shows how the steady state capital stock(s) depend on pensions a. It gives the bifurcation diagram (figure 3.4 in chapter 3) for the chosen parameter values. The highest sustainable transfer is $a = 0.54$.

We also consider the CES example with unproductive public spending financed by lump-sum taxes on the young agents. The steady states as a function of g are plotted in figure A.12. The highest sustainable spending is $g = 0.994$.

Finally, we draw the diagrams of section 4.4 for our specific numerical example. This allows us to show the global dynamics of the economy when

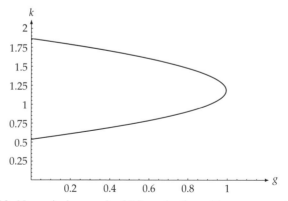

Figure A.12. Numerical example, CES production with government spending.

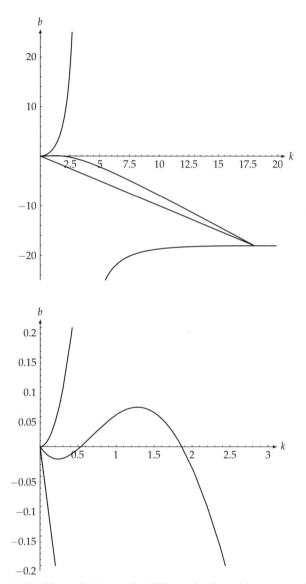

Figure A.13. Numerical example, CES production with constant debt.

the government pursues a constant debt policy as in Diamond (1965). The broad view presented in the top panel of figure A.13 allows us to view the two curves $\bar{b}(k)$ and $\underline{b}(k)$ as well as the constraint $b > -k$. We also plot the steady state curve $\hat{b}(k)$. The two non-trivial steady states with zero debt appear more clearly in the closer view of the bottom panel.

A.5.4 Numerical Solution to Non-linear Forward-looking Models

Let us consider a dynamic model characterized by two non-linear first-order necessary conditions of the form

$$f\left(z_t, z^1_{t-1}, z^2_{t+1}, x_t\right) = 0,$$

$$g\left(z_t, z^1_{t-1}, z^2_{t+1}, x_t\right) = 0,$$

where $z_t = (z^2_t, z^1_t)$ is the vector of endogenous variables at t, including one predetermined variable (z^1_t) and one non-predetermined variable (z^2_t). f and g are functions representing our dynamic model, and x_t is the vector of exogenous variables and parameters.

Since f and g are non-linear, it is not possible in general to solve the model analytically. The general problem is to solve a system of finite difference equations with initial and terminal conditions. Approximating the infinite horizon by a finite one (that means that the transversality conditions on anticipated variables are replaced by the steady state values of these variables at the end of the horizon of simulation), the complete system has as many equations as the number of equations at each period multiplied by the simulation horizon plus the initial and terminal conditions:

$$z^1_0 = z^1_{\text{init}},$$

$$f\left(z_1, z^1_0, z^2_2, x_t\right) = 0,$$

$$g\left(z_1, z^1_0, z^2_2, x_t\right) = 0,$$

$$\vdots \qquad\qquad (S)$$

$$f\left(z_T, z^1_{T-1}, z^2_{T+1}, x_t\right) = 0,$$

$$g\left(z_T, z^1_{T-1}, z^2_{T+1}, x_t\right) = 0,$$

$$z^2_{T+1} = z^2_{\text{steady state}}.$$

When there are few equations and when the equilibrium converges quickly to the steady state (T can be chosen relatively small), this system can be solved by usual numerical algorithms of standard mathematical packages (for instance, the function FindRoot of Mathematica easily finds the solution to the examples of chapter 2).

When the system is more complicated, the system (S) is solved for z_t using a Newton–Raphson relaxation method put forward by Laffargue (1990) and Boucekkine (1995) for solving dynamic non-linear models with perfect foresight. With this technique, the Newton–Raphson improvement at each iteration is computed by triangulation (instead of inversion) of the matrix of the first derivatives of the system. As Boucekkine (1995) shows, this method allows one to characterize the nature of the dynamics of the model (explosivity, saddle-point trajectory, or infinite number of stable solutions) without having to linearize it or to compute the eigenvalues of the linearized system. In particular, it is easy to determine whether the convergence of the algorithm is due to the existence of a saddle-point trajectory or not. Indeed, the algorithm is characterized by explosivity in the case where an infinity of stable solutions exist (see Boucekkine and Le Van (1996)). This explosivity property is in fact common to all convergent relaxation methods. The explosive behavior is revealed by a simple numerical procedure relying on the initialization of the relaxation. Initializing the relaxation with values slightly different from the steady state leads to explosive behavior at the first Newton–Raphson improvement.

This routine is implemented under Gauss with the package Dynare of Juillard (1996).

A.6 STATISTICS

A.6.1 Dynamics of Distributions

Consider a probability distribution function Γ_t on $\mathbb{R}_{++}$:

$$\Gamma_t(h) = \Pr(h_t \leq h).$$

The function Γ_t is defined on $\mathbb{R}_{++}$ with values in $[0, 1]$. It is non-decreasing, with $\Gamma_t(0+) = 0$ and $\Gamma_t(+\infty) = 1$.

We associate to Γ_t the distribution of the logarithms of h_t. This associated distribution Λ_t is defined on $\mathbb{R}$:

$$\Lambda_t(l) = \Gamma_t(\exp l) \quad \Leftrightarrow \quad \Lambda_t(\ln h) = \Gamma_t(h).$$

We consider a linear law of evolution for l_t (which corresponds to log-linear dynamics for h_t):

$$l_{t+1} = a_t l_t + b_t, \qquad a_t > 0.$$

It is possible to describe how the distribution Λ_t changes over time:

$$\Lambda_{t+1}(l) = \Pr(l_{t+1} = a_t l_t + b_t \leq l)$$
$$= \Pr\left(l_t \leq \frac{1}{a_t}(l - b_t)\right)$$
$$= \Lambda_t\left(\frac{1}{a_t}(l - b_t)\right).$$

The mean and the variance of the distribution are

$$\bar{l}_{t+1} = a_t \bar{l}_t + b_t,$$
$$\sigma_{t+1}^2 = a_t^2 \sigma_t^2.$$

Usually, the probability distribution function may also be defined by a density function φ_t:

$$\Gamma_t(h) = \int_0^h \varphi_t(x)\,dx.$$

If $\varphi_t(\cdot)$ is continuous at h, then $\varphi_t(h)$ is the derivatives of $\Gamma_t(\cdot)$ at h:

$$\Gamma_t'(h) = \varphi_t(h).$$

The density function of Λ_t is then

$$\Lambda_t'(l) = \Gamma_t'(\exp l)\exp l = \phi_t(\exp l)\exp l. \tag{A.19}$$

A.6.2 Normal and Log-normal Distributions

In the special case where Λ_t is a normal distribution, its density function is

$$\Lambda_t'(l) = \frac{1}{\sigma_t\sqrt{2\pi}}\exp\left(-\frac{(l-\bar{l}_t)^2}{2\sigma_t^2}\right).$$

It is entirely characterized by the two parameters $\bar{l}_t$ and σ_t. Figure A.14 presents the density function with $\bar{l}_t = 1$, $\sigma_t = 1$.

The original distribution Γ_t is called log-normal, and its density function is given by

$$\Gamma_t'(h) = \varphi_t(h) = \frac{1}{h\sigma_t\sqrt{2\pi}}\exp\left(-\frac{(\ln h - \bar{l}_t)^2}{2\sigma_t^2}\right).$$

This results from the relationship (A.19) between Γ_t' and Λ_t'. One interest of this distribution is that we can express the mean and the variance of the associated log-normal distribution as a function of the parameters of the underlying normal distribution, $\bar{l}_t$ and σ. The mean of the associated log distribution is

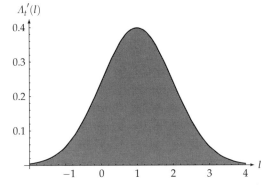

Figure A.14. Density function of a normal distribution.

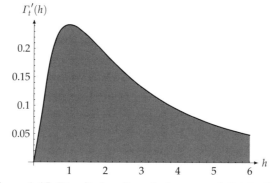

Figure A.15. Density function of a log-normal distribution.

given by

$$\bar{h}_t = \exp\left(\bar{l}_t + \frac{\sigma_t^2}{2}\right), \quad \text{or} \quad \ln \bar{h}_t = \bar{l}_t + \frac{\sigma_t^2}{2},$$

and its variance by

$$\exp\left(2\bar{l}_t + \sigma_t^2\right)\left(\exp \sigma_t^2 - 1\right).$$

Figure A.15 plots the density function of the log-normal distribution.

Many data generating processes in life and social sciences can be characterized by log-normal distributions, such as, e.g., the age of marriage in human populations, and economic data such as the size of enterprises and personal income (see Limpert, Abbt, and Stahel (2001)).

List of Definitions

List of Propositions

List of Assumptions

Bibliography

Abel, Andrew. 1985. "Precautionary saving and accidental bequest." *American Economic Review* 75 (4): 777–791.

———. 1987. "Operative gifts and bequest motives." *American Economic Review* 77 (5): 1037–1047.

Abel, Andrew, Gregory Mankiw, Lawrence Summers, and Richard Zeckhauser. 1989. "Assessing dynamic efficiency: theory and evidence." *Review of Economic Studies* 56 (1): 1–19.

Abel, Andrew and Mark Warshawsky. 1988. "Specification of the Joy of Giving: Insights from Altruism." *Review of Economics and Statistics* 70 (1): 145–149.

Ahmed, Shaghil and John Rogers. 1995. "Government budget deficits and trade deficits. Are present value constraints satisfied in long-term data?" *Journal of Monetary Economics* 36 (2): 351–374.

Aiyagari, Rao. 1989. "Can there be short-period deterministic cycles when people are long lived?" *Quarterly Journal of Economics* 104 (1): 163–185.

Allais, Maurice. 1947. *Economie et Intérêt*. Paris: Imprimerie Nationale.

Altonji, Joseph, Fumio Hayashi, and Laurence Kotlikoff. 1992. "Is the extended family altruistically linked? Direct tests using micro data." *American Economic Review* 82 (5): 1177–1198.

Ambler, Steve. 2000. "Optimal Time Consistent Fiscal Policy with Overlapping Generations." Working Paper, Crefe, Université du Québec à Montréal.

Ando, Albert and Franco Modigliani. 1963. "The 'life cycle' hypothesis of saving: aggregate implications and tests." *American Economic Review* 53 (1): 55–84.

Andreoni, James. 1989. "Giving with impure altruism: applications to charity and Ricardian equivalence." *Journal of Political Economy* 97 (6): 1447–1459.

Araujo, Jorge and Marco Martins. 1999. "Economic growth and finite lifetimes." *Economics Letters* 62 (3): 377–381.

Arrow, Kenneth. 1951. "An extension of the basic theorems of classical welfare economics." In *Proceedings of the Second Berkeley Symposium on Mathematical Statistics and Probability*, edited by J. Neyman, 507–532. University of California Press.

Arrow, Kenneth, Hollis Chenery, B. S. Minhas, and Robert Solow. 1961. "Capital-labor substitution and economic efficiency." *The Review of Economics and Statistics* 43 (3): 225–250.

Arrow, Kenneth and Gerard Débreu. 1954. "Existence of equilibrium for a competitive economy." *Econometrica* 22 (3): 265–290.

Arrow, Kenneth and Mordecai Kurz. 1970. *Public Investment, the Rate of Return, and Optimal Fiscal Policy*. Baltimore: Johns Hopkins University Press.

Arthur, Brian and Geoffrey McNicoll. 1978. "Samuelson, population, and intergenerational transfers." *International Economic Review* 19 (1): 241–246.

Atkinson, Antony. 1971. "Capital taxes, the redistribution of wealth, and individual savings." *Review of Economic Studies* 38 (114): 209–227.

Atkinson, Antony and Agnar Sandmo. 1980. "Welfare implications of the taxation of savings." *Economic Journal* 90 (359): 529–549.

Auerbach, Alan and Laurence Kotlikoff. 1987. *Dynamic Fiscal Policy*. New York and Melbourne: Cambridge University Press.

_____. 1995. *Macroeconomics: An Integrated Approach*. Cincinnati: South Western College Publishing.

Azariadis, Costas. 1993. *Intertemporal Macroeconomics*. Cambridge, MA and Oxford: Blackwell.

_____. 1996. "The economics of poverty traps – part one: complete markets." *Journal of Economic Growth* 1 (4): 449–486.

Azariadis, Costas, James Bullard, and Lee Ohanian. 2001. "Complex eigenvalues and trend reverting fluctuations." Mimeo, UCLA.

Azariadis, Costas and David de la Croix. 2001. "Growth or equality? Losers and gainers from financial reform." Mimeo, UCLA.

Azariadis, Costas and Allan Drazen. 1990. "Threshold externalities in economic development." *Quarterly Journal of Economics* 105 (2): 501–526.

Azariadis, Costas and Luisa Lambertini. 2000. "Volatility in an Economy with Temporary Default Penalties." Mimeo, UCLA.

Azariadis, Costas and Bruce Smith. 1998. "Financial intermediation and regime switching in business cycles." *American Economic Review* 88 (3): 516–536.

Balasko, Yves and Karl Shell. 1981. "The overlapping generations model II: the case of pure exchange with money." *Journal of Economic Theory* 24 (1): 112–142.

Bandiera, Oriana, Gerard Caprio, Patrick Honohan, and Fabio Schiantarelli. 2000. "Does Financial Reform Raise or Reduce Saving?" *Review of Economics and Statistics* 82 (2): 239–263.

Barro, Robert. 1974. "Are government bonds net wealth?" *Journal of Political Economy* 82 (6): 1095–1117.

_____. 1990. "Government spending in a simple model of endogenous growth." *Journal of Political Economy* 98 (5): S103–S125.

Barro, Robert and Gary Becker. 1989. "Fertility choice in a model of economic growth." *Econometrica* 57 (2): 481–501.

Barro, Robert and David Gordon. 1983. "Rules, discretion and reputation in a model of monetary policy." *Journal of Monetary Economics* 12 (1): 101–121.

Barro, Robert and Xavier Sala-I-Martin. 1995. *Economic Growth*. New York, London, and Montreal: McGraw-Hill.

Becker, Gary. 1964. *Human Capital: A Theoretical and Empirical Analysis, with Special Reference to Education*. New York: Columbia University Press.

_____. 1974. "A theory of social interactions." *Journal of Political Economy* 82 (6): 1063–1091.

———. 1992. "Habits, addictions and traditions." *Kyklos* 45 (3): 327–345.

Becker, Gary and Robert Barro. 1988. "A reformulation of the economic theory of fertility." *Quarterly Journal of Economics* 103 (1): 1–25.

Becker, Gary and H. Lewis. 1973. "On the interaction between the quality and quantity of children." *Journal of Political Economy* 81: S279–S288.

Belan, Pascal. 1997. "Systèmes de retraite et redistribution intragénérationnelle?" (With English summary.) *Recherches Economiques de Louvain* 63 (1): 57–78.

Belan, Pascal, Philippe Michel, and Pierre Pestieau. 1998. "Pareto improving social security reform." *Geneva Papers on Risk and Insurance Theory* 23 (2): 119–125.

Bellman, Richard. 1957. *Dynamic Programming*. Princeton: Princeton University Press.

Ben-Porath, Yoram. 1967. "The production of human capital and the life-cycle of earnings." *Journal of Political Economy* 75 (4): 352–365.

Benabou, Roland. 1996. "Heterogeneity, stratification and growth: macroeconomic implications of community structure and school finance." *American Economic Review* 86 (3): 584–609.

Benhabib, Jess and Roger Farmer. 1999. "Indeterminacy and Sunspots in Macroeconomics." In *Handbook of Macroeconomics. Volume 1A*, edited by John Taylor and Michael Woodford. Amsterdam, New York, and Oxford: North-Holland.

Benhabib, Jess and Guy Laroque. 1988. "On competitive cycles in productive economies." *Journal of Economic Theory* 45 (1): 145–170.

Bernheim, Douglas. 1987. "Ricardian equivalence: an evaluation of theory and evidence." *NBER Macroeconomics Annual* 2: 263–303.

Bertocchi, Graziella. 1994. "Safe debt, risky capital." *Econometrica* 62 (244): 493–508.

Bewley, Truman. 1972. "Existence of equilibria in economies with infinitely many commodities." *Journal of Economic Theory* 4 (2): 514–540.

Bisin, Alberto and Thierry Verdier. 2000. "Beyond the melting pot: cultural transmission, marriage, and the evolution of ethnic and religious traits." *Quarterly Journal of Economics* 115 (3): 955–988.

Blackburn, Keith and Giam Petro Cipriani. 2002. "A model of longevity, fertility and growth." *Journal of Economic Dynamics and Control* 26 (1): 187–204.

Blanchard, Olivier. 1985. "Debts, deficits, and finite horizon." *Journal of Political Economy* 93 (2): 223–247.

Blanchard, Olivier and Stanley Fischer. 1989. *Lectures on Macroeconomics*. Cambridge, MA: MIT Press.

Blanchard, Olivier and Charles Kahn. 1980. "The solution of linear difference models under rational expectations." *Econometrica* 48: 1305–1311.

Boucekkine, Raouf. 1995. "An alternative methodology for solving non-linear forward-looking models." *Journal of Economic Dynamics and Control* 19 (4): 711–734.

Boucekkine, Raouf and Cuong Le Van. 1996. "Checking for saddle point stability: an easy test." *Computational Economics* 9 (4): 317–330.

Bouzahzah, Mohamed, David de la Croix, and Frédéric Docquier. 2001. "Policy reforms and growth in computable OLG economies." *Journal of Economic Dynamics and Control*, forthcoming.

Boyd, Richard and Peter Richerson. 1985. *Culture and the Evolutionary Process*. Chicago: University of Chicago Press.

Breyer, Friedrich. 1989. "On the intergenerational Pareto efficiency of pay-as-you-go financed pension systems." *Journal Institutional and Theoretical Economics* 145 (4): 643–658.

Brickman, Philip, Dan Coates, and Ronnie Janoff-Belman. 1978. "Lottery winners and accident victims: Is happiness relative?" *Journal of Personality and Social Psychology* 36: 917–927.

Brock, William. 1970. "On existence of weakly maximal programmes in a multi-sector economy." *Review of Economic Studies* 37 (2): 275–280.

Buiter, Willem and Kenneth Kletzer. 1994. "Ponzi Finance, Government Solvency and the Redundancy or Usefulness of Public Debt." Working Paper 1070, Yale Cowles Foundation.

_____. 1995. "Capital mobility, fiscal policy, and growth under self-financing of human capital formation." *Canadian Journal of Economics* 28: s163–s194.

Bullard, James and Steven Russell. 1999. "An empirically plausible model of low real interest rates and unbacked government debt." *Journal of Monetary Economics* 44 (3): 477–508.

Cardia, Emanuela. 1997. "Replicating Ricardian equivalence tests with simulation series." *American Economic Review* 87 (1): 65–79.

Carroll, Robert. 2000. "The skeptic's dictionary." http://skepdic.com.

Cass, David. 1972. "On capital overaccumulation in the aggregate, neoclassical model of economic growth: a complete characterization." *Journal of Economic Theory* 4 (2): 200–223.

Cavalli-Sforza, Luigi and Marcus Feldman. 1981. *Cultural Transmission and Evolution: A Quantitative Approach*. Princeton: Princeton University Press.

Cazzavillan, Guido and Patrick Pintus. 2001. "Endogenous Labor Supply, Gross Substitutability, and Robustness of Multiple Equilibria in OLG Economies." GREQAM, Marseilles.

Chakraborty, Shankha. 1999. "Endogenous Lifetime and Economic Growth." Mimeo, University of Oregon.

Chamley, Christophe. 1986. "Optimal taxation of capital income in general equilibrium with infinite lives." *Econometrica* 54 (3): 607–622.

Champarnaud, Luc and Philippe Michel. 2000. "Biens culturels, transmission de culture et croissance." *Actualité Economique* 76 (4): 501–520.

Chari, V. V., Lawrence Christiano, and Patrick Kehoe. 1994. "Optimal fiscal policy in a business cycle model." *Journal of Political Economy* 102 (4): 617–652.

Chari, V. V. and Patrick Kehoe. 1990. "Sustainable Plans." *Journal of Political Economy* 98 (4): 784–802.

_____. 1999. "Optimal Fiscal and Monetary Policy." In *Handbook of Macroeconomics. Volume 1C*, edited by John Taylor and Michael Woodford. Amsterdam, New York, and Oxford: North-Holland.

Clark, Andrew, Andrew Oswald, and Peter Warr. 1996. "Is job satisfaction U-shaped in age?" *Journal of Occupational and Organizational Psychology* 69 (1): 57–81.

Coleman, James. 1990. *Foundations of Social Theory*. Cambridge, MA and London: Harvard University Press, Belknap Press.

Cooley, Thomas. 1995. *Economic Growth and Business Cycles*. Princeton: Princeton University Press.

Cremers, Emily. 2001. "General equilibrium with trade balance and real interest rate parity." *Economic Theory* 17 (3): 641–663.

Crettez, Bertrand, Philippe Michel, and Bertrand Wigniolle. 1999. "Debt neutrality and the infinitely-lived representative consumer." Mimeo, Greqam, Marseilles.

——. 2000. "Jusqu'où l'Etat peut-il s'endetter? Une approche par les modèles à générations imbriquées d'agents." Mimeo, Greqam, Marseilles.

Croissant, Yves and Philippe Jean-Pierre. 2001. "Les politiques de transferts sont-elles favorables à la croissances des économies?" *Louvain Economic Review*, forthcoming.

d'Aspremont, Claude, Louis-André Gérard-Varet, and Rodolphe Dos Santos Ferreira. 2000. "Endogenous Business Cycles and Business Formation with Strategic Investment." Working Paper 00/53, CORE, Université Catholique de Louvain.

d'Autume, Antoine and Philippe Michel. 1994. "Education et croissance." (Education and growth. With English summary.) *Revue d'Economie Politique* 104 (4): 457–499.

Dearden, Lorraine, Stephen Machin, and Howard Reed. 1997. "Intergenerational mobility in Britain." *The Economic Journal* 107 (440): 47–66.

Deardorff, Alan. 1976. "The optimum growth rate of population: comment." *International Economic Review* 17 (2): 510–515.

Debreu, Gérard. 1954. "Valuation equilibrium and Pareto optimum." *Proceedings of the National Academy of Sciences* 40 (7): 588–592.

——. 1959. *Theory of Value: An Axiomatic Analysis of Economic Equilibrium.* Cowles Foundation Monographs 17. New Haven: Yale University Press.

De Gregorio, Jose. 1996. "Borrowing constraints, human capital accumulation and growth." *Journal of Monetary Economics* 37 (1): 49–71.

De Gregorio, Jose and Se-Jik Kim. 2000. "Credit markets with differences in abilities: education, distribution, and growth." *International Economic Review* 41 (3): 579–607.

de la Croix, David. 1996. "The dynamics of bequeathed tastes." *Economics Letters* 53 (1): 89–96.

——. 1998. "Growth and the relativity of satisfaction." *Mathematical Social Sciences* 36 (2): 105–125.

——. 2001. "Growth dynamics and education spending: the role of inherited tastes and abilities." *European Economic Review* 45 (8): 1415–1438.

de la Croix, David and Matthias Doepke. 2001. "Inequality and Growth: Why Differential Fertility Matters." Mimeo, UCLA.

de la Croix, David and Omar Licandro. 1995. "Underemployment, irreversibilities, and growth under trade unionism." *Scandinavian Journal of Economics* 97 (3): 385–399.

——. 2000. "Irreversibilities, uncertainty and underemployment equilibria." *Spanish Economic Review* 2 (3): 231–248.

de la Croix, David, Géraldine Mahieu, and Alexandra Rillaers. 2001. "How should retirement policy adjust to the baby bust?" Working Paper 2001/03, IRES, Université Catholique de Louvain.

de la Croix, David and Philippe Michel. 1999. "Optimal growth when tastes are inherited." *Journal of Economic Dynamics and Control* 23 (4): 491–518.

_____. 2001. "Altruism and self-restraint." *Annales d'Economie et de Statistique*, 63-64:233–260.

de la Croix, David and Philippe Monfort. 2000. "Education funding and regional convergence." *Journal of Population Economics* 13 (3): 403–424.

de la Croix, David and Jean-Pierre Urbain. 1998. "Intertemporal substitution in import demand and habit formation." *Journal of Applied Econometrics* 13 (6): 589–612.

Demange, Gabrielle and Guy Laroque. 1999. "Social security and demographic shocks." *Econometrica* 67 (3): 527–542.

_____. 2000. "Social security, optimality and equilibria in a stochastic overlapping generations economy." *Journal of Public Economic Theory* 2 (1): 1–23.

Denison, Edward. 1974. *Accounting for United States Economic Growth, 1929–1969*. Washington: The Brookings Institution.

Devereux, Michael and Ben Lockwood. 1991. "Trade unions, non-binding wage agreements, and capital accumulation." *European Economic Review* 35 (7): 1411–1426.

Diamond, Peter. 1965. "National debt in a neoclassical growth model." *American Economic Review* 55 (5): 1126–1150.

_____. 1977. "A framework for social security analysis." *Journal of Public Economics* 8 (3): 275–298.

Docquier, Frédéric and Philippe Michel. 1999. "Education subsidies and endogenous growth: implications of demographic shocks." *Scandinavian Journal of Economics* 101 (3): 425–440.

Doepke, Matthias. 1999. "The Demographic Transition, Income Distribution, and the Transition from Agriculture to Industry." Mimeo, UCLA.

Douglas, Paul. 1934. *The Theory of Wages*. London: MacMillan.

Duesenberry, James. 1949. *Income, Saving, and the Theory of Consumer Behavior*. Cambridge, MA: Harvard University Press.

Easterlin, Richard. 1971. "Does human fertility adjust to the environment?" *American Economic Review Papers and Proceedings* 61 (2): 399–407.

_____. 1995. "Will raising the incomes of all increase the happiness of all?" *Journal of Economic Behaviour and Organization* 27 (1): 35–46.

Ehrlich, Isaac and Francis Lui. 1991. "Intergenerational trade, longevity, and economic growth." *Journal of Political Economy* 99 (5): 1029–1059.

Elmendorf, Douglas and Gregory Mankiw. 1999. "Government debt." In *Handbook of Macroeconomics. Volume 1C*, edited by John Taylor and Michael Woodford. Amsterdam, New York, and Oxford: North-Holland.

Erosa, Andres and Martin Gervais. 1998. "Optimal Taxation in Life-Cycle Economies." Working Paper 9812, University of Western Ontario.

Farmer, Roger. 1986. "Deficits and cycles." *Journal of Economic Theory* 40 (1): 77–88.

_____. 1993. *The Macroeconomics of Self-Fulfilling Prophecies*. Cambridge, MA and London: The MIT Press.

Feldstein, Martin. 1974. "Social security, induced retirement and aggregate capital accumulation." *Journal of Political Economy* 82 (5): 905–926.

_____. 1985. "The optimal level of social security benefits." *Quarterly Journal of Economics* 10 (2): 303–320.

_____. 1996. "Social security and saving: new time series evidence." *National Tax Journal* 49 (2): 151–164.

Fougère, Maxime and Marcel Mérette. 1999. "Population ageing and economic growth in seven OECD countries." *Economic Modelling* 16 (3): 411–427.

Frankel, Marvin. 1962. "The production function in allocation and growth: a synthesis." *American Economic Review* 52 (5): 995–1022.

Frenkel, Jacob and Assaf Razin. 1986. "Fiscal policy in the world economy." *Journal of Political Economy* 94 (3): 564–594.

Futia, Carl. 1982. "Invariant distributions and the limiting behavior of Markovian economic models." *Econometrica* 50 (2): 377–408.

Gale, David. 1967. "On optimal development in a multi-sector economy." *Review of Economic Studies* 34 (1): 1–18.

———. 1973. "Pure exchange equilibrium in dynamic economic models." *Journal of Economic Theory* 6 (1): 12–36.

Galor, Oded. 1992. "A two-sector overlapping generations model: a global characterization of the dynamical system." *Econometrica* 60 (6): 1351–1386.

———. 1996. "Convergence? Inferences from theoretical models." *The Economic Journal* 106 (437): 1056–1069.

Galor, Oded and Harl Ryder. 1989. "Existence, uniqueness and stability of equilibrium in overlapping generations model with productive capital." *Journal of Economic Theory* 49 (2): 360–375.

Galor, Oded and David Weil. 1996. "The gender gap, fertility and growth." *American Economic Review* 86 (3): 374–387.

Galor, Oded and Joseph Zeira. 1993. "Income distribution and macroeconomics." *Review of Economic Studies* 60 (1): 35–52.

Geanakoplos, John. 1987. "Overlapping generations." In *The New Palgrave: A Dictionary in Economics*, edited by John Eatwell, Murray Milgate, and Peter Newman. London: Macmillan.

Gevers, Louis and Philippe Michel. 1998. "Economic Dynasties with Intermissions." *Games and Economic Behavior* 25 (2): 251–271.

Glomm, Gerhard and B Ravikumar. 1992. "Public versus private investment in human capital: endogenous growth and income inequality." *Journal of Political Economy* 100 (4): 818–834.

Goldin, Claudia. 1994. "How America graduated from high school: 1910 to 1960." Working Paper 4762, National Bureau of Economic Research.

Grandmont, Jean-Michel. 1983. *Money and Value: A Reconsideration of Classical and Neoclassical Monetary Theories (Econometric Society Monographs in Pure Theory, No. 5)*. Cambridge, New York, and Melbourne: Cambridge University Press.

———. 1985. "On endogenous competitive business cycles." *Econometrica* 53 (5): 995–1037.

Grossman, Gene and Noriyuki Yanagawa. 1993. "Asset bubbles and endogenous growth." *Journal of Monetary Economics* 31 (1): 3–19.

Hale, Jack and Huseyin Koçak. 1991. *Dynamics and Bifurcations*. New York: Springer-Verlag.

Hamilton, James and Marjorie Flavin. 1986. "On the limitations of government borrowing: a framework for empirical testing." *American Economic Review* 76 (4): 808–819.

Harrod, Roy. 1942. *Toward a Dynamic Economics: Some Recent Developments of Economic Theory and Their Application to Policy*. London: Macmillan.

Hendricks, Lutz. 1999. "Taxation and long-run growth." *Journal of Monetary Economics* 43 (2): 411–434.

Hercowitz, Zvi and Michael Sampson. 1991. "Output, growth, the real wage, and employment fluctuations." *American Economic Review* 81 (5): 1215–1237.

Hicks, John. 1939. *Value and Capital*. Oxford: Clarendon Press.

———. 1965. *Capital and Growth*. Oxford: Clarendon Press.

Holmgren, Richard. 1996. "Tools for Analyzing Discrete Dynamical Systems." Mathematica code.

Homburg, Stefan. 1990. "The efficiency of unfunded pensions schemes." *Journal of Institutional and Theoretical Economics* 146 (4): 640–647.

———. 1992. *Efficient Economic Growth (Microeconomic Studies)*. Berlin, Heidelberg: Springer-Verlag.

Hopenhayn, Hugo and Edward Prescott. 1992. "Stochastic monotonicity and stationary distribution for dynamic economies." *Econometrica* 60 (6): 1387–1406.

Hu, Sheng. 1979. "Social security, the supply of labor, and capital accumulation." *American Economic Review* 69 (3): 274–283.

Ihori, Toshihiro. 1978. "The golden rule and the role of government in a life-cycle growth model." *American Economic Review* 68 (3): 389–396.

Jacobsen, Hans Jorgen. 2000. "Endogenous, imperfectly competitive business cycles." *European Economic Review* 44 (2): 305–336.

Jappelli, Tullio and Marco Pagano. 1994. "Saving, Growth, and Liquidity Constraints." *Quarterly Journal of Economics* 109 (1): 83–109.

———. 1999. "The welfare effects of liquidity constraints." *Oxford Economic Papers* 51 (3): 410–430.

Jones, Larry and Rodolfo Manuelli. 1990. "A convex model of equilibrium growth: theory and policy implications." *Journal of Political Economy* 98 (5): 1008–1038.

———. 1992. "Finite lifetimes and growth." *Journal of Economic Theory* 58 (2): 171–197.

Jones, Stephen. 1984. *The Economics of Conformism*. Cambridge, MA and Oxford: Basil Blackwell.

———. 2001. "Was an industrial revolution inevitable: economic growth over the very long-run." Mimeo, Stanford University.

Jouvet, Pierre-André, Philippe Michel, and Jean-Pierre Vidal. 2000. "Intergenerational altruism and the environment." *Scandinavian Journal of Economics* 102 (1): 135–150.

Juillard, Michel. 1996. "A Program for the Resolution and Simulation of Dynamic Models with Forward Variables through the Use of a Relaxation Algorithm." Working Paper 9602, CEPREMAP, Paris.

Kaganovich, Michael and Itzhak Zilcha. 1999. "Education, social security, and growth." *Journal of Public Economics* 71 (2): 289–309.

Kaldor, Nicholas. 1963. "Capital accumulation and economic growth." In *Proceedings of a Conference Held by the International Economic Association*, edited by Friedrich Lutz and Douglas Hague. London: Macmillan.

Kehoe, Timothy and David Levine. 1985. "Comparative statics and perfect foresight in infinite horizon economies." *Econometrica* 53 (2): 433–453.

———. 1993. "Debt-constrained asset markets." *Review of Economic Studies* 60 (4): 865–888.

Kimball, Miles. 1987. "Making sense of two-sided altruism." *Journal of Monetary Economics* 20 (2): 301–326.

King, Ian. 1992. "Endogenous growth and government debt." *Southern Economic Journal* 59 (1): 15–21.

King, Ian and Don Ferguson. 1993. "Dynamic inefficiency, endogenous growth and Ponzi games." *Journal of Monetary Economic* 32 (1): 79–104.

King, Robert, Charles Plosser, and Sergio Rebelo. 1990. "Production Growth and Business Cycles: Technical Appendix." Mimeo, University of Rochester.

Klein, Paul and Jose-Victor Rios-Rull. 1999. "Time-Consistent Optimal Fiscal Policies." Mimeo, University of Pennsylvania.

Koopmans, Tjalling. 1965. "The concept of economic growth." In *The Econometric Approach to Development Planning.* Amsterdam: North-Holland.

Kydland, Finn and Edward Prescott. 1977. "Rules rather than discretion: the inconsistency of optimal plans." *Journal of Political Economy* 85 (3): 473–491.

Laffargue, Jean-Pierre. 1990. "Résolution d'un modèle macroéconomique à anticipations rationnelles." (Solution of a macroeconomic model with rational expectations. With English summary.) *Annales d'Economie et de Statistisque* (17): 97–119.

Laitner, John and Thomas Juster. 1996. "New evidence on altruism: a study of TIAA–CREF retirees." *American Economic Review* 86 (4): 893–908.

Laitner, John and Henry Ohlsson. 2001. "Bequest motives: a comparison of Sweden and the United States." *Journal of Public Economics* 79 (1): 205–236.

Levhari, David and Nissan Liviatan. 1972. "On stability in the saddle-point sense." *Journal of Economic Theory* 4 (1): 88–93.

Limpert, Eckhard, Markus Abbt, and Werner Stahel. 2001. "Lognormal distributions across the sciences – keys and clues." *BioScience* 51(5): 341–352.

Ljungqvist, Lars. 1993. "Economic underdevelopment: the case of missing market for human capital." *Journal of Development Economics* 40 (2): 219–239.

Lucas, Robert. 1988. "On the mechanics of economic development." *Journal of Monetary Economics* 22 (1): 3–42.

_____. 1993. "Making a miracle." *Econometrica* 61 (2): 251–272.

Lucas, Robert and Leonard Rapping. 1969. "Real wages, employment and inflation." *Journal of Political Economy* 77 (5): 721–754.

Maddison, Angus. 1992. "A Long-run perspective on saving." *Scandinavian Journal of Economics* 94 (2): 281–196.

_____. 1995. *Monitoring the World Economy 1820–1992.* Paris: OECD.

Malinvaud, Edmond. 1953. "Capital accumulation and efficient allocation of resources." *Econometrica* 21 (2): 233–268.

_____. 1987. "The overlapping generations model in 1947." *Journal of Economic Literature* 25 (1): 103–105.

Mas-Colell, Andreu, Michael Whinston, and Jerry Green. 1995. *Microeconomic Theory.* New York and Oxford: Oxford University Press.

McCallum, Bennett. 1989. "Real business cycle models." In *Modern Business Cycle Theory,* edited by Robert Barro. Cambridge, MA: Harvard University Press.

McCandless, George and Neil Wallace. 1991. *Introduction to Dynamic Macroeconomic Theory – An Overlapping Generations Approach.* Cambridge, MA and London: Harvard University Press.

McKenzie, Lionel. 1986. "Optimal economic growth, turnpike theorems, and comparative dynamics." In *Handbook in Mathematical Economics*, edited by Kenneth Arrow and Michael Intriligator, 1281–1355. Amsterdam: North-Holland.

Michel, Philippe. 1990a. "Some clarifications on the transversality conditions." *Econometrica* 58 (3): 705–723.

———. 1990b. "Criticism of the Social Time-Preference Hypothesis in Optimal Growth." Working Paper 9039, CORE, Université Catholique de Louvain.

———. 1993. "Le modèle à générations imbriquées, un instrument d'analyse macroéconomique." (Overlapping generations models: a tool for macroeconomic analysis. With English summary.) *Revue d'Economie Politique* 103 (2): 191–220.

Michel, Philippe and David de la Croix. 2000. "Myopic and perfect foresight in the OLG model." *Economics Letters* 67 (1): 53–60.

Michel, Philippe and Pierre Pestieau. 1993. "Population growth and optimality: When does serendipity hold?" *Journal of Population Economics* 6 (4): 353–362.

———. 1999. "Social Security and Early Retirement in an Overlapping Generations Growth Model." Working Paper 9951, CORE, Université Catholique de Louvain.

Michel, Philippe and Alain Venditti. 1997. "Optimal growth and cycles in overlapping generations models." *Economic Theory* 9 (3): 511–528.

Michel, Philippe and Jean-Pierre Vidal. 2000. "Economic integration and growth under intergenerational financing of human capital formation." *Journal of Economics* 72 (3): 275–294.

Michel, Philippe and Bertrand Wigniolle. 1993. "Une présentation simple des dynamiques complexes." (A simple presentation of complex dynamics. With English summary.) *Revue Economique* 44 (5): 885–911.

Mountford, Andrew. 1998. "Trade, convergence, and overtaking." *Journal of International Economics* 46 (1): 167–182.

———. 1999. "Trade dynamics and endogenous growth: an overlapping-generations analysis." *Economica* 66 (262): 209–224.

Nehru, Vikram, Eric Swanson, and Ashutosh Dubey. 1995. "A new database on human capital stock in developing and industrial countries: sources, methodology, and results." *Journal of Development Economics* 46 (2): 379–401.

Norman, Loayza, Klaus Schmidt-Hebbel, and Luis Serven. 2000. "What Drives Private Saving across the World?" *Review of Economics and Statistics* 82 (2): 165–181.

Nourry, Carine. 2001. "Stability of equilibria in the overlapping generations model with endogenous labor supply." *Journal of Economic Dynamics and Control* 25: 1647–1663.

Pestieau, Pierre. 1974. "Optimal taxation and discount rate for public investment in a growth setting." *Journal of Public Economics* 3 (3): 217–235.

Phelps, Edmund. 1961. "The golden rule of accumulation: a fable for growthmen." *American Economic Review* 51 (4): 638–643.

———. 1965. "Second essay on the golden rule of accumulation." *American Economic Review* 55 (4): 793–814.

Phelps, Edmund and Karl Shell. 1969. "Public debt, taxation, and capital intensiveness." *Journal of Economic Theory* 1 (3): 230–346.

Pintus, Patrick, Duncan Sands, and Robin de Vilder. 2000. "On the transition from local regular to global irregular fluctuations." *Journal of Economic Dynamics and Control* 24 (2): 247–272.

Pontryagin, Lev. 1966. *Calculus of Variations and Optimal Control Theory*. New York: Wiley.

Postlewaite, Andrew. 1999. "Social Arrangements and Economic Behavior." Mimeo, University of Pennsylvania.

Quah, Danny. 1996. "Empirics for economic growth and convergence." *European Economic Review* 40 (6): 1353–1375.

Radner, Roy. 1972. "Existence of equilibrium of plans, prices, and price expectations in a sequence of markets." *Econometrica* 40 (2): 289–303.

_____. 1991. "Intertemporal general equilibrium." In *Value and Capital: Fifty Years Later*, edited by Lionel McKenzie and Stefano Zamagni, 423–460. New York: New York University Press.

Ramsey, Frank. 1927. "A contribution to the theory of taxation." *Economic Journal* 37 (145): 47–61.

_____. 1928. "A mathematical theory of savings." *Economic Journal* 38 (152): 543–559.

Rankin, Neil and Barbara Roffia. 1999. "Maximum Sustainable Government Debt in the Overlapping Generations Model." Working Paper 2076, CEPR.

Rebelo, Sergio. 1991. "Long-run policy analysis and long-run growth." *Journal of Political Economy* 99 (3): 500–521.

Reichlin, Pietro. 1986. "Equilibrium cycles in an overlapping generations economy with production." *Journal of Economic Theory* 40 (1): 89–102.

Renstrom, Thomas. 1999. "Optimal Dynamic Taxation." In *The Current State of Economic Science*, edited by Shri Dahiya. Rohtak, India: Vedams Books International.

Ricardo, David. 1817. *On the Principles of Political Economy and Taxation*. Cambridge University Press.

Rillaers, Alexandra. 2000. "Education and income inequality: the role of a social protection system." *Journal of Population Economics*, forthcoming.

Rios-Rull, Jose-Victor. 1996. "Life-cycle economies and aggregate fluctuations." *Review of Economic Studies* 63 (3): 465–489.

Rivera-Batiz, Luis and Paul Romer. 1991a. "International trade with endogenous technical change." *European Economic Review* 35 (4): 971–1004.

_____. 1991b. "Economic integration and endogenous growth." *Quarterly Journal of Economics* 106 (2): 531–555.

Romer, Paul. 1986. "Increasing returns and long-run growth." *Journal of Political Economy* 94 (5): 1002–1037.

_____. 1989. "Capital accumulation in the theory of long-run growth." In *Modern Business Cycle Theory*, edited by Robert Barro. Cambridge, MA: Harvard University Press.

Ryder, Harl and Geoffrey Heal. 1973. "Optimal growth with inter-temporally dependent preferences." *Review of Economic Studies* 40 (1): 1–31.

Saint-Paul, Gilles. 1992. "Fiscal policy in an endogenous growth model." *Quarterly Journal of Economics* 107 (4): 1243–1259.

Sala-I-Martin, Xavier. 1996. "A positive theory of social security." *Journal of Economic Growth* 1 (2): 277–304.

Samuelson, Paul. 1958. "An exact consumption-loan model of interest with or without the social contrivance of money." *Journal of Political Economy* 66 (6): 467–482.

————. 1975a. "Optimum social security in a life-cycle growth model." *International Economic Review* 16 (3): 539–544.

————. 1975b. "The optimum growth rate of population." *International Economic Review* 16 (3): 531–537.

————. 1976. "The optimum growth rate for population: agreement and evaluations." *International Economic Review* 17 (2): 516–525.

Samwick, Andrew. 2000. "Is pension reform conductive to higher saving?" *Review of Economics and Satistics* 82 (2): 264–272.

Schultz, Theodore. 1961. "Investment in human capital." *American Economic Review* 51 (1): 1–17.

Seater, John. 1993. "Ricardian equivalence." *Journal of Economic Literature* 31 (1): 142–190.

Shell, Karl. 1971. "Notes on the economics of infinity." *Journal of Political Economy* 79 (5): 1002–1011.

Solon, Gary. 1992. "Intergenerational income mobility in the United States." *American Economic Review* 82 (3): 393–408.

Solow, Robert. 1956. "A contribution to the theory of economic growth." *Quarterly Journal of Economics* 70 (1): 65–94.

————. 1957. "Technical change and the aggregate production function." *Review of Economics and Statistics* 39 (3): 312–320.

————. 1960. "Investment and technological progress." In *Mathematical Methods in the Social Sciences 1959*, edited by Kenneth Arrow, Samuel Karlin, and Patrick Suppes, 89–104. Stanford, CA: Stanford University Press.

Sosin, Kim and Loretta Fairchild. 1984. "Nonhomotheticity and technological bias in production." *Review of Economics and Statistics* 66 (1): 44–50.

Starr, Ross. 1987. "Sequence economies." In *The New Palgrave: A Dictionary in Economics*, edited by John Eatwell, Murray Milgate, and Peter Newman. London: Macmillan.

Stein, Jerome. 1969. "A minimal role of government in achieving optimal growth." *Economica* 36 (142): 139–150.

Stokey, Nancy and Robert Lucas. 1989. *Recursive Methods in Economic Dynamics*. Cambridge, MA, and London: Harvard University Press.

Thibault, Emmanuel. 2000. "Existence of equilibrium in an OLG model with production and altruistic preferences." *Economic Theory* 15 (3): 709–715.

Tirole, Jean. 1985. "Asset bubbles and overlapping generations." *Econometrica* 53 (6): 1499–1528.

Uhlig, Harald. 1998. "Capital income taxation and the sustainability of permanent primary deficits." In *Market Behaviour and Macroeconomic Modelling*, edited by Steven Brakman, Hans van Ees, and Simon Kuipers. London: Macmillan.

Uzawa, Hirofumi. 1965. "Optimal technical change in an aggregative model of economic growth." *International Economic Review* 6 (1): 18–31.

Veblen, Thorstein. 1934. *The Theory of the Leisure Class*. New York: Modern Library.

Weddepohl, Claus and Mehmet Yildirim. 1993. "Fixed price equilibria in an overlapping generations model with investment." *Journal of Economics* 57 (7): 37–68.

Weil, Philippe. 1987. "Love thy children: reflections on the Barro debt neutrality theorem." *Journal of Monetary Economics* 19 (3): 377–391.

————. 1989. "Overlapping families of infinitely-lived agents." *Journal of Public Economics* 38 (2): 183–198.

————. 1994. "The Transition from Unfunded to Funded Social Security Might Not Be As Painful As You Think." ECARE, Université Libre de Bruxelles, Belgium.

Wiggins, Stephen. 1990. *Introduction to Applied Nonlinear Dynamic Systems and Chaos*. New York: Springer-Verlag.

Wigniolle, Bertrand. 1994. "Capital humain, innovation et hétérogénéité dans une économie en croissance." Ph.D. dissertation, Université de Paris 1.

Wilcox, David. 1989. "The sustainability of government deficits: implications of the present value borrowing constraint." *Journal of Money, Credit and Banking* 21 (3): 291–306.

Wilhelm, Mark. 1996. "Bequest behavior and the effect of heir's earnings: testing the altruistic model of bequests." *American Economic Review* 86 (4): 874–892.

Woodford, Michael. 1986. "Stationary sunspot equilibria in a finance constrained economy." *Journal of Economic Theory* 40 (1): 128–137.

Zhang, Jie, Jusen Zhang, and Ronald Lee. 2001. "Mortality decline and long-run economic growth." *Journal of Public Economics* 80 (3): 485–507.

Author Index

Subject Index